NAMIBIA AND SOUTHERN AFRICA

A PUBLICATION OF THE GRADUATE INSTITUTE
OF INTERNATIONAL STUDIES,
GENEVA

Also published in this series:

The United States and the Politicization of the World Bank
Bartram S. Brown

Trade Negotiations in the OECD
David J. Blair

World Financial Markets after 1992
Hans Genberg and Alexander K. Swoboda

Succession Between International Organizations
Patrick R. Myers

Ten Years of Turbulence
Barbara Barnouin and Yu Changgen

The Islamic Movement in Egypt
Walid Mahmoud Abdelnasser

The International Organization of Hunger
Peter Uvin

NAMIBIA AND SOUTHERN AFRICA

REGIONAL DYNAMICS OF DECOLONIZATION
1945–90

Ronald Dreyer

Routledge
Taylor & Francis Group

LONDON AND NEW YORK

First published 1994 by Kegan Paul International Ltd

2 Park Square, Milton Park, Abingdon, Oxon OX14 4RN
711 Third Avenue, New York, NY 10017, USA

Routledge is an imprint of the Taylor & Francis Group, an informa business

First issued in paperback 2016

British Libary Cataloguing in Publication Data
   Dreyer, Ronald
      Namibia and Southern Africa: Regional
      Dynamics of Decolonization, 1945–90. –
      (Publication of the Graduate Institute
      of International Studies, Geneva)
      I. Title   II. Series
      968.8103

   Library of Congress Cataloging-in-Publication Data
   Namibia and southern Africa: regional dynamics of
   decolonization 1945–1990. Ronald Dreyer
       300pp   21cm
   Includes bibliographical references and index
   ISBN 0 7103 0471 4
   1. Namibia–politics and government 1945–1990.
   2. Namibia–Relations–Africa, Southern
   3. Africa, Southern–Relations-Namibia.   I. Title.
   DT1648 074 1993
   968.810   dc20   93–14190
                                                        CIP

   ISBN 13: 978-0-7103-0471-1 (hbk)
   ISBN 13: 978-1-138-97669-6 (pbk)

to Marni

CONTENTS

vii

MAPS

ABBREVIATIONS

AAPSO	Afro-Asian Peoples Solidarity Organization
ACN	Action Christian National
ANC	African National Congress
BOSS	Bureau of State Security
BPP	Bechuanaland People's Party
CDA	Christian Democratic Action (for Social Justice)
CIA	Central Intelligence Agency
CLSTP	Liberation Committee for São Tomé and Principe
CONCP	Conference of Nationalist Organizations of the Portuguese Colonies
CONSAS	Constellation of Southern African States
COREMO	Revolutionary Committee of Mozambique
CPSA	Communist Party of South Africa
DTA	Democratic Turnhalle Alliance
ELNA	National Liberation Army of Angola
ELP	Portuguese Liberation Army
FACCP	African Front against Portuguese Colonialism
FAPLA	People's Armed Forces for the Liberation of Angola
FCN	Federal Convention of Namibia
FLEC	Front for the Liberation of the Enclave of Cabinda
FNLA	National Front for the Liberation of Angola
FRELIMO	Mozambique Liberation Front
GRAE	Revolutionary Government in Exile
JMC	Joint Monitoring Commission
JMCs	Joint Management Centres
ICU	Industrial and Commercial Workers' Union

IDAF	International Defence and Aid Fund (for Southern Africa)
LLA	Lesotho Liberation Army
MFA	Armed Forces Movement (Portugal)
MLGICV	Movement for the Liberation of Guinea and the Cape Verde Islands
MNR	Mozambique National Resistance
MPC	Multi-Party Conference
MPLA	People's Movement for the Liberation of Angola
NAPDO	Namibia African People's Democratic Organization
NNDP	Namibia National Democratic Party
NNF	Namibia National Front
NPF	National Patriotic Front
NSMS	National Security Management System
OAU	Organization of African Unity
OPC	Ovamboland People's Congress
OPO	Ovamboland People's Organization
OSPAAL	Afro-Asian, and Latin American Peoples' Solidarity Organization
PAC	Pan-Africanist Congress
PAFMECA	Pan-African Freedom Movement of Central Africa
PAFMECSA	Pan-African Freedom Movement of Central and Southern Africa
PAIGC	African Independence Party of Guinea Bissau and Cape Verde Islands
PDA	Democratic Party of Angola
PIDE	International Police for the Defence of the State (Portugal)
PLAN	People's Liberation Army of Namibia
RENAMO	see MNR
SACU	Southern African Customs Union
SADCC	Southern African Development Coordination Conference
SADF	South African Defence Force
SAIC	South African Indian Congress
SAP	South African Police
SAUF	South African United Front
SWANLIF	South West Africa National Liberation Front

SWANP	South West Africa National Party
SWANPA	South West Africa Progressive Association
SWANU	South West Africa National Union
SSC	State Security Council
SWAPO	South West Africa People's Organization
SWAPO-D	SWAPO-Democrats
SWATF	South West African Territorial Force
TGNU	Transitional Government of National Unity
UDENAMO	National Democratic Union of Mozambique
UDF	United Democratic Front (Namibia)
UNIA	Universal Negro Improvement Association
UNIAS	Union of Non-Independent African States
UNHCR	United Nations High Commissioner for Refugees
UNIN	United Nations Institute for Namibia
UNIP	United National Independence Party
UNITA	National Union for the Total Independence of Angola
UNTA	National Union of Angolan Workers
UNTAG	United Nations Transitional Assistance Group
UPA	Union of the Peoples of Angola
ZANU	Zimbabwe African National Union
ZAPU	Zimbabwe African People's Union

PREFACE

The idea for examining the regional dynamics of Namibia's decolonization arose in early 1985 as a result of my ongoing interest in southwestern Africa since I had witnessed the first South African invasion of Angola in 1975/76 as a delegate of the International Committee of the Red Cross. The research was undertaken as part of a post-doctoral project supported by the Swiss National Science Foundation. This enabled me to conduct extensive research in the region, notably in the Frontline states.

Extremely helpful exchanges of ideas with colleagues working at the United Nations Institute for Namibia in Lusaka, at the University of Zimbabwe and the Centro de Estudos Africanos in Maputo enabled me to formulate the hypotheses which are pertinent for the understanding of Namibia's decolonization from a regional vantage point. They were followed by extensive research in the region's archives and libraries, thus supplementing preliminary research carried out in Geneva, England and Portugal. Moreover, Frontline state diplomats and members of southern African liberation movements gave me invaluable insights into the sometimes complex relationships between liberation movements on one hand, and between SWAPO and the Frontline states on the other. Their openness has been greatly appreciated, and I thank all the individuals who have thus contributed to the successful conclusion of the research.

However, a special word of appreciation goes to the editors of *Facts and Reports* published by the Holland Committee on Southern Africa. Their selection of press cuttings on the region enabled me to examine in detail the political dynamics of the region, especially concerning the period immediately preceding the independence of Namibia.

My greatest indebtedness goes to Dr Marni Pigott, my wife, friend, and colleague. Her suggestions and comments on drafts of the manuscript, but above all, her patience, were invaluable.

Nyon, Switzerland, January 1993

Map 1 Southern Africa

Source: Susanna Smith, *Front Line Africa, the Right to a Future* (Oxford, Oxfam, 1990), with modifications by the author.

Map 2 Namibia

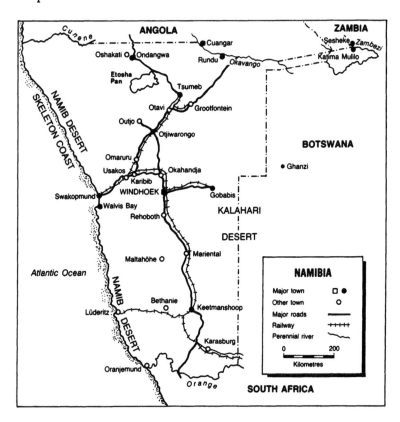

Source: United Nations Institute for Namibia, *Namibia: Perspectives for National Reconstruction and Development* (Lusaka, UIVIN, 1986), with modifications by the author.

Map 3 Angola/Northern Namibia

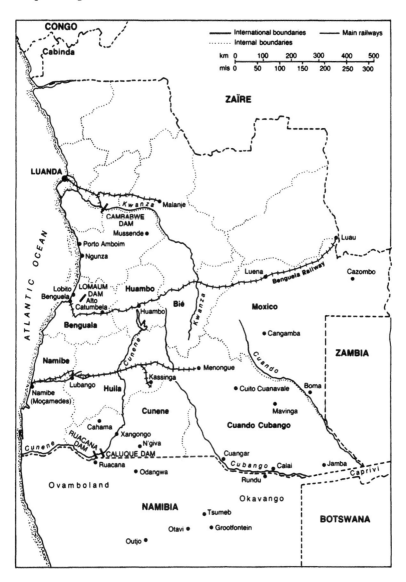

Source: Joseph Hanlon, *Beggar Your Neighbours. Apartheid Power in Southern Africa* (London/Bloomington, CIIR/Indiana University Press, 1986), with modifications by the author.

xvii

INTRODUCTION

The independence of Namibia on 21 March 1990 signalled the
end of more than a century of colonial rule, first by Germany
from 1884 to 1914 in the wake of the European partition of
Africa, followed by 75 years of South African occupation which
profoundly marked Namibia's twentieth century history. The
independence of the country in March 1990 also signalled an
end to the struggle of the Namibian people against colonial
rule. Political mobilization inside Namibia, and diplomatic
initiatives at the United Nations since the late 1950s had been
complemented by the armed struggle of the South West African
People's Organization (SWAPO) since 1966.

The internal and international dimensions to Namibia's
decolonization in the broad sense as a historical process leading
to independence[1] is well trodden ground for both historians
and social scientists.[2] However, studies of the internal dynamics of occupation, resistance and collaboration and of international diplomatic efforts as a result of Namibia's unique position in United Nations diplomacy do not explain satisfactorily
– either on their own, or in combination – the complexity
of decolonization and nationalism in Namibia. For Namibian
independence was preceded by open warfare opposing South
Africa and Angola, prolonged negotiations and a peace agreement between South Africa, Angola and Cuba in December
1988. And it was this *regional* peace settlement, contained in
the New York Accords, which was neither signed by SWAPO
as the only Namibian nationalist movement recognized by the
United Nations nor any other Namibian political party, which
provided the framework for South African withdrawal from
Namibia and the subsequent transition to independence under

1

United Nations supervision. But the regional dimension to Namibia's decolonization is not confined to the military conflict between South Africa and Angola and its solution in 1988. The web of regional interactions which are of importance to the understanding of Namibian decolonization can be traced back to the end of the Second World War. In particular, the history of South African occupation should be placed and analysed in the context of the evolving policies of Pretoria's regional economic and military domination culminating in the Total National Strategy which became South African official policy after P.W. Botha had become South African prime minister in 1978. Similarly, the study of the politics of liberation go beyond the analysis of the resistance to South African occupation inside Namibia. SWAPO's existence as an exile movement during almost twenty years raises questions about the organization of the struggle from its regional bases and the nature and form of its relations with host countries and other liberation movements.

The main argument of this study is the following: *regional dynamics of Namibia's decolonization from 1945 to 1990 interacted with and at times determined, both the internal dynamics of colonization, collaboration and resistance and the international dimension of United Nations diplomacy and superpower politics.* A regional approach to the study of Namibia's recent history – ranging from the study of cross-border movements to regional diplomatic, economic and military strategies – thus complements and enlarges existing avenues of research which focus on the internal and international-diplomatic dimensions of Namibia's colonization and liberation.

The regional dimension to Namibia's decolonization already became apparent in the wake of the Second World War. A South African plan to annex South West Africa was not only opposed by Namibians but also by regional actors such as Tshekedi Khama, a chief in the neighbouring British Bechuanaland protectorate and opposition movements inside South Africa. This is the theme of *chapter one* which shows that regional opposition to the annexation of Namibia by South Africa after the Second World War contributed significantly to the rejection of Pretoria's plan by the United Nations General Assembly in December 1946, signalling the beginning of U.N. involvement in Namibian decolonization. But the regional

2

dimension to early Namibian decolonization was not confined to the sphere of United Nations diplomacy.

South African opposition groups and trade unions were directly involved in the formative phase of Namibian nationalism as a force 'seeking to create a progressive independent state and government in Namibia and to foster a spirit of collective purpose among all the people of Namibia'.[3] While South African trade union officials inside Namibia introduced Namibian contract workers in Luederitz to the rudiments of trade union organization in the late 1940s, Namibian students and workers living in South Africa developed relationships with members of the Communist Party, the African National Congress and the Liberal Party during the 1950s. The form and nature of the relationship between Namibian expatriates and South African opposition groups and the extent to which the latter influenced the birth of modern Namibian political movements will be examined in *chapter two*. The chapter also analyses the first years of exile politics of SWAPO and to a lesser extent of the South West Africa National Union (SWANU), from 1960 to 1966. At the same time, the South African police, together with the British colonial authorities in the Bechuanaland protectorate and the Rhodesians, engaged in police cooperation against Namibian and South African refugees in transit to Tanzania, while police collaboration between South Africa and Portugal against Namibians and Angolans marked the beginnings of almost thirty years of South African counterinsurgency warfare beyond Namibia's borders.

Cooperation between SWAPO and other nationalist movements of southern Africa in the late sixties and early seventies and collaboration between South Africa and Portugal to maintain their respective colonial rule in Namibia and Angola intensified with the launching of SWAPO's armed struggle and the revocation of South Africa's former League of Nations' mandate over Namibia in 1966. Most significantly, political alignments of SWAPO with other southern African liberation movements within the Afro-Asian Peoples Solidarity Organization (AAPSO) overshadowed, but did not exclude, more discrete relationships with movements outside AAPSO's orbit, such as SWAPO's relationship with UNITA (National Union for the Total Independence of Angola). The launching of the armed struggle by SWAPO in Namibia and the intensification of

3

MPLA's (People's Movement for the Liberation of Angola) military activities in Angola also led to increased cooperation between colonizers. Military and police collaboration between South Africa and Portugal intensified and was complemented with economic cooperation and joint infrastructure projects such as the Cunene hydroelectric scheme on the Namibian Angolan border. This web of regional interactions, which increasingly permeated the politics of liberation and colonization, will be examined in *chapter three*. The fall of the Caetano government in Portugal in 1974 and the rapid decolonization of Mozambique and Angola also signalled a shift in regional alliances concerning Namibia. *Chapter four* analyses how the South African government and SWAPO responded to the new realities in southern Africa. In particular, it examines South African military collaboration with UNITA and FNLA (National Front for the Liberation of Angola), the two Angolan nationalist movements opposed to MPLA, who became Pretoria's allies in the South African invasion of Angola in 1975/76. The independence of Angola under the MPLA government and South African military defeat against Angolan and Cuban troops backed by Soviet equipment also led to a rethinking of American policy towards southern Africa. The American government, who feared further Cuban and above all Soviet involvement in southern Africa, advocated a negotiated settlement of the decolonization conflicts in Namibia and Rhodesia. Supported by its western allies, the Carter administration engaged in parallel negotiations with South Africa, SWAPO and the Frontline states resulting in the adoption of Security Council resolution 435 of 1978. In this context, *chapter five* examines the as yet little explored involvement of the five majority ruled southern African states (Angola, Botswana, Mozambique, Tanzania, Zambia) in the negotiations leading to the adoption of resolution 435 and in efforts to implement the settlement plan from 1978 to 1981. In particular, it attempts to highlight the relationship between SWAPO and the Frontline states who supported the movement's struggle. But SWAPO's policy options were at times constrained by Frontline state pressure in favour of the western settlement plan underlying resolution 435. Chapter five also draws attention to a new South African regional policy, embodied in the Total National Strategy, which coincided with the coming to power of P. W. Botha as South

4

African prime minister in 1978 and which prevented the implementation of resolution 435.

The South Africans were able to reinforce their claims to the continued occupation of Namibia after the Reagan administration had introduced the notion of 'linkage' in 1981, in accordance with which the independence of Namibia would have to be linked to the withdrawal of Cuban troops from Angola. From 1981, linkage, P. W. Botha's Total National Strategy as reflected in South African-UNITA destabilization of Angola and Angolan-Cuban resistance set the parameters of a regional conflict which is analysed in *chapters six and seven*. Both resistance inside Namibia to South African occupation and the diplomatic efforts to implement resolution 435 were subordinated to the war in southern Angola, the outcome of which was to provide the basis for Namibian independence in 1990.

The study of Namibia's decolonization from 1945 to 1990 from a *regional perspective* highlights aspects which may challenge some assumptions of the historiography which has evolved out of the liberation struggle. SWAPO's collaboration with UNITA before 1975, Frontline state pressure on SWAPO during the negotiations leading to the adoption of Resolution 435 in 1978 and the fact that SWAPO as Namibia's leading nationalist movement which in addition had been engaged in armed struggle for more than a decade, only played a marginal role in the negotiations leading to the New York Accords of December 1988, were decisive features of Namibia's liberation struggle. However, they often were deliberately underplayed by a historiography which depicts the history of Namibia's liberation primarily as the history of SWAPO's struggle. In this respect, the word of caution issued by the late Aquino de Bragança in relation to Mozambique's history of liberation one month before his tragic death in October 1986, should be remembered:

> While the enemies of the Mozambican revolution can deliberately distort its history, the same can be done by those who, out of sympathy, support, solidarity, seek to defend it. Unfortunately, the commitment can sometimes blind one to realities and only make one see the idealized version of that reality.[4]

In this sense, a regional approach to the study of Namibian

decolonization raises questions, the answers to which may not always correspond to accepted interpretations of the liberation struggle. It can, however, add some additional elements allowing for the better understanding of Namibia's unique history.

CHAPTER ONE

INCORPORATION OF NAMIBIA INTO SOUTH AFRICA. REGIONAL DIMENSIONS TO UNITED NATIONS DIPLOMACY. 1945–6

On 14 December 1946, the United Nations General Assembly decided to reject a South African demand for the incorporation of Namibia into South Africa thereby signalling the beginning of United Nations opposition to South Africa's rule in Namibia which she had occupied since 1915. The South African plan for annexation was opposed not only by the United Nations General Assembly and the majority of Namibia's inhabitants, but also by regional actors. Tshekedi Khama, a chief in the neighbouring British Bechuanaland protectorate and South African opposition groups, the African National Congress (ANC) and the Communist Party of South Africa in particular, opposed Pretoria's plan for the annexation of Namibia and South African regional expansionism in general and got involved in a campaign at the United Nations against Namibia's annexation. Thirty years before the Front Line States played an important role in the negotiation of Security Council Resolution 435 of 1978, Chief Tshekedi Khama of Bechuanaland and South African opposition groups contributed to the rejection of Pretoria's proposal for incorporation, highlighting a regional dimension to the emergence of Namibia as an issue of United Nations diplomacy, a distinguishing feature of Namibian decolonization since the Second World War.

South African expansionism before the Second World War

Since the second half of the nineteenth century, the two Boer Republics, the Transavaal and Orange Free State as well as the Cape colony had advocated and pursued a policy of territorial expansion. The expansionist movement of the Boer settlers from the Cape to the Transvaal in the 1830s extended to Namibia, Angola, Zimbabwe and Malawi. Attempts by the Transvaal government in the 1880s to expand eastwards to the Kalahari desert were frustrated by the proclamation of a British protectorate over Bechuanaland in 1885, a move also designed to prevent German eastward expansion from South West Africa. To the east of the Transvaal, the Kruger government directly administered Swaziland between 1894 and 1902, when Swaziland became a British colony in the aftermath of the Anglo-Boer War. To the north, Transvaal expansionism was limited by the British South Africa Company which administered Northern and Southern Rhodesia. Cecil Rhodes initially planned to extend direct company rule as far north as the southern part of the Belgian Congo, embracing at the same time the Portuguese colonies of Angola and Mozambique.[1]

The government of the Cape colony had played with the idea of a British protectorate covering Namibia, Bechuanaland and the Transvaal since 1874, two years after the Cape had been granted the status of a self-governing colony. And convinced of Namibia's economic profitability, the Cape argued for the territory's annexation. But the metropolitan government only approved the annexation of the port of Walvis Bay in 1878, recognizing its strategic significance 'as the only port of entrance to very large regions in which the [Cape] colony is materially interested'.[2] Walvis Bay was declared a part of the Cape colony in 1884, a decision which Pretoria was to use a century later for legitimizing its claim to ownership over the Bay and which was to prove to be a major obstacle in the indirect negotiations between South Africa and SWAPO leading to Security Council Resolution 435 of 1978. During the German rule over Namibia from 1884 to 1915, successive Cape governments continued to call for the territory's annexation. But London was not prepared to sanction Cape expansionism as it did not want to jeopardize Anglo-German relations over

8

a distant territory of little importance to the metropolitan government.[3].

South African expansionism, 'a persistent element in the political traditions of the Cape and the two Republics',[4] continued to dominate Pretoria's regional policy in its manifestation as both territorial expansionism and economic control. Since the establishment of the Union of South Africa in 1910, the South African Customs Union had linked the economies of the High Commission Territories Bechuanaland, Basutoland and Swaziland to the South African economy and the South Africa Act of 1909 provided for the eventual incorporation of the three territories into the Union.

Pretoria pursued a de facto incorporation of Namibia since South African troops had invaded German South West Africa in 1915. After five years of military occupation whereby South Africa notably conquered Ovamboland, which had never been controlled by Germany, Namibia was placed under a class C mandate of the League of Nations in December 1920, a compromise between South Africa's, New Zealand's and Australia's claims for annexation of the former German territories and the American president Wilson's opposition to annexation.[5] Accordingly, Pretoria would administer the territory as an *integral* part of South Africa subject only to vague international supervision such as the submission of annual reports to the League of Nations. To the South African prime minister Smuts, the status of South West Africa 'amounted to annexation in all but name',[6] and Pretoria embarked on a systematic policy of de facto integration of the territory into the Union both economically and politically.

Namibia became part of the Southern African Customs Union in 1921 and the territory's railways and harbours were integrated into the South African network in 1922. More significantly, Pretoria viewed Namibia as an outlet for white settlement. Land concessionary companies were expropriated and unallocated land was declared Crown land. The influx of settlers from South Africa was encouraged and subsidized with the result that the settler population had doubled between 1914 and 1925 despite the repatriation of 6,000 Germans.[7] This policy also concerned the settlement of approximately 1900 Angola-Boers who had been living in the south of Angola and who were resettled on territory which had belonged to the Hereros.

Land spoliation of Namibia's African population was inherent to white settlement. In 1922, Pretoria formally instituted the system of native reserves, based on existing reserves which had been introduced during German rule and on the Union Land Settlement Act of 1913. Concomitantly Pretoria introduced discriminatory laws analogous to the ones prevailing in South Africa.

While resistance to South African rule by the Bondelzwarts in 1922, the Rehoboth people in 1925 and the Impumbu in Ovamboland in 1932 were crushed, economic integration and land spoliation were complemented in 1934 by open calls – by settlers and Union politicians – for the full incorporation of South West Africa into the Union as its fifth province. But Pretoria, undoubtedly under the influence of general Smuts, who then was minister of justice, was not prepared to alienate the League of Nations and change the legal status of territory. However, the South African prime minister Hertzog assured his followers that South West Africa would become the Union's fifth province once the mandate ceased to exist.[8]

The plan for incorporation and opposition by Namibians

To the South African government, the end of the Second World War presented an opportune occasion to abolish the mandate. In March 1945 Smuts, who had again become prime minister in 1939, stated in parliament that 'the mandate will have to be abolished and the territory can be incorporated as a province of the Union'.[9] Smuts was convinced that 'if ever there were a territory which was part of the Union from every point of view, it is South West [Africa] . . . It was really the territory of the old Cape. Both historically and from the point of view of the defence of South-West Africa, it is an integral portion of South Africa . . . Administratively it is already a part of the Union. We have such a strong case that I am prepared to plead it to the best of my ability and I hope to succeed. If I do not succeed I shall fall back on the status quo',[10] i.e. continue to administer the territory as a mandate. Smuts was prisoner of his own role in history. He wanted to annex Namibia. But as a founding father of the League of Nations mandate system he was not prepared to do so without the approval of international public opinion as reflected in the newly established United Nations.

In a reply to a renewed call for incorporation by settlers in 1943, Smuts had already pointed out that since the mandate was an international agreement, South Africa could not act unilaterally.[11]

But from the beginning, Smuts was aware that he would face opposition within the United Nations. When he attended its founding conference in San Francisco in May 1945, he reported to his deputy that the United Nations had 'a strong humanitarian tendency, finding expression in provisions for equal rights all round and other somewhat embarrassing proposals so far as we [are] concerned'.[12] In order to circumvent the contradiction between the United Nations call for 'equal rights and self-determination of peoples' as well as 'respect for human rights and fundamental freedoms for all',[13] and the Union's policy of racial discrimination, the South African government attempted to legitimize its claim for incorporation by organizing a referendum among *all* inhabitants of Namibia.[14]

The all-white Legislative Assembly of south west Africa voted unanimously for incorporation in May 1946. Pretoria also organized a 'referendum' among the territory's African population. But the South African authorities only consulted headmen whom they asked to sign a document stating that 'our people have been happy and have prospered under the rule of the government of the Union of South Africa and that we should like that government to continue to rule us; that we do not wish any other government, or people to rule us and that we should like our country to become part of the Union of South Africa'.[15] Moreover, the headmen who were consulted, were given a block vote equal to the number of individuals they claimed to have authority over. As a result, the South African government claimed that 208,850 inhabitants were in favour of annexation 33,520 were against, while 56,790 were not consulted.[16]

However, it soon became apparent that the majority of Namibians had refused annexation and opposition to incorporation soon became known beyond Namibia's borders as Frederick Maherero, the Paramount Chief of the Hereros, lived in exile in Bechuanaland.[17] Herero chiefs who still lived inside Namibia informed Frederick Maherero that 'the Hereros refused, the Nama refused, the Ovambos refused and the Berg Damaras refused. We were divided into tribal groups and each tribe was asked separately; all refused'.[18] They urged Frederick Maherero to return to his country because 'the heritage of your father's orphans is about to be taken away from them'. In Maherero's absence and living in scattered reserves, they were not able to oppose incorporation and they needed him as 'a unifying factor'.[19] But Frederick Maherero refused to return because of Pretoria's policy of land spoliation and racial discrimination. He argued that as long as the Hereros did not have sufficient land and were scattered over numerous small reserves, their traditional land being occupied by settlers, he was not prepared to return. His return also was conditional on the improvement of the Africans' living conditions in the country, an eventuality which he ruled out if Namibia were incorporated into South Africa.[20] For 'as it is, conditions in South West Africa today have become akin to those under which natives live in the Union'.[21]

Frederick Maherero and some of the Namibian refugees in Bechuanaland lived in the tribal area controlled by Tshekedi Khama, the chief of the Bangwato. And Tshekedi skillfully used Namibian opposition to annexation in his own campaign against what he perceived to be Pretoria's regional expansionism not only towards Namibia but also towards Bechuanaland.

Opposition by Tshekedi Khama

Tshekedi Khama who had ruled over the Bangwato tribe, Botswana's largest tribal area which is adjoining Zimbabwe, since 1925,[22] had known about South Africa's plan to annex Namibia since September 1945. And in January 1946, he asked the British high commissioner to forward a telegram of protest to the United Nations.[23] But London refused to support Tshekedi officially[24] on the grounds that 'the question of South Africa is not at present before U.N.O. and there is, therefore, no case for such action'.[25] Nevertheless, Tshekedi Khama, supported by his fellow chiefs and assisted by the South African lawyer Douglas Buchanan who was his legal adviser, started a campaign against Namibia's annexation.

Against the background of South African calls for the incorporation of the High Commission territories as a reward for South African war efforts,[26] Tshekedi's campaign was dominated by the fear that Namibia's incorporation into South Africa would lead to the encirclement of Bechuanaland by South Africa and the Rhodesias and would ultimately result in Botswana's annexation by South Africa. For if Namibia were part of the Union, Bechuanaland 'would then be barred in not only from the south, east and north, but from the west and our only hope for a free and open route would be lost to us and the economic development of the territory strangled at its birth'.[27]

In order to forestall this eventuality and to ensure that Bechuanaland could be 'politically and economically independent of the Union', Tshekedi advocated the establishment of a corridor from Bechuanaland to Walvis Bay. Tshekedi and his fellow chiefs pointed out in a memorandum that due to Botswana's mineral wealth 'as yet untapped', the country would have a potential for industrial development. But the latter would depend on a free trade route which did not exist. The country's railway line was 'owned and controlled by the Rhodesian Railways in conjunction with the Union Government Railways' and it would be 'neither in the interest of the Union Government, nor the Government of Southern Rhodesia to assist in the development of our territory, in fact the policy of the Union has been and is, the negation thereof'. The only alternative route which would depend neither on South Africa, nor on Southern Rhodesia, would lead through South West Africa to the Atlantic Ocean. The fact that the question of the territory's incorporation into South Africa was going to be discussed at the United Nations, would therefore provide 'the opportune occasion to decide this problem for all time'.[28]

In addition to Tshekedi's fear of encirclement, which he thought could be avoided through the establishment of a corridor across Namibia to the Atlantic Ocean, the chief accused South Africa of openly preventing Botswana's development 'with the definite objective of forcing the inhabitants of Bechuanaland to seek employment in the Union'.[29] As a result, Bechuanaland would be placed 'in a position where she ultimately [would] have no alternative but to be forced for economic considerations to come into the Union of South Africa. This is the present position of the sister High Commission Territories in South Africa especially Basutoland'.[30]

Tshekedi also spoke out against the 'notorious policy of native administration' in South Africa in an effort to convince the British government 'that the Union of South Africa cannot,

13

in the true interest of the welfare of the native peoples of South West Africa . . . [and] South Africa to be entrusted with more and more territories principally inhabited by native peoples'.[31] Pretoria's policy towards Namibia's African population was contrary to the clauses of the League of Nations mandate,[32] and would prevent 14,000 Herero refugees then living in Bechuanaland from returning to Namibia.[33]

For Tshekedi, a *direct* British mandate over South West Africa was the preferred alternative to incorporation. Failing this, the compromise suggested by Tshekedi was *partition*. This proposal envisaged the southern part of Namibia being incorporated into South Africa, while the northern part would be a British or failing the latter, a United Nations mandate 'so as to provide the Bechuanaland Protectorate and incidentally Rhodesia, with free access to and a free port on, the West Coast of Africa and an opportunity to the displaced persons to return to their homeland'.[34] Tshekedi argued his case for partition along ethnic lines. 'The southern portion of South West Africa is inhabited by the Nama, or Hottentot and the Bastards tribes. The Bastards are coloured and the Hottentot have ceased to exist as a tribe and they are perhaps more akin to the Coloured than the Bantu'. As the Rehoboth Basters had accepted Pretoria's plan for incorporation, Tshekedi asked his fellow chiefs whether it was not 'reasonable therefore to suggest that the southern [part] may be annexed and the central and northern parts of South West Africa remain as a mandate under UNO?'[35]

The way in which Tshekedi articulated his opposition to the annexation of Namibia by South Africa reveals the nature of his involvement. While he sympathized with the plight of the Namibian people, Tshekedi skillfully used the issue of Namibia in order to expose Botswana's vulnerability in relation to South Africa. Thirty three years before his nephew Seretse Khama proposed the establishment of the Southern African Development Coordination Conference (SADCC) in 1979, the fear of Botswana's economic and ultimately political strangulation by South Africa dominated Tshekedi's campaign. Whereas Pretoria intended to profit from the demise of the League of Nations by wanting to annex Namibia as its fifth province, Tshekedi Khama saw in the uncertain status of Namibia in the wake of the Second World War a possibility for furthering what he perceived – twenty years before Botswana's independence – as the country's 'national interest'. By associating all but one of Botswana's chiefs to his protest, he transformed what had been a personal campaign into a national one, representing 'the first example of nationally coordinated political action in the twentieth century history of Bechuanaland'.[36] While Tshekedi undoubtedly hoped that the support of his fellow chiefs would add weight to his arguments, it remains doubtful that Tshekedi himself consciously sought to fight a 'national' campaign. As far as Namibia was concerned, Tshekedi did not hesitate to advocate partition along ethnic lines in order to establish a corridor from Bechuanaland to the Atlantic Ocean thereby breaking his country's landlocked position and dependence of South Africa.

South African opposition

Namibia's incorporation was also opposed from within South Africa, notably by the African National Congress and the Communist Party of South Africa. After the South African delegate at the United Nations had announced in January 1946 that his government wanted to annex Namibia, A. B. Xuma, the president-general of the African National Congress (ANC), sent a telegram of protest to the United Nations.[37] Xuma also supported Tshekedi Khama in his campaign against the annexation of Namibia and feared incorporation of Botswana. According to Xuma, 'we Africans in the Union are interested in all the territories surrounding us, in fact all the territories in Africa'. The ANC was 'especially interested in British territories because we feel in them and through them the British government has an opportunity of showing the Dominion of the Union of South Africa how all His Majesty's subjects should be treated as citizens of the Empire with every opportunity for development'. Bechuanaland and the two other High Commission territories should not be incorporated into South Africa 'because of the anti-African policy of the Union government'. And 'South West Africa . . . must not be incorporated into the Union because only the whites – members of the Legislature – will gain by such incorporation. The Africans will be merely added to our system of oppression and discrimination'.[38]

Tshekedi was also supported by Prof. Z. K. Matthews, who was an influential member of the ANC and himself of Botswana origin. He had met Tshekedi for the first time when he was a student at Lovedale in South Africa in 1916 and they subsequently became friends.[39] Matthews argued that 'before the anti-democratic elements in the Union native policy have been rooted out of this country, it would be criminal for any more people of colour to be brought under the jurisdiction of the Union Government' and that a United Nations trusteeship over Namibia would 'undoubtedly have a wholesome influence on the development of Union native policy'.[40]

R. T. Bokwe, another member of the ANC executive, shared Matthew's optimism concerning the impact of a U.N. trusteeship agreement for Namibia on South Africa's domestic policy. For Bokwe, a trusteeship agreement 'would not only be the means of serving the best interest of the native population of that country but would indirectly help us in the Union because with the protecting hand of Britain over the Protectorates on the one hand and that of the Trusteeship Council [over South West Africa] on the other, . . . the Union of South Africa may hesitate to pursue further its present policy which can only end in permanent injury to good relations between the Black and White races in Africa'.[41]

D. D. T. Jabavu, the president of the All African Convention, also supported Tshekedi in his campaign against South African expansionism towards Namibia and the High Commission territories. He urged Tshekedi, who planned to travel to England for arguing his case, to use every opportunity to mobilize British public opinion against 'the power of Field Marshal Smuts in his effort to enlarge his sphere of unjust methods to Africans yet happily outside his reach [sic]'.[42]

While Jabavu – at least in his letter to Tshekedi – seemed to be unaware of the conditions which prevailed in Namibia precisely because of the introduction of discriminatory legislation analogous to the one in South Africa, the positive role ascribed to Britain by Xuma and Bokwe undoubtedly added weight to the arguments of those who were critical of ANC leaders, in particular the ANC Youth League formed in 1944. The group of militants of the Youth League including Nelson Mandela and Oliver Tambo accused the ANC of having been unable 'in the last twenty years to advance the national cause [of South Africa] in a manner commensurate with the demands of the times . . . [and of being] a loose association of people who

16

merely react negatively to given conditions, able neither to assert the national will, nor to resist it openly'.[43] But as the Youth League did not split from the ANC, it did not appear to make a separate policy statement against Namibia's incorporation into South Africa. But its Africanist policy orientation, namely that 'we believe that national liberation of Africans will be achieved by Africans themselves',[44] makes it unlikely that the ANC Youth League would have even considered that Britain could play a positive role in southern Africa.

While the ANC Youth League spoke out – in general terms – for national liberation led by Africans, the Communist Party argued for independence. Already in 1932, the Communist Party of South Africa had protested against the bombing of the village of the Ovambo chief Impumbu by the South African air force and in 1934, the party urged members of the ANC and the Industrial and Commercial Workers's Union (ICU) to join in a campaign for the immediate withdrawal of all armed forces from Namibia.[45]

In January 1946, the Communist Party protested against Namibia's annexation because of the Union Government's 'failure to fulfil obligations of trusteeship towards the non-white peoples and its undemocratic and oppressive treatment of its own African population'. The Communist party therefore 'strongly urged' that South West Africa should be placed under a United Nations trusteeship agreement as a 'first step towards democratic independence'.[46] The Party's protest to the United Nations also reflects on the relationship between the Communist Party and the ANC in 1946. Moses Kotane, the Party's secretary-general who had been a member of the ANC national executive since 1945,[47] was aware that Xuma, the president of the ANC, had sent a telegram of protest at the same time. Kotane profited from the occasion to spell out some of his party's criticism towards the ANC and to congratulate Xuma for having protested against Pretoria's plan of annexing Namibia: 'My quarrel with you and Congress has been over the fact that you and Congress leadership generally let things go by default, that you do not speak up when you should and when it is necessary that you should. However, well done this time, sir. The Government will gnash its teeth but the Africans will appreciate your action deeply'.[48] In October 1946, the Communist Party asked for 'the assistance of the Trusteeship Council to lead the territory towards independence'.[49]

Tshekedi Khama and the United Nations

While Pretoria sought United Nations approval for Namibia's incorporation, both South African opposition groups and Tshekedi Khama attempted to influence the outcome of the General Assembly debates which took place from October to December 1946.

Already in February 1946, Tshekedi had informed the Anti Slavery Society in London about his opposition to Pretoria's plan. In his reply, the Society's secretary promised that he would approach a high official of the United States State Department whom he had met during the General Assembly session in London in January 1946. He told Tshekedi that he had also informed Britain's representative in the U.N Trusteeship Council (Fourth Committee) about Tshekedi's opposition and had asked him to use his personal influence against the South African claim for Namibia's annexation.[50]

Tshekedi and his legal adviser Buchanan were trying to obtain a travel permit in order to present their case personally in London. But by then the British government had already decided – a decision unknown to Tshekedi – to back South Africa's claim for incorporation. The Cabinet had in fact been in favour of the South African claim since April 1946 and decided on 13 May to inform Pretoria of its conditional support. These conditions required the South African government to consult *all* inhabitants of Namibia using 'methods agreeable to the United Nations'.[51] Accordingly, the high commissioner was instructed not to give Tshekedi any assistance. He told the chief unofficially that his attempts to come to England would provoke a hostile attitude from the British government with the possible result that it would not oppose the transfer of the High Commission territories to South Africa. And Smuts warned the British government that if Tshekedi were allowed to visit England, the South African government could introduce steps in parliament for the transfer of Bechuanaland, Basutoland and Swaziland in terms of the South Africa Act of 1909. As concerned Namibia specifically, Tshekedi realized that London 'was not prepared to argue against the demand to be made by

General Smuts at next U.N.O. Conference'.[52] As to Tshekedi's fear of encirclement, the British government argued that if South West Africa were part of the Union, 'the position of the Bechuanaland Protectorate . . . would not in fact be essentially different from that of Basutoland which is entirely surrounded by Union territory, or of Southern Rhodesia which depends for access to the sea on routes through the Union, or foreign territory'.[53]

Faced with London's refusal to support their claim against Namibia's incorporation, Tshekedi and Buchanan began to explore possible alternative channels. They approached the Anti Slavery Society for guidance on how to approach the British parliament,[54] and they also requested the British government to send the Bechuanaland chiefs' memorandum against Namibia's incorporation to the Dominions' delegations – Canada, Australia, New Zealand and India – at the United Nations. For 'all these governments have repudiated the idea of territorial aggrandizement and supported the principle of the protection of backward people until such times as they can maintain themselves'.[55]

Buchanan personally approached the Indian High Commission in South Africa asking if the Indian U.N delegation could present their case against Namibia's annexation.[56] Buchanan's initiative was not incidental. On one hand, India had already protested against South Africa's announcement in January 1946 that it wanted to incorporate Namibia and organize a 'referendum' to this effect.[57] On the other hand, the Indian government had recently initiated proceedings at the U.N. against Pretoria's discriminatory policy towards South Africa's Indian minority which had culminated in the Asiatic Land Tenure and Indian Representation Act of 1946.[58]

In addition to contacting governments considered sympathetic to their cause, Tshekedi wanted his case against Namibia's incorporation to be known by the public opinion in England, the United States and South Africa. He hoped that 'friends will take this matter up in the press to keep the pressure on'. Probably still hoping to obtain London's support, Tshekedi argued that without public influence, the British government would do nothing to put their case before the United Nations.[59] While Buchanan inquired about 'the correct method of conducting a press campaign',[60] Tshekedi gave extensive interviews to

the press,[61] to which he also released some of his correspondence with the British high commissioner and he asked a South
African friend to 'send to the *New York Times* some of our
contentions'.[62]

After South Africa had presented the results of the 'consultation' in Namibia, showing that 70% of the inhabitants had
voted in favour of incorporation, India who enjoyed strong
support 'both in the [General] Assembly and in the public',[63]
and who had imposed an economic boycott on South Africa
because of Pretoria's treatment of the Indian minority, took
the lead in United Nations' opposition to Pretoria's claim for
incorporation during the General Assembly debates from October to December 1946. Smuts, who personally presented South
Africa's case at the United Nations,[64] admitted that 'prospects
look pretty bad'[65] despite the support of Attlee the British prime
minister. Smuts complained that 'the Conference, while not
disliking South Africa, dislikes its colour bars and its racial
outlook . . . It is against annexation and prefers U.N.O.
trusteeship'.[66]

For Buchanan, the 'consultation' of Namibians was an
'absolute swindle'. He believed that it was organized mainly
because the British government had informed Smuts that the
consent of Namibia's population was the condition for London's support of Pretoria.[67] Tshekedi, for his part, was confident that the South African proposal for incorporation would
be defeated and that 'Bechuanaland would have played a very
big part in bringing this about'.[68] Nevertheless, Tshekedi envisaged the possibility of the General Assembly voting in favour
of incorporation. In this eventuality, Bechuanaland should seek
closer association with Southern Rhodesia 'so that the fight for
a free port, to which Rhodesia has only become alive, could
be made jointly with Rhodesia'.[69] But Buchanan was sceptical
about Rhodesia's intentions. He feared that the Rhodesians
would make 'common cause with the Union Whites against
all Africans whether in the Union, in the Rhodesias, in the
Protectorates, or elsewhere in Africa'.[70]

The government in Salisbury – like Tshekedi – wanted to
take advantage of the issue of Namibia's incorporation into
South Africa to negotiate for the establishment of a corridor
through Namibia to the Atlantic as Beira would not be satisfac-
tory as an outlet for Rhodesian exports.[71] Plans for a rail link

between Rhodesia and the Atlantic had existed since the early 1920s after South Africa had opened a railway from Walvis Bay to Gobabis near the Bechuanaland border in 1924.[72] A survey was carried out in 1931. But technical problems, doubts about the line's profitability and South African opposition[73] led the project to be temporarily abandoned. The Rhodesian government resuscitated the project of a corridor to the Atlantic after the Second World War. From a political point of view, 'we cannot be shut in by foreigners and goodness knows what the Union will do after Smuts goes'. Economically, a port on the Atlantic coast would allow coal from Wankie to be competitive on the international market instead of using the longer route to Beira in Mozambique.[74]

But as in the case of Tshekedi Khama, London was not willing to support the Rhodesian government. While Britain supported Pretoria's claim for Namibia's annexation, which excluded the establishment of a corridor through Namibia, London argued – not without cynicism – that it could not back the Rhodesian claim for a corridor , as 'we might be giving the impression that we were supporting the Union government's proposal for imperialistic reasons, i.e. in order to secure a piece of the territory for a British colony'.[75]

While Tshekedi and Buchanan who had been prevented from leaving southern Africa, relied on India to defend the case against Pretoria, Xuma, the president of the ANC lobbied personally against Namibia's annexation to South Africa.[76] He had joined members of the South African Indian Congress who backed India's case against the South African government's treatment of the Indian minority.[77] In a statement to the United Nations, written in New York, Xuma protested against incorporation of Namibia on behalf of not only the people of Namibia and South Africa, but also on behalf of those of the High Commission territories Bechuanaland, Lesotho and Swaziland.[78]

The Communist Party and its Youth League, South African local opposition groups and trade unions[79] added their names and weight to the protest against Namibia's incorporation by sending letters and telegrams to the United Nations. They notably condemned South African policy inside Namibia and asked for the territory to be placed under a U.N. trusteeship.[80] And the Transvaal Council of Non-European Trade Unions sent a letter of protest in conjunction with the League of Coloured People, the Pan-African Federation and the West African National Secretariat which had been established in the wake of the Fifth Pan-African Congress held at Manchester in October 1945.[81] This may explain in part why South African trade unions who were not active in Namibia in 1946, voiced their opposition to the annexation of the territory. The Manchester Congress, 'a landmark in the history of Pan-Africanism and decolonization',[82] had assigned to trade unions a leading role in the decolonization process.[83] The Congress had situated Pretoria's domestic and regional policies in the broader context of anti-colonial struggle. The resolution on southern Africa emphasized that 'the struggle of our brothers in South Africa is an integral part of the common struggle for national liberation throughout Africa'.[84]

The involvement of South African trade unions and opposition groups in the Namibian question has to be seen above all in the light of the radicalization of the resistance *inside* South Africa during the Second World War. In this context, it can be argued that the involvement of trade unions, ANC and the Communist Party against Namibia's annexation was linked to their support of India's campaign against Pretoria's policy towards the Indian minority. Both issues were debated at the United Nations at the same time. This presented a unique occasion for exposing and weakening the South African government in the international arena. For Smuts was caught in a fundamental contradiction which could easily be exploited. As coauthor to the preamble of the U.N. Charter which 'reaffirmed faith in fundamental human rights' and called for 'social progress and better standards of life in larger freedom', Smuts could not, at the same time, credibly defend his government's policies in South Africa and Namibia. The General Assembly spoke out against Pretoria's treatment of the Indian minority on 7 December 1946 and rejected South Africa's claim for the incorporation of Namibia by 37 votes to nil with nine abstentions[85] one week later on 14 December 1946.

South African opposition groups saw the United Nations debate on Namibia's incorporation into South Africa as an occasion to weaken the South African government on the international scene. Tshekedi Khama opposed Namibia's annexation primarily because he wanted to break Botswana's situation as a landlocked country and avoid its encirclement and eventual annexation by South Africa. Although Tshekedi's claim that he had played a significant role in bringing about South Africa's defeat[86] remains open to further investigation,[87] the involvement of Tshekedi and to a lesser extent of South African opposition groups against Namibia's incorporation was important. Tshekedi helped to expose the situation *inside* Namibia which was little known and which was in contrast with the yearly reports which the South African government had submitted to the League of Nations. Furthermore, in November 1946 Tshekedi contacted the Reverend Michael Scott recently released from jail in South Africa and acquainted him with the Namibian issue.[88] And it was Scott who became a indefatigable advocate of Namibian *anti-colonialism* at the United Nations.[89]

While Tshekedi and South African opposition groups brought Namibian anti-colonialism to international attention in the wake of the Second World War, regional actors also informed the formation of Namibian nationalism defined as a force 'seeking to create a progressive independent state and government in Namibia and to foster a spirit of collective purpose among all the people of Namibia'[90] from the early fifties. The dynamics of resistance inside South Africa contributed significantly to the formation of the South West Africa People's Organization (SWAPO) and the South West Africa National Union (SWANU), both of whom engaged in cooperation with other southern African nationalist movements from the early sixties.

CHAPTER TWO

REGIONAL DYNAMICS OF NAMIBIAN NATIONALISM. 1949–66

As much as southern African regional actors contributed to the emergence of Namibia as an issue of United Nations diplomacy, the regional dimension complemented significantly the local dynamics of anti-colonialism, nationalism and their repression inside Namibia. During the fifties, the dynamics of resistance in South Africa and leaders of South African opposition movements played an important role in the very formation of Namibian nationalism as reflected in the formation of SWAPO and SWANU. The rapid decolonization in Africa in the early sixties also accelerated the movement for national emancipation in southern Africa where exile politics and the preparation for armed struggle became its salient feature.

While the dynamics of resistance inside South Africa played an important role in the formative phase of Namibian nationalism, nationalist movements from Namibia, South Africa and Angola attempted to coordinate their activities from the early sixties. Two features characterized the relationships between southern African liberation movements from the outset. Political cooperation and solidarity in Pan-African forums such as the Pan-African Freedom Movement of Central and Southern Africa (PAFMECSA) and in regional groupings like the South African United Front, was complemented by tactical cooperation in the field, ranging from day-to-day contact in transit camps in Botswana to attempts of military collaboration between SWAPO and Holden Roberto's National Front for the Liberation of Angola (FNLA) in northern Angola.

SWAPO's alliance with FNLA in the early sixties and to a certain extent with ZANU of Zimbabwe and PAC of South Africa in the 'Congo Alliance' from 1963 to 1964, – though

24

short-lived – is important to the understanding of SWAPO's relationships with other southern African liberation movements. It created the basis for personal relationships which were to exist concomitantly with and independently of, SWAPO's later political alignments with MPLA, ANC, ZAPU and FRELIMO.

The launching of the armed struggle in Angola and South Africa in 1961 and the radicalization of the anti-colonial and nationalist struggle in Namibia precipitated the reaction of South Africa and Portugal. As much as the politics of liberation went beyond the confines of Namibia, efforts of the colonizers to preserve colonial rule were not limited to repressive measures inside the colonial borders. South Africa, the British authorities in Botswana and Southern Rhodesia increasingly engaged in police cooperation against refugees from South Africa and Namibia in the wake of the Sharpeville massacre of March 1960 and the repression of SWAPO's and SWANU's activities following the Windhoek shootings of December 1959.

Angola was to be the prime focus of cooperation between colonizers. Efforts by South Africa and Portugal to contain Namibian and Angolan nationalist movements mirrored attempts by Lisbon to maintain colonial rule. They also reflected the emergence of a new South African regional strategy in the wake of Sharpeville and the rapid decolonization of Africa, notably the creation of circles of buffer territories around a 'white' core area inside South Africa.

South African opposition movements and Namibian nationalism. 1949–60

While South African opposition groups and trade unions had expressed their opposition to Pretoria's plans for the annexation of Namibia in the context of their own opposition to South Africa's domestic and regional policies in the wake of the Second World War, they became directly involved in the emergence of Namibian nationalism. On one hand, South African trade union officials inside Namibia initiated Namibian contract workers to trade union militancy. On the other hand, Namibian workers and students in South Africa developed relationships with members of the ANC, the Communist Party and the Liberal Party, leading to the establishment of the Ovamboland People's Congress[1] in Cape Town in 1957.

South African trade unions in Namibia

Against the background of an expanding mining sector and fishing industry in Namibia after the Second World War, South African trade unionists of the Food and Canning Workers' Union became involved in Namibia from 1949. Formed by Ray Alexander (Ray Simons) in 1941, the Food and Canning Workers' Union rapidly spread in the eastern and western Cape;[2] and in 1942, Alexander set up a branch in Port Nolloth near the Namibian border. Following the establishment of fish processing factories in Luederitz and Walvis Bay,[3] the union spread its activities to Namibia where no labour legislation existed. After Alexander had met the administrator of the territory who agreed to an investigation by the Food and Canning Workers' Union, the union's president Frank Marquard – instead of Ray Alexander who was expecting a child – set up a branch in Luederitz in 1949.[4] But according to Alexander, Marquard made no headway,[5] and the workers asked for assistance by Alexander, probably because she was known for her trade union activities in the northwestern Cape province.

In 1952, Ray Alexander who then was secretary of the union, went to Luederitz where she found working conditions 'far below those which are . . . considered adequate and normal by factory management in South Africa'.[6] In spite of being followed by the South Africa 'Special Branch', Alexander managed to transmit some basic principles of trade union organization to the workers and four days after her arrival in Luederitz, management agreed to wage increases.[7] And in May 1952, the Legislative Council of the territory introduced labour legislation. While a *Factories, Machinery and Building Work Ordinance* reduced working hours from sixty to forty six hours a week,[8] a *Wage and Industrial Conciliation Ordinance* allowed for the registration of trade unions and conciliation procedures between workers and employers.[9]

According to the *Clarion*, 'it was due largely to continuous pressure from the union that industrial legislation has been introduced in the territory'.[10] Although Alexander campaigned successfully for the introduction of labour legislation and was not opposed by management, the police prevented her from continuing to organize workers in Luederitz and from initiating trade union activities in Walvis Bay.[11] After her trip to Luederitz, communications between the Luederitz branch and the Cape Town head office were cut. Alexander, who was a member of the Communist Party, was prohibited from attending meetings under the provisions of the *Suppression of Communism Act* and she had to resign from her post as secretary of the Food and Canning Workers' Union. Inside Namibia, the union suffered from police harassment and had to cease its activities after two strikes in fish canneries in Luederitz and Walvis Bay in 1953 during which three Ovambo workers were killed.[12]

While the suppression of the strikes put a temporary end to trade union activities inside Namibia, contacts between Namibian workers and the Food and Canning Workers' Union were maintained inside South Africa. In December 1953, Alexander secretly met with Andimba (Herman) Toivo ya Toivo, an Ovambo worker in Cape Town and a fellow worker from Luederitz, initiating a *personal* relationship with Namibian workers in Cape Town which was to contribute to the formation of the Ovamboland People's Congress in 1957.

South African opposition groups and the formation of SWAPO and SWANU

At the same time as South African trade unionists attempted to introduce trade union organization in Namibia, political movements inside Namibia and in South Africa contributed to the emergence of the South West Africa People's Organization (SWAPO) and the South West Africa People's Union (SWANU). In Namibia, anti-colonial resistance during the fifties was led by Chief Hosea Kutako of the Herero Chiefs Council and reflected in numerous petitions to the United Nations. Supported by the Nama, Ovambo and Damara and represented at the United Nations by Michael Scott, the Herero Chief's Council also collaborated with SWAPO's forerunner, the Ovamboland People's Organization (OPO) and SWANU in 1959, both of whom had developed from the dynamics of resistance inside South Africa.

In 1952, Namibians studying in South Africa[13] set up the

27

South West Africa Student Body in Windhoek. The students had been exposed to the 1952 Defiance Campaign in South Africa and one of the South West Africa Student Body's founders and member of the body's executive, Jariretundu Kozonguizi, who subsequently became the president of SWANU, participated in the activities of the ANC student branch at Fort Hare University.[14] By 1956, the South West Africa Student Body had developed into the South West Africa Progressive Association (SWAPA). The Association notably campaigned for better education for African children and gave advice as to the procedures to be followed for admittance to South African schools. According to Hamutenya and Geingob, the Student Body and the Progressive Association were unable to create a significant social base. The Student Body only comprised students who were able to attend schools in South Africa and the Progressive Association was 'a small club of teachers, clerical workers and other quasi-intellectuals in Windhoek'.[15] Ruth First, who at the beginning of the sixties saw SWANU as the leading Namibian nationalist movement, argued that the Progressive Association was the breeding ground for 'a national political movement to lead the struggle for freedom and independence'.[16]

As the Progressive Association, which evolved into SWANU in 1959, could not claim any substantial following in its own right, it attempted to broaden its social base. Inside Namibia, Kozonguizi who had joined the Herero Chiefs Council in 1954, succeeded, to a certain extent, to bridge the gap between the elders who opposed South African rule by petitions to the United Nations and sending delegations to the authorities with the younger generation 'anxious to replace tribal divisions with an aggressive and popular nationalism'.[17] In South Africa, Kozonguizi, who had again enrolled as a student at Fort Hare University[18] where he was on the executive of the ANC student branch, met Toivo ya Toivo, who had met Ray Alexander in December 1953 and who was instrumental in organizing Namibian workers and some students in Cape Town.

Andimba Toivo ya Toivo had found employment as a clerk for a furniture dealer in Cape Town, escaping, like fellow Namibians, contract work on South African mines. Moreover, Toivo ya Toivo like Sam Nujoma who had met with the former several times in Cape Town, had been politicized in part

28

through their contacts with the traditional leaders Hosea Kutako and David Witbooi.[19] In 1957, Toivo ya Toivo organized some of the two hundred Namibians who stayed in Cape Town into the Ovamboland People's Congress. The organization grew out of an informal support network among Namibian workers many of whom had deserted contract work on South African mines and were staying in Cape Town illegally.[20] From the outset, the program of OPC was targeted at combating the system of contract labour. Moreover, it was not ethnically defined as non-Ovambo students in South Africa, such as Jarir-etundu Kozonguizi and Ottile Shimming Abrahams identified with the goals of OPC.[21] In 1958, OPC was transformed into the Ovamboland People's Organization (OPO). While the abolition of the contract labour system was the primary aim of OPO, nationalist aspirations increasingly permeated the organization. According to Hamutenya and Geingob, the leaders of both OPO and the Progressive Association thought that the contract system was an issue around which 'the African workers in Namibia could be organized and politicized'.[22]

OPC and OPO also had the support from members of South African opposition groups, in particular of the Communist Party, the Liberal Party and of the African National Congress. However, the form and scope of their assistance differed, throwing some light on the early relationship between ANC and SWAPO which developed out of OPO in April 1960.[23]

The relationship between members of OPC/OPO and of the Communist Party were of a personal nature such as the relationship between ya Toivo, Ray Alexander and her husband Jack Simons since Toivo ya Toivo and Alexander had met in Cape Town in 1953. Namibian expatriates met in the Simons' house where OPC allegedly was formed. The involvement of the Communist party which had been illegal since the Suppression of the Communism Act in 1950, in the formation of OPC/OPO was given importance ex post facto by the South African prime minister Vorster in 1975,[24] who described SWAPO as being 'the child of four communists: Jack Simons, Ben Turok, H. Sachs and Fred Carreson'.[25]

The Liberal Party, by contrast, seemed to have played a role in the formative phase of OPO/SWAPO, which is generally underestimated. In 1958, a small group of the Namibians in Cape Town had come into contact with members of the Liberal

Party through Joseph Nkatlo, a former member of ANC and the Communist Party who now was the vice-chairman of the Liberal Party in Cape Town. Nkatlo who had met the Namibians through Toivo ya Toivo, acted as a middleman. The Namibians of OPO wanted to join the Liberal Party as full members – but without loosing their identity as members of OPO – in order to acquire methods of political organization.[26] Furthermore, in 1960 SWAPO used the Liberal Party's newspaper *Contact* for exposing the precarious living conditions in northern Namibia under South African colonial rule.[27]

Collaboration between OPO and the Liberal Party can be explained if seen in the South African political context of the late fifties. As far as the Liberal Party was concerned, it no doubt improved its Africanist image and countered earlier criticism that it was a 'white' Party with a few black 'stooges'.[28] In addition, the Namibians were perceived by members of the Liberal Party, and by Patrick Duncan who was chairman of the party's Cape Town branch in particular, as being receptive to the Liberal Party's ideas.[29] While this was no doubt true concerning the important role which the United Nations should play in the liberation of southern Africa, there is no evidence suggesting that the Namibians identified ideologically with the anti-Communist stand of the Liberal Party. Some argue that reasons of practical expedience played an important role in the affiliation of Namibians to the Liberal Party. Since the party had a strong following among Cape Coloureds who did not need work permits in Cape Town, membership of the Liberal Party would have enabled Namibians who were often illegally in Cape Town, to pass on the authorities off as Coloureds and circumvent restrictive labour legislation on Africans.[30]

The African National Congress did not have a decisive influence on the formation of OPC/OPO. On one hand, ANC was not firmly established in Cape Town. It was traditionally weak in the Western Cape due to the fact that Africans, a large proportion of whom were contract workers from the Transkei, constituted a minority of the area's population.[31] On the other hand, members of the ANC probably identified more easily with the Namibians who were members of the South West Africa Progressive Association and SWANU and who, in the eyes of some members of ANC, had probably articulated the ideas of nationalism and national liberation better than the

Namibian workers in Cape Town who formed the core of OPC/ OPO. However, it has to be emphasized that sympathy of ANC members such as Ruth First for SWANU, were not necessarily a reflection of ANC policy. In 1959, Oliver Tambo who had a lawyer's practice with Nelson Mandela, was attorney of OPO. Shortly after the Windhoek shootings of December 1959,[32] OPO had contacted Tambo in Johannesburg in order to assist the organization against the deportation of its leaders, notably Sam Nujoma its president and Jacob Kuhangua its secretary-general who had launched OPO in Windhoek in April 1959.[33] In the event, Tambo, who had flown to Windhoek, was refused entry on the grounds that South African 'Natives' would need a permit to enter South West Africa.[34] Furthermore, institutional cooperation between ANC and both SWANU and SWAPO was reflected in the affiliation of the three organizations in the South African United Front from 1960 to 1962.

Regional politics of liberation and colonization. 1960–6

The South African United Front. 1960–62

The formation of the South African United Front between ANC, PAC, SAIC, SWANU and – for a short period – SWAPO was the direct result of the beginning of South African and Namibian exile politics in the wake of the Sharpeville massacre, the banning of ANC and PAC in South Africa and increased repression inside Namibia after the Windhoek shootings of December 1959.

After the South African authorities had declared the state of emergency inside South Africa on 30 March 1960, the ANC Executive ordered its vice-president, Oliver Tambo, who had escaped a police round up, to leave the country.[35] Tambo and Tennison Makiwane who had already been abroad organizing the British Anti-apartheid movement, met Nana Mahomo, Peter Molotsi of the PAC and Dr. Yusuf Dadoo of the South African Indian Congress in Accra in April 1960. Encouraged by Kwame Nkrumah and other African leaders and anxious to present a united front, they agreed to work together in principle. While they rejected suggestions for creating a government-in-exile, they reached a formal agreement of cooperation during the Second Conference of Independent African States,

31

held in Addis Ababa in June 1960, establishing the South African United Front which was subsequently joined by SWANU and SWAPO. By the end of 1960, the Front had established offices in London, Accra, Cairo and Dar es Salaam and it sent delegations to African and Asian countries as well as to the United Nations.

During the 1960 General Assembly session, Oliver Tambo testified together with Nujoma, Kerina and Kozonguizi[36] against South African colonial policy. Replying to a delegate who thought that the ANC was a Namibian nationalist movement, Tambo pointed out that Namibians and South Africans fought the same struggle. Living on the two sides of the border, they suffered under the same government which was enforcing the same policies.[37]

But the United Front's activities centered on South Africa. In February 1961, it announced in London that the United Front was to launch a campaign against the recruiting of labour in southern African states for the South African mines. As a result, the government of Tanzania in one of Nyerere's first acts as prime minister , cancelled an agreement with the Witwatersrand Native Labour Organization for the recruitment of 10,000 to 12,000 men a year for the Rand mines.[38] As a result of another initiative by the United Front, Tanzania, Ghana, Nigeria, India, Ceylon and Malaya supported the Front's call for opposing an attempt by the South African government to join the Commonwealth unless it agreed to abandon its policy of apartheid.[39] The South African United Front also issued a call for economic sanctions against South Africa,[40] and in October 1961, the Front demanded South Africa's expulsion from the United Nations.[41]

African leaders inside South Africa approved the existence of the United Front. They supported Oliver Tambo who was in New York lobbying against South African occupation of Namibia.[42] But from the beginning, the Front's existence was overshadowed by the local dynamics of resistance inside South Africa, the split between ANC and PAC in particular. The South African United Front was therefore faced with the dilemma that the image of unity which the Front presented abroad, did not exist inside South Africa. And in January 1962, ANC and PAC representatives in Dar es Salaam announced that the Front had been dissolved, a decision which was confirmed by representatives of the two organizations as well as SAIC and SWANU in London on 13 March.[43] The deepening divisions between ANC and PAC inside South Africa,[44] and leadership quarrels abroad were the main reason for the Front's break up. The contradiction between the United Front's purpose and the reality of resistance inside South Africa was recognized by Tambo who accused PAC of dividing the opposition inside South Africa and adopting a similar conduct abroad.[45]

The role of Namibian nationalist movements in the South African United Front appeared to be peripheral. SWAPO was only affiliated during a short period in 1961,[46] and it can be argued that SWANU's membership in the Front was above all the result of Kozunguizi's personal involvement with the ANC abroad – he had joined the British Boycott Movement in 1959 – and as a former member of the organization. More importantly, Namibian participation in the United Front was overshadowed by increasing rivalry between SWANU and SWAPO in the early 1960s.

Initially, SWANU and OPO had closely collaborated. On one hand, Sam Nujoma who had launched OPO together with Jacob Kuhangua in Windhoek in April 1959, became a member of SWANU's executive in September 1959.[47] On the other hand, the two organizations joined hands in organizing a defiance campaign in protest against forced removals from Windhoek's 'old location' to a new township, which came to be known as 'Katatura' ('We have no dwelling place').[48]

However, collaboration between SWANU and OPO was short-lived. While it is still difficult to determine the exact reasons for the disagreement between the two organizations, a conflict of personalities between OPO and SWANU leaders abroad served as catalyst for tensions which led OPO to leave SWANU and to establish the South West Africa People's Organization (SWAPO) in April 1960. In particular, Kerina suggested in a letter to Nujoma in early 1960 that the Ovamboland People's Organization (OPO) should rid itself of its ethnical label and reconstitute itself as South West African National Congress.[49] After an attempt made by Nujoma and Kozonguizi while in Monrovia, to unite SWANU and OPO, had failed, the OPO reconstituted itself as South West African People's Organization in June 1960.

SWANU's involvement in tribal politics and personality

clashes were decisive in precipitating the split between SWAPO and SWANU. In 1959 and 1960, SWANU and OPO/SWAPO were not the only anti-colonial groups in Namibia. A third force, the Herero Chiefs Council under Chief Hosea Kutako, had been the main forum of nationalist protest against South African rule.[50] The Herero Chiefs Council now distanced itself from SWANU because of the latter's involvement in tribal matters. SWANU leaders had notably opposed the nomination of Clemens Kapuuo as a deputy to the aging Chief Kutako, as they considered Kapuuo as a collaborator of the South Africans. Furthermore, SWANU got involved in a tribal dispute between the Chief's Council and the Mbabenderu, a Herero speaking group. [51] This no doubt alienated SWANU from the Herero population base. Moreover, the Herero Chiefs Council and SWAPO increased their cooperation in the early 1960,[52] a fact which no doubt further isolated SWANU.

Growing dissensions between SWANU on one hand and the Herero Chiefs Council and SWAPO on the other, were compounded by personality clashes between Kozonguizi, the president of SWANU and Kerina, the then chairman of SWAPO (Sam Nujoma was SWAPO's president), both of whom had been the first two Namibian petitioners at the United Nations representing, together with the Reverend Michael Scott, representing the Herero Chiefs Council.[53] Kerina eventually left SWAPO in 1962 and SWANU rapidly lost influence in Namibia, especially after a last attempt to unite SWAPO and SWANU in 1963 in a South West Africa National Liberation Front (SWANLIF) had failed.[54] From the beginning, SWAPO thus was in a stronger position than SWANU in the different regional alignments other than the United Front.

Pan-African organizations

In addition to Namibian affiliation with the short-lived South African United Front, both SWAPO and SWANU participated in Pan-African conferences, such as the *All African Peoples' Conference* and SWANU had become a member of the *Afro-Asian Peoples' Solidarity Organization (AAPSO)* in 1959,[55] which had been established in the wake of the Afro-Asian Peoples Conference held in Cairo in December 1957. SWAPO was not affiliated to AAPSO until SWANU's expulsion from the organization in 1967 against the background of Sino-Soviet rivalry which was to play an important role in determining regional political alliances between southern African liberation movements from the late 1960s.

Both SWAPO and SWANU were also members of the *Pan-African Freedom Movement for East, Central and Southern Africa (PAFMECSA)*. Established in 1958 as the Pan-African Freedom Movement for East and Central Africa (PAFMECA), this 'loose but effective grouping of the political parties of all East and Central African territories'[56] attempted to achieve regional political cooperation in East and Central Africa. It provided significant assistance for the United National Independence Party (UNIP) of Zambia in the first general elections in Northern Rhodesia in 1962 and for the Kenya National Union (KANU) in the Kenyan elections in 1963. At PAFMECA's fourth conference held in Addis Ababa in February 1962 and chaired by Kenneth Kaunda, PAFMECA was enlarged so as to include nationalist movements of southern Africa. Renamed PAFMECSA with Julius Nyerere as its leading figure,[57] the Pan-African Freedom Movement for East, Central and Southern Africa became increasingly identified with the liberation of white ruled southern Africa. Dar es Salaam, where PAFMECSA offices had been established, became 'an open city for liberation movements and freedom fighters'.[58] By the end of 1961, PAFMECA shared premises with SWAPO, the South African United Front, a branch of UNIP of Zambia and UDENAMO of Mozambique; and most southern African nationalist movements became affiliates of PAFMECSA. UNIP, UDENAMO and the Malawi Congress Party had already joined in 1961. They were followed in 1962 by ANC, PAC, SWANU , SWAPO, the Basutoland African Congress and the Bechuanaland People's Party[50] as well as the Union of the Peoples of Angola (UPA),[60] and ZAPU.[61] Although a Coordinating Freedom Council, the forerunner of the OAU's Liberation Committee, provided some direct financial assistance to the liberation movements, estimated at a £1,000 a year per movement,[62] the significance of PAFMECSA to southern African liberation movements was largely symbolic. In terms of PAFMECSA's second constitution, adopted at the Addis Ababa conference of February 1962, liberation movements were represented on an equal footing with governments of independent states. More importantly,

PAFMECSA recognized the legitimacy of the armed struggle. A clause advocating non-violence contained in its first constitution, was dropped from the 1962 Constitution. Perhaps most importantly, PAFMECSA established the principle of collective responsibility for the liberation of southern Africa,[63] the most important objective after Pan-Africanism being 'to unite the people of Eastern, Central and Southern Africa in order to rid these countries of imperialism, white supremacy, exploitation and social degradation by stepped up nationalist activities to attain self-determination and establish democratic governments for the social and economic well-being of the people'.[64]

But solidarity between liberation movements and independent African states in political forums were only a part of the regional dynamics of nationalism in southern Africa and Namibia. More important than political solidarity in Pan-African organizations, tactical alliances and day-to-day collaboration between liberation movements in the field reflected the scope for and limitations of, regional solidarity in the liberation of southern Africa. In the case of Namibia, tactical cooperation between SWAPO and to some extent SWANU, with ANC and PAC of South Africa in Botswana and SWAPO, FNLA and PAC in Angola was confronted by collaboration between the colonizers, between South Africa and the British authorities in Botswana and the Central African Federation, but primarily between South Africa and the Portuguese in Angola.

The beginning of exile politics in Bechuanaland

Bechuanaland (Botswana from 1966), due to the fact that it shares borders with both Namibia and South Africa, was the natural meeting point for Namibians and South Africans who left their countries in the wake of the banning of ANC and PAC in South Africa in 1960 and the police repression inside Namibia following the Windhoek shootings of December 1959. Moreover, Bechuanaland became an important transit place for volunteers who were to undergo military training in Tanzania, Ghana, Egypt, Algeria and socialist countries, the Soviet Union in particular, as a result of ANC's, PAC's and SWAPO's decision to embark on armed struggle.

In South Africa, the ANC national executive decided in June 1961 to establish Umkhonto we Sizwe ('Spear of the Nation' in

Zulu), which formally launched its sabotage campaign with bomb attacks on electric power stations and government offices in Port Elizabeth and Johannesburg on 16 December 1961. PAC did not really begin to plan for guerrilla war before August 1962, after its leader Leballo had been released from jail, two months after the first group of volunteers recruited by Umkonto had escaped South Africa for military training in Tanzania. Over the next year, more than a dozen groups attempted to reach Dar es Salaam, first through Bechuanaland, Northern Rhodesia (Zambia) and Southern Rhodesia (Zimbabwe) and later, as the danger of being intercepted grew, by charter aircraft from Francistown in Bechuanaland to Dar es Salaam.[65]

Policy shifts from political action to armed struggle also took place in Namibia and decisively influenced the regional dynamics of Namibian decolonization. SWAPO had discarded its early policy of advocating a United Nations trusteeship in September 1960,[66] and subsequently called for the 'temporary administration of the country by a United Nations Commission composed of African states, to arrange for free general elections . . . [and] independence not later than 1963'. SWAPO also called for the establishment of a United Nations police force, the release of all political prisoners and the disarmament of all South African military and para-military personnel and its withdrawal to South Africa.[67] While SWAPO's demands would be reflected, to a great extent, in Security Council Resolution 435 of 1978, which was to provide the basis for the Namibian independence process in 1989, SWAPO did not want to rely exclusively on United Nations action. According to Hamutenya and Geingob, 'by 1962, SWAPO had come to the realization that to rely on the United Nations' intervention to liberate Namibia was to leave this liberation to mere chance. SWAPO decided that political and military efforts in pursuit of national liberation were not contradictory, but rather they were complementary and should be pursued concurrently'.[68]

Accordingly, SWAPO initiated a military training program. On one hand, volunteers who had entered Namibia from Tanzania in 1962, successfully recruited 'hundreds of cadres for military training and academic education'.[69] On the other hand, a first despatch of 200 Namibians left for military training in the United Arab Republic (Egypt) in the same year. In Bechuanaland, SWAPO volunteers were initially very close to the men of PAC with whom they often shared accommodation.[70] But as PAC was plagued by its internal divisions and had little credibility with the other movements, SWAPO cooperated mostly with ANC. They travelled jointly to the refugee camps in Tanzania where they also shared training facilities. However, SWAPO did not interfere – and this remained its policy – with the internal divisions between ANC and PAC.[71] After spending some time in the Kongwa camp in Tanzania, guerrillas were then sent for further training in Ghana, Algeria, Egypt and the Soviet Union and from 1965 also to the People's Republic of China and North Korea. However, most SWAPO volunteers underwent training in Africa.[72]

While Bechuanaland was primarily a transit place for both Namibian and South African volunteers, there were plans for the establishment of military camps inside Bechuanaland near the Namibian border. In 1961, Patrick Duncan who had been the head of the Cape Town branch of the Liberal Party of South Africa and who was close to SWAPO, tried to raise funds in order to set up a SWAPO camp in the northwestern part of Bechuanaland near the Namibian border. For Duncan believed that it was essential to have bases in the contiguous territories in order to facilitate the liberation first of Namibia, then of South Africa. Duncan was supported by Andreas Shipanga, secretary of the Cape Town branch of SWAPO, who was also then member of the Liberal Party. But according to Duncan's biographer, the plan was opposed by David Astor, a friend of Duncan, who helped to finance the Liberal Party, as well as by Michael Scott and Colin Legum. Scott did not want to take sides with SWAPO against SWANU by supporting the establishment of SWAPO bases in Bechuanaland and Legum argued that a large sum of money should not be invested in a project that might already be known by the police who would be able to intercept people going to and returning from the camp.[73]

While Duncan's plan for the establishment of a SWAPO camp near the Botswana-Namibian border never materialized, the newly independent African states such as Tanzania (Tanganyika until 1964) and Ghana met their facilities at the disposal of the guerrillas. The military training of southern African nationalists was financed above all by the Soviet Union and

China on a bilateral basis directly with the liberation movements. In particular, they channeled their aid through the African Asian Peoples Solidarity Organization (AAPSO), which had been founded in Cairo in 1958. AAPSO was important for the liberation movements, as the national branches of AAPSO channelled aid to the liberation movements.[74] Both the Soviet Union and China were members of AAPSO in the 1960s.[75] Bilateral Soviet and Chinese aid to the liberation movement thus existed outside the framework of the Organization of African Unity and its 'Coordinating Committee for the Liberation of Africa, which was responsible for channeling aid from African countries to liberation movements from 1963. However, details concerning Soviet and Chinese aid to the liberation movements were not published and thus remain subject to speculation.[76]

Apart from aid by the socialist countries for guerrilla training, scholarships obtained from western governments and multinational corporations[77] enabled Namibian and South African refugees to justify their travels from Bechuanaland to Tanzania, with the British colonial authorities in Bechuanaland, the Rhodesias and Nyasaland. However, Namibian refugees in Bechuanaland had sometimes left Namibia only with a vague promise of scholarships. In 1963, 54 refugees were reported to be in Bechuanaland while waiting for their scholarships which had not come forward.[78] This presented SWAPO with some logistical problems, as the Namibian refugees then in transit in Francistown were uncertain about their official status. In the 1960s, scholarships in Europe and the United States were very popular among southern African nationalists, even more as it was difficult to obtain work in the newly independent states of southern Africa, such as Tanganyika (1961) and Zambia (1964). In the United States, they were able to benefit from private – largely church sponsored – and government scholarships programmes.[79] However, as a result of colonial collaboration against the emerging liberation movements, it became increasingly difficult for Namibian and South African refugees to reach their destination of either studies or military training.

British colonial collaboration with South Africa against Namibian nationalists

Attempts by members of SWAPO, SWANU, ANC and PAC to reach Tanzania through the Rhodesias (Zambia and Zimbabwe) were indeed prevented by the governments of the Central African Federation (Northern and Southern Rhodesia, Nyasaland) on one hand and as a result of collaboration between South African and British colonial police in Bechuanaland on the other. Between 1961 and 1962, only 360 ANC men succeeded in reaching ANC camps abroad,[80] and many Namibians were arrested before being deported either to Namibia, or South Africa.

In January 1963, a group of Namibians was arrested in Bulawayo where they were sentenced to two months imprisonment.[81] One of them, Maxton Joseph who was SWAPO's first representative in Bechuanaland, was deported to Pretoria where he was jailed for an additional two years.[82] SWAPO's president Sam Nujoma and six other Namibians were also arrested in Bulawayo in the same month,[83] while Andreas Shipanga, together with Dr. Kenneth Abrahams and two other Namibians were stopped by the South African police *inside* Bechuanaland when they attempted to travel from Ghanzi near the Namibian border to Francistown. Chief Husea Kutako, who had already opposed Namibia's incorporation into South Africa in 1946 and was head of the Herero Chiefs Council, one of the three anti-colonial Namibian groupings at the beginning of the 1960s, did not mince his words when speaking about British-South African collaboration against Namibians: 'What we know in South West Africa is that the South African police often go to Bechuanaland in the same way they travel in the four provinces of South Africa and in South West Africa. We believe the South African police go to Bechuanaland with the consent of the British government to spy on movements of the refugees. The British authorities in Bechuanaland act as police and handmaidens for Dr. Verwoerd. They shamefully do the same thing in Bechuanaland as that which they do in Southern Rhodesia of returning refugees to the South African government. The only difference is that the refugees in Bechuanaland are handed secretly to the South African police while there is an extradition [treaty] between the South African government and Southern

Rhodesia'.[84] And in 1964, SWAPO accused the British authorities in Bechuanaland of deporting 154 Namibian refugees who had crossed the border.[85]

In addition to collaboration between South African and British colonial police in Bechuanaland and infiltration of South African agents into the refugee community living at what was known as the White House in the township of Francistown,[86] Namibian and South African refugees were also exposed to the hostility of Bechuanaland's settler community. The pressure of the white community was 'a traumatic experience of South, or South West Africans arriving at Francistown where they found themselves surrounded by hostile whites',[87] who were reported to have dynamited a refugee center near Francistown and set fire to an airplane which was about to fly refugees out of Bechuanaland.[88]

South African-British collaboration in Bechuanaland was not restricted to the control of Namibian and South African political activists. In 1958, the minister of defense of the Union of South Africa had requested the British government to grant to the South African Defence Forces transit facilities from South Africa through Bechuanaland to the Eastern Caprivi strip where South Africa intended to establish a military training school so as 'to enable the combined armed forces of the Union and South West Africa to adapt themselves to the true conditions of war which may arise in tropical parts'.[89] While the British government turned down Pretoria's request, it nevertheless allowed the South African forces to reconnoitre an emergency route from the Caprivi strip through Bechuanaland to Namibia and was reported to consider sympathetically requests by Pretoria to send vehicles to Namibia across Bechuanaland. Manoeuvers which were described by the South African defence ministry as large-scale exercises, took place in the Eastern Caprivi strip in August 1959.[90]

From the point of view of Pretoria, the military buildup in Namibia and the collaboration between South Africa and the British colonial governments against Namibian and South African refugees has to be seen in the light of a shift in Pretoria's perception of its own position in southern Africa. In the wake of the Sharpeville massacre of March 1960 and in the light of the rapid decolonization of Africa, Pretoria began to perceive a direct threat to the apartheid system both internally and through the emergence of an anti-apartheid front of African states through the Organization of African Unity, through its Liberation Committee in particular.[91] For Pretoria, 'the emergence of black states forced South Africa's front line down from the Middle east 'gateway' [Suez] to Rhodesia. The old doctrine of meeting the enemy in the far north had to be abandoned'.[92]

As a result of Sharpeville, the South African government nearly tripled its defence expenditures from 22 million pound sterling in 1960–61 to over 60 million in 1962–63,[93] principally geared to suppress the internal challenge to the regime. Described as the 'politics of security' and justified on the grounds of combating communism,[94] repression inside South Africa was complemented by the emergence of a regional southern African policy which was to culminate seventeen years later in the Total National Strategy.

In the eyes of prime minister Verwoerd, apartheid should not be confined to South Africa and its 'homelands', but would include the High Commission Territories of Bechuanaland, Basutoland and Swaziland which Pretoria had wanted to annex since the establishment of the Union of South Africa in 1910. Linked to South Africa through a Customs Union since 1910,[95] and being an outlet for the expanding South African economy for which it provided labour, the three High Commission territories, if drawn into the homeland design, would, according to Verwoerd, also 'prevent the adoption of policies in the Territories which ran counter to separate development'.[96] Although Britain opposed incorporation of Bechuanaland, Basutoland (Lesotho) and Swaziland and was ready to decolonize, Verwoerd still wanted to create political and economic ties between the three countries, even politically independent and South Africa. In 1963, he proposed the establishment of a commonwealth which would be a consultative body composed of Bechuanaland, Basutoland, Swaziland, South West Africa, Southern Rhodesia and 'independent' homelands. Economic links would be maintained through a common market type organization. According to the well informed South African academics Venter and Geldenhuys, 'Dr. Verwoerd's commonwealth-cum-common market design . . . would have surrounded South Africa with a group of virtual client states'.[97]

While Pretoria's attempts to draw the High Commission Territories into the apartheid design failed, South Africa consolidated her position in Namibia which was already a de facto fifth province of South Africa because of its economic and political integration into the Republic. A 'Commission of Inquiry into South West African Affairs', established in 1962 and headed by Odendaal, a former administrator of the Transvaal, prepared a plan for Namibia's future administrative structure.[98] The Commission proposed the establishment of ten different homelands, or ethnic 'nations' inside Namibia which were gradually to be given 'independence', eight for Africans, one for the Rehoboth community and one for the 'Coloureds'. A 'white' South West Africa was to be integrated more closely into the Republic. One of the aims of this strategy which implied the application of apartheid to Namibia, was to maximize ethnic differentiation and tribalization and break up nationally based movements.[99] The bantustanization of Namibia would thus reinforce the *cordon sanitaire* protecting South Africa from the impact of decolonization and external pressures for political change in both Namibia and South Africa.[100]

But the South African government did not immediately implement the recommendations of the Odendaal Commission. In 1960, the Security Council had voted an arms embargo against South Africa while Ethiopia and Liberia had instituted proceedings in the International Court of Justice against South Africa's occupation of Namibia. But the Court rejected Ethiopia's and Liberia's contentions in 1966, a fact which led to the revocation of South Africa's mandate over Namibia by the General Assembly in October 1966. However, in the logic of setting up a *cordon sanitaire* around South Africa, it embarked on the militarization of the territory. In 1939, Pretoria had extended the Union's defence legislation to Namibia and had integrated the defense of the territory and the Union in a single structure.[101] Taking advantage of the fact that Walvis Bay, Namibia's only deep water harbour was exempt from the provisions of the League of Nations mandate, because it had been a Cape enclave during the German occupation of Namibia, South Africa had constructed a military airfield near Walvis Bay in 1940.[102] Large scale military exercises took place in the eastern Caprivi in 1959 and by 1965, two new air bases had been built near Katima Mulilo in the Eastern Caprivi and in Rundu on the Angolan border in Okavango in addition to the airports which already existed at Windhoek, Grootfontein, Walvis Bay and Odangwa in Ovamboland.[103]

While the militarization of Namibia in the early 1960s was the outcome in part of Pretoria's policy of creating buffer territories around South Africa, it also served the more immediate objective of repressing SWAPO's and SWANU's activities inside the country, as evidenced by the establishment of a military camp in Ovamboland and the maintenance of a regiment of the Armoured Corps of the Citizen Force in Windhoek.[104] But the repression of Namibian nationalist movements was not confined to police action inside the territory and collaboration with British police in Bechuanaland and Southern Rhodesia. Increasingly, Angola became the focus of cooperation between SWAPO and Angolan nationalist movements and between South African and Portuguese police, laying the basis for the dynamics of a regional conflict in southwestern Africa.

Namibian nationalism and Angola

Cooperation between Nambian and Angolan liberation movements was a distinguishing feature of regional dynamics in southwestern Africa from the early 1960s, underpinned as it was by ethnic kinship and the contract labour system. On one hand, ethnic kinship between the Ovambo of northern Namibia and the Kwanyama of southern Angola characterized constant cross border interactions between northern Namibia and southern Angola. On the other hand, southern Angola was an important labour reservoir for Namibian and South African mines.[105]

Contract workers from Angola had worked in mines in Namibia since the early 1920s. They had constituted an important part of the work force in the diamond mines near Luederitz throughout the mandated period with the exception of the economic depression when employment was generally low. For as a result of population pressure on scarce resources and the ensuing shortfall in subsistence production, rather than administrative measures, Angolans looked for employment in Namibia's mining and fishing industries.[106] The double pattern of demand for labour by the mining and fishing industry and the supply of labour largely as a result of pressures on a fragile subsistence economy continued after the Second World War.

44

In 1946, between 5,000 and 6,000 contract workers, approximately half of Namibia's contract labourers, came from Angola.[107] Migration from Angola to the mines and fisheries in Namibia accelerated in the early sixties,[108] and in 1971 more than 40% of the contract workers in Namibia were from Angola.[109]

They were exposed to an increasingly militant worker consciousness among Namibians which arose not only out of the hard working conditions inside Namibia but also of external influences such as 'the symbolic role of the United Nations, whose claim to legal authority has been instrumental in destroying the legitimacy of colonial rule'.[110] As the issue of contract work was the initial platform of OPO, Angolan workers were no doubt influenced by OPO/SWAPO, not only concerning its campaign for the abolition of contract work, but also in regard to SWAPO's anti-colonialism in general. SWAPO was also credited by the Portuguese with a following among the Kwanyama in the area of N'Giva north of the Namibian border,[111] and in 1962, the South African police prevented SWAPO organizers from infiltrating southern Angola.[112]

As much as the ideas of Namibian nationalism penetrated southern Angola through contract labour and ethnic Ovambo kinship, two factors which were to become important ten years later during a general strike in Namibia of 1971/72, SWAPO also cooperated with Angolan nationalists, in particular with Holden Roberto's National Front for the Liberation of Angola (FNLA). The movement had developed out of the Bakongo peasant uprising against the Portuguese in the north of Angola in 1961 and was formed in March 1962 as a result of a merger between Holden Roberto's Union of the Peoples of Angola (UPA) and the Democratic Party of Angola (PDA).[113] In 1962, Jacob Kuhangua, SWAPO's secretary-general, had talks with members of the Provisional Government of the Republic of Angola which had been established in March 1962, leaders of the National Liberation Army of Angola (ELNA) of which Roberto was commander in chief and the General League of Angolan Workers (UNTA) which had been in existence in Leopoldville since 1960. SWAPO subsequently signed a joint declaration with FNLA, which was to assume the name of Revolutionary Government in Exile (GRAE) in April 1962. As they were 'facing common problems', SWAPO and FNLA notably called for strong military collaboration against the Portuguese in Angola and the South Africans in Namibia. In so doing , they hoped to prepare the ground for a future 'Federation of Independent States of Angola, Botswana and South West Africa' under a central government which would eventually become part of the 'Federal States of Africa'.[114]

What were the reasons for an alliance between SWAPO and FNLA in a Pan-African context? While the movement's alliance with SWAPO fuelled speculations in the press that Roberto wanted to gain supporters in the extreme south of Angola, SWAPO's statement in the United Nations that they had signed a joint declaration calling for military collaboration because they were facing common problems, suggests that FNLA and SWAPO perceived certain common features in their opposition to colonial rule. The origins of the two movements were rural and ethnically defined, the initial basis for support being the Ovambo in case of SWAPO and the Bakongo in the case of UPA/FNLA. Both SWAPO and UPA subscribed to Pan-Africanist ideas and attempted to broaden their ethnic platform and evolve into nationalist movements; and the movements faced rival nationalist organizations in the Movimento Popular de Libertação de Angola (MPLA) and the South West Africa National Union (SWANU).[115]

In addition to and partly as a result of the features which they shared, more immediate concerns prompted the collaboration between the two movements who were separated by approximately 1,000 kilometres. The possibility of FNLA's activities spreading south certainly played a role in the calculations of both FNLA and SWAPO. But as far as Holden Roberto and FNLA was concerned, it can be argued that the dynamics of the struggle inside Angola, namely FNLA's rivalry with MPLA which had launched the armed struggle in Luanda in February 1961, was the main reason for reaching agreement with SWAPO. Roberto probably saw the alliance with SWAPO as a means of strengthening FNLA by gaining subcontinental and Pan-African influence, thus opposing MPLA which had allied itself with the Mozambique Liberation Front (FRELIMO), the African Independence Party of Guinea Bissau and Cape Verde (PAIGC) and the Liberation Committee for São Tomé and Principe (CLSTP) in the Conference of Nationalist Organizations of the Portuguese Colonies (CONCP) established in Casablanca in April 1961. Already in January 1962, Roberto had attempted to form an alliance with the Liberation Movement of Guinea and the Cape Verde Islands (MLGICV) and to establish a Front africain contre le colonialisme portugais (FACCP) which never went beyond the stage of a joint communiqué.[116]

The joint declaration of FNLA and SWAPO which called for a Federation of Independent States of Angola, Botswana and South West Africa under a central government which could become part of the 'Federal States of Africa', seems clearly to have been designed to enhance FNLA's and Roberto's personal standing within the Pan-African movement. Roberto, who had participated at the Second All African Peoples'Conference in Tunis in January 1960, had been elected on the Conference's Steering committee before being replaced one year later by MPLA's Mario de Andrade. And at PAFMECA's Conference in Addis Ababa in February 1962, during which the organiz-ation was enlarged so as to include southern African liberation movements, UPA was the only Angolan movement to be repre-sented and was the only Angolan organization to belong to PAFMECSA. UPA/FNLA's alliance with SWAPO certainly gave UPA publicity and was viewed by the South Africa liberal weekly newspaper *Contact* as 'a most significant development in the freedom movement in southern Africa'.[117]

SWAPO may have thought that FNLA would be able to carry the struggle to southern Angola, especially in the light of Roberto's efforts to broaden UPA's social basis by appointing men from central and southern Angola to positions of responsi-bility in UPA. In March 1961, Roberto had contacted Jonas Savimbi, a student from central Angola, who belonged to a prominent Ovimbundu family from Chilesso in Bié district and who had fled to Europe where he enrolled for studies at the University of Lausanne, Switzerland. After some hesitation, as he did not want to commit himself either to MPLA, or UPA, Savimbi accepted to become secretary-general of UPA in Nov-ember 1961.

As much as Roberto's appointment of Savimbi 'did much to blunt charges that it [UPA] was tribalist',[118] Savimbi's position as secretary-general of UPA and subsequently as foreign minis-ter of GRAE, also laid the basis for personal contacts between the SWAPO leadership and Savimbi, which developed into an almost ten year long working relationship between SWAPO and UNITA from its formation in 1966 to 1975.

In 1963, the existing alliance between SWAPO and GRAE was joined by other southern African liberation movements who formed the short-lived Congo Alliance. This alliance came into being not only as a result of Roberto's attempts to broaden his influence, but also has to be seen in the context of the emergence of the Organization of African Unity. Adoula, the president of Congo-Léopoldville who wanted to assume a Pan-African role as Congo-Léopoldville had occupied a leading place within the Monrovia group of African states,[119] supported Roberto's initiative to invite southern African liberation movements, one per territory, to establish their politico-military headquarters in Léopoldville. After talks with leaders of the southern African movements, Roberto proposed that the União Democratica Nacional de Moçambique (UDENAMO), the Pan-Africanist Congress of South Africa, led by its London representative Nana Mahomo, SWAPO and the Zimbabwe African National Union (ZANU), led by Ndabaningi Sithole and which broke away from ZAPU in August 1963, join the new alliance. The Adoula government promised to extend financial assistance to the five movements of the Congo-Alliance until the OAU Liberation Fund would be operational.

According to Marcum, three criteria guided Roberto's choice of UDENAMO, PAC, SWAPO and the emergent ZANU into the Congo Alliance. Membership in the CONCP alliance (CLSTP, PAIGC, FRELIMO, MPLA, ANC) automatically disqualified a movement from becoming member of the Congo Alliance. In addition, Roberto and UPA/GRAE would have had a 'natural affinity' with the four other movements of the Congo Alliance because they 'were uni-racial and sceptical of intellectuals and multiracialism and nationalist and wary of ideological issues'.[120] However, Marcum's assertions about the common features of the five movements are not convincing. Affiliation to the Congo Alliance was above all of circumstantial nature. As FRELIMO was a member of CONCP which had established a working relationship with ANC since 1962, Roberto logically drew UDENAMO of Mozambique and PAC of South Africa into the Congo-Alliance. But membership in CONCP was not a criterion for selection as far as ZANU and SWAPO were concerned.

In the case of Zimbabwe, ZANU's instead of ZAPU's affiliation to the Congo-Alliance can be seen as a corollary of policy differences and leadership struggle within ZAPU which led to the formation of ZANU in August 1963. It can be argued that Sithole, Mugabe and Takawira saw the Congo Alliance as a means of strengthening their position in Africa against Nkomo whose leadership they contested. In particular, they contested Nkomo's idea of setting up a government-in-exile as opposed to waging the struggle from within Zimbabwe. Nkomo's idea of a government-in-exile was also opposed by Nyerere and Kaunda. And this opposition 'acted as a catalyst for those who had been growing increasingly discontented with his [Nkomo's] leadership'.[121] After ZANU's break from ZAPU in August 1963, Sithole persuaded Roberto to recognize ZANU as a member of the Congo Alliance, a role which was contested by representatives of ZAPU until the collapse of the Congo Alliance in mid–1964.[122]

As far as SWAPO was concerned, the *existing* alliance with GRAE was probably the main reason for SWAPO's participation in the Congo Alliance. In addition to strengthening ties with Roberto and GRAE's foreign minister Savimbi, the Congo-Alliance also laid the basis for the relationship between SWAPO and ZANU which, according to SWAPO, was always excellent.[123] SWAPO's membership of the alliance also points to SWAPO's position in regard to the ANC. As the two movements belonged to two antagonistic alliances, it can be argued that the relationship between SWAPO and ANC in the early sixties were mainly the result of networks between individuals which had been created in Botswana and Tanzania and which ran parallel to SWAPO's and ANC's official alignments.

Some members of the Congo-Alliance also attempted to engage in military collaboration. Guerillas from the Mozambican UDENAMO, PAC and SWAPO started military training with Roberto's men at FNLA's camp at Kinkuzu in northern Angola. The volunteers expected to receive military instructions in combat alongside Angolans, following which some of them would be attached to the National Liberation Army of Angola (ELNA). But from the outset, the project was handicapped by poor organization and a lack of discipline, especially among Angolans and South Africans.[124] According to Marcum, the FNLA, on whose support SWAPO, UDENAMO and PAC had counted, 'offered a demoralizing example of politico-military improvisation and indiscipline'.[125] The military training scheme collapsed and the Congo-Alliance had disintegrated by May 1964. In the same year, the OAU Liberation Committee withdrew its recognition of FNLA on the grounds that its armed struggle had waned and because it was identified more with an ethnic Congolese than Pan-Angolan movement.[126]

South African-Portuguese collaboration in Angola. 1960–4

As much as FNLA, SWAPO, PAC and UDENAMO saw military collaboration as a means of carrying the struggle southwards, the Congo Alliance, despite its ephemeral existence and ineffectiveness, fuelled Luso-South African military collaboration in repressing any signs of nationalism.

The formation of SWAPO and reported 'stirrings of discontent' among the Ovambo on the Angolan side of the border in 1961,[127] signalled the beginning of military cooperation between the Portuguese and South Africa. South African police notably attempted to control the activities of SWAPO in Ovamboland, where SWAPO leaders who had been deported to Ovamboland in the wake of the Windhoek shootings of December 1959 and the police repression in the country, had established a network of committees.[128] In 1961, the South African authorities started fencing the border with Angola, a move which was resented by the peasants who attempted to remove the fences as soon as they had been put up. In addition, the Portuguese authorities, in collaboration with the South Africans, had confiscated several thousand Namibian cattle grazing to the north of Namibia's colonial border. The resulting confrontations between the peasants and the colonial administration gave SWAPO 'further ammunition with which to fight the system'.[129] In 1962, the South African police controlling the border prevented SWAPO organizers from infiltrating into southern Angola and increasingly cooperated with the Policia International de Defesa de Estado (PIDE) in their common attempts to prevent nationalist movements from taking root north of the Namibian border, where SWAPO was reported by the Portuguese to have a following in the area around N'Giva.[130]

Already in June 1960, Nujoma had complained to the United Nations that South Africa carried out military operations in northwestern Namibia in the northern Kaokoveld near the Cunene river.[131] And in 1962, he testified in the UN Fourth Committee that two SWAPO men had been arrested in the Federation of Rhodesia-Nyasaland before being deported to Namibia, from where they were escorted to Angola. The men were reported to have been killed by Angolan settlers.[132] But Luso-South African military cooperation in the early sixties was not confined to the Namibia-Angola border region. The South African defence minister had visited Lisbon in the wake of the 1961 uprising in the north of Angola. Although the Portuguese were able to contain the uprising,[133] the South Africans assisted the Portuguese in surveilling the border between Angola and Katanga, while the Katanga secessionists were materially assisted by both South Africa and the Portuguese.[134] In the words of Kuhangua, SWAPO's secretary-general, Pretoria 'had organized a group of fighters which it had sent to fight in Angola, knowing that if the rebellion was successful in Angola, it would then spread out to South West Africa'.[135]

Although the spectre of a generalized rebellion in Angola and Namibia was perhaps an improbable scenario to the Portuguese and South Africans in 1961, their cooperation in Angola and especially in Mozambique because of its proximity to South Africa – several meetings between South African and Portuguese military took place in Mozambique in 1963 and 1964 – blended into their respective overall policy designs. For South Africa, assistance to Portugal in the Angolan rebellion in 1961 was in line with Pretoria's apartheid policy, namely to create circles of buffer territories around the 'white' core area inside South Africa. The Portuguese portrayed collaboration with South Africa in terms of their role as a member of the Western defence alliance NATO, rather than as an attempt to maintain colonial rule.

According to Melo Antunes, who had been a Portuguese officer in southern Angola and who participated in the negotiations of the Alvor agreement of January 1975 between MPLA, FNLA and UNITA, before becoming foreign minister of Portugal, the fundamental ideological premise of the Salazar and later Caetano regime for collaboration with South Africa was that the Portuguese saw their colonial empire as a bedrock for the defense of western Europe and even to some extent the United States, against Soviet expansionism in Africa. And all

51

forms of Portuguese cooperation with South Africa would have derived from the ideological premise of their common defense of western civilization in Africa.[136]

South Africa, for her part, portrayed herself as champion of western values in Africa, anti-communism being a legitimizing ideology since the Nationalist Party had come to power in 1948.[137] The common mission of South Africa and Portugal in defense of western civilization was clearly expressed by the South African foreign minister in 1970: 'We are two friendly countries and we are perfectly identified with each other as defenders of civilization in Africa. We have a common mission to fulfil and we are fulfilling it'.[138]

But despite numerous speculations on a defense alliance, there is no evidence that military collaboration between South Africa and Portugal and later Rhodesia has ever been formalized.[139] As a result of Portugal's traditional role in Africa as a weak partner and client state of Britain and later of South Africa especially as far as Mozambique was concerned, Portugal was determined to demonstrate to the outside world its sovereignty and independence. The Portuguese government limited its commitment to South Africa to vague statements such as that it was 'prepared to negotiate nonaggression agreements with the governments of countries and territories which are contiguous to the Portuguese overseas provinces . . . [and] did not rule out provisions calling for cooperation in all fields which may be of mutual interest'.[140] South Africa's position is resumed by the much quoted remark of Vorster in 1967 that South Africa was 'good friends with both Portugal and Rhodesia and good friends do not need a pact. Good friends know what their duty is if a neighbour's house is on fire'.[141]

As far as Angola was concerned, military collaboration between South Africa and Portugal increased significantly with the opening of MPLA's third military region in the east of Angola,[142] and the launching of SWAPO's armed struggle in 1966. Moreover, South Africa and Portugal increasingly engaged in economic collaboration and in joint infrastructure ventures such as the construction of a hydroelectric scheme in southern Angola.

The launching of SWAPO's armed struggle in August 1966 set the scene for a regional dimension of Namibian nationalism which assumed the form of political alignments with southern

African liberation movements against the background of Sino-Soviet rivalry, tactical military cooperation with UNITA , both complemented by a subregional cross-border dynamics resulting from the 1971 general strike in Namibia and a parallel Ovambo peasant uprising.

CHAPTER THREE

COOPERATION BETWEEN LIBERATION MOVEMENTS AND BETWEEN COLONIZERS. 1966–74

After SWAPO's president Sam Nujoma had announced on 18 July 1966 that SWAPO would launch the armed struggle,[1] the first important engagement between SWAPO guerrillas and the South African police took place in Ovamboland on 26 August 1966[2] after South African security forces had attacked SWAPO's base at Omgulumbashe. The scene was set for the rapid escalation of the dynamics of resistance and repression inside Namibia. South African forces killed two SWAPO fighters and captured twenty-seven during the engagement on 26 August and captured the camp which had been SWAPO's first base inside Namibia and which had been equipped and fortified for eleven months.[3] By the end of August, according to ya-Otto of SWAPO, 'the entire north was flooded with South African troops in helicopters and armoured cars, combing the bush for guerillas, terrorizing and arresting hundreds of villagers'.[4] On 27 September, SWAPO retaliated with a surprise attack on government buildings at Oshikango on the Namibian-Angolan border.[5] SWAPO fighters raided the property of pro-South African chiefs in Ovamboland in November and December 1966 and attacks spread to the Grootfontein region.[6] But by December 1966, South African police had clamped down on SWAPO by arresting its leaders who were still inside Namibia, among them the organization's acting president Nathaniel Mahuilili, its acting secretary-general John ya-Otto, the regional secretary for Ovamboland Andimba Toivo ya Toivo and the secretary for external relations Jason Mutumbulua.[7] Arrested under the Suppression of Communism Act which was applied for the first time to Namibia, 37 Namibians were charged under the Terrorism Act (No.83 of 1967), which had been promulgated in July 1967. The Act was made retroactive to June 1962 and covered both South Africa and Namibia.[8]

But in addition to both the local dynamics of the conflict and its international ramifications highlighted by the UN General Assembly's decision in October 1966 to revoke South Africa's mandate over Namibia (GA resolution 2145 (XXI), 27.10.1966), a web of regional interactions increasingly permeated the politics of liberation and repression. On one hand, political alignments of SWAPO with other southern African liberation movements within the Afro-Asian Peoples Solidarity Organization (AAPSO) overshadowed but did not exclude more discrete relationships with movements outside AAPSO's orbit, with UNITA of Angola in particular. On the other hand, the spreading of MPLA's armed struggle to eastern Angola, with the southeast of the country becoming a transit route for SWAPO guerillas from Zambia to northern Namibia, led to increased cooperation between South Africa and Portugal. Military and police collaboration which had existed since the early sixties, was intensified and increasingly complemented with economic cooperation. While South African private investment in the Angolan economy remained relatively low, South African capital significantly contributed to joint infrastructure projects, notably the Cunene hydroelectric scheme on the Namibian Angolan border.

Namibia and the Afro-Asian solidarity movement

The liberation of southern Africa was of primary concern to the Organization of African Unity and its Liberation Committee. Most southern African liberation movements had also been affiliated through the Pan-African movement in PAFMECSA. However, the most important political alignments of southern African liberation movements appear to have taken place within the transcontinental Afro-Asian Peoples Solidarity Organization (AAPSO).

Established in the wake of the Afro-Asian Peoples Solidarity Conference held in Cairo from 26 December 1957 to 1st January 1958 and with its headquarters in the Egyptian capital, AAPSO was important for the liberation movements. In particular, the organization's national branches were the institutional expression of bilateral links between the socialist countries and the liberation movements, the Soviet Solidarity Committee being the executing agent of the Soviet bilateral aid to liberation movements.[9]

As much as affiliation to AAPSO was important for the liberation movements because it could help to secure material aid which the Liberation Committee of the OAU could not provide,[10] AAPSO at the same time created and exacerbated rivalries between liberation movements. It was within AAPSO that Soviet Chinese rivalry over the leadership of the anti-colonial and anti-imperialist struggle in the Third World was fought out between 1961 and 1967.

For Nikita Khrushchev, the Soviet policy with regard to Africa and the Third World in general, had a twofold objective: extending Soviet influence in the Third World, by accepting the principles of nonalignment as formulated at the Bandung conference in 1955, while at the same time searching for a global arrangement with the United States in terms of strategic parity and expressed in the formula of 'peaceful coexistence'. However, this balancing act between Third World activism and superpower policy proved to be perilous as evidenced by the Cuban missile crisis of November 1962. China was quick to exploit Krushchev's climb down during the missile crises and the signing of the Nuclear non-proliferation treaty between the United States and the Soviet Union in 1963. The Chinese leadership whose aim was to isolate the Soviet Union from the Third World countries, not only denounced collusion between the United States and the Soviet Union. China also contended that the Soviet Union was 'white', 'European' and 'developed'. She could therefore not grasp – contrary to China – the real problems which Third World countries had to face.[11] China emphasized the importance of the anti colonial and anti-imperialist struggle while the Soviet Union stressed the significance of disarmament and world peace to which the anti colonial struggle would be subordinated.

The African-Asian Peoples Solidarity Organization became a central forum for Sino-Soviet rivalry. Among African countries, China initially had the support of Nyerere of Tanzania. At the third plenary assembly meeting of AAPSO, held in Moshi in February 1963, Nyerere alluded to Soviet-American collusion. He pointed out that the world was witnessing a second 'scramble for Africa', a coming international class struggle between rich and poor 'with capitalist and socialist countries on both sides of the conflict'.[12] The Chinese themselves reverted to racist arguments by stating that the Soviet people would never support the anti-imperialist struggle because they were white.[13] While China enjoyed some support by African states at the Moshi conference, nine months later, the Soviet Union scored a major success at a meeting of the AAPSO's Council in Nicosia, Cyprus. The Council approved the signing of the Nuclear Non-Proliferation Treaty between the Soviet Union and the United States and the principle of peaceful coexistence. African delegates who grew impatient with China's increasingly virulent attacks against the Soviet Union, were not prepared to accept China's stand against non-proliferation[14] and 'most African delegates, many of whom had previously supported the Chinese, now moved over to the Soviet camp'.[15]

From 1964 to 1967, ideological infighting between the Soviet Union and China dominated the work of AAPSO which led to disillusionment of African delegates with the organization. However, the ideological rift between the Soviet Union and China within AAPSO was important as it determined regional political alignments between southern African liberation movements, in particular as concerned Namibia.

AAPSO's fourth plenary conference held at Winneba in Ghana in 1965, decided to hold AAPSO's next plenary meeting in Peking. This decision prepared the ground for transforming the Sino-Soviet ideological dispute into an organizational split which resulted in China leaving AAPSO in 1967. The Soviet Union tried to change the venue from Peking to Algiers. As a result of pressure from the Soviet Union, undoubtedly aided by the Cultural Revolution which tended to restrict Chinese foreign commitments,[16] the Council of AAPSO, at a meeting held in Nicosia, Cyprus in February 1967, reversed the previous decision to held the next Assembly in Peking. Instead, it proposed Algiers.[17] The Chinese, who did not participate at the Council meeting , objected and declared the decision to be illegal. The Chinese Committee for Afro-Asian Solidarity announced that it would go ahead in its preparations for the conference to take place in China as planned. At the same time, China dissociated herself from AAPSO. For the Chinese, the organization's permanent secretariat in Cairo 'has degenerated into a tool of the Soviet revisionists for implementing their counterrevolutionary lines . . . [and China] shall henceforth have nothing to do with this organ'.[18] But neither the Peking, nor the Algiers conference took place. While China was too deeply involved in the Cultural Revolution to host a meeting, there was not sufficient support from AAPSO members for the conference to be held in Algiers as proposed by the Soviet Union.

While AAPSO's Council meeting in Nicosia had formalized the split between the Soviet Union and China who withdrew from the central organization,[19] one of the resolutions of the Nicosia Council Meeting directly concerned Namibia. In its eighth organizational resolution concerning membership within AAPSO, the Council decided to expel SWANU from the organization and to accept SWAPO as a new member[20]

Two related factors help to explain SWANU's expulsion from and SWAPO's admission to the now Soviet controlled AAPSO, namely SWANU's pro-Chinese stance and the recognition of SWAPO as the sole Namibian liberation movement by the Organization of African Unity. SWANU's expulsion from AAPSO had been precipitated by an increasingly pro-Chinese attitude of Kozonguizi who had been SWANU's president until his resignation in 1966. Already in 1960, while in China on a visit, Kozonguizi was criticized by his rival Kerina, then chairman of SWAPO, for his alignment with socialist countries. Kozonguizi had made a speech over radio Peking, deploring the handling of the Namibia issue by the United Nations.[21] Moreover, at an earlier AAPSO conference at Havana in January 1966,[22] Kozonguizi condemned 'Soviet-American collusion under the guise of peaceful coexistence,'[23] and he aligned himself with the Chinese by backing the Chinese delegation in its opposition to any mention of 'peaceful coexistence' appearing in the Conference's resolutions[24]

Kozonguizi's pro-Chinese position at Havana reverberated at the Nicosia meeting of the Council of AAPSO which was now Soviet dominated. According to Gibson, the pro-Soviet faction at the meeting was led by the ANC, while SWANU who was a member of the AAPSO Executive Committee and the Bechuanaland People's Party proved to be staunch supporters of China. During the debates, the ANC delegate attacked SWANU for being a virtually nonexistent 'student group' which was seeking to undermine AAPSO. Referring to Kozonguizi's speech in Havana as an example of SWANU's negative attitude, the ANC delegate called for SWANU's expulsion from AAPSO. Despite SWANU's protests that such a move would be unconstitutional, a vote was called. SWANU was expelled by twenty-five votes to nil and SWAPO admitted instead.[25]

The Nicosia meeting sealed a new alliance of southern African liberation movements, namely MPLA, FRELIMO, PAIGC, ANC, ZAPU, and SWAPO. Presenting a common front in Africa and Europe,[26] the six liberation movements also enjoyed recognition by international solidarity organizations which set them apart from other southern African nationalist movements such as ZANU, PAC, FNLA, and UNITA. At the 'First International Conference of Solidarity with the Fighting People of Southern Africa and the Portuguese Colonies' organized by AAPSO and the World Peace Council in Khartoum in January 1969, the conference resolution called for the recognition of MPLA, PAIGC, FRELIMO, ANC, SWAPO and ZAPU as 'the sole official and legitimate authorities' of the territories in which they were fighting.[27] Henceforth known as the 'Authentic Six', they not only enjoyed material and political support of the Soviet Union, but also presented a common front on the international scene, much to the irritation of the OAU Liberation Committee who also channelled aid to those movements who were not part of the Khartoum alliance.[28] PAC, ZANU, UNITA and the *Comite Revolucionario de Moçambique* (COREMO) who all enjoyed Chinese support, condemned the Khartoum conference as an attempt 'to control the liberation struggle of the Portuguese colonies and southern Africa in order to further Soviet cooperation with the United States for their joint domination of the world'.[29] While SWANU and FNLA were associated with this grouping, there never was any formal 'anti-Khartoum alliance'. Joint declarations condemning the Khartoum alliance and statements of solidarity were the most visible sign of cooperation between southern African nationalist movements excluded from the Khartoum alliance.[30]

However, the Khartoum alliance of the 'Authentic Six' and the informal grouping of other southern African nationalist organizations only give a very partial picture of the dynamics of interaction between liberation movements in southern Africa. The liberation movements were indeed critical of political alliances as, in the words of Oliver Tambo 'the Afro-Asian

59

revolution, which AAPSO was formed to accelerate, remains – and will yet remain – an unfinished revolution, especially if the mighty anti-imperialist forces continue in their present state of disunity and if 'massive' or 'increased ' material assistance to fighting peoples ends where it begins, in speeches and resolutions'.[31] In addition to ideological affinities and traditional ties with the Soviet Union, existing patterns of cooperation and, particularly as far as SWAPO was concerned, recognition by the Organization of African Unity played a role in determining the grouping of MPLA, FRELIMO, PAIGC, ANC, SWAPO and ZAPU in the Khartoum alliance. Moreover, cooperation within the Khartoum alliance did not prevent its members from either receiving Chinese support, or from working with liberation movements outside the alliance. The relationships between FRELIMO and ZANU and between SWAPO and UNITA are cases in point.

ANC and MPLA because of their traditional links with Moscow were the pivots of the Khartoum alliance. The Angolan Communist Party which had evolved out of the Portuguese sister party in 1955, was instrumental in the establishment of MPLA in 1956, a common front of emerging nationalist movements. And Nikita Krushchev pledged solidarity with MPLA in 1961 in response to MPLA's request for assistance.[32] However, Soviet aid was slow to materialize. It was temporarily withdrawn in 1963 because FNLA/GRAE then enjoyed the exclusive recognition of the OAU, a fact which prompted MPLA's cooperation with Cuba. Soviet aid in fact remained moderate until the large scale Soviet intervention in Angola in 1975.[33]

Links between Moscow and the ANC were the result of the long relationship between the Communist Parties of the Soviet Union and South Africa which date back to 1921.[34] And one year after the launching of Umkhonto we Sizwe (MK) in 1961, established as a result of a joint initiative by the CP and ANC, the Communist Party managed to secure aid from the Soviet Union and its allies which was estimated at $2.8 million.[35]

While ANC and to some extent, MPLA were the obvious allies within the pro-Soviet Khartoum alliance because of their existing links with the Soviet Union through the communist party, their affiliation to the alliance with PAIGC, FRELIMO and ZAPU can be explained in terms of existing alliances.

MPLA, FRELIMO, PAIGC were linked in the CONCP alliance. CONCP had set up a working relationship with ANC in 1962,[36] and had also established close links with ZAPU.[37] ZAPU in turn was closely linked to ANC. ZAPU was also backed by the Soviet Union who saw it as the original nationalist movement, from which ZANU had subsequently split. And the Soviet leaders had developed good working relations with Nkomo.[38] In July 1967, a joint ZAPU-ANC military force had entered Zimbabwe in the Victoria Falls region. And in August, Tambo of the ANC and Chikerema of ZAPU, in a joint statement, confirmed the existence of a common military front.[39]

SWAPO's affiliation to the Khartoum alliance – as well as its admittance to AAPSO in 1967 – were determined above all by the fact that SWAPO was the only Namibian nationalist movement recognized by the OAU, which also was the crucial factor determining recognition of African liberation movements by the Soviet Union. Initially, SWAPO and SWANU both enjoyed OAU recognition and they were to receive equal allocations from the first budget of the Liberation Committee. However, commitment to armed struggle was a prerequisite for receiving funds. SWANU did not commit itself to taking this step,[40] and by mid-1965 SWAPO was the only Namibian nationalist movement qualifying for OAU assistance.[41] Moreover, it is alleged by some that SWAPO was recognized as a beneficiary of OUA aid as a result of Sam Nujoma's friendship with the then Tanzanian foreign minister and chairman of the OAU Liberation Committee Oscar Kambona.[42]

While SWAPO's position as Namibia's only liberation movement recognized by the OAU seemed to determine its inclusion in the Khartoum alliance, it can be argued that ideological factors played a very minor role as far as SWAPO's relationship with the Soviet Union and indeed with the other liberation movements belonging to the Khartoum alliance was concerned. SWAPO was by no means anti-Chinese. SWAPO volunteers had been trained in China since the early sixties and SWAPO adopted elements of the Maoist conception of guerrilla warfare.[43] Furthermore, political cooperation within the alliance with MPLA, PAIGC, FRELIMO, ANC and ZAPU did not prevent SWAPO from collaborating with liberation movements outside the orbit of AAPSO and the Khartoum alliance, particularly as there existed no previously established formal links with either CONCP, ANC, or ZAPU. According to SWAPO, the relationship with ZANU had always been excellent.[44] It probably dated back to 1963 when both movements were affiliated to the Congo alliance. However, the relationship between SWAPO and PAC, another member of the Congo alliance, had deteriorated. In 1967, representatives of PAC courted unsuccessfully Nujoma during a meeting in London.[45] And in 1972, SWAPO refused requests that it should assist PAC units in their attempts to reach Botswana through the Caprivi strip.[46] SWAPO did not renew its collaboration with FNLA. However, it cooperated with UNITA which was to become the source of some tension between SWAPO and MPLA.

SWAPO and UNITA

Personal links between SWAPO and Savimbi had existed since 1962, when SWAPO had formed an alliance with Roberto's GRAE of which Savimbi was foreign minister. These personal contacts were maintained, even after Savimbi had resigned from GRAE in 1964 because of disagreement with Holden Roberto.[47] After Savimbi had announced his resignation during the OAU's second summit in Cairo in July 1964, he contacted the SWAPO office: 'I knew them: they were friends. They welcomed me and suggested we should work together'.[48] Contact was maintained during 1965 with UNITA's co-founder Tony Fernandes establishing contacts with SWAPO in Dar es Salaam, where they were were waiting for permission from the Zambian government to use Zambia as a rear base for raids into Namibia.[49] SWAPO's association with UNITA intensified from March 1966 when UNITA was formally launched.

According to the Savimbi biographer Fred Bridgland, SWAPO hid Savimbi and ten followers in a refugee camp near Dar es Salaam from July to September 1966, after they had returned to Africa from China where they had been trained in guerilla warfare. However, MPLA members who were in a nearby transit camp, suspected UNITA's presence in the SWAPO camp and complained to the OAU Liberation Committee. And SWAPO was instructed to hand over any Angolans in their camp to MPLA. According to Bridgland, Sam Nujoma managed to conceal the presence of Savimbi and his men in the camp by arguing that some SWAPO members spoke Portuguese. As a result of ethnic kinship between the Ovambo living on the Namibian and Angolan side of the border, they would have been brought up in southern Angola. After the the Zambian government had lifted its restrictions on the presence of African liberation movements in Zambia in October 1966, SWAPO and UNITA guerrillas travelled together from Tanzania to Lusaka, from where UNITA fighters were sent by Savimbi to Angola.[50] SWAPO also helped to train UNITA's first fighters in southern Angola.[51]

Collaboration between SWAPO and UNITA was based on personal contacts and to a certain extent, on ethnic affinity. Ethnic kinship should indeed not be underestimated as a contributing factor to SWAPO-UNITA cooperation, ethnicity being 'a factor which cannot be ignored in liberation politics and organizations'.[52] In particular, the Kwanyama Ovambo community lived on both sides of the Namibian-Angolan border and some Kwanyama were members of UNITA.[53] For example, Kashaka (Antonio) Vakulukuta, who was a leader of the Kwanyama living in Angola, had joined UNITA in the early 1970s and he was credited with support among Namibians living south of the border.[54] However, as far as SWAPO is concerned, the importance of ethnicity in its policies and in the composition of its leadership, is often exaggerated. Admittedly, SWAPO evolved out of the ethnically based Ovamboland People's Organization (OPO) and its principal popular support in Ovamboland. But from the beginning, SWAPO closely collaborated with members of other ethnic groups. In the early 1960s, SWAPO notably cooperated with the Herero Chiefs Council. This collaboration with a traditional non-Ovambo body, such as the Herero Chief's Council, persuaded members of the Herero community to join SWAPO.[55] In 1966, SWAPO and its leadership not only comprised Ovambo and Herero, but also Rehoboth and Baster people and the Lozi from Zambia through the Caprivi African National Union which had merged with SWAPO in 1964.[56]

Personal contacts[57] and ethnic affinity facilitated the main purpose of SWAPO-UNITA collaboration which, from the point of view of SWAPO, was above all a tactical necessity. SWAPO guerillas who wanted to penetrate Ovamboland from Zambia without entering the heavily armed and sparsely populated Caprivi strip, crossed UNITA controlled territory in southeast

Angola. And SWAPO depended on UNITA's clearance for enabling it to pass through the area.[58] Moreover, Savimbi alleged that UNITA had put a training camp at the disposal of SWAPO in UNITA controlled territory.[59] And after UNITA had opened an office at N'Ggiva near the Namibian border in June 1974,[60] Namibian refugees, who were not all members of SWAPO, often contacted UNITA officials who at times spoke the same language, rather than cadres of MPLA who did not have an office in N'Giva in 1974.[61] UNITA helped SWAPO activists to reach Zambia,[62] and as the situation in southern Angola was of great confusion at the time, some Namibians may have enrolled with UNITA which was on a recruitment drive in the region.

Although SWAPO had explained to MPLA the reasons for its collaboration with UNITA, namely to guarantee a transit route for PLAN fighters through southeast Angola to Namibia,[63] cooperation with UNITA created tensions with SWAPO's political ally MPLA. SWAPO and MPLA leaders discussed the issue at the 1970 Non-Aligned summit conference in Lusaka. According to Peter Katjavivi who participated at the meeting, 'there was a tense exchange with Nujoma demanding evidence of SWAPO collaborating with UNITA. Nothing was resolved, but there was no break in relations between the two organizations'.[64] However, when one of MPLA's leaders, Daniel Chipenda, was asked in 1969 about MPLA's cooperation with other liberation movements, he replied that they did not cooperate with anyone in Namibia.[65] Significantly, MPLA did not send any message of support to SWAPO's Consultative Congress held in Tanga, Tanzania at the close of 1970. The conference was attended by SWAPO's other political allies FRELIMO and ANC while ZAPU sent a message of support.[66]

Moreover, it has been alleged that SWAPO and MPLA clashed militarily in 1972,[67] and in 1975 MPLA claimed that they were fighting soldiers of SWAPO in southern Angola.[68] The fact that there could be the possibility of SWAPO and MPLA forces clashing militarily before the independence of Angola, while the two movements, at the same time, presented a united political front in solidarity meetings, should not be dismissed lightly. It highlights one aspect of the reality of the liberation struggle which is often overlooked. Perceptions of collaboration with other liberation movements by combatants of the Peoples

Liberation Army of Namibia (PLAN) did not necessarily correspond to the image of regional solidarity held by SWAPO's political leadership. Difficulties in communication with SWAPO headquarters in Lusaka due to geographical factors left PLAN a certain degree of autonomy. This no doubt helps to explain that SWAPO's cooperation with both MPLA and UNITA was not mutually exclusive at the time.

Although the extent of collaboration between SWAPO and UNITA should not be overestimated – SWAPO cadres worked closely with MPLA activists[69] – it was important enough to provoke MPLA's public protest. In a note to the Zambian government in June 1973, in which MPLA's president Dr. Agostinho Neto asked Zambia to intensify her actions against UNITA, Neto pointed out that Zambia should 'take into account that it is SWAPO which is the large-scale supplier of arms to UNITA and which provides Zambian travel documents for it, under the completely false pretext that UNITA should control southeast Angola which is a vital passage to Namibia.[70]

While the tactical exigency of a transit route through Angola reflected SWAPO's need for cooperation with UNITA, Savimbi's motives for working with SWAPO were less straightforward. Long established personal contacts as well as regional and ethnic affinities between some of the leaders of SWAPO and UNITA, accounted for much of Savimbi's motives for cooperating with SWAPO.[71] But this cooperation was of an opportunistic nature. Not only did Savimbi collaborate with the Portuguese army and police in order to fight MPLA,[72] but he betrayed SWAPO in 1975 by providing information on the location of SWAPO bases in Angola as a quid pro quo for South African assistance to UNITA against MPLA.[73]

Collaboration between South Africa and Portugal

SWAPO's relationship with other southern African liberation movements, characterized by a blend of political cooperation against the background of the Sino-Soviet rivalry in the Afro-Asian Peoples Solidarity Movement, personal relationships and ethnic kinship as well as military considerations, was paralleled by collaboration between South Africa and Portugal. In the logic of Pretoria's conception of maintaining the status quo inside South Africa by surrounding itself with a layer of buffer

65

territories and Lisbon's attempt to cling to its colonial empire, it was military cooperation which dominated the relationship between South Africa and Portugal. South African capital increasingly penetrated Angola and military cooperation between the two countries was accompanied by joint infrastructure projects, notably the construction of a huge hydroelectric complex covering southern Angola and northern Namibia, the Cunene dam scheme.

Military cooperation

Military collaboration between South Africa and Portugal which had begun in the early sixties, intensified in 1966, coinciding with the launching of the armed struggle by SWAPO and the opening of MPLA's third military region in east Angola.[74] According to an Angolan eyewitness, South African helicopters flew daily into Angola and the Portuguese arrested suspected SWAPO guerillas who were passing through Angolan territory on their way to Namibia.[75]

One month after SWAPO had launched its armed struggle in August 1966, the South African police and Portuguese troops intercepted a SWAPO commando inside Angola on the Namibian border.[76] In 1967, P.W. Botha, South Africa's then minister of defence and the South African Defence Forces' Chief of Staff made a visit to Lisbon. One year later, South Africa was allowed to operate an air unit in eastern Angola and a joint Portuguese-South African commando centre was established at Cuito Cuanavale, a small town in southeast Angola which twenty years later was to play a crucial role in modifying the regional military balance of power in southwestern Africa in favour of Angola and against South Africa.

Military cooperation between South Africa and Portugal was further strengthened in 1971 and 1972, when South Africa covertly supplied arms, helicopters and a limited number of pilots to the Portuguese forces in Angola.[77] From Cuito Cuanavale, which was also a South African helicopter base,[78] the helicopters were used to escort Portuguese troops who by then only moved in convoys of fifty to a hundred vehicles.[79] It was reported that South African army units were operating directly in the Cuando Cubango district in the south east, in the Moxico district in central Angola and that they had established bases in south west Angola and near Luso in the north east of the country.[80] MPLA accused both South Africa and Portugal of using chemical products in Angola's liberated areas.[81]

At the same time as South Africa started intervening in Angola using Namibia as a springboard, the militarization of Namibia and in particular the construction of an air base in the eastern Caprivi strip in 1965, also affected Rhodesia and Zambia. Rhodesian Hunter jet fighters and Canberra bombers reportedly used the airfield in the Caprivi strip;[82] and in 1965, the Zambian president Kaunda qualified the construction of the base in the Caprivi strip as 'a direct threat to Zambia's integrity'.[83] The base at Katima Mulilo which is situated more than a thousand kilometres north of Pretoria, was to become an important military forward position enabling South Africa to apply its regional military strategies to her neighbours.

In 1971, after heavy fighting between SWAPO and South Africa in the Caprivi strip and in the light of repeated accusations that Zambia harboured SWAPO guerillas, South Africa closed the border between the strip and Zambia,[84] and South African paramilitary units crossed into Zambia in October 1971.[85] The South African prime minister Vorster justified the incursion on the grounds that 'if terrorists come into our territory and attack our people, we reserve the right to pursue them wherever they might flee'.[86] Pretoria had initiated its policy of 'hot pursuit', which it subsequently used as one justification for the South African invasion of Angola in 1975 and which would be characteristic of incursions into the Front Line States in the context of Pretoria's Total National Strategy from the late seventies.

At the same time, the Caprivi strip became the springboard for supporting dissident movements in Pretoria's attempts to destabilize presumed host countries to ANC and SWAPO guerrillas, a policy which was to become notorious from the late 1970s. Against the background of secessionist sentiments among the Lozi (Barotse) in western Zambia, South Africa recruited a hundred Zambians for military training in Namibia in December 1972 before infiltrating them back into Zambia. Four of the ringleaders including the former mayor of Livingstone, were arrested and convicted of treason for allegedly plotting to overthrow the government. This attempt by Pretoria to foster dissident movements preceded a more serious incursion by an armed gang who returned from Namibia to Zambia via Angola in 1975. Led by a former Zambian government official and known as the 'Mushala gang', it was to create serious disorder in the North Western Province which was qualified by Kaunda as a small civil war.[87]

Economic collaboration

Military cooperation with Portugal and the beginnings of destabilization policies against independent southern African countries, were complemented by an increasing penetration of South African capital into Angola and joint infrastructure projects, notably the Cunene dam scheme.

Trade between Ango'a and South Africa was traditionally weak.[88] So was involvement of South African capital with the exception of diamond extraction by DIAMANG which was partly controlled by de Beers.[89] But a trade agreement between Portugal and South Africa of October 1964, coupled with Lisbon's decision, in April 1965, to abandon its traditionally restrictive policies on foreign investment in her colonies, led to an influx of South African and western capital into the Angolan economy, in particular into the extraction industry.[90] But South African *private* investment in the Angolan economy with the exception of mineral extraction, remained low,[91] despite the affirmation by the South African press that 'South African companies are exporting capital and know-how to Angola to take part in the tremendous development opportunities that exist for investors in this rapidly growing territory'.[92] There still seemed to persist 'an unmistakable apprehension on the part of the Portuguese lest they be 'swamped' by foreigners and in particular by South Africans'.[93] Although trade between the two countries doubled between 1964 and 1972, it remained modest,[94] South Africa being Angola's seventh ranking supplier after Portugal, West Germany, the United States, the United Kingdom, France and Japan.

South African capital participation was more important in joint infra structural schemes. Against the background of the nationalist uprising and its strategy of containing it, the Portuguese government hired South African contractors in 1962 for building a 3000 miles road complex in southern Angola at a cost of 160 million dollars.[95] In 1969, South African and Portuguese officials met to discuss the further development of road communications. Only a section from Sa da Bandeira (Lubango) to the Namibian border remained to be built in order to complete a strategic highway from Luanda To Beira in Mozambique via the Cape.[96]

The Cunene river dam scheme

But more important, because of its potential implications for the maintenance of South African control of Namibia and Portuguese colonial rule over Angola, was the ambitious project to build a hydroelectric complex along the river Cunene covering an area of 130,000 square kilometres, 95,000 of which are in Angola. The regulation of the flow of the Cunene, which rises in central Angola on the plateau near Huambo before running southwards to the Namibian border and then turning to the Atlantic coast, was presented by South Africa and Portugal as a way of promoting Namibia's and Angola's economic development. The Portuguese promoters of the scheme defined the aim of the project as being 'the transformation of physical conditions so as to promote local development and agriculture and the settling of the population in centres properly equipped for the improvement of their social and general living conditions [and] the provision of economic and social infrastructures and equipment to support the development of southern Angola'.[97]

The history of the Cunene dam scheme in fact dates back to the end of the nineteenth century when the German emperor and the king of Portugal signed a treaty delimitating the border between Angola and German South West Africa, thus putting an end to a dispute over water rights. In 1926, South Africa reached a new border agreement with Portugal and in a parallel accord, South Africa was given the right to build a dam inside Angola in order to guarantee Namibia's water supply. But disagreements between the South African and Portuguese members of a technical commission set up to investigate the project, led to the lapse of the agreement. Discussions were revived in 1962 on South Africa's initiative.

For Pretoria, the immediate aim was to reach an agreement in terms of which the water of the Cunene could be used to complement an existing scheme of canals in Ovamboland. But the South African initiative went beyond purely technical considerations. It has to be seen in the context of Namibia's integration into South Africa in the early sixties. The Odendaal Commission, which had drawn up a development plan for Namibia along the lines of apartheid, also analyzed the water power needs of the territory. After the Commission had visited northern Namibia and Angola, it proposed that the South African government seek as a matter of urgency the cooperation of the Portuguese government. Electricity drawn from the Cunene would be an important contribution for the economic development of South West Africa, for the irrigation of Ovamboland and the generating of electricity for the mining industries in particular.[98] A preliminary contract concerning a common Cunene development program was signed in 1964. But final agreement on the first phase of the construction was not reached before 1969.[99]

The first phase of the ambitious Cunene project, the total cost of which was estimated at $648 mio,[100] was financed almost entirely by South Africa with loans from West German, British, French, Dutch and Luxemburg banks.[101] Work started on the construction of a regulating dam at Gove south of Nova Lisboa (Huambo). The dam with an artificial lake of 179 square km was finished in 1973. Another important feature of the project was the construction of a power house at the Ruacana Falls on the Namibian-Angolan border completed in 1974 and a dam at Caluque, less than 20 km north of Ruacana inside Angola. Construction of the Caluque dam could not be completed before the independence of Angola and 'protection' of the Caluque dam which is instrumental for regulating the water supply to Ovamboland, was to be a pretext for the South African invasion of Angola in 1975.

But economic considerations such as the provision of water for Ovamboland and southern Angola and the generating of electricity for the Tsumeb and Rössing mines in Namibia and Cassinga mines in Angola concealed underlying political motives. For both South Africa and Portugal, the Cunene dam scheme was designed to strengthen their control over Namibia and Angola. While for Pretoria, the scheme was part of Namibia's incorporation into South Africa in order to reinforce the *cordon sanitaire* protecting South Africa from political change, Portugal's underlying motives can be seen in the light of Lisbon's policy of large-scale 'white' settlement and the resettlement of the African population in order to isolate nationalist forces in southern Angola.

While emigration to the colonies and land settlement had played a prominent role in Portuguese colonial policy since the thirties, the Portuguese government renewed its efforts to encourage intensive land settlement in Angola to ensure the continuation of Portuguese colonial control after armed revolt had erupted in Angola in 1961.[102] The Cunene dam scheme, once completed, would irrigate 125,000 hectares of land and enable over 6,000 families to settle on 20 hectare plots.[103] Land settlement, made possible by the Cunene dam scheme, like the Cabora Bassa dam in Mozambique, could thus help to ensure that the colonies would continue to provide protected markets for Portugal who could not compete internationally and provide foreign exchange for the metropolis through the export of minerals . According to official estimates, the regulation of the flow of the Cunene would allow for the eventual settlement of 500,000 people, an unrealistic assumption in the light of the fact that Portugal was nearing full employment due to massive emigration to western Europe.[104]

But the Cunene scheme also had an impact on the African population, as it threatened to disrupt the economic existence of the African population living in the south of Angola. In 1969, the Portuguese government ceded large tracts of land in the Cunene valley to South African settlers in order to derive supplementary income for her colonial wars.[105] More importantly, the flooding of the Gove artificial lake in 1973 and the freeing of land for settlers, forced pastoralists out of the region. This compounded the problems of Angolans, caused by an existing strategy of resettling them as a result of the Portuguese counterinsurgency program.

Angolans were resettled either in *aldeamentos* (strategic resettlements), or *reordenamentos rurais* (rural resettlements). Located generally in the east and to a lesser extent in the northwest of the country, strategic resettlements were large villages organized by the army. Often surrounded by barbed wire, they regrouped formerly dispersed Africans in order to isolate them from combatants. Rural resettlements were situated outside the immediate fighting zones with the alleged purpose of promoting economic and social development rather than preventing guerilla infiltration of the rural population. Rural resettlement officially began in 1962. In southern Angola, resettlement failed and proved to be a miscalculation by the Portuguese. On one hand, guerilla warfare had not even remotely touched the area. On the other hand, the resettlement program was resented by Africans. Contrary to the stated aim of the rural resettlement program which was to promote economic and social development, the traditionally conservative Angolan pastoralists of the south saw the resettlement program as yet another attempt to rob them of their lands and traditional way of life. Resettlement implied the installment in fixed settlements and therefore represented economic ruin for 37,000 seminomad pastoralists who lived in southern Angola. As a result, the people of the south of Angola were open to nationalist appeals, probably more because of the threats to their lifestyles by the resettlement program than by prospects of political independence. By the end of 1968, MPLA started an intensive campaign of politicization in the region which was to lead three years later to the opening of its sixth military region in January 1972.[106]

The Cunene dam scheme was opposed by SWAPO, MPLA and UNITA. UNITA condemned South African apartheid and Portuguese colonial policies in general, South Africa's involvement in the scheme representing 'a step forward towards the consolidation of apartheid in Namibia and oppression in southern Africa'.[107] SWAPO and MPLA particularly referred to the scheme's implications for the nationalist struggle and cooperation between Namibians and Angolans. For SWAPO, the clearing of bush land on both sides of the border, which would precede the creation of white settlement, especially in Angola, would have as a consequence the creation of a buffer-strip between the two countries. 'This, again, will make the communications between Namibians and Angolans more difficult because of the 'white belt' they will have to cross'.[108] Nujoma pointed out that the real purpose of the project was to strengthen the position of white settlers in southern Angola and northern Namibia. Many of these settlers would join the Portuguese or South African army, increasing the politics of repression in both Angola and Namibia. 'SWAPO was completely opposed to such schemes which were of a military rather than economic nature. It would do its utmost to thwart the Cunene River project and help the freedom fighters in Mozambique to destroy the Cabora Bassa dam'.[109]

SWAPO's apprehensions were echoed by MPLA. In addition to strengthening South Africa's and Portugal's economies, reinforcing South Africa's position as a White industrial base of a backward Black Africa in particular, investments in the Cunene project would be 'aimed at consolidating the position of settler domination in southern Africa, functioning as a link in a cordon the South African regime is trying to fashion against the advance of the national liberation movements and also representing a permanent threat to the independent African states'.[110] The fact that both SWAPO and MPLA linked the Cunene dam scheme to their struggle, became part of a further development of the regional dynamics in northern Namibia and southern Angola, which was expressed in a general strike in Namibia and a simultaneous Ovambo cross-border peasant uprising in December 1971 and January 1972.

The Namibian General Strike and its Repercussions on Angola. 1971–2

A strike in Namibia which began among contract workers in Walvis Bay,[111] led to a subregional dynamics on the Namibian-Angolan border involving contract workers, peasants, liberation movements and the colonizers South Africa and Portugal. From Walvis Bay, the strike quickly spread to the copper mines in northern Namibia and to the diamond mines in the south of the country. While workers in the commercial and industrial sectors joined the strike, it was estimated that over 22,000 contract workers – 25,000 if farm workers were included – took strike action, representing over half of the 43,000 contract workers of a total work force of 50,000 in 1971.[112]

As forty per cent of the contract workers were from Angola, coupled with the fact that 18,000 men had returned to Ovamboland as a result of the strike, repercussions on Angola were inevitable. The strike was joined by 600 workers on the Cunene project who came out in sympathy,[113] and one week after the strike had started, pickets were put up at the border to prevent strike breakers from Angola from entering Namibia. In Ondangwa at the Namibian-Angolan border thousands of workers who had returned, were detained in a large fenced-in field.

They were released by labour officials to return to their villages just as the first group of strike breakers arrived from Angola. The South African police stood by watching a bloody battle between the strikers and the strike breakers from Angola, before dispersing the crowd with tear gas.[114]

More importantly, the presence of politicized contract workers among the peasantry in Ovamboland led to a broadening of the resistance. The general strike merged with a peasant revolt on both sides of the border. At meetings, speakers increasingly articulated peasant grievances against the colonial administrations. In the first half of January 1972, several attacks on the property of headmen took place on the Namibian side of the border after they had called in the South African police to break up meetings. In mid-January 1972, the border fence was cut at 21 places and destroyed along 100 km. At the same time and partly in reaction to South African police intervention, people were attacking property of headmen and destroying stock control posts as well as government offices.[115]

On the Angolan side of the border, the Kwanyama of the Cunene district protested against the Portuguese system of taxation, fees and forced labour. They destroyed cattle vaccination stations and schools and attempts were made to destroy four administrative posts whereby a number of Portuguese and South African soldiers as well as African militia men collaborating with the administration were killed.[116]

The peasant revolt in the Ukwanyama region on both sides of the border has to be seen in the context of general peasant discontent with administrative measures. Opposition to administrative harassment, coupled with resistance to resettlement, were founded in a tradition of resistance against colonial rule, in particular among the Kwanyama who lived on both sides of the border. Mandume, the last Kwanyama king, had opposed Portuguese rule until 1915 and was killed in 1917 by a South African expedition completing the conquest of Ovamboland which had never been controlled by Germany.[117] Moreover, the Ukwanyama area was overpopulated, a reality exacerbated by the influx of settlers in southern Angola and cut into half by the border fence along the international boundary line, thus depriving the Kwanyama of traditional cattle grazing ground. According to testimonies from Ovamboland, peasants from the

Namibian side of the border cut the border fence primarily in order to reach grazing ground inside Angola.[118]

By February 1972, the 'cross-colonial-border' peasant revolt and the strike had been repressed by South Africa and Angola both individually and sometimes in joint action. The South African government reached a new labour agreement with the employers which was signed on 20 January, after short discussions with representatives of the Ovambo and Kavango Legislative Councils. While the agreement abolished the recruiting agency SWANLA, the function of which was taken over by the Ovambo Legislative Council, it left the essential features of contract work intact, notably low wages, restriction to compounds, separation of families and restrictions on mobility.[119]

South African police contingents moved into Ovamboland on 12 January 1972 and were reinforced by army units a fortnight later, signalling the start of South African Defence Force involvement in Ovamboland.[120] Further police reinforcements arrived in early February by which time the South African government had issued emergency regulations for Ovamboland. According to South African figures, these measures led to the arrest of 213 people,[121] and to a campaign of intimidation and terror by police and army units.

The Portuguese were sufficiently alarmed by the peasant revolt in the far south of the colony to send large numbers of heavily armed troops, four battalions according to some reports, to the border.[122] The uprising had come as a surprise to the Portuguese.[123] They probably feared the opening of a new military front by MPLA in an area which had assumed new strategic importance because of the construction of the Cunene dam scheme, an eventuality which would stretch existing Portuguese military resources. Moreover, the area was reported of being infiltrated with hundreds of PIDE agents.[124] Described by the censored Portuguese press as a worrying situation created by subversion and even terrorism, high officials including Angola's governor general Rebocho Vaz, flew to the region to assess the situation.[125] And the governor agreed to some of the peasants' demands, in particular the alleviation of taxes.[126] According to MPLA, South Africa assisted the Portuguese in suppressing the revolt by sending two helicopters with policemen. The objective was to protect traditional chiefs who were siding with the Portuguese authorities on their side of the border. At the same time, South African units who were outstripped by the events, also solicited Portuguese help.[127]

Although the strike and the peasant revolt had been broken by mid-February 1972,[128] they helped to intensify the struggle of both SWAPO and MPLA. Political consciousness among the Ovambo peasantry was increased during the strike and the peasant revolt. And previously apolitical people joined SWAPO while turning away from traditional chiefs who had lost credibility because of their collaboration with South Africa during the events.[129]

This confirmed the success of SWAPO as a mass party. For since its inception, SWAPO, then the Ovamboland People's Organization, had put the abolition of contract work, which concerned the majority of Ovambo men, at a centre of its political activities. According to Hamutenya and Geingob, the leaders of OPO, as well as the Progressive Association as the forerunner of SWANU, 'felt that the oppressive and exploitative conditions and long-standing abuse to which the Africans were subjected in the contract system, were the most immediate and burning issues around which the African workers in Namibia could be organized and politicized'.[130] But contrary to SWANU, SWAPO was able to command mass support. According to the Finnish author Kiljunen, it owed its success to three related factors: firstly, SWAPO also operated inside the country where it managed to establish and maintain a broad network of branches and activists; secondly, the organization was able to rally people from different ethnic origins and thirdly, SWAPO enjoyed support not only among intellectuals, but precisely among the contract workers.[131] The question as to whether the Ovambo contract workers supported SWAPO because of ethnic kinship with SWAPO leaders or merely because of their socio-economic condition as contract workers, remains open to debate, as the two cannot be separated.

The mass support for SWAPO was confirmed during the strike of 1971 and 1972. Although SWAPO was not responsible for organizing the strike, many of the strikers were members or supporters of SWAPO;[132] and Namibian students, who played an leading role in organizing the strike in Windhoek, worked through local SWAPO branches.[133] The fact that often illiterate peasants in Ovamboland decided to join SWAPO after the strike in 1972, could only reinforce SWAPO's claim to a mass party.

The peasant revolt and the strike also informed MPLA's struggle. MPLA announced in February 1972 that it had opened it's sixth military region covering the districts of Cunene, Huila and Moçamedes, as the MPLA militants who had been active in the region since 1968 'were now satisfied that the objective conditions there were suitable for the commencement of the armed struggle'.[134] According to a MPLA war communiqué, the population of the Cunene district had taken advantage of favourable circumstances due to the strike in Namibia to commence 'armed struggle against Portuguese colonialism in coordination with the struggle being waged in Namibia against the South African racists'.[135] However, the opening of new military front in the south of Angola was of merely declaratory nature. By the end of 1972, MPLA had not managed to start military action as such, its activities being concentrated on politicizing people through clandestine committees.[136] And it was only after the signature of the Alvor agreement in January 1975 that MPLA opened an office at N'Giva near the Namibian border.[137]

For SWAPO, on the contrary, the combined effects of the Namibian general strike and the peasant uprising on the Namibian-Angolan border consolidated SWAPO's position as Namibia's leading national liberation movement. The increased popular support enabled SWAPO to have a stronger material support base among Namibian and southern Angolan peasants for guerrilla incursions by the People's Liberation Army of Namibia. More importantly, however, the 'armed struggle' by SWAPO was to gain momentum as a result of Angola's decolonization and independence in 1975. The decolonization of Angola in the wake of the overthrow of the Caetano regime in Portugal in 1974 also led South Africa to look for new allies in the region and it increasingly involved extra-regional actors in the southern African conflict.

CHAPTER FOUR

NAMIBIA-ANGOLA.
SHIFTING ALLIANCES. 1974–6

The fall of the Caetano regime in Portugal in April 1974 and the rapid decolonization of Mozambique and Angola, had a decisive impact on both the regional politics of liberation and Pretoria's attempts to maintain – in the absence of Portugal's help – South Africa's domination of the region. In particular, the shift of the liberation movements' 'frontline' to the borders of South Africa and Namibia, shook the very foundations of South Africa's regional policies embedded in the concept of buffer states, which now had to be reformulated.

From the South African point of view, the impending independence of Angola implied that Namibia now became a strategically important buffer territory protecting South Africa from nationalist forces. The fact that Portugal was ending both its operations against Angolan nationalist movements and its military cooperation with South Africa, led to a reassessment of South Africa's role in southwestern Africa which culminated in the invasion of Angola in 1975/76.

While the Vorster government initially adopted a conciliatory attitude towards Mozambique, notably by withholding support in a coup attempt by right-wing settlers to topple the provisional FRELIMO government and also pressed the Smith regime in Rhodesia for a political settlement of the war for independence which appeared unwinnable for the Rhodesian settlers,[2] this policy of détente did not apply to South Africa and Angola and only partially to Namibia.

Inside Namibia, South Africa acknowledged the inevitability of some form of independence but was determined to control the decolonization process. This implied, on the one hand, preventing SWAPO from coming to power and on the other, establishing a pro-South African administration, thereby ensuring that Namibia would remain a buffer territory protecting South Africa. Limited political and constitutional reforms, increased repression and the militarization of the territory were the expression of this policy.

On the regional level, in a first ad hoc response to the decolonization of Angola, plans were drawn up for the establishment of a cross-border buffer territory – a Greater Ovamboland – in northern Namibia and southern Angola. More importantly, however, Pretoria's strategists were determined to prevent the pro-Soviet MPLA from coming to power. The South African invasion of Angola in 1975/76, with Namibia being the springboard and close collaboration with UNITA and FNLA, both before and during the invasion, were the reflection of South Africa's new regional policy in southwestern Africa. While the South African invasion of Angola led to the internationalization of the conflict in Angola, it also influenced SWAPO's regional politics of liberation. It signalled an end to SWAPO-UNITA cooperation and a shift from Zambia to Angola as primary host state for SWAPO from 1976.

'Détente' and the Turnhalle Conference

On the regional level, Pretoria responded to the decolonization of Angola and Mozambique with a two pronged approach of militarization and political/diplomatic initiatives. On one hand, South Africa expanded its military capacity by increasing the defence budget by 150% from 1973/74 to 1974/75.[3] On the other hand, the Vorster government adopted the political/diplomatic initiative which came to be known as 'outward movement' or 'détente'. In September 1974, Vorster visited several Francophone African countries. And in a speech to parliament in October 1974, Vorster emphasized that southern Africa was at a crossroads and would have to choose between peace and escalating violence. The cost of confrontation would be too high a price to pay for southern Africa. In an attempt to revive the earlier Verwoerdian idea of a regional common market, Vorster proposed a South African controlled 'United Nations of Southern African States'. They would comprise South Africa and its 'independent' Bantustans, Namibia, Rhodesia, Zambia, as well as Botswana, Lesotho and Swaziland which were already linked – with Namibia – to South Africa through the Southern African Customs Union (SACU) and hopefully Mozambique and Angola.[4]

Concerning Namibia, Vorster indicated a change in policy for the first time in a speech to his constituency in Nigel, Transvaal in June 1974. He pointed out that 'it is not the government of South Africa's task or function to decide the future of South West Africa, but South Africa will also not permit any outsider to do so.' This decision would be left to 'every individual and the *peoples* [emphasis added]' in the territory.[5] While Vorster's statement was a euphemism for direct South African control of any process for Namibian self-determination, his reference to the 'peoples' rather than the people of Namibia reflects the essence of the Vorster government's approach to Namibian self-determination. In the logic of apartheid, ethnicity was at the heart of Namibian self-determination, in line with the recommendations of the Odendaal Commission in 1964. South African *control* of Namibian independence along ethnic lines set the scene for differing interpretations of Namibian self-determination by Pretoria on one hand and SWAPO, the United Nations and the Western powers on the other hand.

While the Vorster government had formally abandoned the idea of annexing Namibia in November 1972,[6] the Frontline states and Zambia in particular, were involved in Pretoria's policy reformulation towards Namibia and southern Africa in general.[7] Secret contacts between the Zambian government and the Portuguese over the conflict of Mozambique had existed since 1973 and indirect contacts between the Zambian government and Pretoria were established in March 1974.[8] When the South African and Zambian foreign ministers met for the first time in New York during the UN General Assembly in late September 1974, they discussed South Africa's policies towards Rhodesia and Namibia. Changwa, the Zambian foreign minister, wanted to know whether South Africa would be willing to withdraw its support for the Smith regime in Rhodesia as well as to withdraw from Namibia and place it under UN responsibility.[9] At the same time, Kaunda's special assistant Mark Chonah, Marquard de Villiers, who had informed Vorster about the contacts between the Portuguese and Kaunda of 1973 and van den Bergh, the head of the South African Bureau of

State Security (BOSS), had been drafting a document entitled 'Towards the Summit: An Approach to Peaceful Change in Southern Africa'. Known as the 'détente scenario', the document laid out Zambia's conditions for a negotiated settlement in Zimbabwe and Namibia.[10]

As far as Namibia was concerned, the document called for South Africa to reaffirm its willingness to grant self-determination to Namibia in accordance with the will of the majority of the country's population; to guarantee SWAPO freedom as a political movement in Namibia, to cease floggings and other forms of corporal punishment and to allow Namibians outside the country to return and participate in 'normal political activities'. In return, Zambia and 'friends' would undertake to persuade SWAPO 'to declare themselves as a party not committed to violence provided that the South African government allows their registration as a political party and allows them to function freely as such'. If these conditions were met, SWAPO should 'desist from armed struggle'. SWAPO was not consulted by the Zambian government who soon after the drafting of the memorandum ordered the movement to stop fighting from Zambian territory, initiating a restrictive policy towards SWAPO which was ultimately to result in the transfer of its headquarters from Lusaka to Luanda in June 1976. The détente scenario preceded both Vorster's 'crossroads' speech of 25 October 1974 and Kaunda's reply on the following day in which he hailed Vorster's speech as 'the voice of reason, for which Africa and the world had waited for many years'. Kaunda later admitted that the two speeches had been carefully orchestrated as part of the détente 'scenario'.[11] The Frontline states endorsed Kaunda's policy of détente but *not* the secret document which had been drafted in early October.[12]

In a parallel and probably not unrelated development inside Namibia, the leader of the South West Africa National Party, apparently under pressure from Pretoria,[13] announced in September 1974 plans to hold constitutional talks about the future of Namibia. The proposal, which was discussed through party meetings and through a multiracial territorial Advisory Council which had been established in 1972/73, gathered momentum in early 1975, partly as a response to increased international pressure. The United States, Britain and France, who had vetoed the expulsion of South Africa from the United Nations in October 1974, endorsed a Security Council resolution two months later which gave South Africa five and a half months to 'take the necessary steps to effect the withdrawal . . . of its illegal administration maintained in Namibia'.[14] The resolution also called on South Africa to abolish discriminatory laws and release political prisoners.

However, the South African government was not ready to end its occupation of Namibia. Although it was, in theory, committed to Namibia's self-determination, its goal was 'to pave the way for a moderate and stable Namibia which could leave the *cordon sanitaire* [protecting South Africa] intact'.[15] In practice, this meant that Pretoria attempted to impose its own version of Namibia's 'self-determination'. The Namibian nation would be based not on a unitary non-racial state but on ethnically defined and administratively autonomous regional entities along the lines of the South African homelands. In order to avert international pressure for Namibian independence, Pretoria decided to convene a constitutional conference to discuss Namibian self-determination along this ethnic model.

However, this ethnic version of nationhood close to the concept of apartheid now termed 'separate development', was unacceptable to both SWAPO and the United Nations. Moreover, it run counter to the the general trend of decolonization in Africa which favoured the creation of unitary nation states and the abnegation of ethnic identity as an element of nation building. From the outset, the South African plan for Namibian self-determination based on ethnicity was above all a strategy to exclude SWAPO and to a certain extent the United Nations, from the decolonization process in Namibia, over which South Africa wanted to keep control. Moreover, to depict the southern African political dynamics in racial terms, conformed to the South African government's *Weltanschauung*, which did not enjoy international legitimacy.

In September 1975, the South African government convened a multiracial constitutional conference, the Turnhalle Conference, in a converted gymnasium in Windhoek. 146 delegates of the eleven population groups of Namibia officially proclaimed by Pretoria, issued a declaration of intent calling for a draft constitution. The purpose was to create a form of government which would guarantee each population group administrative autonomy, while at the same time protecting minority rights.

While the United States and its allies opposed the Turnhalle proposals and were to back the call for elections supervised by the United Nations from 1976, the proposals were also rejected by SWAPO and other parties such as SWANU, the Volksparty, NAPDO and the Damara Tribal Executive Committee. SWAPO called the talks 'a farce . . . aimed at perpetuation of white minority rule under which South African domination would continue'.[16] It issued its own constitutional proposals which called for a directly elected legislature, a bill of rights and an independent judiciary. At the same time, SWAPO intensified its political campaign inside Namibia. It boycotted an election for an Ovambo Assembly in January 1975. In August, the Chief Minister of Ovamboland, Chief Filemon Elifas who had won the January elections, was assassinated by an unknown gunman. The Chief's assassination, for which SWAPO was held responsible, led to increased repression, whereby virtually the entire leadership of SWAPO which operated legally inside Namibia, was detained.[17] A political trial in Swakopmund which was aimed at intimidating Namibian nationalists,[18] reflected Pretoria's determination to exclude SWAPO from the decolonization process. Increased militarization of the territory aimed at preventing SWAPO incursions and limiting popular support for the movement in the north of the country,[19] complemented both police repression and the attempts to create a power structure opposed to SWAPO.

Militarization of Namibia

After the Revolution in Portugal which had brought an end to military cooperation with Portugal in Angola, the SADF rapidly expanded its presence in northern Namibia. In June 1974, the army had taken over complete control of the border regions from the South African police. At this date, 15,000 troops and counterinsurgency units were reported to be in Namibia.[20] Operations against SWAPO in the border areas became the responsibility of the South African Defence Force (SADF) directly responsible to headquarters in Pretoria. And SWAPO alleged in August 1974 that South Africa had established a three mile wide security strip along the northern border between Angola and Ovamboland in an effort to stop the mass exodus of Namibians to Angola.[21]

At the same time as reinforcing the presence of South African troops in Namibia, the SADF started creating tribal armies. A San (Bushman) ethnic unit later called 201 Battalion, consisting of San people from the Caprivi and Angola, was formed in the Caprivi Strip in 1974. And battalions were formed among the Ovambo (101 Battalion) and Kavango (202 Battalion) in 1975.[22] The San Battalion was to be part of the first South African column invading Angola in October 1975. The South African policy of maintaining a 'cordon sanitaire' around South Africa to guarantee the status quo inside South Africa, was not, however, confined to Namibia. In the wake of the Revolution in Portugal in April 1974, attempts to influence Angolan decolonization complemented South African policies inside Namibia. One such response was the attempt to create a cross-border buffer territory in northern Namibia and southern Angola – a Greater Ovamboland – which preceded direct South African military intervention in Angola in South Africa's attempt to prevent MPLA from coming to power.

The Greater Ovamboland scheme

In order to maintain a buffer territory in Angola and to preempt SWAPO from taking advantage of the Angolan decolonization, Pretoria envisaged the partition of Namibia into two 'autonomous' states. An Ovambo state comprising the Ovambo in both northern Namibia and southern Angola, if the Angolan government's consent for the cession of the territory could be obtained and a loose confederation of Namibia's other ethnic groups, including 'whites' who laid claim to about two-thirds of the Namibian territory. In the logic of apartheid, this region could be linked to South Africa as a 'sovereign independent state'. The Namibians other than the Ovambo and the white population would constitute themselves into separate 'states' who could join a loose federation with the 'white' core area.

The plan for a Greater Ovamboland (Groot Owambo) was revealed in October 1974 by the Commissioner for the Indigenous People of South West Africa, Jannie de Wet who had designed the scheme. The concept of ethnic states inside Namibia was not new. It reflected the apartheid design for the territory by the Odendaal Commission which had proposed in the early sixties the establishment of ten different homelands or ethnic 'nations' which would be gradually given independence and which would be linked to a 'white' South West Africa.[23] Its novelty lay in the establishment of an Ovambo 'state' extending across the colonial borders. A Greater Ovamboland comprising both northern Namibia and southern Angola would constitute a buffer territory *par excellence*. According to de Wet, the estimated 350,000 Ovambo in Namibia could amalgamate with the 120,000 Ovambo in southern Angola, provided that the government of an independent Angola would agree.[24]

In early 1975, South Africa took practical steps to implement the Greater Ovamboland scheme by infiltrating Namibian Ovambos into Angola to instigate separatist feelings among the population. In September, Pastor Kornelius Ndjomba, the Chief Minister of Ovamboland who had succeeded the assassinated Chief Filemeon Elifas, was reported to have been taken to southern Angola by the South Africans where he spoke in favour of the scheme.[25] The infiltrations were reported from a number of sources ranging from MPLA and SWAPO to UNITA and the Portuguese who were still in control of the administration in southern Angola.[26] SWAPO opposed the scheme on the grounds that South Africa could thereby cut off SWAPO's military wing PLAN from a future support base inside Angola.[27] More fundamentally, the plan for a cross-border ethnic Ovambo state was in conflict with SWAPO's stand for a non-racial unitary state in Namibia. The president of MPLA, Agostinho Neto claimed in July 1975 that South Africa was planning to take over the Cunene province in southern Angola and he accused South Africa of mobilizing the population in the area 'into forming a new country with an ethnic grouping of Ovambo'.[28] And N'Gola Kabunga of FNLA, who was the minister of interior of Angola's transitional government formed in January 1975,[29] may have referred to the Greater Ovamboland scheme, when he accused Pretoria in April 1975 of making military preparations and waiting 'for a time of internal confusion [in Angola] to annex the Cunene district to Namibia'.[30]

UNITA on the other hand, supported the scheme,[31] and UNITA activists spread rumours of Ovambo unity in the Cunene district where the organization had opened an office in June 1974. UNITA's support for the Greater Ovamboland scheme, which never materialized,[32] coincided with the beginnings of military cooperation between the SADF and UNITA, a move which was to become an outstanding feature of South Africa's invasion of Angola from October 1975 to March 1976.

UNITA, FNLA, the United States and South Africa

The decolonization of Angola and in particular the fact that Portugal had ended both its military operations against the nationalist movements and its collaboration with South Africa in southern Angola, led Pretoria's strategists to reassess their policy towards Angola. Collaboration between SADF, FNLA and above all UNITA, which was based on requests by the two movements for South African help, was an essential component of this policy.

The Defence Force and Military Intelligence felt strongly that South Africa should involve itself in some way to influence events in Angola. Military intelligence had put out feelers to the three liberation movements, in order to ascertain their attitudes towards South Africa. According to Geldenhuys, MPLA 'was found implacably hostile, whereas the other two organizations, UNITA in particular, proved quite amenable. Should MPLA come to power, . . . South Africa's security interests in Namibia might be seriously jeopardized'.[33] MPLA had indeed pledged its unconditional support to SWAPO as well as the Zimbabwean and South African liberation movements after Angolan independence. The SADF feared that MPLA support to SWAPO would enable the movement to intensify its military operations in Namibia and there was also mention of SWAPO training two to three thousand Namibian refugees in camps north of the border.[34] The minister of defence P.W. Botha suggested to Vorster in April 1975 that South Africa should assist anti-MPLA forces;[35] and in June, the SADF submitted a document outlining different policy options towards Angola to Botha who in turn handed the paper for a final decision to Vorster.[36] The scene was now set for South African collaboration with UNITA and FNLA.

It should be noted from the outset that the rapprochement and subsequent collaboration between SADF, FNLA and UNITA was as much the outcome of initiatives by UNITA and

FNLA seeking South African help against MPLA, as of Pretoria's overtures to FNLA and UNITA in an attempt to prevent MPLA from coming to power. In November 1974, UNITA's representative in Luanda announced that future relations between Angola and South Africa should be based upon mutual respect and non-interference. More significantly, he stated that as much as Angolans had fought for their independence alone, Namibians should be expected to do the same, in effect implying that UNITA would be ready to renounce its cooperation with SWAPO.[37] In January 1975, the Zambian press quoted Savimbi as saying that he favoured dialogue with South Africa,[38] and two months later, the first direct contact between Savimbi and a South African intelligence officer was reported to have taken place in Paris.[39] At a second meeting in Lusaka in April, Savimbi requested arms from South Africa. The demand was refused because the leader of UNITA was at that time unwilling to form an alliance with FNLA, the other Angolan nationalist movement favoured by South Africa.[40] In a press conference in Luanda on 3 May 1975, Savimbi hailed the South African prime minister Vorster as a responsible leader. He emphasized that armed struggle would not solve the problems of Namibia and Zimbabwe and that he favoured a policy of dialogue and 'détente'. As far as UNITA's relationship with SWAPO was concerned, Savimbi admitted that SWAPO had helped UNITA and had 'shed blood with us', but that it would not be possible to help SWAPO as Angola had problems of its own.[41] Cooperation between the two movements had come to an end, at least formally and Savimbi's declaration undoubtedly pleased South Africa.

Holden Roberto's FNLA who had been SWAPO's ally in the early sixties, also distanced itself from SWAPO. Daniel Chipenda, a former MPLA leader who had been expelled from the movement in February 1975 after he had lost a power struggle against MPLA's president Dr. Agostinho Neto, joined Holden Roberto's FNLA with 2,000 MPLA soldiers loyal to him personally. And Chipenda had talks with South African officials in Windhoek at the end of May 1975.[42] Chipenda who was of Ovimbundu origin, tried with his followers to establish a power base in southern Angola which as yet had been untouched by FNLA. He returned to Windhoek in July for three days when he met General Hendrik van den Bergh, the head of BOSS and close advisor to Vorster, who had been involved in discussions with the Zambian government over 'détente'. This meeting took place shortly after Holden Roberto had met with South African officials in Kinshasa.[43] As a result of these talks, Roberto agreed to Chipenda's visit to Windhoek in order to secure military support from South Africa.[44] On the South African side, the discussions were led by General Van den Bergh. After FNLA had undertaken to cooperate militarily with UNITA, South Africa started with the delivery of second-hand light machine guns, rifles and mortars to FNLA in August;[45] and if van den Bergh had had his way, South African involvement in the Angolan civil war would not have gone further.[46]

Savimbi's decision to ally himself with South Africa has to be viewed against the background of the political stalemate and the escalation of the armed conflict between MPLA, FNLA and UNITA. While MPLA and FNLA had clashed militarily since March 1975 when FNLA forces attacked MPLA positions around Luanda,[47] UNITA's military involvement began with the moving southwards of MPLA forces in July 1975. Aware that it was much weaker militarily than MPLA and FNLA, UNITA had largely kept out of the conflict except for a number of minor clashes in regions where it was predominant.[48] However, the situation changed dramatically in July. MPLA forces advanced to the south of the country and the port of Lobito – the terminal of the Benguela railway – came under their control. And in August, the three movements were involved in heavy fighting on the Namibian border,[49] which led to the occupation of the Ruacana dam by South Africa, followed by the temporary occupation of N'Giva (Pereira d'Eça), the district capital of Cunene, on 22 August. But at the same time, UNITA and MPLA formed an ephemeral alliance in Lisbon on 17th August. According to Heimer, MPLA not only wanted to consolidate its own positions but also to make UNITA understand that it could not remain neutral in the conflict.[50] Immediately after the signing of the accord, Savimbi was informed of the South African military assistance to FNLA and having learned that Pretoria was willing to extend its support to UNITA, Savimbi broke his agreement with MPLA under the pretext that the UNITA delegation in Lisbon had exceeded its mandate. Savimbi was convinced that FNLA was in a position to gain the upper hand against MPLA.[51] He again asked for South African military help and now accepted to ally himself with FNLA after he had been informed that the United States were about to increase considerably their involvement in Angola.

The United States had played a low-key role in Angola since the early 1960s, arming FNLA which was supported by Zaire, the principal American ally in Central Africa. What were then the reasons for the United States to get substantially involved in the complex Angolan civil war? Again, the Zairean factor is crucial in explaining why the United States stepped up its assistance to FNLA and later to UNITA. Holden Roberto's FNLA was 'little more than an extension of Mobutu's own armed force', Roberto himself being linked to the Zairean president through marriage.[52] Mobutu openly supported FNLA against its rival movement MPLA. Moreover, after the collapse of the Portuguese colonial empire, Zaire became a privileged partner of the United States in Central Africa in terms of the 'Nixon doctrine' whereby the United States wanted to rely on regional allies such as Zaire and South Africa, in order to secure its world wide engagements.[53] This view was no doubt reinforced by Zaire's economic importance to the United States with American investments in that country amounting to approximately 800 million dollars.[54] Moreover, president Mobutu appeared to have some influential private lines of communication with Washington. This would have enabled him to prevent the administration from making realistic assessments as far as the developments in Angola were concerned, combined as it was with a general ignorance of events in the region by American policy makers.[55]

In January 1975, the '40 Committee' of the American National Security Council authorized a covered fund of 300,000 dollars for FNLA, which was the movement with the largest army.[56] No doubt, the '40 Committee,' hoped that American help to FNLA would bolster the position of FNLA's protector Zaire, which was facing a major economic crisis.

Rumours of heavy CIA involvement in favour of FNLA circulated almost immediately afterwards in Luanda and alarmed not only MPLA, but also its ally, the Soviet Union. Although there is no conclusive evidence, the American initiative in favour of FNLA no doubt helped triggering a substantial increase in Soviet aid to MPLA from March 1975. The argument, that the United States acted in response to Soviet and Cuban expansionism, does therefore not withstand scrutiny.[57]

In July, the National Security Council allocated an additional 14 million dollars to UNITA and FNLA,[58] despite voices inside the administration which argued strongly against American involvement.[59] Covert aid in military hardware to FNLA and UNITA which now also received American aid, was valued at more than $30 million by the end of 1975.[60] The CIA closely collaborated with BOSS of South Africa. Top CIA officials 'welcomed their [South Africa's] arrival in the war' and in October 1975, for instance, arms for UNITA were transferred from CIA to South African planes on Zairean soil.[61] However, the American covert military aid came to an end in December 1975, when the majority of the Senate, 'sensing a congruence of conscience and a promising election-year issue', voted by 54 votes to 22 to ban further covert aid to Angola (Clark Amendment).[62]

While units of FNLA and UNITA, together with armoured squadrons from Zaire, launched attacks against MPLA positions in central Angola,[63] the South African military set up several training camps, one for the Chipenda faction of FNLA at Mapupa in the south east of the country in late August and two camps for UNITA at Calombo south of Bié (Silva Porto) in central Angola,[64] and at Cuvelai, 200 km north of the Namibian border.[65] A South African liaison officer who was subsequently joined by nineteen instructors, was received by Savimbi at his headquarters in Bié on 24 September in order to discuss South African aid and training for UNITA as well as the defence of Huambo (Nova Lisboa) against an MPLA offensive and on 5 October, UNITA and the South African instructors managed to stop FAPLA from advancing on the town.[66]

As a quid pro quo for South African help, Savimbi provided information on the location of SWAPO bases in southern Angola and Zambia,[67] and broke with SWAPO.[68] Savimbi's alignment with South Africa was in line with his previous opportunistic policy stands. As easily as he had earlier collaborated with the Portuguese against MPLA, Savimbi now renounced the long-standing relationship with SWAPO. Savimbi's turn to South Africa signalled the beginning of close military cooperation which was to last until 1989. As far as South Africa was concerned, the despatch of advisors to UNITA and

FNLA 'meant that South Africa had actually entered the Angolan civil war supporting two of the three belligerent'.[69]

South African, Soviet and Cuban intervention in Angola

South Africa's collusion with UNITA and FNLA, which was tacitly supported by Zambia and Zaire,[70] prepared the ground for a large-scale direct intervention by the South African Defence Force. The despatch of advisors to UNITA and FNLA and small-scale incursions from July to September, were followed by direct SADF intervention in collaboration with UNITA and FNLA units from October to Angola's independence on 11 November 1975. Substantial reinforcements in troops and material and a drive to Luanda in November and December 1975 was followed by military defeat and the withdrawal of SADF from Angola in March 1976.

The decision to intervene directly in the Angolan civil war appears to have been taken by the South African government in July or August 1975,[71] after the military had won the day against van den Bergh who was against direct South African involvement in Angola. Although conclusive evidence is as yet not available, the viewpoint of the military that their direct intervention in Angola would enable them to give a *coup de grace* to SWAPO, which in turn would allow Pretoria to put into practice its 'Turnhalle Conference' strategy of putting into place a pro-South African government before granting independence to the territory,[72] probably convinced Vorster to back direct South African intervention in Angola. South African units first entered Angola in July, after UNITA men had attacked and robbed a South African engineer who worked at the construction site of the Caluque dam which was part of the joint South African-Portuguese Cunene hydroelectric scheme. South African army units occupied the dam and the village of Caluque where MPLA, FNLA and UNITA had offices. While FNLA and UNITA were only disarmed, the MPLA office was sacked and MPLA prisoners were taken.[73] On 9 August, South African forces permanently occupied the Caluque dam about 25 km north of the Namibian border with a force of several hundred men comprising a detachment from an Infantry Battalion stationed at Walvis Bay.[74]

South African intervention escalated sharply at the end of

August against the background of fighting between MPLA and UNITA. After MPLA had driven UNITA out of N'Giva 40 km inside Angola on 25 August, South African troops occupied N'Giva for several days. It was the first clear manifestation of Pretoria's decision to intervene in the Angolan civil war on behalf of UNITA against MPLA. The South African occupation of N'Giva was not necessary for the protection of the Caluque dam which had been Pretoria's official reason for sending troops into Angola in the first instance.[75]

South African involvement in the Angolan civil war further escalated in September. Not only did the SADF dispatch instructors and weapons to UNITA and FNLA and help UNITA in holding Huambo against FAPLA forces, but they also set up a regular supply route north from Rundu in Okavango in Namibia. The South African military now devised a four-phase plan for offensive operations with the capture of Luanda being the ultimate goal. The decision to move from one stage to the other was left to Vorster and P.W. Botha. This meant that P.W. Botha and the prime minister were 'the two principal (if not the only) political decision makers who were to control South Africa's military involvement in the Angolan war'.[76] The Department of Foreign Affairs was opposed to South African military intervention fearing that South African military intervention would lead to an increase in Soviet involvement and would jeopardize 'détente'. It wanted South Africa to adopt the same attitude of non-interference as it had displayed when the Portuguese left Mozambique, but it was by and large excluded from the decision making process and 'the Defence Force saw the Angolan war very much as *its* responsibility'.[77] The scene was set for the invasion of Angola.

On 14 October, a unit comprising about a thousand followers of Daniel Chipenda, together with the Bushman unit which had been set up in 1974 and French mercenaries, all under South African command, crossed into Angola at the Angolan border town of Cuangar, 140 km west of Rundu. Five days later, the 'Zulu column', or 'Brigada Chipenda', dislodged MPLA from N'Giva, which had been retaken by MPLA after the South African withdrawal in early September. On 21 October, the column was reinforced by regular South African troops sent from the Namibian border post of Ruacana and former members of the Portuguese army and police in Angola, who had regrouped under the 'Portuguese Liberation Army' (ELP) at Xangongo (Roçadas), about 70 km north of the Namibian border. Encountering practically no resistance, the Zulu column swept rapidly northwards. Lubango (Sa da Bandeira) fell on 24 October, Moçamedes two days later and by 7 November, the town of Benguela and the port of Lobito were in South African hands.

While the Zulu column made its rapid advances in the south west of Angola, South Africa organized a second combat group this time consisting of South African, UNITA and FNLA troops to the east. The 'Foxbat' column moved rapidly up to Cela in central Angola north of Huambo before joining up with the Zulu column at Lobito on 8 November.[78] At the same time, American equipment was flown to UNITA and FNLA via Zaire. In October 1975, arms for UNITA were transferred from CIA to South African planes on Zairean soil.[79] Within a month, MPLA had lost virtually all the territory which it had gained in August and September.

After the capture of Lobito, the two South African columns which had joined each other, separated again. The 'Foxbat' column returned to central Angola where it continued its advance, whereas the Zulu column which had first invaded Angola on 14 October, resumed its offensive along the coast. On the eve of Angolan independence on 11 November, the South Africans were at Ngunza (Novo Redondo),[80] some 300 km south of Luanda, which was the furthest point north on the coast reached by the Zulu column during the invasion.[81]

When MPLA declared the People's Republic of Angola in Luanda and UNITA/FNLA set up a Democratic People's Republic of Angola in Huambo on 11 November, the MPLA southern front had collapsed. In the interior, the combined UNITA/South African forces controlled almost the entire Benguela railway. South of the railway, they occupied large parts of the Moxico province. By that time, South Africa had committed more than the 2,000 troops – as officially admitted after the invasion – to Angola.[82] Faced with the strength and the size of the South African advance, MPLA leaders quickly realized that they could not defend the position without significant outside support.

In addition to the South African/UNITA advance from the south, MPLA faced a Zairean backed offensive on Luanda by FNLA, which the South Africans decided to support with avi-

93

ation and South African manned artillery.[83] According to Savimbi, the South Africans were confident that FNLA forces would defeat the MPLA forces and that Holden Roberto would be in Luanda the next day.[84] However, Steenkamp who provides the most detailed account of the South African invasion (Operation 'Savannah'), claims that high ranking field commanders such as Ben Roos and Constand Viljoen advised Roberto against attacking Luanda, an advice which seemed to have been discounted in Pretoria.[85] The offensive was launched on 9 November but repelled by the materially superior forces of MPLA who were now backed by heavy Soviet artillery and newly arrived Cuban combat troops.[86] Large-scale Cuban intervention and the sending of Soviet material and advisers indeed tipped the military balance in favour of MPLA who was facing a two-front attack by South African columns from the south and FNLA from the north. In particular, heavy Soviet weapons, notably the 122 mm rocket launcher 'Stalin Organ', had arrived in Luanda on 9 November, while 400 Russian advisors were reported to have arrived in the Angolan capital on 13 November.[87]

The Soviet Union had already provided modest political, ideological and military support to MPLA since the early 1960s, as MPLA had evolved in part out of the Angolan branch of the Portuguese Communist party in 1956. It stepped up its military support in early 1975 after having momentarily suspended its aid to MPLA because of the leadership struggle between Neto and Chipenda. Aid was resumed after Chipenda's expulsion from MPLA in February 1975 and increased substantially in March in response to a request by Neto for Soviet military aid following the payment of 300,000 dollars in covert financial aid to FNLA by the CIA in January 1975.

From March 1975 Soviet aid in favour of MPLA increased proportionally to the intensification of military activities by FNLA who was supported not only by the United States, but also by Zaire and China. With the South African invasion of southern Angola in October 1975 in favour of UNITA and FNLA (Chipenda), Soviet support reached a peak between November 1975 and January 1976 with the sending of tons of sophisticated arms including tanks.[88]

What were then the reasons for large-scale Soviet intervention in Angola to ensure that MPLA would form the first government of independent Angola? Although the exact reasons and process leading to the Soviet decision to commit large quantities of military equipment and several hundred military advisors to Angola from 1975 remain the subject of speculation in the absence of conclusive documentary evidence, it is nevertheless possible to sketch the main causes which accounted for the escalation of Soviet help to MPLA in 1975. From an ideological point of view, the decision to intervene on a large scale in Angola did not represent a break with past policies, whereby the Soviet Union claimed to support liberation movements against imperialism. The coup d'Etat in Portugal of April 1974 with its revolutionary potentials,[89] and the victories of Marxist oriented régimes in Mozambique, Guinea Bissau and Cap Verde as well as São Tomé and Principe helped to shape the Soviet view prevailing in the seventies that trends in Africa favoured the expansion of socialism at the expense of imperialism. The 'revolutionary-democratic' school became official Soviet state policy towards the Third World countries at the 25th Congress of the Soviet Communist Party in February 1976.[90] To ensure the coming to power of MPLA in Angola could only reinforce this tendency.[91] From a geopolitical point of view, a decisive intervention on behalf of MPLA was probably seen as enhancing the Soviet position in Africa against the United States but above all against China. For Soviet assistance was not only directed against South African intervention in Angola but also against 'American imperialism' and 'domestic reaction [against MPLA by FNLA] supported by Peking'.[92] Massive Soviet involvement in the Angolan civil war presented an opportunity of weakening the United States, even more as there was little chance of a super power military conflict in the aftermath of the Vietnam War in a region where the interests of both the Soviet Union and the United States had traditionally been minor and where super power rivalry did therefore not threaten détente in Europe.[93]

To counteract the Chinese presence in Angola and its assistance to FNLA in particular, was probably more important in the eyes of the Soviet leadership. Holden Roberto had visited Peking in 1973 and over hundred Chinese military instructors arrived in Kinshasa at the end of May for the training of FNLA soldiers, soon followed by an estimated 450 tons of weaponry.[94] To contain Chinese influence in Africa which had already been a major issue in the sixties,[95] was therefore an important factor accounting for the escalation of Soviet involvement in conjunction with Cuba.

Cuban ties with MPLA dated back to the early 1960s, when MPLA leaders studied in Cuba. Cuban involvement in Africa started when Ernesto Che Guevara led a guerrilla group against Moise Tshombe, the leader of the Katanga secession during the 1960 Congo crisis. In 1965, Che Guevara met the MPLA leadership in Brazzaville, which had become the headquarter of MPLA and started training MPLA military and political cadres during the same year.[96] But the question of military aid to MPLA did not arise before 1975. In April 1975, the MPLA requested the Cuban government to send military advisers to complement the Soviet military aid and to counter the escalation of FNLA military activities. Cuban advisers were reported to have been involved in fighting in May 1975. An MPLA delegation visiting Cuba sought additional military assistance in early August; and according to Maxwell, Fidel Castro authorized the planning of a sea and airlift of troops, equipment and supplies to Angola in mid-August,[97] after he had secured agreement to send Cuban troops into Angola from a Portuguese delegation of the Portuguese Armed Forces Movement (MFA) which had visited Havana in July.[98] Another 200 Cuban infantry instructors were reported to have arrived in Luanda in August.[99] According to the Cuban born author Dominguez, war games were held in Cuba at the end of August; and high ranking Cuban military commanders began preparing for war at the beginning of September.[100] Several hundred further instructors arrived in Angola by sea in October; and according to Wolfers and Bergerol, the first two planes of Cuban combat troops arrived in Luanda between 8 and 10 November, where they helped repelling the FNLA attack backed by South African artillery,[101] followed by the landing of reinforcements at Porto Amboim on 14 November and the arrival of three Cuban troop ships carrying an artillery regiment in Luanda on 27 November. And according to Fidel Castro, 36,000 Cuban troops were in Angola at the peak of 'Operation Carlotta' in January 1976.[102]

According to the Colombian writer Gabriel Garcia Marquez, who was the only source close to the Cuban government relating the unfolding of Operation 'Carlotta', the large-scale involvement of Cuban troops was not decided before 5 November, in response to the South African invasion and following a request from MPLA. In addition, Marquez claims that Cuba acted independently of the Soviet government which would have been informed after the decision to commit Cuban combat troops had been taken.[103] In the words of Fidel Castro: 'The South Africans were there. They held more than half of Angola's territory and we had only one unit when the situation broke out. There was no choice but to send more troops, since that unit could not be left there, alone and isolated . . . This wasn't a drawn-up plan, but a situation that cropped up – an unforeseen, unexpected situation. Little did we think that South Africa, considering its international disrepute, would dare launch its troops against Angola'.[104]

While Fidel Castro did not deny the presence of Cuban troops in Angola at the time of South Africa's invasion as alleged by Marquez, the sequence of events reconstituted by the Cuban born Dominguez and corroborated by other analysts,[105] suggests that the decision of large-scale Cuban military intervention was taken in July/August 1975. Moreover, the extent to which Cuba coordinated its action with the Soviet Union, is not clear. The two opposite views that Cuba acted at the request of the Soviet Union or, inversely, that its decision to intervene was taken completely independently from Moscow, as alleged by Marquez, are both doubtful. On one hand, Fidel Castro always demonstrated a relative autonomy of action with regard to the Soviet Union. According to a Soviet diplomat who defected in 1978, the initiative of intervening in Angola was taken by Cuba, which then convinced the Soviet leadership to support the Cuban intervention.[106] On the other hand, the importance of the operation was such that Cuba would hardly have taken such a decision without consulting its Soviet ally,[107] on whom it relied for ensuring the shipment of weaponry to Angola. In the absence of documentary evidence, the reason for Cuba's decision to launch Operation 'Carlotta' remains the subject of speculation. Nevertheless, it can be argued that internationalist solidarity,[108] and the personal commitment of Fidel Castro to Angola[109] were among the most important factors leading to Operation 'Carlotta', which prevented the coming to power of the South African and United States backed UNITA/FNLA alliance in November 1975.

Whereas Cuban and Soviet military assistance had enabled

MPLA to repel the FNLA attack on Luanda on the eve of Angola's independence on 11 November 1975, the advance of the Zulu column was stopped at the Queve River between Ngunza (Sumbe/Novo Redondo) and Porto Amboim some 300 km south of Luanda on 20 November, largely as a result of the deployment of the 122 mm rocket launchers and of Cuban reinforcements which had arrived at Porto Amboim on 14 November. In the interior, UNITA forces backed by South African troops continued to make advances until mid-December, when a newly formed South African unit 'X-Ray' helped UNITA to retake Luena (Luso) on the Benguela railway in Central Angola. However, the South Africans failed to take Luau (Texeira de Sousa) on the Zaire border.[110] The advance of another newly formed South African/UNITA column 'Orange' was stopped at Mussende, 300 km east of Porto Amboim.[111]

These military reverses were compounded by a series of diplomatic setbacks for South Africa. An increasing number of African states recognized MPLA as the new government of Angola. More importantly, the American Senate voted to end covert military assistance to anti-MPLA forces (Clark Amendment), which implied in turn an end to the collaboration with the CIA on which South Africa had relied. According to Geldenhuys, South Africa now decided that it would not proceed with phase four of the operation which called for the capture of Luanda, after it had learned that the American Senate was blocking further US involvement in the conflict. The decision to withdraw was taken some time around the end of December and beginning of January 1976,[112] after Savimbi with the concurrence of Kaunda had flown to Pretoria on 20 December in an attempt to persuade South Africa to stay on.[113] On 5 January, South African troops began withdrawing from Huambo at the same time as the FNLA front in the north collapsed. As MPLA forces started an offensive in the south in the middle of January, South African forces began moving towards the Namibian border on 22 January, withdrawing first to a 50 km strip north of Namibia.[114] They left Angola altogether on 27 March 1976, after they had reached an agreement with MPLA under which the South Africans would withdraw in exchange for the MPLA guaranteeing the security of the Cunene dam.[115] They were followed by approximately 3,500 refugees who had been grouped in the Angolan town of Calai on the Kavango river opposite Rundu.[116] Cuban forces were on the Namibian border at the beginning of April.

Pretoria argued that its decision to withdraw was due to the fact that American aid was not forthcoming. The question whether the South Africans would have achieved a victory in Angola, if more aid had been forthcoming, is debatable in the face of the massive Cuban and Soviet help to MPLA. The fact remains that South Africa suffered a military setback if not defeat. This was implicitly acknowledged by Vorster in late December when he told the press that the Soviet Union was sending sophisticated weapons to Angola. He acknowledged that 'only big powers can affect this arsenal. It is certainly beyond our limits'.[117] And the commander of the South African detachment during the unsuccessful FNLA attack on Luanda on the eve of Angolan independence, confided that he 'hated to lose'.[118]

What then was the rationale for Pretoria's decision to commit South Africa militarily in Angola, thereby running the risk of jeopardizing the policy of 'détente' with black Africa? Vorster's statement in January 1976 that South Africa had intervened in Angola in order to prevent the Soviet Union from having 'a string of Marxist states across Africa from Angola to Tanzania'[119] appears to be an *ex post facto* justification. Although anti-communism had played an important role in the ideology of the Nationalist government since its coming to power in 1948, as a reason for South African military intervention in Angola, anti-communism was relatively unimportant despite the rhetoric. Likewise, the argument that 'hot pursuit' operations against SWAPO were a decisive factor for South African intervention[120] does not explain the large-scale South African military intervention and the plan for the capture of Luanda.

The argument that South Africa intervened in Angola in order to save détente is equally unconvincing. According to this argument, détente was presented as a policy of gradual and controlled change in southern Africa which could be jeopardized by Cuban and Soviet intervention on behalf of a potentially hostile MPLA.[121] However, when South African troops invaded Angola in October 1975, the Cuban intervention and large scale shipments of Soviet arms had not yet materialized. Furthermore, the Department of Foreign Affairs was from the outset opposed to military intervention in Angola. Although

Zambia, who was South Africa's main partner for détente, supported the South African invasion, Foreign Affairs officials feared, that attacking a black African state could jeopardize détente, undermine its often declared commitment to non-interference and provoke a deeper involvement of the Soviet Union in response to South Africa's military intervention.[122]

Foreign Affairs were largely excluded from participating in the decisions taken in respect to Angola,[123] and the fact that the military saw South African involvement in Angola as their responsibility, is crucial for understanding the motives underlying the operation. The South African military thought that they could engineer a military stalemate between MPLA, FNLA and UNITA and prevent MPLA from coming to power. A pro South African government in Luanda would hopefully deny bases to SWAPO and ANC. The 'cordon sanitaire' protecting Namibia and South Africa from attacks by SWAPO and ANC who both were political allies of MPLA, could thus be kept intact.[124] But carried away by their initial military successes, the South Africans probably overestimated both their own military capacity and those of their allies UNITA and FNLA. Furthermore, they did not foresee the large-scale Cuban intervention and massive shipment of Soviet arms on behalf of MPLA. What at first appeared to be a low risk *military* venture with no clear political objectives in Angola[125] other than preventing MPLA from coming to power, turned into a psychologically traumatic experience for South Africa. For the first time, South African regional military hegemony was put into question. And the failed invasion of Angola was an important factor accounting for the development of a new defensive strategy, the Total National Strategy which was to characterize South African regional policy from the late 1970s to 1989.[126]

The South African invasion of Angola and SWAPO

While South African military intervention in Angola and the SADF defeat against MPLA and Cuban forces set the stage for a thirteen year war between South Africa and MPLA government forces, the South African invasion also accelerated the shift of SWAPO's alliances with the Angolan nationalist movements away from UNITA towards closer collaboration with MPLA. Until August 1975, SWAPO was politically allied to MPLA while it had maintained a close working relationship with UNITA. And it was not until 1976, that SWAPO had realigned itself completely with MPLA.

The Angolan government had promised assistance to SWAPO as early as July 1975 in the event of MPLA coming to power.[127] At the same time, the South African military asserted that MPLA had promised training and equipment for SWAPO, if the latter assisted MPLA in the Angolan civil war.[128] In September 1975, the South African officer commanding South West Africa, Brigadier Marais, told the press that MPLA was prepared to help SWAPO to liberate Namibia provided that SWAPO assisted them in Angola.[129] However, the reality of SWAPO's changing alliances reveals a more complex picture.

For example, MPLA publicly announced in September 1975 that its forces were facing soldiers of SWAPO in southern Angola.[130] SWAPO officially refuted the accusation but did not issue any statement of solidarity with MPLA. Rather, SWAPO officials insisted that they would not support any movement in Angola.[131] After South Africa had occupied N'Giva the capital of the Cunene province in September 1975, elements of SWAPO, with units of the FNLA Chipenda faction and UNITA, reoccupied the town for a few days at the end of September before being forced out again by MPLA on 2 October.[132]

In another instance, Savimbi alleged that his movement had provided a training camp to SWAPO in the zone controlled by UNITA in defiance of a decision by the Angolan transitional government which comprised MPLA, FNLA and UNITA to expel SWAPO from Angola in May 1975.[133] Savimbi was also reported as having said in December 1975 that UNITA followers were killed or taken prisoner by South African troops because they harboured SWAPO guerillas.[134] UNITA claimed in February 1976 that approximately 3,000 SWAPO guerillas were in the UNITA held region of Angola. Although relations were becoming strained because SWAPO's president Sam Nujoma had paid tribute to MPLA's victory in the Angolan war, UNITA would continue to harbour SWAPO guerillas.[135]

Allegations about the collaboration between units of SWAPO and UNITA – and even South Africa – against MPLA also surfaced during an internal crisis of SWAPO from 1975 to 1976, as the SWAPO Youth League, backed by the then secretary of information and publicity Andreas Shipanga and PLAN fighters in Zambia took issue with SWAPO's exile leadership in Lusaka. In a document entitled 'Why we have to meet directly the Liberation Committee of the OAU' of March 1976, PLAN fighters alleged that weapons intended for SWAPO had been handed over to UNITA and according to some sources, the weapons had been diverted to UNITA by the government of Zambia who supported Savimbi during the Angolan war in 1975.[136] Shipanga alleges that the weapons were handed to UNITA by SWAPO,[137] thereby corroborating an earlier criticism by Neto in 1973 that SWAPO would be a large-scale supplier of arms to UNITA. PLAN guerillas also alleged that some commanders had forced them alongside the South Africans against MPLA in battles along the Benguela railway line.[138] And thirty plan fighters were reported to have died in a battle at Luena.[139]

While Sam Nujoma denied Savimbi's claim that UNITA was harbouring SWAPO guerrillas,[140] SWAPO decided to lend exclusive support to MPLA only in early February 1976 after one week of talks with the MPLA leadership in Luanda.[141] In an interview in March 1976, Nujoma publicly stated SWAPO's position. It had always recognized MPLA as the authentic representative of the Angolan people. There have been long-standing military links between the two organizations, although SWAPO, for a number of logistic reasons, had to maintain certain relations with UNITA. And he pointed out that SWAPO would never forget that Daniel Chipenda of FNLA had denounced dozens of clandestine cadres of SWAPO to the South Africans.[142] In April 1976, SWAPO fighters were reported to have led MPLA and Cuban forces to UNITA hideouts in southeast Angola.[143] SWAPO also helped to consolidate MPLA's position against UNITA in the Cunene province which MPLA effectively occupied at the beginning of April 1976.[144] MPLA put a SWAPO unit in charge of security of the Caluque dam on the Cunene river as one condition for providing SWAPO with material assistance and the use of training camp facilities in southern Angola,[145] and according to Vakulukuta, the Kwanyama leader from Angola who had joined UNITA in the early 1970s, SWAPO signalled the location of UNITA bases in the Cunene region to MPLA. However, Vakulukuta's UNITA forces, which at the time included former members of SWAPO who may have split from the organization during the conflict in Angola and were personally loyal to Vakulukuta,[146] attacked SWAPO units and dislodged them from Caluque.[147] But after two counteroffensives by MPLA and Cuban troops in August and November 1976, in which SWAPO denied any participation,[148] the Cunene province came under the control of MPLA. In June, SWAPO, whose movements were at times restricted by the Zambian government, transferred its headquarters from Lusaka to Luanda.[149] At the same time, PLAN fighters attacked a UNITA camp in Namibia where some of Savimbi's followers had withdrawn after their defeat in the Angolan civil war,[150] and from where Savimbi with South African help reorganized his resistance against the Angolan government.

The independence of Angola also had as a consequence the reinforcement of the cooperation between SWAPO and ANC who from 1976 both had their military training camps and education centres inside Angola.[151] On one hand, they shared facilities and helped each other out with material. On the other hand, a close relation between the ANC and the SWAPO leadership was initiated. The collaboration between SWAPO and ANC had been slow to develop, despite the fact that the two movements were political allies in the Khartoum alliance which regrouped the self-proclaimed authentic six liberation movements of southern and Portuguese speaking Africa. But differences in the development of ideological perspectives were an important factor accounting for a relatively cool relationship before Angolan independence. Before the adoption of its first political programme in 1976 which pledged SWAPO to 'a vanguard party capable of safeguarding national independence and of building a classless, non-exploitative society based on the ideals and principles of scientific socialism',[152] the ANC did not see any clear ideological dimension in SWAPO's policy. Inversely, the ideological and political alignment of the ANC with the South African Communist Party prevented SWAPO – or at least some of its Africanist members – from identifying closely with ANC.[153] But from 1976, MPLA, ANC and SWAPO were allied on the political and ideological levels as well as in the field.

The independence of Angola thus introduced a fundamental shift in the balance of power in southern Africa which had important implications for Namibia. On the *local* level inside

Namibia, MPLA's victory in Angola and its support for SWAPO enabled the latter to intensify substantially the armed struggle. This in turn led to increasing repression inside Namibia. At the same time, Pretoria attempted to impose ethnically based constitutional reforms in order to create a political alternative to SWAPO. On the *international* level, the independence of Mozambique and Angola led to the reformulation of the United States, policy towards southern Africa. Seeking a political settlement of the conflicts in the region, the western countries in collaboration with the Frontline states initiated a process of negotiations for Namibian independence culminating in the adoption of Security Council resolution 435 of 1978. But these initiatives came into conflict with Pretoria's emerging *regional* policy embedded in the Total National Strategy, which placed military containment of SWAPO and ANC and the weakening of potential host states above any negotiated settlement.

CHAPTER FIVE

REGIONAL DYNAMICS OF NEGOTIATIONS: THE FRONTLINE STATES AND NAMIBIA. 1976–81

Following the independence of Angola, the Namibian conflict intensified on the local level while attempts to reach a solution were made simultaneously inside Namibia, on the international as well as on the regional levels. SWAPO who could now rely on rear bases in Angola, was able to step up considerably its armed struggle, leading to an escalation of the conflict with South Africa and the further militarization of Namibia. Concomitantly, the South Africans increased their efforts to control Namibian decolonization through political means, notably by weakening SWAPO as a political force in favour of pro-South African political parties willing to accept a South African controlled transition to independence on Pretoria's terms.

With the large scale intervention of Cuban troops and sending of Soviet arms and advisors to Angola, Namibian decolonization also assumed an international dimension. The American secretary of state Henry Kissinger, who feared further Cuban and Soviet involvement in southern Africa, urged a negotiated settlement in Zimbabwe and Namibia acceptable to all parties of the conflicts.

While Western countries known as the 'Contact Group' or the 'Western Five' (Canada, France, Federal Republic of Germany, United Kingdom, United States) were instrumental in formulating the terms of a settlement contained in Security Council Resolution 435 of 1978, five majority ruled southern African states, the Frontline states (Angola, Botswana, Mozambique, Tanzania, Zambia) played a crucial and as yet little explored role in the negotiations leading to resolution 435. In particular, Frontline state pressure on SWAPO played an important if not determining role in SWAPO's acceptance of the resolution.

However, South Africa refused to agree to the implementation of resolution 435. The South African government under the premiership of the former minister of defence P. W. Botha who had replaced Vorster as prime minister in September 1978, adopted a hard line approach to Namibia and southern Africa in general. A negotiated settlement of the conflict in Namibia and the possibility of a 'Marxist' SWAPO government coming to power was an anathema to the South African defence establishment which put into practice a new comprehensive strategy, the Total National Strategy. It paved the way for direct confrontation between Angola and South Africa to which Namibian decolonization was subordinated from the early 1980s.

SWAPO and South Africa

The intensification of SWAPO's armed struggle prompted the South African Defence Force to declare the border regions of Ovambo, Kavango and Caprivi 'security districts' under military control in May 1976. At the same time, the South Africans announced plans to establish a one kilometre wide no-man's land free firing zone along the entire border between Namibia and Angola, uprooting several thousand peasants living in the border area.[1] During the biggest military operation as yet launched against SWAPO, the SADF admitted in June 1976 that SWAPO fighters had penetrated south of Ovamboland.[2] By 1977, the SADF claimed to be intercepting SWAPO guerillas in roughly 100 clashes a month and according to South African sources, SWAPO had 2,000 men in Angola, 1,400 in Zambia and 300 inside Namibia.[3]

In response to the escalation of SWAPO's armed struggle, South Africa increased its military presence inside Namibia. In 1976, the United Nations estimated that South Africa had a total of 45,000 troops in Namibia – three times as many as in 1974 – including 1,900 counterinsurgency police and approximately 26,000 logistic support forces.[4] However, not all troops were regular South African units. Increasingly, the SADF relied on ethnic battalions or 'tribal armies' which formed the skeleton of the future South West Africa Territory Force (SWATF) established in 1980. After a San (Bushmen) unit later called 201

Battalion had been formed in 1974, an Ovambo and a Kavango Battalion (Battalion 101 and 202) were established in 1975. In addition, Coloured infantry troops from the Cape province operated in Namibia in 1977 the same year as the SADF set up a 'multi-ethnic' battalion (Battalion 41 renamed later Battalion 911), which also included Whites and was presented as Namibia's first integrated indigenous battalion.[5] Lastly and this conferred a special regional dimension to the militarization of Namibia, the South Africans set up a special counterinsurgency unit which was integrated into the SADF, the 'Buffalo Unit' or 32 Battalion.

The Buffalo or 32 Battalion, which was formed a few months after the South Africans had left Angolan soil in March 1976, comprised a number of mercenaries from western countries and Australia, as well as 3,500 Angolan followers of Chipenda who after having collaborated with the SADF during the South African invasion of Angola, had fled with many of his followers to Namibia in January 1976. The 32 Battalion had its main operational base at Bagani (Buffalo) in the western Caprivi strip and it was under the command of white South African officers. The Buffalo Battalion was to operate almost exclusively inside Angola, in the Cunene province in southwest Angola in particular, where it was engaged in operations against SWAPO and became notorious for perpetrating atrocities against the civilian population from the late 1970s.[6]

But the escalation of military repression by South Africa against SWAPO in Namibia and Angola did not preclude SWAPO from intensifying its political activities inside Namibia, where it acted legally, in spite of SWAPO's public statement 'that armed resistance to the South African occupation in our country is the only viable and effective means left to us to achieve genuine liberation in Namibia'.[7] Likewise, Pretoria continued in its attempts to impose a South African controlled decolonization of Namibia whereby SWAPO would be marginalized.

SWAPO and the Turnhalle Conference

After the first meeting of the Turnhalle Conference in September 1975 which had excluded SWAPO who called the Turnhalle talks a 'farce . . . aimed at the perpetuation of white minority

107

rule under which South African domination would continue',[8] a committee set up by the Conference began to work on a draft constitution for Namibia which was presented in March 1977. Significantly, it was based on ethnic lines and called for a 'three-tier' system of administration on the national, regional and local levels. A 60 member *national* assembly drawn from each ethnic group[9] would be appointed by the second-tier regional legislative assemblies and tribal councils which represented Namibia's eleven official ethnic communities. One delegate from each ethnic group would be on a Minister's Council headed by a president appointed by the South African state president. In addition, Pretoria was to retain power over crucial ministries such as defence, foreign affairs and finance.[10] Moreover, the national executive, the Council of Ministers, was to reach decisions by consensus. Accordingly, each minister could block policy initiatives. In practice, this would have amounted to the power of veto by the white community who could thereby prevent any fundamental changes in the constitutional scheme.[11]

While the three-tier administrative system was to form the basis of South African colonial administration in Namibia until independence, the Turnhalle constitutional proposals were opposed by SWAPO and several other political parties who were active inside Namibia. While SWAPO declared that it would 'under no circumstances accept the South African plan to impose on our people a weak and fearful confederation of Bantustans, a confederation which will be incapable of contradicting neocolonial orders from Pretoria',[12] the question of whether to support or oppose the Turnhalle proposals divided the other Namibian opponents to South African rule. Four Nama communities from the south of Namibia led by Pastor Hendrick Witbooi,[13] and representing 80% of the 37,000 Nama in southern Namibia declared their support for SWAPO in 1976. 'Our choice is clear. We join unconditionally in the genuine nationalist platform of SWAPO created by our fellow-countrymen and not Turnhalle, the platform created by our enemy, the South African government'.[14]

While the Namibia National Front (NNF) which was dominated by SWANU[15] wanted to present an alternative to both the Turnhalle Constitutional Conference and SWAPO, Dirk Mudge, who had been the deputy leader of the South African

National Party in Namibia and who had been asked by the territory's Legislative Assembly to convene the Turnhalle Constitutional Conference in 1975,[16] formed the Democratic Turnhalle Alliance (DTA) in late 1977.[17] The DTA received considerable financial assistance from South Africa and it supported the South African controlled independence of Namibia along ethnic lines. It proposed the introduction of some reforms of the apartheid legislation such as higher wages, an end to job reservation and residential segregation. But from the outset, DTA symbolized the colonial collaborator to which not only SWAPO but also the United Nations were opposed.[18] Furthermore, the Democratic Turnhalle Alliance was also opposed by the western permanent members of the Security Council, the United States, Britain and France, who became involved in prolonged negotiations which, from the beginning, involved the Frontline states and which led to Security Council Resolution 435 of September 1978.

Reformulation of American policy towards southern Africa

The independence of Angola not only led to an escalation of the conflict between South Africa and SWAPO inside Namibia. It also prompted a reformulation of American policy towards southern Africa. In particular, the Soviet intervention in Angola came as shock to the American secretary of state Henry Kissinger. Impressed with the facility with which the Soviet Union was able to set up a base several thousand kilometres away from the Soviet Union,[19] Kissinger declared in San Francisco in February 1976 that the United States would not tolerate a repetition of the Angolan scenario.[20] In order to preempt any further Cuban and Soviet military intervention in southern Africa, the United States now reversed their previous policy of bolstering the white minority regimes.[21] The United States now favoured the independence of Zimbabwe and Namibia so as to prevent an internationalization of the conflicts in Namibia and Zimbabwe and thus forestall any further Cuban and Soviet military action in southern Africa. While the Soviet Union concluded treaties of friendship with Angola and Mozambique in 1976 and 1977 and decided to strengthen the liberation movements as the trends in Africa would favour the expansion of socialism at the expense of imperialism,[22] Cuba, though not

109

intending to invade any African countries, was in favour of 'the forced expulsion' of the South African troops from Namibia and the establishment of a SWAPO government.[23]

Already in January 1976, the United States, Britain and France as the permanent members of the Security Council, who traditionally opposed resolutions condemning the white regimes in southern Africa, but now realized that they had to support majority rule in southern Africa if they wanted to safeguard their long term economic interests in the region,[24] had endorsed a strongly worded resolution on Namibia. The resolution which provided the framework for the negotiations leading to Resolution 435 of 1978, notably called for South African withdrawal from Namibia within six months, the release of all political prisoners, the abolition of all racially discriminatory and political repressive laws and practices, an unconditional amnesty for Namibian exiles and elections under United Nations supervision. Furthermore, if South Africa did not comply with the resolution within six months, the Security Council would consider 'the appropriate measures to be taken under the Charter of the United Nations',[25] a euphemism for the threat of sanctions.

American support for Resolution 385 also signalled the start of Kissinger's personal shuttle diplomacy to southern Africa, in order to find a negotiated settlement of the conflicts in Zimbabwe and Namibia. In a speech in Lusaka on 27 April 1976, Kissinger declared that his journey would 'usher in a new area in American policy . . . We support self-determination, majority rule, equal rights and human dignity for all the people of southern Africa'. Kissinger presented a ten point plan for the achievement of majority rule in Zimbabwe and asked the South African government to put pressure to bear on the regime of Ian Smith. He also called for majority rule in Namibia. In particular, he reiterated the Security Council's demand for free elections under United Nations supervision and called on Pretoria to commit itself to a definite timetable for independence.[26] It was Kissinger's Lusaka speech, Resolution 385 and the possible threat that the western countries would support the call for sanctions in case of noncompliance with the resolution, that prompted the South African government to commit itself through a Constitutional Committee of the Turnhalle Conference to Namibian independence by 31 December 1978. For in the words of Geldenhuys, 'the Damocles sword of sanctions dangles over South Africa's head as long as it retains control of Namibia. Sanctions (or the threat of sanctions) are indeed the ultimate pressure being brought to bear on South Africa'.[27] The threat of sanctions was indeed used by the western countries during the negotiations leading to Resolution 435 of 1978.

While Kissinger's speech set the parametres for western diplomatic involvement in Zimbabwe and Namibia, the choice of Lusaka as a venue for delivering his speech was not fortuitous. His specific aim was to involve the African governments of the region in the settlement of both the conflicts in Zimbabwe and Namibia. A point which he made more explicitly when stating that the United States would be 'prepared to work with the international community and *especially with African leaders*, to determine what further steps would improve prospects for a rapid and acceptable transition to Namibian independence [emphasis added]'.[28] And in fact, the diplomatic efforts of the Frontline States, namely Angola, Botswana, Mozambique, Tanzania and Zambia, played a key role in the negotiations leading to Resolution 435 and subsequent attempts at its implementation from 1978 to 1982.

The foundations of Frontline state diplomacy

Initially suggested by the Tanzanian president Julius Nyerere,[29] the Frontline states were established in 1974 as in informal alliance between Botswana, Mozambique,[30] Tanzania and Zambia. They attempted to coordinate their policies towards the liberation of southern Africa. The fundamental document underlying Frontline state diplomacy towards Zimbabwe and Namibia was the *Manifesto on Southern Africa* issued by the Fifth Summit Conference of East and Central African States in Lusaka from 14 to 16 April 1969.[31] Written by Nyerere[32], the Lusaka Manifesto was an attempt to redefine the OAU's policy towards the liberation of southern Africa in the light of continuing resistance to change by the white minority regimes, existing policy divergences between those African states who favoured armed struggled and those who advocated direct contact with Pretoria,[33] and the OAU's failure to contribute effectively to the liberation of southern Africa through its Liberation Committee.[34] The Manifesto introduced a twofold strategy for the liber-

111

ation of southern Africa which was to determine future Front-line state diplomacy towards Namibia:

We can neither surrender nor compromise. We have always preferred and we still prefer, to achieve it [liber-ation] without physical violence. *We would prefer to negotiate rather than destroy, to talk rather than kill.* We do not advocate violence . . . If peaceful progress to emancipation were possible, or if changed circumstances would make it possi-ble in the future, we would urge our brothers in the resis-tance movements to use peaceful methods of struggle even at the cost of some compromise on the timing of change. But while peaceful progress is blocked by actions of those at present in power in the states of Southern Africa, we have no choice but to give to the peoples of those territor-ies all the support of which we are capable in their struggle against their oppressors [emphasis added].[35]

The double emphasis of the Manifesto on 'negotiation if possi-ble and support for armed struggle if necessary' justified in the eyes of the Frontline states the détente exercise of 1974 in which Zambia both played the role of host state to SWAPO, ANC and the Zimbabwean liberation movements, while Kaunda engaged at the same time in discussions with the South African government. Support for the politics of liberation and attempts to seek a diplomatic *rapprochement* with Pretoria in the framework of détente was also reflected in Zambia's attitude towards SWAPO from 1974 to 1976.

Zambia and SWAPO. 1974–6

With President Kaunda's support for the liberation of southern Africa and because of its geographical position bordering Zim-babwe, Namibia and Botswana,[36] Zambia played an important role as a host state to SWAPO before Angola's independence. SWAPO's headquarters were in Lusaka and PLAN fighters infiltrated into Namibia from Zambia either directly into the Caprivi strip or after crossing southeast Angola. SWAPO had established a health and education centre known as the 'Old Farm' inside Zambia in the 1960s, where in 1969 there were 4,000 Namibian refugees. Furthermore, Zambia was the desti-nation of over 6,000 Namibian refugees who left the country

112

between June 1974 and January 1975 as a result of relaxed border controls with Angola in the wake of the Revolution in Portugal in 1974.[37]

Zambia's support for the liberation of Namibia was also reflected in the establishment in 1976 of the United Nations Institute for Namibia in Lusaka. The rationale for the creation of such an Institute was that Namibia had a severe shortage of Namibian qualified personnel as a result of South Africa's policies. A special effort thus had to be made to create the nucleus of a public service, in which Namibians, who had been excluded from adequate training and schooling inside Namibia, could play a significant role. Sean MacBride, the then United Nations Commissioner for Namibia, suggested to the United Nations Council for Namibia in February 1974 that a research and training institute for Namibians should be established in Africa.[38] The proposal was endorsed by the General Assembly in December 1974.[39] The United Nations Institute for Namibia (UNIN) was inaugurated on 26 August 1976, Namibia day, in celebration of the launching of SWAPO's armed struggle in 1966.

UNIN had close links with SWAPO. For 'the Institute is a liberation support organization and close cooperation with and support and confidence by SWAPO have helped to make the Institute a success'.[40] However, the lack of systematic secondary and even full primary education, experienced by many UNIN students who had fled Namibia, made the task of creating a high standard of teaching and training very difficult. This problem was compounded with political complications such as the relationship between SWAPO and Zambia. Although the degrees conferred by UNIN were degrees of the University of Zambia, there were undercurrents which made the beginnings of UNIN difficult.[41]

While the Zambian government in general supported the liberation of Namibia, its actual policy towards SWAPO was more complex. SWAPO faced a serious internal rebellion in 1976, the origins of which go back to 1974 when thousands of Namibian refugees left the country. On one hand, the influx of refugees into Zambia created logistical problems for SWAPO. On the other hand, some refugees who had been active in the SWAPO Youth League inside Namibia, openly criticized SWAPO's external leadership accusing it of incompetence and

113

corruption and demanding changes.[42] Their demand for a new Party Congress – the last congress had taken place in Tanga, Tanzania in 1969 – was supported by prominent SWAPO members such as the secretary for information Andreas Shipanga and, to a lesser extent, the secretary for labour Salomon Mifima. While the SWAPO external leadership suspected that 'the motive and ultimate aim of these dissidents was to seize power',[43] an open rebellion of PLAn fighters brought the crisis to a head in early 1976 and involved the Zambian government directly.

The Zambian authorities had ordered SWAPO to stop fighting from Zambian soil soon after South African and Zambian officials had drafted the document outlining a scenario for détente in October 1974.[44] They continued to exert pressures on SWAPO in 1975. According to Shipanga, orders were given in April 1975 that all SWAPO guerillas be photographed and their identities recorded.[45] Shipanga further alleged that after the orders to halt military activities had been issued, the entire front was at a complete standstill by May 1975 and that Namibians were photographed and fingerprinted by the Zambian authorities in June.[46] In September, it was reported that a consignment of Soviet arms for SWAPO had been confiscated[47]. And it was also alleged that the Zambian government had put pressure to bear on SWAPO to release six South African soldiers who had been captured by PLAN fighters in an engagement in July 1975.[48]

SWAPO's compliance both with the order to suspend combat activities and to accept identity controls was criticized by PLAN fighters who accused the SWAPO leadership of weakness.[49] At one base, Central base, the discontent of PLAN fighters turned into open rebellion from March to April 1976.[50] In a document entitled 'Why We Have to Meet Directly the Liberation Committee of the OAU' of 23 March, they complained of being starved and being left without arms which they alleged had been given to UNITA.[51] When they met a OAU delegation in Lusaka, they were disarmed and detained while a group of about fifty other PLAN fighters, who had attempted to free them, were stopped by the Zambian army.[52] According to sources sympathetic to the SWAPO dissidents, members of the SWAPO executive committee then requested officials of the Zambian ministry of interior to arrest Shipanga, Mifima and leaders of the SWAPO Youth League whom they considered to be the leaders of the rebellion.[53] Shipanga and ten other dissidents were arrested on 21 April 1976 and deported to Tanzania where they were detained until 1978.[54] Furthermore, the Zambian army was reported to have detained a thousand Namibians – 700 according to SWAPO – in July 1976.[55] The majority of them were subsequently released and reintegrated into SWAPO.[56]

While President Nyerere of Tanzania justified the detention of the SWAPO dissidents in Tanzania by the fact that the headquarters of the OAU Liberation Committee, responsible for OAU policy towards the liberation movements, was based in Dar es Salaam,[57] the Zambian government's restrictive policy towards SWAPO and its tough stand towards the SWAPO dissidents in particular, reflect the potential contradictions between Zambia's policy towards South Africa and its policies as a host state to liberation movements. On one hand, Kaunda was clearly not willing to jeopardize the détente exercise with South Africa in 1974 and 1975. As a landlocked country, Zambia depended on neighbouring territories as transit routes for its trade, for the export of copper in particular. The repeated closures of its border with Rhodesia and the inability to use the Benguela railway in Angola, increased Zambia's dependency on South Africa. Moreover, Kaunda emphasized that the policy of dialogue with the Vorster government was in line with the spirit of the Lusaka Manifesto which called for negotiations if possible and armed struggle if necessary. In reply to critics of Zambia because of its discussions with the Pretoria government, Vernon Mwaanga, Zambia's foreign minister in 1975, replied that 'if South Africa is the colonial authority as we believe she is in Zimbabwe and Namibia, what is wrong with talking to a colonial authority about granting independence to the people that she oppresses or to the people that are under her colonial domination?'[58] On the other hand, the Zambian army's heavy handed approach towards the SWAPO dissidents illustrates Kaunda's resolve to keep the liberation movements united which was one of the basic goals of the OAU's Liberation Committee, to assert Zambian control over the activities of liberation movements active inside Zambia,[59] and to prevent a repetition of the bloody revolt analogous to the one of the Zimbabwe National Union (ZANU) which had led to the assassination of ZANU's chairman Herbert Chitepo in Lusaka in March 1975.[60] Furthermore, both Zambia and Tanzania were no doubt anxious to prevent dissensions within SWAPO at the very time when Kissinger was engaged in his shuttle diplomacy over southern Africa.

As far as SWAPO was concerned, the Zambian attitude during the SWAPO internal crisis had illustrated SWAPO's reliance and dependence on the host state. While the Zambian army helped the SWAPO leadership to overcome its internal crisis, at the same time, the Zambian authorities curtailed SWAPO's room for manoeuvre, a fact which probably weighed heavily in SWAPO's decision to move its headquarters from Lusaka to Luanda in 1976. Angola now was the main rear base for SWAPO's armed struggle. But at the same time and contrary to what is often assumed, the Angolan government and president Neto in particular, also played a crucial role in finding a negotiated settlement of the Namibian conflict.

Mediating the Namibian conflict: the Western Contact Group and the Frontline states

After Kissinger's attempts to find a negotiated settlement in Namibia had stalled in October 1976,[61] the administration under President Carter decided to lend active support to the implementation of Resolution 385 which had earlier been accepted unanimously by the Security Council in January 1976 and which called for the South African withdrawal from Namibia and United Nations supervised elections for independence. Soon after president Carter's inauguration in January 1977, the American ambassador to the United Nations Andrew Young and his deputy, Donald McHenry, played an important role in constituting an informal grouping which became known as the Western Contact Group. The exact origins of the Contact Group are uncertain. According to one author, who interviewed members of the Contact Group, the idea originated either with Young's deputy McHenry, or Gerald Helman who then worked in the Bureau of international organizations in the American State Department, or indeed Julius Nyerere who would have suggested the idea to Young in early 1977.[62] The Contact Group comprised the three permanent western members of the Security Council, the United States, the United Kingdom and France, as well as Canada and the Federal Republic of Germany, who were temporary members of the Security Council. And the constitution of the Contact Group in early 1977 laid the basis for protracted negotiations and shuttle diplomacy of the Group between the South African government, SWAPO and the Frontline states.

As far as Great Britain was concerned, the new foreign secretary of the labour government, Dr. David Owen, was determined to be less accommodating towards the South African government than his predecessors of the Conservative governments in particular, had been. Owen notably wanted to see a clearer commitment by Britain, than in the past, in favour of change inside South Africa. According to Owen, Britain should demonstrate clearly that it was committed to help to bring about majority rule in South Africa.[63] An active British role in the negotiations for Namibia's independence would illustrate this commitment. Moreover, Owen saw a close link between the negotiations over Namibian independence and the decolonization of Zimbabwe, to which he subordinated the Namibian issue.[64] At the same time, however, Britain had close and important economic links with South Africa, a reality which made opposition to apartheid and the South African government often more rhetorical than real. In 1977, the Group's initiative over Namibia lay not with Britain, but the United States, Canada and the Federal Republic of Germany. They conceived of Namibian independence, with hindsight correctly, as a stage preceding fundamental change inside South Africa.[65]

In February 1977, the Contact Group, led by the American deputy ambassador to the United Nations Donald McHenry who became the effective chairman of the group, held discussions with both the Frontline states and South Africa in New York in order to develop an approach acceptable to all parties. SWAPO was initially excluded from the talks. According to Cyrus Vance, 'contact with SWAPO was difficult, partly because its leaders were so frequently out of reach, but also because of its suspicions about our motives'.[66]

While the Carter administration's efforts to find a settlement of the conflict in Namibia represented a continuation of the efforts which had been initiated by Henry Kissinger, both the rationale underlying the new American initiative and the methods being contemplated to persuade South Africa to withdraw from Namibia differed substantially from Kissinger's approach and contributed to the Frontline states' willingness to cooperate with the Contact Group.

The Ford administration and its secretary of state Kissinger had defended a 'globalist' approach to Third World conflicts, just as the Reagan administration would during the period from 1981 to 1988. Accordingly, all third world conflicts were subordinated to the global east-west confrontation. American involvement in supporting UNITA and FNLA in Angola and seeking a negotiated settlement in Zimbabwe and Namibia were seen simply as a response to Soviet expansionism. While the Carter administration shared the perception of a Soviet and Cuban threat in southern Africa, it was initially opposed to simply subordinating local and regional conflicts in southern Africa to east-west rivalry. Cyrus Vance and Andrew Young were opposed to the globalist approach to American policy in Africa. For Vance, 'the most effective policies towards Africa are affirmative policies . . . A negative, reactive American policy that seeks only to oppose Soviet or Cuban involvement in Africa would be futile. Our best course is to help resolve problems which create opportunities for external intervention'.[67] Accordingly, Vance and Young believed that South African withdrawal from Namibia 'was necessary if we were to get the Cuban troops out of Angola'. For the escalation of the conflict in Namibia would increase the risk of South Africa carrying the war into Angola. A Cuban-South African conflict could spill over into Rhodesia with the risk of a general war in southern Africa 'in which we would be virtually powerless to prevent immense damage to American political, economic and strategic interests'.[68] In addition and contrary to Kissinger's approach to southern Africa, the Carter administration was 'committed to majority rule, self-determination and racial equality as a matter of fairness and basic human rights',[69] and Namibian independence could serve as a model for change in South Africa.[70]

Western pressure on South Africa to withdraw from Namibia was limited, however, by their refusal to support mandatory sanctions against South Africa. Vance clearly outlined the dilemma which the sanctions issue presented to the American administration: 'Without a strategy for Namibian independence, the Western nations would soon be faced with the dilemma of how to respond to African demands for mandatory sanctions against South Africa. If there were no credible negotiating initiative, the Africans would be able to force a Security Council vote. We would then either damage our relations with black Africa by vetoing the resolution, which would be at odds with the Carter administration's African policy, or by approving it, destroy the negotiating process and harm important western economic interests in South Africa'.[71] Vance, Carter and Young were opposed to sanctions which was an issue which divided the State Department;[72] and fear of having to impose sanctions against South Africa set the limits of western pressure on South Africa.

The Frontline states

The Frontline states, who had been recognized by the OAU as a formal ad hoc Committee of the organization's assembly of heads of states in 1975,[73] and to whom the OAU effectively delegated its authority over southern Africa[74] concentrated their efforts for conflict resolution in Zimbabwe. Frontline state support for the western initiative over Namibia only emerged gradually as they wanted to have assurances that the Contact Group was in a position to bring pressure to bear on South Africa to agree to Namibian independence.[75] But several factors contributed to te Frontline states' support of the Contact Group. *Firstly*, the Carter administration who led the Group took a stronger stand in favour of majority rule and human rights than the previous Ford administration. *Secondly* and more importantly, the five members of the Contact Group were all major trading partner of South Africa. They therefore possessed – at least in theory – an undeniable potential of leverage over Pretoria,[76] especially concerning the imposition of sanctions. The western countries effectively used the threat of imposing sanctions against South Africa in April 1977, as a result of which the Vorster government dropped the Turnhalle constitutional proposals and accepted the principle of elections for a constituent assembly, of universal suffrage and of United Nations involvement.[77] This no doubt gave credence to the view that the United States and its allies were willing to bring pressure to bear on South Africa. *Thirdly*, the nature of the military confrontation between South Africa and SWAPO rend-

119

ered the prospects of Namibian independence brought about through the armed struggle unlikely. The scale and capabilities of South African counterinsurgency prevented SWAPO from sustaining an effective armed struggle, contrary to what was the case in Zimbabwe. The Frontline states considered military action an unlikely option for bringing about Namibian independence. They therefore decided to give negotiations leading to United Nations supervised elections a chance.[78] However, Frontline states unanimity in public did not preclude the existence of policy differences concerning Namibia among themselves.

As far as *Angola* was concerned, the country's president Dr. Agostinho Neto, who did not often attend Frontline meetings,[79] was sceptical about the negotiations. If the decision had been left to Angola, it would have decided against Frontline state involvement in the western initiative. However, the Angolan government was willing to accommodate the majority of the Frontline states,[80] and Neto who was eager to reduce the South African military threat on Angola's borders, took a leading role in the Frontline effort at mediation between SWAPO and South Africa. Neto and the Angolan leadership actually 'proved to be vigorous supporters of a negotiated solution' and Vance intended to maintain a close relationship with Angola on the Namibian question because of Neto's perceived influence over Nujoma.[81]

Botswana's role as a Frontline state was constrained because of its position as a landlocked country between South Africa, Namibia and Zimbabwe with a small outlet to Zambia across the Zambezi. Nevertheless, Botswana had aligned itself with the independent countries to the north since its independence in 1966. In 1969, President Seretse Khama declared his support for the Lusaka Manifesto.[82] In 1974, he supported détente cautiously, emphasizing that the white minority régimes should first demonstrate their willingness to change their racial policies.[83] But he was prepared to support armed struggle if negotiations failed.[84] Already in September 1973, the president of Botswana had declared that his government had 'always recognized the right of the black citizens of these [minority ruled] countries to achieve their full human rights and has expressed support for their efforts to do so. It is the wish of Botswana that these rights be achieved by peaceful means, but where this is not possible, the Government has publicly expressed its understanding when the people concerned decide to resort to violent means'.[85]

In the early seventies, the liberation struggle in Namibia was not a policy priority for the Botswana government and SWAPO enjoyed less support than the Zimbabwean and Angolan liberation movements.[86] However, with Angolan independence the question of Namibian independence gained in importance. After Botswana had joined the United Nations Council for Namibia in December 1974, Seretse Khama publicly denounced South African occupation of Namibia and the Turnhalle constitutional proposals.[87] Although the Botswana government disliked what they perceived as SWAPO's and particularly Sam Nujoma's intransigence, it welcomed the Contact Group's initiative. According to Botswana's foreign minister at that time, Botswana had always appealed to South Africa's allies to put pressure to bear on the Pretoria régime.[88]

The president of *Mozambique* Samora Machel backed the Frontline state position in favour of a negotiated settlement of the Namibian conflict. Two factors seemed to have played a role in FRELIMO's support for the Contact Group's initiative. On one hand, the Mozambican government, in common with other Frontline states, had serious reservations about SWAPO's ability to achieve a military victory over South Africa. This was important in Mozambique's assessment of the Namibian situation which, in point of fact, Machel believed would be resolved before Zimbabwe achieved independence. In addition, FRELIMO always had good relations with some sectors of the American administration.[89] And Mozambican diplomats were credited subsequently with playing an important role in pressuring the western countries to persuade South Africa to comply with Security Council Resolution 435 of September 1987.[90]

Tanzania, as a result of Nyerere's long-standing commitment to the liberation of southern Africa[91] was, together with Angola, to play the most prominent role in the Frontline states mediation efforts over Namibia. Although Nyerere was also initially sceptical about the western initiative,[92] he believed that the Contact Group would be able and willing to bring sufficient pressure to bear on South Africa to withdraw from Namibia,[93] even more as the Carter administration had 'given its word of honour to deliver South Africa'.[94] Like the other Frontline states, Tanzania realized that the chances for forcing the South Africans out of Namibia militarily were very slim and that a diplomatic initiative led by the more sympathetic Carter administration could be successful. When asked his opinion of western involvement in southern Africa during a visit to the United States in August 1977, Nyerere pointed out that 'we can put the necessary kind of pressures, combined pressures, your pressures, our pressures, to bear on the South Africans with regard to Namibia and Rhodesia and achieve independence quickly'.[95]

Zambia's preference for a negotiated solution to the Namibian conflict had already been noticeable in its attempts at a rapprochement with South Africa during the détente period from 1974 to 1975. And Kaunda supported the Western initiative. However, contrary to the case of Zimbabwe, direct Zambian diplomatic involvement over Namibia was discrete. No doubt, the pressures which were brought to bear on Zambia by the Rhodesians, who attacked Zambia militarily in 1977 and 1978, explain that the independence of Namibia was not the immediate policy priority of the Zambian government.

The task now facing the Frontline states was to convince the SWAPO leadership to accept a compromise solution for Namibian independence mediated by South Africa's allies. Frontline state pressure on SWAPO to compromise over crucial issues such as the South African troop withdrawal from Namibia and the control of the South African claimed harbour of Walvis Bay, became a salient feature of the negotiations leading to SWAPO's acceptance of a settlement plan proposed by the Contact group in April 1978, which was to form the basis of Security Council Resolution 435 of 29 September 1978 and ten years later the transition period leading to Namibian independence in March 1990.

The Frontline states and SWAPO. 1977–8

The relationship between the Frontline states and SWAPO in the negotiations leading to the adoption of Security Council Resolution 435 of September 1978 were often difficult. It was an asymmetrical relationship between a liberation movement who depended on the support of its neighbours in its struggle against South Africa and the Frontline states who, although sympathetic to SWAPO's cause, put a lot of pressure to bear on SWAPO, so that it would accept a compromise solution proposed by the Contact Group and ultimately reflected in Resolution 435. Whereas the Contact Group attempted to persuade the South African government to accept Namibian independence under the supervision of the United Nations, the role played by the Frontline states was crucial in persuading SWAPO to accept the plan.

However, the western plan for a settlement under the United Nations supervision as it emerged in 1978, was only a second best solution for some of SWAPO's leaders. SWAPO, like other nationalist movements which had reverted to armed struggle, had reservations about the Lusaka Manifesto with its two-pronged approach of negotiations if possible and armed struggle if necessary.[96] They tended to view negotiations for independence as being prejudicial to the armed struggle and as an attempt to seek a neocolonial solution that would create new problems. Nevertheless, the liberation movements generally refrained from criticizing the Manifesto, as they depended on its signatories, on Tanzania and Zambia in particular, for their continuing support as host states.[97] Some members of the SWAPO leadership believed that a negotiated settlement over Namibia which involved the mediation of South Africa's allies would not satisfy SWAPO's aspirations. They preferred the military option, even more as the eastern European countries and the Soviet Union in particular, did not support the western initiative to the point of alienating the Frontline states who were seeking a compromise solution.[98] But the Soviet Union was not in a position to prevent either SWAPO from engaging in negotiations or the Frontline states to bring pressure to bear on SWAPO to compromise.[99] In addition, some states such as Ethiopia and Libya had warned SWAPO that negotiations would lead to elections and SWAPO had to be sure that they wanted this outcome.[100] Publicly, Nujoma stated that SWAPO had explored all peaceful options to achieve Namibian independence. But confronted with South African oppression in Namibia, SWAPO was committed to the armed struggle as the only viable and effective alternative to negotiations, 'unless all the conditions that have led to our war of national liberation have been eliminated'.[101] Furthermore, SWAPO had 'not been in the struggle for more than sixteen years and made all the many supreme sacrifices that we have made in order to come and accept electoral traps set up for us [by the western initiative] to fall into and thereby opening the way for a neocolonial solution in Namibia[102'].

Nevertheless, SWAPO never outright rejected negotiations and Nujoma had publicly declared in February 1977 that he was willing to meet the South African prime minister Vorster.[103] According to Ngarikutuke Tjiriange, who as SWAPO's secretary for legal affairs had participated in all the negotiations leading to the adoption of Resolution 435, SWAPO's initial negotiating position was that no political process could take place in Namibia while South Africa was administering the territory, that elections could not take place while South African troops and the South African police remained in Namibia, that all armed groups such as citizen groups should be disarmed and that Walvis Bay should be an integral part of Namibia.[104] South African troop withdrawal from Namibia and the ownership and control of the South African claimed port of Walvis Bay were particularly sensitive issues to SWAPO.

Sovereignty over Walvis Bay which is Namibia's only developed deep-water port was claimed by both SWAPO and South Africa. The 1,124 square km (434 square miles) territory of Walvis Bay had been annexed by Britain in 1878 and was part of the Cape colony during the German occupation of Namibia from 1884 to 1914. The Bay was excluded from the terms of the League of Nations mandate over the territory which had been conferred to South Africa in the wake of the First World War. According to the South West Africa Act of 1922, Walvis Bay was legally part of the Cape province but should be administered as if it belonged to South West Africa. After the Second World War, the South African government used the Bay's exclusion from the mandate's provision to militarize the surrounding territory. And the Vorster government declared in 31 August 1977 that Pretoria not only claimed sovereignty over Walvis Bay but was to *administer* the Bay as an integral part of the Cape province. For Pretoria, this meant that Walvis Bay was South African territory and therefore not negotiable. For SWAPO on the contrary, the Bay was an integral part of Namibia irrespective of its colonial history. In particular, SWAPO based its claim on the principle of estoppel, which means that South Africa, by administering Walvis Bay as part of South West Africa for 60 years, had in fact abandoned its claim to South African sovereignty over the Bay. Moreover, in view of the principle of the self-determination of peoples combined with the fact that Walvis Bay belonged geographically, economically and historically to Namibia, South Africa would not be entitled to recolonize the territory of the Bay.[105] SWAPO was not prepared to compromise on the issue. The American secretary of state Vance recognized that the positions of SWAPO and Pretoria were 'diametrically and immovably' opposed and that if the negotiations had to solve the issue of Walvis Bay, the western initiative 'could be destroyed'.[106] On the issue of South Africa troop withdrawal from Namibia, SWAPO insisted that *all* troops should be withdrawn before independence elections took place,[107] and that the United Nations should assume *direct* legal responsibility over Namibia during the transition period. Agreement on South African troop withdrawal would be crucial. And the questions both of South African troop withdrawal and the sovereignty of Walvis Bay became the two key issues over which pressure on SWAPO to compromise was brought to bear by the Frontline states.

After a second round of talks between the Contact Group and South Africa in June 1977, the Frontline states persuaded Nujoma to meet with the Group in New York on 8 August 1977. According to Vance, president Neto, who was worried about the South African military threat on Angola's southern border, 'was particularly helpful' and president Nyerere 'added his arguments . . . as he was anxious to stop the fighting in Namibia and Rhodesia before it widened'.[108] Nyerere met with president Carter prior to the meeting between SWAPO and the Contact Group. The American deputy ambassador to the United Nations McHenry who led the Contact Group presented a settlement plan which notably provided for free elections open to all Namibian political parties and the presence of a UN special representative who, together with a South African appointed administrator general, would supervise an interim government. All discriminatory laws would be abolished, all political prisoners released and exiles allowed to return. South Africa would begin a phased withdrawal of its troops which would be completed upon independence. However, South Africa had not presented a timetable for troop withdrawal and

125

the Contact Group conceived of the United Nations presence in the form of a monitoring group of about 1,000 rather than a large peacekeeping force.

Nyerere accepted the principles of elections and universal suffrage but pointed out to the Americans that the main concern of SWAPO and the Frontline states was that the elections should be free and fair. The answer would be to strengthen the role played by the United Nations who should assume legal responsibility for the territory during the transition period with an administrative staff to replace the South Africans and the local authorities. According to Vance, Nyerere insisted that there should be a large UN peacekeeping force and that South Africa would have to withdraw *all* of its troops. The Frontline states would accept a small South African military presence until independence as a face-saving device for the Vorster government. However, on independence day SWAPO would have to take power from the United Nations and not from South Africa. If the Frontline states were convinced that the United Nations would control and supervise the transitional phase, they would urge SWAPO to accept the western plan and to observe a cease-fire with South Africa. Nyerere also accepted Carter's argument that SWAPO should show more flexibility if the Contact Group were to continue serious negotiations with the South Africans.[109]

Pressurized by the Frontline states, SWAPO had little choice but to accept the principle of western mediation. The SWAPO delegation who met the Contact group in New York in August, had told the Group that it appreciated the western initiative to assist the United Nations to implement resolution 385 of January 1976. But SWAPO feared correctly that the attitude of the South African government would be the main obstacle to a negotiated settlement of Namibian independence.[110] SWAPO continued to ask for a total South African troop withdrawal before independence and for the deployment of a large UN peacekeeping force as a condition for accepting the western settlement plan.[111] The negotiation process reached a stalemate at the end of 1977 over the question of South African troop withdrawal, the size of the UN force and the status of Walvis Bay. Both South Africa and SWAPO rejected a compromise proposal worked out by the Contact Group, namely that a token South African force of 1,500 could remain in Namibia but be confined to a single base and operate under UN monitoring until independence, a UN military presence of approximately 2,000 and the deferment of the Walvis Bay issue until after independence.[112]

Again under pressure from the Frontline states, SWAPO agreed to a gradual withdrawal of South African troops to a level of 1,500 to 3,000.[113] But when the Contact Group had presented new proposals at 'proximity' talks, which South Africa and SWAPO were to attend separately in February 1978, Nujoma demanded that the South African troops should be based at Karasburg in the south of Namibia and he declared that SWAPO's demand that Walvis Bay was an integral part of Namibia, was not negotiable.[114] Pretoria rejected SWAPO's demand that the South African forces be confined to the south of Namibia and it again insisted that Walvis Bay was legally part of South Africa and that the issue should be settled between Pretoria and an independent Namibian government. More importantly, the South African foreign minister 'Pik' Botha abruptly withdrew from the talks declaring that the western proposals contained the serious risk that Namibia would be overrun and governed by Marxist terrorists. And after a cabinet meeting on 14 February, Vorster, who was probably under pressure by hardliners such the minister of defence P. W. Botha,[115] announced that South Africa would carry out its own solution for independence through the internal parties and hinted at the possibility of granting unilateral independence by 31 December 1978.[116] The South African move raised increasing doubts as to Pretoria's sincerity to reach an agreement. Furthermore, the assassination of Chief Clemens Kapuuo in March 1978,[117] which weakened the Democratic Turnhalle Alliance of which he was one of the main leaders, increased the likelihood of Pretoria refusing international negotiations and choosing an internal settlement. To the Contact Group, it meant that 'we could not tolerate further delays'.[118]

In late March, the Group presented revised proposals to Pretoria which were to form the basis of the 'Proposal for a settlement of the Namibian situation' which the Group submitted to the Security Council on 10 April 1978 and which were to be the main body of Security Council Resolution 435 of September 1978.[119] According to the new proposals, the South African appointed administrator general would retain control of the Namibian police, who would be accompanied by UN observers; the size of the UN peacekeeping force and monitoring group would be decided by the UN special representative but South Africa would be consulted on the national composition of the United Nations force; South African forces could be concentrated at two bases in the north of Namibia rather than in the south as demanded by SWAPO; the Contact Group would take into account the wishes of the constituent assembly if it asked the South African forces to remain in Namibia. The Group also stated its intention to exclude Walvis Bay from the settlement. Its status would be negotiated after independence.[120]

The South African government formally accepted the proposals on 25 April. But it associated its acceptance with new conditions. A reduced South African force would have to be allowed to remain in Namibia after independence if requested to do so by the Constituent Assembly, all hostilities would have to end before South Africa would withdraw its troops and South African police would maintain law and order during the transition period.[121] 'South Africa's ability to raise a steady stream of new issues' became the central problem for the Contact Group,[122] and it raised questions about Pretoria's sincerity in surrendering the territory. Deon Geldenhuys, a South African academic and foreign affairs consultant to P. W. Botha in the early 1980s, qualified South Africa's 'tendency to raise new issues, or exaggerate existing ones just as others have been resolved', as 'an outstanding feature of South African conduct of the Namibian negotiations' with the purpose 'to stall negotiations and to win time'.[123]

Pretoria's strategy of delaying solution did not go unnoticed by SWAPO as the South Africans arrested nine members of SWAPO's internal wing on the same day as Pretoria announced its acceptance of the western proposals on 25 April 1975. Nujoma was annoyed, because he felt that the Contact Group had pushed SWAPO into a settlement by presenting the proposals to the South African government and the Security Council. Immediately after Pretoria's acceptance of the western proposals had been known, Nujoma told the Frontline states that he could not accept the proposals. However, the Frontline states refused to back him and at a meeting with Cyrus Vance, Don McHenry and the Nigerian foreign minister Joseph

Garba[124] on 27 April 1978, Nujoma had to tell the American secretary of state that he would not reject the proposals. He intended, however, to seek substantial changes. He again reiterated his demand that the South African troops should be located in the south of Namibia and that Walvis Bay which was an integral part of Namibia, should be included in the western proposals.[125]

The entire negotiation process nearly broke down after South African planes had bombarded Kassinga, a SWAPO refugee camp 250 km north of the Namibian border in Angola on 4 May, killing over 600 people.[126] The South African raid highlighted how little Pretoria was prepared to accept a negotiated settlement which could bring SWAPO to power. As a result of the Kassinga raid, Andrew Young and McHenry were extremely sceptical about the intentions of the South African government.[127] More importantly, the raid showed the growing importance of the military, led by P. W. Botha who was opposed to concessions in Namibia, in South African foreign policy making.[128] Nujoma immediately broke off the negotiations and returned to Angola. The entire central committee of SWAPO met in Luanda and was very reluctant to continue participating in the negotiations,[129] even more as Pretoria was planning to hold its own internal elections for a constituent assembly in December 1978.

The Kassinga raid thus presented a formidable challenge to Frontline state diplomacy and a great deal of persuasion was needed to bring SWAPO back to the negotiating table. According to Vance, the Angolans who were making an exceptional effort in dissuading Nujoma from blocking the western proposals, were furious.[130] And President Nyerere took the initiative of a compromise solution over Walvis Bay which would satisfy SWAPO. The Tanzanian president suggested that the status of Walvis Bay should be the object of a separate Security Council resolution which should support the integration of Walvis Bay into Namibia, as the Bay belonged to the country from a historical and geographical point of view. However, the resolution would not back SWAPO's position that Walvis Bay was an integral part of Namibia also from a legal point of view. In addition, the issue of Walvis Bay should be discussed after independence between the governments of South Africa and Namibia.[131] Nyerere told the Americans that the question of

Walvis Bay and the location of South African troops during the transition period were the only 'irreducible' problems which had to be solved. SWAPO insisted that the status of Walvis Bay was not negotiable,[132] and according to Tjiriange, SWAPO's principal negotiator, SWAPO had deadlocked on the issue.[133] However, the Tanzanian president could persuade Nujoma to meet the Contact Group in Luanda in June.

In Luanda, the Western Group refused to endorse SWAPO's stand that Walvis Bay should be part of the settlement[134], but backed Nyerere's idea of a separate Security Council resolution on the issue. The Frontline states and Angola in particular, also put pressure to bear on SWAPO concerning the location of South African troops. The Contact Group was not prepared to reopen negotiations with the South African government on the subject, as Pretoria had refused a suggestion to concentrate all troops in one base. But the Group was prepared to ask the UN secretary-general to designate a peace-keeping force big enough to monitor South African bases. The Frontline states supported this position and according to Vance, the Angolan representatives insisted that the meeting between SWAPO, the Frontline states and the Contact Group should not adjourn until SWAPO had accepted the group's position.[135]

The contentious issues of Walvis Bay and the location of South African troops inside Namibia illustrate the asymetrical relationship between SWAPO and the Frontline states, Tanzania and Angola in particular. At one point, Nujoma was summoned from East Berlin to Dar es Salaam where Nyerere told him 'unceremoniously' to accept the compromise over Namibia and over Walvis Bay in particular. Angola added its voice by arguing that the existence of territorial enclaves was not unusual, the American base of Guantanamo in Cuba being an example.[136] During the course of the negotiations, Nyerere also told Nujoma that 'if you can't fight, you have to negotiate'.[137] The Frontline stand was that as SWAPO was not in a position to liberate Namibia militarily, it had to negotiate and they did not hesitate to employ a combination or persuasion, pressure and subtle threats to convince SWAPO to accept the settlement.[138]

SWAPO's room for manoeuvre was limited. On 12 July, it agreed to both the location of South African troops at two bases (at Oshivelo and Grootfontein) and the Walvis Bay question. In the official and somehow ambiguous wording of SWAPO, the organization 'allowed the issue to stand over until after independence on the undertaking that the West would endorse a Security Council resolution explicitly recognizing Walvis Bay as Namibian territory'.[139] A Resolution was voted on 27 July.[140] The resolution did not explicitly condemn the South African claim to sovereignty over the Walvis Bay. It declared that Namibia's territorial integrity and unity must be assured through the reintegration of Walvis Bay into the territory and that, pending the attainment of this objective, South Africa must not use Walvis Bay in any manner prejudicial to the independence of Namibia or the viability of its economy. Furthermore, it declared that the Security Council would lend its full support to the initiation of steps necessary to ensure early integration of Walvis Bay into Namibia. Resolution 432 was a compromise. In the words of Vance, it did 'not prejudice the legal position of any party' and the western Contact Group would encourage negotiations on the subject between the governments of South Africa and Namibia after independence.[141] While South Africa restated its claim to sovereignty over Walvis Bay, SWAPO later justified its acceptance of the compromise solution arguing that the question should be solved after independence. It argued that this would reflect the strategy of 'phased struggle'. The primary goal would be to achieve formal independence, even without a prior, or simultaneous, settlement of the secondary issue of Walvis Bay.[142]

But what were the real reasons behind SWAPO's decision to accept the western settlement plan? The repression inside Namibia, the South African raid on Kassinga and Pretoria's subsequent decision to hold *internal* elections for a constituent assembly under South African control in December, clearly indicated South Africa's unwillingness to accept a settlement with SWAPO. The pressure of the Frontline states which was brought to bear on SWAPO by Tanzania and Angola in particular, led to a policy debate within SWAPO and almost caused a split within SWAPO's leadership.[143] According to some observers, the then secretary for foreign affairs Peter Mueshihange and an important minority group within the National Executive, supported the military option, while SWAPO's president Nujoma had a personal preference for a negotiated settlement.[144] To some, such as Tjiriange, the western proposals

131

were a compromise which neither SWAPO nor the South Africans liked. But the fact that Pretoria had formally accepted the proposals, presented a diplomatic score for SWAPO.[145] To others, it proved painful for SWAPO to accept the western settlement plan and the resolution on Walvis Bay. However, SWAPO's room for manoeuvre was limited, as it wanted to avoid any confrontation with the Frontline states[146] on whose support it depended. Moreover and perhaps more importantly, SWAPO was convinced that it would win elections held under United Nations supervision.

While the role of the Frontline states was crucial in persuading SWAPO to accept the clauses of the western plan, which was subsequently integrated into Security Council resolution 435 of September 1978, Frontline state pressure on SWAPO has to be explained in the overall context of the liberation struggle in southern Africa. To the Frontline leaders, the conflicts in Namibia and Zimbabwe were linked. They perceived the struggles in Namibia and Zimbabwe essentially as struggles against South Africa.[147] In particular, they feared that a failure in the negotiations over Namibia would almost certainly lead to a breakdown of negotiations over Zimbabwe.[148] In March 1978, Ian Smith, Bishop Muzorewa and Sithole had reached an agreement which paved the way for an internal settlement in Rhodesia which would exclude the Patriotic Front, an umbrella organization under which Robert Mugabe's ZANU and Joshua Nkomo's ZAPU had united. The Frontline leaders most probably believed that a breakdown of the negotiations over Namibia, which could lead to the implementation of an internal settlement which excluded SWAPO, would give a boost to a similar settlement in Rhodesia. This would mean a continuation of the war by ZANU and ZAPU guerillas, a war which had inflicted considerable economic hardship on Zambia, Botswana and Mozambique who had closed its borders with Rhodesia in 1976. Angola, on the other hand, had a direct security interest in South African withdrawal from Namibia. The escalation of direct military attacks by the SADF on Angola in 1977 and 1978, South African support to UNITA and a plan for a military operation to be launched against Angola simultaneously from Zaire and Namibia, which was discovered in February 1977, increased the urgency for the Angolan government to give a chance to any solution likely to remove the South African threat on its borders.

The breakdown of the settlement. 1978–81

From the acceptance of the western proposals by SWAPO in July 1978 to the breakdown of the negotiations, which were again mediated by the Frontline states and the Contact Group, in 1981, the regional dynamics of Namibian decolonization evolved along two lines. On one hand, the Frontline states continued to be involved in the attempts to reach a diplomatic solution to Namibian independence. On the other hand and more decisively, the South African policy towards Namibia and regarding southern Africa in general, underwent a significant change, when the defence minister P. W. Botha succeeded John Vorster as prime minister on 20 September 1978. Until South Africa's decision in 1988 to effectively withdraw from Namibia, the question of Namibian decolonization has to be analysed in the context of a new comprehensive South African strategy, the Total National Strategy, which started to unfold from the late 1970s.

The Frontline states and Security Council Resolution 435

After SWAPO had accepted the western proposals on 12 July 1978, the Security Council requested the secretary-general to appoint a special representative for Namibia and asked the secretary-general to submit recommendations for the implementation of the proposals.[149] The Finnish diplomat Martti Attisaari relinquished his post as United Nations commissioner for Namibia and visited the territory in August. Based on Attisaari's recommendations, the secretary-general Kurt Waldheim sent a report to the Security Council on 29 August. Together with the western proposals of 10 April, the two documents were to form the basis of Security Council Resolution 435 of 29 September 1978. While the South African government had already rejected Waldheim's report on 20 September, arguing that it 'deviated substantially' from the Contact Group's proposal,[150] SWAPO accepted the report not as a result of its own initiative, but under pressure from Angola and Nigeria in early September.[151] In the middle of September,

133

Angola and Zambia ordered SWAPO to suspend its military operations from their territories in order to facilitate a negotiated settlement,[152] and military operations were suspended until December 1978.[153] This confirmed the pattern of the Namibian negotiations, whereby SWAPO was given little chance to assert its own positions.

But South Africa proceeded with its plans for internal elections for a constituent assembly without SWAPO's participation in December, signalling its opposition to United Nations supervised elections.[154] Nevertheless, the Frontline states efforts to reach a negotiated settlement continued in 1979 and SWAPO, who was under continuing pressure from Angola and Zambia,[155] decided to stand by its acceptance of the United Nations plan. In 1979, the presidents of the two Frontline states, President Neto in particular, played an important role in trying to find a compromise solution to a new issue raised by the South Africans, in what the United Nations undersecretary-general Brian Urquhart, who participated in the negotiations, qualified as 'their perennial search for a new and insurmountable obstacle to progress'.[156]

The issue now at stake was the implementation of a cease-fire and the stationing of SWAPO forces inside Namibia. The western settlement plan embodied in Resolution 435 called for 'a cessation of all hostile acts by all parties and the restriction of South African and SWAPO armed forces to base'[157] without mentioning where the SWAPO bases were to be located. The South African government, while appearing to agree to the main elements of the UN plan, 'once again . . . raised new issues that prevented implementation'.[158] It rejected SWAPO's demand that its guerilla forces should be concentrated in designated locations inside Namibia and claimed that SWAPO had no bases inside Namibia. Accordingly, the term 'restriction to base' could only apply to SWAPO bases outside Namibia.[159] In addition, Pretoria wanted SWAPO to accept that its forces in Angola and Zambia would be monitored by the United Nations before a cease-fire could be concluded and before the UN peace-keeping force arrived in Namibia, a condition which SWAPO rejected immediately.[160] The South Africans also objected to a modified United Nations proposal submitted in February 1979. Accordingly, SWAPO forces inside Namibia at the time of the cease-fire would be restricted to designated locations while

PLAN fighters in the neighbouring countries would be restricted to base there. Waldheim was seeking the agreement of Angola, Zambia and Botswana for UNTAG liaison offices to be established in their countries in order to facilitate the implementation of the plan.[161] But the plan did not provide for a UN monitoring force in the neighbouring countries, as Angola considered a UN presence on its territory as an infringement of its sovereignty.[162] The fact that there was no provision for UN monitoring in the three Frontline states was used by Pretoria as yet another pretext to avoid implementation of Resolution 435. The South Africans argued that the plan would not prevent SWAPO guerillas from entering Namibia during the electoral process. SWAPO accepted the UN plan in February. But South Africa would not agree to any SWAPO forces to be based inside Namibia, even if they were monitored by United Nation forces.[163]

In order to break the deadlock, Neto proposed the establishment of a 100 km wide demilitarized zone – 50 km deep on each side – along the 1,400 km border separating Namibia from Angola and Zambia, with the exception of the Caprivi strip where it would be narrower, during talks with the American chief negotiator Donald McHenry in Luanda in July 1979, two months before Neto's death in September.[164] The Angolan president now also agreed to the presence of UN forces inside Angola.[165] SWAPO guerrillas inside the demilitarized zone at the time of the cease-fire would have the choice of either being escorted beyond the demilitarized zone or being disarmed and remain as civilians.[166] The other Frontline states accepted the principle of a demilitarized zone in August. At the same time, they put pressure to bear on SWAPO to drop its demand for bases inside Namibia at the time of the cease-fire,[167] and to accept to base its forces *outside* the demilitarized zone.[168] The Frontline leaders told the UN undersecretary-general Brian Urquhart that they could 'bring SWAPO into line', provided that South Africa accepted the demilitarized zone.[169]

Following a now familiar pattern, the South African government did not commit itself and manoeuvred on details in order to prevent implementation of Resolution 435.[170] And Robert Mugabe's independence election victory in Zimbabwe in March 1980 made the prospects for settlement seem even more elusive. For the South Africans, the negotiations were 'a game of procrastination'.[171] Nevertheless, the Frontline states remained committed to the UN plan. According to Urquhart, Frontline leaders of Tanzania, Zambia and Botswana were prepared to do anything within reason to meet outstanding South African difficulties on the implementation of the Namibian settlement plan.[172] Angola, despite its public support for SWAPO and ANC,[173] held secret bilateral talks with South Africa on the island of Sal in the Cape Verde Islands in summer 1980 with a view to arranging direct talks between Pretoria and SWAPO.[174] Already in 1977, South Africa and Angola had been engaged in secret talks in order to negotiate a South African withdrawal from the Angolan-Namibian border.[175] Angolan and South African middle rank officials were reported to have secretly met near the border in order to reach agreement over the working of the Caluque dam on the Cunene river in February 1979.[176] And South Africans and Angolans were reported to have met secretly in Paris in March 1980, raising the possibility of a meeting between South Africa, SWAPO and Namibia's internal parties.[177]

A meeting between the Frontline states, the Contact Group, South Africa, SWAPO and internal parties took place in Geneva in January 1981. Although all parties had accepted the terms of Resolution 435, the Geneva 'Pre-implementation meeting' collapsed within one week. On one hand, South Africa again raised new issues to prevent implementation centering around a presumed UN partiality towards SWAPO. The demands included rescinding the General Assembly Resolution naming SWAPO as the sole and authentic Namibian liberation movement with observer status at the United Nations and ending UN financing of SWAPO. On the other hand and related to the latter, South Africa's main concern was to strengthen the role of the internal parties and to promote them as alternative negotiating partners to SWAPO. It became clear that Pretoria had no intention of reaching an agreement. The South African administrator general Danie Hough ended the meeting declaring that it was 'premature' to further discuss the date for implementing the UN settlement plan.[178] The abortive Geneva meeting, which put an end to four years of diplomatic efforts by the Frontline states and the western Contact Group, confirmed Pretoria's strategy since 1975, namely the creation of a political power structure inside Namibia which would present an alternative to SWAPO. Furthermore, the victory of Robert Mugabe in the elections for Zimbabwean independence undoubtedly strengthened the arguments of those who were opposed to concessions in Namibia and, in particular, to SWAPO coming to power. For since the former minister of defence P. W. Botha had become prime minister in 1978, the influence of the military in policy making had increased significantly, reflected in a new comprehensive regional and domestic strategy for the defence of the apartheid state, the Total National Strategy which had been taking shape from the mid seventies.

The South African response. The Total National Strategy

The origins of the Total National Strategy are linked to the response by the South African military establishment to the rise of guerilla warfare both by SWAPO and ANC from the early seventies. According to Geldenhuys, 'it was against the background of growing threats to South Africa's security that the military began talking of a 'total onslaught' on the Republic and of the need for a counter-strategy. The latter opened the door for the military to involve itself with major decision making on both foreign and domestic matters'.[179] The Concept of 'total strategy' which implied the mobilizing of all the country's resources for its defence, was first mooted in a White Paper on Defence in 1973. South African strategists were of the opinion that there existed an 'escalating' threat against the country which would compel the government 'to strive for full military preparedness at an increased rate'.[180]

But it was not before 1977 that Pretoria's military strategists first publicly called for the adoption of their Total Strategy, justified by the demise of the Portuguese colonies in Africa, the unsuccessful invasion of Angola of 1975/76 and the Soweto uprising of June 1976, which all called for a reformulation of South Africa's domestic and regional policies. While the aim of the new policy was to assert the century old concept of South African regional hegemony and white supremacy, the evolving strategy was defensive in nature. It was basically conceived as a survival strategy against the presumed subversion of the South African state by internal and external forces. In order to counter what South African security strategists qualified as a 'total onslaught' against South Africa by liberation

137

movements and hostile southern African states, which would be orchestrated by Moscow, Pretoria's top military commanders asked for the totality of state structures and functions to be deployed.[181] This meant that the four power bases of the South African state – political/diplomatic, economic, social/psychological and military – were integrated into a single National Security Management System (NSMS). The main decision making body of this system was the State Security Council (SSC) and its subsidiaries. The SSC supervised a network of 15 internal and external Joint Management Centres (JMCs). While ten internal Joint Management Centres, which were decentralized to the community level, played an important role in opposing community based resistance, an eleventh centre dealt with Walvis Bay and four centres covered Namibia and unspecified southern African countries.[182] Within the National Security Management System, the most important role accrued to the military who had now become an 'active participant in political decision making'.[183] According to the prime minister P. W. Botha, 'the maintenance of effective decision making by the state rests on a strong defence force to guarantee orderly government as well as efficient, clean administration.[184]

On the regional level, the Total National Strategy as formulated in 1979 was a two-pronged approach to preserve South African regional hegemony in defence of the status quo inside South Africa. Military and economic coercion of neighbouring states would ensure that they did not serve as springboards for liberation movements and that they remained politically and economically weak. For in the logic of the Total National Strategy, weak states which were economically dependent on South Africa, would not support sanctions against South Africa which would have devastating results for them. They would thus shield the Republic from punitive international economic action.[185] But the Total Strategy on the regional level not only comprised coercive measures. South Africa also attempted to establish political and economic control in southern Africa through security arrangements such as nonaggression pacts and incentive measures like preferential trade agreements and development aid.

The idea of an economic grouping between southern African states including Namibia, which was already a member of the South African dominated Southern African Customs Union

(SACU) and the 'independent' Bantustans, – a Constellation of Southern African States (CONSAS) – was an important element in the first phase of the Total National Strategy, put forward by Botha in 1979. A pro-South African Zimbabwe, the second most developed country in the region after South Africa, was perceived by Pretoria as the key to success of the CONSAS idea.[186] However, the independence elections in Zimbabwe in 1980 were won by Robert Mugabe's Zimbabwe African National Union (ZANU) and the new Zimbabwean government joined the Southern African Development Coordination Conference (SADCC) which was established in 1980. As the first development objective of SADCC was 'the reduction of economic dependence, particularly, but not only on the Republic of South Africa',[187] SADCC was an anathema to a South African controlled regional economic order.

The independence of Zimbabwe under Mugabe and the establishment of SADCC thus prevented the scheme of a South Africa dominated Constellation of Southern African States from being put into practice. It precipitated a shift in South African regional policy towards coercive strategies. From 1980 and 1981, Pretoria had turned to 'destabilization tactics in a fairly generalized and indiscriminate manner',[188] aimed primarily at Angola, Mozambique and Lesotho.[189] In Pretoria's logic, those countries of southern Africa which supported ANC/PAC and SWAPO and advocated sanctions as well as South Africa's international isolation, were committed to the destabilization of the Republic. South Africa would therefore be justified in destabilizing or 'reciprocating in kind'. The aim of destabilizing South Africa's neighbours would be 'to effect profound political changes in the target state. They may or may not involve structural change – which means dislodging the regime in power – but certainly involve major changes in the target state's behaviour, specifically towards the "destabilizer" [South Africa]'.[190]

The Total National Strategy became official state policy in 1979 and dominated South Africa's regional and domestic policies until its phasing out was announced by the South African government in November 1989.[191] However, the origins of the Total National Strategy and destabilization of southern African states, using Namibia as a springboard, were already present in Angola and, to a certain extent, in Zambia from the mid-seventies.

Zambia

South Africa had initiated the policy of hot pursuit against SWAPO guerrillas who operated from Zambia in 1971. And against the background of secessionist sentiments among the Lozi (Barotse) in western Zambia, it had recruited Zambians for military training in Namibia in December 1972 before infiltrating them back into Zambia.[192] More seriously, the SADF again trained a Zambian dissident group led by Adamson Mushala, a former official of Zambia's United National Independence Party (UNIP) in 1975. The group known as the Mushala gang was sent back to Zambia in December 1975, in an unsuccessful attempt to exploit the dissatisfaction in former Barotseland.[193] The gang skirmished with Zambian forces, blew up a bridge and kept South Africa informed about SWAPO movements.[194] When South African helicopter gunships attacked SWAPO camps at Sialola and Shatotua in western Zambia near the Caprivi strip in July 1976, killing twenty four people,[195] the South Africans may have had access to information of the Mushala gang, as they seemed to be familiar with the layout and the defences of the camps.[196] There is no clear evidence as to South Africa's support for the Mushala gang after 1976. The gang engaged in low level banditry disrupting the Western province in what Kaunda called 'a small civil war'[197] until Mushala was killed by Zambian security forces in November 1982.[198]

Zambia was also the target of direct attacks by the South African army. In August 1976, Pretoria admitted to an attack on a Zambian border village,[199] and SWAPO claimed at the same time that the South African air force was operating against guerillas in Zimbabwe.[200] In 1977, the Zambian government accused the South Africans of having opened fire on the Sesheke border town with the Caprivi strip.[201] After SWAPO had launched a rocket attack on the Katima Mulilo base in the Caprivi strip in August 1978, South Africa retaliated by mounting a 'follow-up' operation 30 km inside Zambia,[202] and by attacking Sesheke, claiming that Zambian troops had been involved in the attack, an allegation which was denied by

Zambian authorities.[203] The Zambian government accused South Africa of provoking SWAPO and the Frontline states into an open confrontation which could prejudice the nego-tiations of the UN settlement plan.[204]. SWAPO's attack on Katima Mulilo and South Africa's retaliation, illustrate the fra-gility of the settlement plan. Its acceptance by SWAPO did not preclude the continuation of fighting. South Africa's reprisals clearly indicate, as did the attack on Kassinga in May 1978, that the South African military were playing an increasingly dominant role in foreign policy formulation and seemed little concerned with the implications of cross-border attacks on the outcome of the diplomatic negotiations.

In 1979, president Kaunda alleged that the SADF were inten-sifying their attacks on Zambia to a point where the Zambian government had to divert financial resources for increasing its defence capacities[205] after a renewed South African incursion into Zambia in March 1979.[206] In October, 600 South African troops crossed into Zambia from the Caprivi strip, at the same time as 400 Rhodesian troops entered southeast Zambia. Two South African battalions invaded Zambia in April 1980. Although many men were withdrawn by May, South African troops stayed in Zambia until the end of the year.[207]

Angola

While South African destabilization often assumed the form of economic coercion, such as in the case of Zimbabwe, Lesotho and Mozambique, South African destabilization tactics were from the outset different in the case of Angola. The country was neither integrated into the South African communication network, nor was Angola economically dependent on south Africa. Military destabilization, using Namibia as a spring-board, was thus the means for Pretoria's attempt to change the Angolan government's policy towards South Africa, namely to increase the costs of its support for SWAPO and ANC to such an extent that it would be forced to revise its position. This, in turn, would enable South Africa to eliminate SWAPO mili-tarily, or at least weaken it politically to the extent that a pro-South African régime shielding the Republic from external threats, would emerge in Namibia. Increasing South African

141

support for UNITA and direct military intervention by the SADF were the expression of this policy.

According to Savimbi, regular South African assistance to UNITA did not commence before 1980;[208] but UNITA forces had been trained by the SADF inside Namibia since 1976,[209] and they relied on SADF rear bases for logistical support which – according to pro-South African sources – started in 1977;[210] and which was provided on a large scale from late 1978 or early 1979.[211] Direct interventions by the SADF in Angola had resumed soon after the South Africans had withdrawn from the country on 27 March 1976. According to Hanlon, the South Africans staged 17 raids into Angolan territory between April and July 1976,[212] and the Angolan government recorded 41 'acts of aggression' ranging from airspace violation to infiltration during the year.[213]

A plan for a four-pronged invasion from Zaire, Namibia, the enclave of Cabinda and from the sea planned for September 1977, was uncovered in February 1977 by the Angolan government as a result of leaks from Zairean sources. 'Operation Cobra' involved UNITA, the Front for the Liberation of Cabinda (FLEC) and was supported regionally by South Africa, Zaire and Senegal where much of the planning was done.[214] The plan was also backed by France, who had oil interests in Cabinda and the United States who planned to participate in the operation from Zaire.[215] 'Operation Cobra' never materialized. But the plan shows that South Africa was as unwilling as before its invasion of 1975/76 to accept the MPLA government and was again prepared to invade Angola. Prime minister Vorster declared in Cape Town on 28 May 1977 that South Africa was prepared to fight Soviet imperialism alongside other African states who shared more concern over the threat than did the United States.[216]

The military's involvement in policy making over Namibia and Angola became clear during the protracted negotiations leading to Security Council Resolution 435. The South African raid in Kassinga whereby over 600 Namibian refugees were killed, was the first large-scale military operation in Angola since the South African invasion of 1975. The decision to launch large-scale military operations into Angola had been taken at a meeting in Vorster's seaside cottage near Port Elizabeth in December 1977. Although Vorster himself was said to be 'not wildly enthusiastic' about cross-border operations, the military convinced him that pre-emptive attacks on SWAPO bases inside Angola would be necessary to stop PLAN fighters from crossing into Namibia.[217] While the driving force behind the political decision to launch the attack on Kassinga (Operation Reindeer) was the Defence Force, supported by P. W. Botha,[218] the SADF also cooperated with UNITA, who was reported to have infiltrated SWAPO and transmitted intelligence reports.[219] The decision in late 1977 to embark on large-scale military operations against Angola and to attack a SWAPO refugee camp in May 1978, clearly indicate that the majority of South Africa's decision makers had no intention of withdrawing from Namibia. Keeping the negotiations going was above all a diplomatic ploy to avoid the possibility of economic sanctions against South Africa.[220]

Pretoria's decision to reject the UN settlement plan in September 1978 also reflects the increasingly important role played by the military. Officially, Vorster announced the South African decision on the very day he resigned as prime minister on 20 September. But the actual decision to reject the Waldheim proposals had been taken by the Cabinet, chaired by P. W. Botha instead of Vorster on 6 September 1978,[221] whose position had been weakened following a scandal surrounding the government's involvement in a covert propaganda offensive.[222] Botha had always been against concessions in Namibia and as one of the architects of the 1975 invasion of Angola, he was personally responsible for many of the institutional and administrative changes which allowed for the implementation of the Total National Strategy.

With the Total National Strategy becoming official state policy in 1979, attacks on Angola intensified. In September 1979, the South African air force bombarded Lubango, the provincial capital of the Huila province more than 200 km north of the border as well as Xangongo in the Cunene province. And in June 1980, the SADF launched 'Operation Smokeshell', which amounted to a full-scale invasion of parts of the Cunene and Cuando Cubango provinces, involving a larger military force than the 1975 invasion.[223] While South Africa claimed that it had destroyed SWAPO's operational headquarters in Angola,[224] 'Operation Smokeshell' was only partly directed against SWAPO. It was also aimed at capturing key points inside the proposed demilitarized zone which was still the object of negotiations with the Contact Group and the United Nations, as well as installing UNITA in the south of the country.[225] In September 1980, the South Africans captured Mavinga in the Cuando Cubango province, thus enabling Savimbi to set up his forward headquarters in south east Angola.[226] The scene was set for joint South African-UNITA destabilization of Angola. The issue of Namibian independence was increasingly subordinated to the regional dynamics of conflict in Angola and to the American notion of linkage according to which the independence of Namibia was subject to the withdrawal of Cuban troops from Angola.

CHAPTER SIX

NAMIBIA-ANGOLA.
'LINKAGE' AND WAR. 1981-7

After the breakdown of the UN settlement plan in January 1981, the new American administration under Ronald Reagan who had succeeded Carter in January 1981, took a policy initiative over Namibia which gave South Africa another pretext to postpone any international settlement. By linking the issue of Namibian independence to prior or simultaneous Cuban withdrawal from Angola, the regional military conflict between Angola, who was supported by Cuba and South Africa who backed UNITA, dominated the regional dynamics of Namibian decolonization. As a result, the decolonization of Namibia was from now on subordinated to the dynamics of conflict in southern Angola. This also meant that with the exception of Angola and, to a certain extent, Zambia, the importance of the Frontline states as a collective mediator between SWAPO and the South African government, declined. Although the Frontline states formally rejected any linkage between the conflicts in Angola and Namibia, both resistance inside Namibia to South African occupation and the diplomatic efforts to implement resolution 435 were in fact subordinated to the issue of linking Namibian independence to the withdrawal of Cuban troops from Angola. Linkage, the total National Strategy as reflected in South African-UNITA destabilization of Angola and Angolan-Cuban resistance set the parameters of a regional conflict, the outcome of which would provide the context for Namibian independence.

The introduction of linkage

After Ronald Reagan had taken office in January 1981, Chester Crocker, who was the designated assistant secretary of state for African affairs, suggested in a secret State Department memorandum of February 1981 which was subsequently leaked to the press, that the independence of Namibia should be tied 'to a withdrawal of Cuban forces from Angola and a commitment by the Marxist leaders in Angola to share power with western backed guerillas'.[1] The underlying rationale for the new American policy of linking Namibian independence to Cuban withdrawal from Angola was to apply the global policy of competition with the Soviet Union to the regional level. For according to Crocker, 'the real choice we will face in South Africa in the 1980s concerns our readiness to compete with our global adversary in the politics of a changing region whose future depends on those who participate in shaping it'.[2] Although Crocker and the Reagan administration were better disposed towards the South African government than their predecessors, Crocker did not back the 'internal' solution for Namibian independence. For 'the United States and its allies have nothing to gain from backing a South African client government in circumstances that assure a continuation of internationalized warfare'.[3] Senior members of the administration were interested above all in Cuban withdrawal from Angola. But Crocker, who was also strongly opposed to the Cuban and Soviet presence in Angola,[4] argued that if the demand for Cuban withdrawal from Angola were to have any credibility, it would have to be linked with the question of Namibian independence. In April 1981, the United States, Britain and France had notably vetoed Security Council resolutions calling for sanctions against South Africa and condemning South African raids on Angola. Linkage was 'a marriage of convenience'[5] between those who saw Cuban withdrawal from Angola as a policy priority and United States commitment to an internationally recognized independence of Namibia since it had supported Security Council Resolution 385 in January 1976.

Despite the breakdown of the Pre-implementation meeting in Geneva in January 1981, attempts to implement Resolution 435 therefore continued. But in order to obtain the agreement of the South African government, Crocker and his team attempted to alter the contents of the Resolution in favour of South Africa. Crocker argued that Pretoria held the key to a settlement in Namibia. South Africa would therefore need a 'minimum of confidence' in any settlement if it were to be implemented.[6] When the Contact Group met in London and in Rome in April and May 1981 to review the situation concerning Namibia, they agreed to 'strengthen' Resolution 435 by taking measures which would increase the confidence of all the parties in the settlement plan.[7] Aimed at accommodating the South African government, the Group submitted a proposal in October 1981, according to which the constitution should be worked out before independence elections. After the Frontline states and SWAPO had made counterproposals in November, the western Group submitted a new proposal in December 1981, now calling for half of the members to be elected by proportional representation and half from single-member constituencies. Both SWAPO and the Frontline states rejected the proposal. They argued that apart from being extremely complicated to implement, it would undermine the electoral strength of SWAPO by favouring tribal and white minority groups.[8] According to SWAPO, the proposal was intended to have the white vote counted as a bloc via proportional representation, while at the same time giving black candidates opposed to SWAPO a chance to appeal for votes on ethnic bases.[9] A compromise solution was reached in July 1982. The Contact Group informed the secretary-general on 12 July 1982 that all parties had agreed on 'Principles concerning the constitution and the constituent assembly for an independent Namibia'. The contentious issues of electoral procedures was not mentioned explicitly. The letter only stated that the parties agreed that the issue 'must be settled in accordance with the terms of Security Council Resolution 435'.[10]

Significantly in the light of the outcome of the elections of November 1989, the 'Principles concerning the constituent assembly' stated that the assembly 'will adopt the Constitution as a whole by a two-third majority of its total membership',[11] a clause which had originated with Chester Crocker and the International Organizations' section of the state department.[12] This was probably seen by Crocker as one of the 'confidence building' measures needed to persuade Pretoria to agree to a settlement. At the same time, SWAPO most probably thought that it could afford to compromise on the issue as most observers agreed that SWAPO would win UN supervised elections by an overwhelming majority. But it was the issue of linkage which prevented any solution from being reached. The South African government now insisted that Cuban withdrawal from Angola was a precondition for implementing Resolution 435. Inversely, Angola and Cuba had maintained since February 1982 that Cuban troops would only be withdrawn from Angola, once South Africa had ceased its military threats against the Angolan government and implemented Resolution 435. For Cuban troops were in Angola to protect the country from South African attacks from Namibia. Reconciling and satisfying the two diametrically opposed security concerns was the task of Crocker's diplomacy. Linkage, and the escalating military conflict opposing South Africa and UNITA to the Angolan government forces backed by Cuba and the Soviet Union, overshadowed the question of Namibian independence, which was increasingly subordinated to a prior settlement of the military conflict in southern Angola.

As far as the members of the Contact Group other than the United States were concerned, the introduction of linkage gave rise to tensions within the group. It precipitated the end of the Contact Group as a collective mediator in Namibian decolonization. After the unsuccessful 'Pre-implementation meeting' held in Geneva in January 1981, efforts by the contact group to help reaching a settlement nevertheless continued. However, the members of the Contact Group other than the United States did not support the attempt by the new Reagan administration to link Namibian independence to a prior withdrawal of Cuban troops from Angola. Britain, Canada, France and the Federal Republic of Germany were united in rejecting the idea of linkage. After the successful decolonization of Zimbabwe, the British government was eager to implement Security Council Resolution 435. In this it was supported by the German government, which, because of Germany's historic ties with Namibia, also wanted to see a rapid end to the conflict. The new socialist government in France was ideologically more inclined in favour of SWAPO and against Pretoria than its predecessor had been. In this, it was supported by the Canadian government of Pierre Trudeau.[13]

Tensions between the United States and the other members of the Contact Group surfaced again in 1982, after an agreement on most of the conditions for implementing Resolution 435 was reached in July. However, Washington, supported as it was by Pretoria, made the Cuban withdrawal from Angola a precondition for implementing Namibia's decolonization, as set out in Resolution 435.[14] The differences within the Contact Group came to a head in 1983. At a United Nations sponsored international conference on Namibia, held in Paris in April 1983, the French foreign minister Claude Cheysson severely criticized the idea of 'linkage' and France suspended its participation in the Contact Group in December 1983.[15] International mediation in the Namibian conflict was now dominated by the United States. In 1984 and 1985, Britain, Canada, France, and Germany all reaffirmed their opposition to Washington's and Pretoria's attempts to link Namibian independence with a Cuban troop withdrawal from Angola. However, they seemed to accept that the United States were conducting the diplomatic efforts over a Namibian settlement.[16] They realized that only Washington had the necessary leverage to put pressure to bear on Pretoria to compromise.[17] While Chester Crocker initially maintained close contact with the other four of the Group,[18] the five members of the Contact Group ceased to meet in early 1985, leaving it to the United States to take new initiatives concerning the implementation of Resolution 435.[19]

Destabilization of Angola

When the Reagan administration presented the linkage idea to the South African government in June 1981, 'Pretoria immediately seized upon this handy new delaying issue'.[20] For in the past, South Africa had never made the Cuban withdrawal from Angola a precondition for its acceptance of the UN settlement plan for Namibia. Linkage provided a justification for delaying UN supervised elections, and for strengthening an anti-SWAPO, and pro-South African power structure in Namibia. The military thought a Cuban withdrawal from Angola would never take place.[21] Linkage thus provided an additional pretext for perpetuating the occupation of Namibia, and intensifying attacks on Angola.

At the same time as seizing on the linkage issue, the South

African military reverted to open destabilization of the region after Pretoria's idea of a Constellation of Southern African States had collapsed in the wake of Zimbabwean independence, and the formation of SADCC. In August 1981, the SADF mounted their biggest military operation since Angola's independence. During 'Operation Protea', more than 5,000 South African troops occupied all the main towns in the Cunene province in the southwest of Angola for several weeks. Angolan government troops (FAPLA) were able to stop the South African advance 110 km north of the Namibian border. But several thousand South African troops continued to occupy a 70 km wide strip in the southern Cunene province.[22] This led to a quasi permanent occupation until end of August 1988, only briefly interrupted in 1985.

Officially presented as a preemptive strike against SWAPO, and the installation of a Soviet built early warning radar system and ground-to-air missiles, 'Operation Protea' illustrated two important features of the Total National Strategy as applied to Angola. Unlike the destabilization of other southern African states, where South Africa either supported dissident groups – the Mozambique National Resistance Movement (MNR or RENAMO), and the Lesotho Liberation Army (LLA)[23] – or staged commando raids, South African forces were engaged in conventional warfare with Angolan troops.

In addition to direct intervention, South Africa also supported UNITA which it had helped to rebuild, and to reinstal itself in the southeast of Angola in 1980. In particular, it enabled the men of Savimbi to take Mavinga which became UNITA's forward base, and later a central target for several offensives by FAPLA. This in turn provided the South African military with the pretext to intervene inside Angola in defence of UNITA from 1985. UNITA forces had been trained by the SADF inside Namibia since 1976,[24] and they relied on SADF rear bases for logistical support which had been reported in 1977, and which started on a large scale in late 1978 or early 1979.[25] In addition to supporting UNITA, Pretoria also relied on the Buffalo or 32 Battalion, the special counterinsurgency force which had been created in 1976, and which consisted of former followers of FNLA, and mercenaries. Supported by the 54 Paratroop Battalion, and South African Air Force squadrons based at Ondangwa in northern Namibia, the 32 Battalion operated almost exclusively inside Angola, in the Cunene province in particular, where it became notorious for its atrocities against the civilian population. According to a defector, the Battalion's operations inside Angola ranged from small commando raids against SWAPO guerillas, attacks on Namibian refugee camps and units of the Angolan armed forces, to 'cleaning-up' operations directed at the local civilian population.[26]

The 32 Battalion also acted as an important liaison between regular South African troops, and UNITA forces. In the Cuando Cubango province in southeast Angola, members of the Battalion served as instructors to UNITA, and took part in joint operations.[27] According to the testimony of another defector, the 32 Battalion was carrying out operations which would later be claimed by UNITA.[28] By 1981, South African had established its military supremacy in southern Angola where it occupied the Cunene province in the west, and supported UNITA which again controlled the sparsely populated Cuando Cubango province in southeast Angola.

Militarization of Namibia

As a result of the implementation of the Total National Strategy, South Africa also intensified its repressive policies inside Namibia. After SWAPO had stepped up its armed struggle in response to the internal elections held in December 1978, during which the SADF had openly supported DTA, South Africa intensified the military buildup inside Namibia. The South African army later acknowledged that the number of 'incidents' had increased from 500 in 1978 to more than 900 in 1979, and that there had been more than 300 'contacts' with PLAN fighters, an increase of almost 100% as compared to 1978.[29] In September 1979, 10,000 to 12,000 South African combat troops were reported to be engaged in the north of the country 'in one of the biggest operations in the fifteen year war against nationalist guerillas'.[30] By the end of the year, the number of troops in the territory had increased to 30,000 men, a fifty per cent increase from 1978.[31] A de facto martial law which had previously covered northern Namibia and the Caprivi Strip, was now extended as far south as Windhoek, covering practically half of the country, and affecting eighty per cent of its population.[32] The military asserted the need for what they qualified as hard-hitting preventive and punitive action against SWAPO.[33] And the defence minister General Malan told Chester Crocker on his first visit as undersecretary of state designate to South Africa in April 1981, that South Africa would not tolerate a SWAPO victory. The foreign minister Roelof 'Pik' Botha added his voice by stating that his government was convinced that SWAPO was 'Marxist'. If in power, it would nationalize the entire country and cause a civil war, an eventuality which would force South Africa to invade Namibia. South Africa would rather prefer an indefinite low-level conflict.[34]

In order to carry out military and police repression inside Namibia, Pretoria relied on the South West Africa Territory Force (SWATF), and the South African Police (SAP). Set up in 1980, and composed of eighty per cent Namibians, the SWATF comprised a number of SADF units, and different tribal armies which had been formed in the 1970s. While the SADF maintained overall control, the South African Police engaged in counter-insurgency operations against SWAPO and alleged supporters. The best known – and most feared – of the police units engaged in 'internal warfare' was Koevoet ('crowbar'). Created in 1978, and known as the Namibian equivalent of 32 Battalion, Koevoet consisted mostly of Namibians from the north of the country with white South African police commanders, and engaged in assassinations and sabotage activities, which were attributed to SWAPO.[35]

This hard-line attitude was paralleled with a 'winning of the hearts and minds campaign' whereby South African military personnel engaged in civilian duties in schools, hospitals, and social services in northern Namibia. However, this strategy was not successful in the same way as the attempts to set up a credible pro-South African, and anti-SWAPO alternative political power structure failed to gain any substantial popular support. In February 1982, the Democratic Turnhalle Alliance which was the umbrella organization for the majority of Namibia's political parties, lost the support of its essential Ovambo constituent group which was seen as playing a pivotal role in any anti-SWAPO coalition.[36] The South African administrator general, first appointed in 1977, dissolved the 'National Assembly', and 'Council of Ministers', and assumed direct rule over the territory in February 1983.

The responses of SWAPO and the Frontline states

The South Africans were confident in early 1982 that they would 'eventually eliminate SWAPO as fighting force'.[37] But despite the setbacks suffered as a result of the South African incursions into Angola, SWAPO managed to intensify the armed struggle inside Namibia. According to SADF estimates, SWAPO had 6,000 troops, and it launched a general offensive in April 1982, which was described by the South Africans as the largest military operation ever mounted by the organization. More than a hundred PLAN fighters penetrated into the white farming area of Tsumeb in northern Namibia, and by the end of April, SWAPO was reported to dominate the military situation in the farming area around Grootfontein, Otavi, and Outjo, many white farmers having fled.[38] According to Steenkamp, it took 'about two months of unremitting effort [by the South Africans] before the raid ended', claiming the death of ten South African soldiers and policemen.[39] However, the scale and capabilities of South African counterinsurgency were too great for SWAPO to establish 'liberated areas', and to wage a guerilla war similar to those which had been fought in Angola, Mozambique, and Zimbabwe. And contrary to what many assumed at the time, the independence of these three countries did not engender a 'domino' effect with the rapid liberation of Namibia and South Africa.[40]

SWAPO, the Angolan government, the other Frontline states, and the OAU, like the four members of the western Contact group other than the United States, rejected the 'linkage' idea. According to the Tanzanian foreign minister Ahmed Salim, linkage had in fact 'deadlocked' the mediation efforts of the Frontline states.[41] In a joint communiqué issued in Lusaka on 4 September 1982, SWAPO, and the presidents of the Frontline states declared that linkage constituted not only an interference into Angola's internal affairs but it was an attempt by the United States and South Africa to obstruct the process of negotiations.[42] For the Frontline states, the question of the Cuban presence in Angola was a bilateral issue between the Angola and Cuban governments. The Frontline state leaders decided that the Angolan government should take the leading Frontline role in the negotiations over Namibia, because it was the principal state of the region affected by the outcome of these negotiations.[43] According to Crocker, the collective diplomatic involvement of the Frontline states declined after September 1982, as they rejected linkage.[44] Furthermore, the Frontline states had much less leverage in southwestern Africa than had been the case in Zimbabwe. Despite their sometimes virulent verbal attacks on 'linkage', the Frontline states had no tangible means to influence the outcome of the conflict in southern Angola.[45] However, the Angolan president dos Santos consulted with President Samora Machel of Mozambique, and Kenneth Kaunda of Zambia, with both of whom he had close personal links.[46] As far as Zimbabwe was concerned, Robert Mugabe was at times the sharpest critic of American diplomacy over the Namibian, and Angolan conflicts.[47] However, he did not play an active role in mediating between the South Africans and Angolans. In spite of his generally hostile attitude towards the South African government, he nevertheless was to welcome a cease-fire agreement between Angola and South Africa in 1984, as it would be aimed at achieving peace in southern Africa from which Zimbabwe could also benefit.[48] Contrary to Mozambique, which was Zimbabwe's close ally, neither the Zimbabwean government, nor its army could do much to oppose either South African occupation of Namibia, or destabilization of Angola. But this did not preclude Zimbabwean political, and probably material support for SWAPO. Contrary to negotiations around the formulation and implementation of Security Council Resolution 435 from 1977 to 1981, the importance of the Frontline states as a collective mediator in Namibian decolonization, had declined. From now on, the government of Angola which was most directly affected by South African destabilization from Namibian territory, was the main regional actor involved in negotiations with South Africa concerning the war in Angola and the independence of Namibia which was increasingly subordinated to the outcome of the latter.

Destabilization and negotiation. 1981–4

While international diplomatic efforts to resolve both the Namibian question and the conflict in southern Angola were unsuccessful, South Africa failed to suppress SWAPO militarily. It therefore increased its pressure on Angola, in order to force the Angolan government to abandon its support for SWAPO.

Following the pattern of destabilization in line with the Total National Strategy, South African conventional and counterinsurgency forces intervened directly, while South Africa stepped up its support for UNITA, raising the estimated total cost of destruction to over $10 billion from 1975 to 1983.[49] In addition, the cost of maintaining the Cuban troops in the country was estimated at $250 million a year[50] which were drawn from Angola's oil revenues, and prevented the government in engaging in any substantial development programme.

In supporting surrogate armies in both Angola and Mozambique, where RENAMO carried out increasingly devastating attacks on the country's infrastructure and civilian population, Pretoria's objective was not to overthrow the existing governments, but to weaken them to the extent that they would change their policies towards the South Africa.[51] For Mozambique and Angola presented a double danger to Pretoria. Not only did they support liberation movements, but they were the only states in the region ruled by Marxist-Leninist parties which were committed to a process of socialist transformation. If successful, they would pose a 'direct ideological challenge and potential alternative to apartheid capitalism'.[52]

But in contrast to Mozambique, where the SADF did not intervene directly, South Africa escalated its conventional warfare in Angola which built up to 'Operation Askari' in December 1983.[53] Aimed at capturing Lubango more than 200 km north of the Namibian border, South African strategists saw the possibility of a full assault on Luanda. But the South African offensive encountered unexpectedly strong Angolan resistance. FAPLA forces had been substantially reinforced with Soviet made weaponry, and for the first time they used heavy tanks in offensive action. Operation Askari showed the limits of South African action in Angola. In particular, the South Africans were faced with indirect Soviet opposition. On one hand, the offensive revealed the weakness of the South African air force against Soviet built radar assisted defenses. On the other hand, the Soviet Union, who had monitored the military build up leading to Askari, had warned South Africa through its ambassador at the United Nations in November that it would not tolerate any attempt by the SADF to challenge the Cuban positions south of Luanda, and in January 1984,

155

the Soviet Union and Cuba assured the Angolan government of their continued military support.[54]

However, a hardening of positions on the battleground did not preclude South Africa and Angola from negotiating. Despite the fact that Luanda had formally rejected 'linkage', the negotiating process had never completely stopped. Although a settlement of the Namibian question seemed more remote than ever against the background of the escalating war in Angola, Chester Crocker and other American officials held eight rounds of talks with Angolan leaders in an unsuccessful attempt to sell the linkage approach from 1981 to 1983.[55] Angola, and Cuba maintained that Cuban troops would be withdrawn from Angola only after South Africa had left Namibia, and had ceased its support for UNITA. Nevertheless, the Angolan government had never been opposed to negotiations, as evidenced by its mediating role during the prolonged negotiations leading to the adoption of Resolution 435 in 1978. Direct talks between South African and Angolan officials took place in the Cape Verde islands in December 1982. The discussions between 'Pik' Botha, the South African foreign minister, and the Angolan government aimed – as would the negotiations six years later – at producing a phased withdrawal of all foreign troops from Angola, and a timetable for Namibian independence. But the negotiations were opposed by the military on the South African State Security Council. They feared a deal involving a South African withdrawal from Angola without a linked Cuban withdrawal.[56] A next round of secret talks was held in January 1983. But in response to a major SWAPO offensive from its bases in Angola, South Africa only sent low-key officials to a third meeting held in February, and the meeting remained inconclusive.

The talks were resumed one year later. After the South African prime minister P. W. Botha had announced in January 1984 that SADF had begun to withdraw from southern Angola, a cease-fire between Angola, and South Africa was proclaimed in Lusaka on 16 February 1984. In addition to the cease-fire, the Lusaka Accord between 'Pik' Botha, the Angolan minister of interior Alexandre Rodrigues, and Chester Crocker also called for a limited South African withdrawal from the western triangular part of southern Angola stretching from the Cunene to the Cubango river along the Namibian border, with Kassinga

250 km north of the border as its apex. For the South Africans had refused even to discuss the issue of their support for UNITA which controlled southeast Angola. South Africa and Angola agreed, however, that neither UNITA nor SWAPO should be allowed into the area from which South African forces were to withdraw, and both parties agreed to establish a Joint Monitoring Commission (JMC), consisting of 300 FAPLA, and 300 SADF troops[57] on the border with Namibia. United States officials qualified the talks as a 'confidence building exercise' which would lead to a Cuban troop withdrawal from Angola, and to Namibian independence.[58] The Angolan government was concerned in the first place with the withdrawal of South African troops from Angola. This would precede the implementation of Resolution 435 which should be the object of direct negotiations between South Africa and SWAPO. Concerning linkage, and the Cuban withdrawal from the country, Luanda reaffirmed its position of February 1982, namely that Cuban troops would be withdrawn from Angola, once South Africa had ceased its military threats against Angola, and its support for UNITA, and had implemented Resolution 435.[59]

A cease-fire, and the announcement of a limited South African withdrawal from Angola suited both parties. The cease-fire enabled Angolan government troops to concentrate on fighting UNITA forces which were intensifying their operations in the north of the country. For Pretoria, the cease-fire agreement reflected in part the setback suffered by South Africa during Operation Askari, 'a sobering experience for the SADF'.[60] However, South Africa maintained that the estimated 25,000 Cuban troops would have to withdraw from Angola before any settlement over Namibia could be reached. The Lusaka accord did not prevent the South African defence minister General Malan from visiting Savimbi at his headquarters in Jamba in southeast Angola, and pledging South Africa's continuing support.

But the Lusaka Accord was not favourable to SWAPO who was not party to the agreement. Despite Angolan claims that the disengagement of South African troops from Angola was a first step towards a cease-fire between South Africa and SWAPO, followed by independence elections,[61] Angola's pledge to a cease-fire, and the restriction of SWAPO's movements in the zone of South African withdrawal inside Angola,

157

slowed down the military operations of SWAPO. South Africa claimed in March 1984 that joint SADF-Angolan patrols had intercepted SWAPO guerillas 33 times.[62] Angola's immediate security interests, namely to end South African aggression from Namibia, appeared to outweigh its political commitment of supporting SWAPO's armed struggle, a factor which led to disagreements between the SWAPO leadership, and the Angolan government.[63] Yet, during the initial period of the cease-fire, SWAPO was reported to have infiltrated 800 men into Namibia, and PLAN attacked the South African air force base at Ondangwa in March 1984.[64]

From the South African point of view, both the cease-fire agreement with Angola, and the announcement of its withdrawal from Angola should be situated in the broader context of Pretoria's Total National Strategy. For one month after the Lusaka accord on Angola, P. W. Botha and the Mozambican president Samora Machel signed a nonaggression treaty, the Nkomati Accord, which provided, most importantly, for the cessation of the Mozambican government's support to the ANC, and of South African support to RENAMO.[65] The original Total National Strategy called not only for military, but also for diplomatic and economic actions in order to create a South African dominated interdependence in southern Africa. This was initially reflected in the idea of a Constellation of Southern African States. But the CONSAS idea did not succeed, and the Total National Strategy was subsequently blurred by 'military quick fix solutions', and the apparent absence of 'formative action' on the regional level 'now began to be recognized by a number of leading [South African] academics with close links to the government'.[66] One of them argued that one of the risks of destabilization would be that 'the target state might well call on outside military support to counter South African destabilization . . . [and] Cuban troops, East German advisers, and Soviet arms would be the prime candidates'.[67]

This became apparent in the case of Angola where the Soviet warning that it would not tolerate a South African advance in Angola beyond a certain point, clearly showed to the military the limits of an indiscriminate destabilization policy, and their regional expansionism. This realization coupled with the failure of Operation Askari, helps to explain why P. W. Botha announced a withdrawal of South African troops from Angola in January 1984, and why, momentarily, and without yet breaking the deadlock over linkage, a diplomatic approach to the conflict in Angola prevailed.[68]

The Frontline states who expressed their understanding of Angola's and Mozambique's decisions to reach an agreement with South Africa, publicly expressed their hopes that a South African withdrawal from Angola would lead to the implementation of Resolution 435.[69] Although, as Salim Ahmed Salim of Tanzania stated, the Frontline states were neither optimistic nor pessimistic, anything that could bring about a breakthrough in the implementation of Resolution 435 would be welcome.[70] And in its instructions to the Tanzanian delegation at a meeting between the foreign ministers of the Frontline states, and those of the Scandinavian countries in Stockholm in June 1984, the Tanzanian government emphasized its rejection of linkage. Furthermore, it reiterated its adherence to the spirit of the Lusaka Manifesto, namely that the 'preference is for a peaceful solution, and Resolution 435 presents that opportunity, but because of South African intransigence to implement Resolution 435, the war of liberation continues, and the Frontline states will continue to give support to SWAPO'.[71]

However, this did not preclude initiatives by individual members of the Frontline states. In April 1984, Kenneth Kaunda, who had met P. W. Botha in 1981, and who attempted to brake the linkage deadlock over Namibia,[72] took the initiative to host talks between SWAPO, and South Africa, and Namibia's 'internal parties' grouped in the South African sponsored 'Multi-Party Conference' (MPC), which had been established in November 1983. Kaunda had the backing of the Angolan government, but not of the other Frontline states. Kaunda had managed to persuade SWAPO that they meet Namibia's internal parties, most of which SWAPO considered as collaborators of the South African colonial régime. But the talks broke down because of the South African delegation's insistence on linkage, and its refusal to agree to the immediate implementation of Resolution 435. However, the issue which brought the talks to a failure was the insistence by the MPC delegates that the United Nations should cease to recognize SWAPO as sole representative of the Namibian people, and acknowledge Namibia's internal parties on an equal basis with SWAPO. This should be done *before* any decision concerning the implementation of Resolution 435 could be made. This was contrary to the United Nations position, also accepted by SWAPO, that the exclusive recognition of SWAPO would fall away once agreement was reached. Furthermore, representatives of the MPC defected from the alliance during the talks, and joined the SWAPO delegation, thereby highlighting the little support which the South African sponsored MPC commanded.[73] Kaunda's initiative was unsuccessful, showing that South Africa, through the voice of the 'internal' parties which it sponsored or tolerated, was not yet ready to agree to Namibian independence, which could bring SWAPO and other political parties of Namibia in a, from now on, common search for Namibian independence. The basis for intra-Namibian dialogue had been created. This gives credence to the view held by Kaunda, and to a certain extent shared by the Angolan president dos Santos, that the failure of the talks were a setback to, rather than the end of, the negotiating process over Namibia.[74]

The diplomatic respite regarding Angola, Mozambique, and Namibia was short-lived. While South Africa violated the clauses of the Nkomati Accord by increasing its support for RENAMO, the SADF withdrew its troops from Angola as late as April 1985, only to reenter again in September to save UNITA from defeat against Angolan government troops. Concomitantly, Pretoria reinforced its attempt to foster its own 'internal' solution for Namibia.

Inside Namibia: the Transitional Government of National Unity

In April 1985, at the same time as South Africa withdrew its troops from Angola, Pretoria announced the formation of a new government in Namibia, a 'Transitional Government of National Unity' (TGNU) formed by representatives of the Multi Party Conference, a coalition between the Democratic Turnhalle Alliance (DTA), and five other parties opposed to SWAPO.[75] Representatives of the six parties were also members of an non elected 'Legislative Assembly', and a 'Constitutional Council' nominated from the Assembly. Although the formation of TGNU in June 1985 brought an end to a two year period of direct South African rule, Pretoria's overall control continued. The South African parliament retained direct control over finances by voting the finances which kept Namibia solvent in face of the territory's declining economy,[76] decisions concerning foreign affairs, and security continued to be made in Pretoria. Furthermore, all the votes of the 62 member legislative assembly had to be ratified by Louis Pienaar, the new South African administrator general from July 1985. When the TGNU was formed in June 1985, it presented the same flaws as all the previous attempts by Pretoria since 1975 to impose a South African solution on the Namibian people. The Transitional Government of National Unity lacked legitimacy. It had no popular mandate, and from the beginning, it lacked substantial popular support. The TGNU was a collection of a few minority parties prepared to collaborate with South Africa.[77] However, to back an unpopular, inefficient, and divided government was the backbone of Pretoria's policy for a future pro-South African Namibia.

Finding a political solution which would exclude SWAPO from coming to power was paralleled by military repression. In 1984, 83.1% Afrikaans speaking white South Africans interviewed (63.1% English-speakers) were confident that in the long run, South Africa would win the war against SWAPO.[78] The South African defence budget for 1984–85 rose by more than 21%, and military expenditure for Namibia was estimated at between $500 to 600,000 a day.[79] Officially, 35,000 troops were stationed in Nambia in 1986 with unofficial estimates indicating the much higher number of 80,000. Concomitantly, South Africa's regional destabilization policy towards Angola intensified. Direct interventions by SADF, and increased support for UNITA, which also benefitted from American military aid from 1986, poised the conflict in Angola for further escalation.

South Africa and Angola: towards a military stalemate. 1985–7

Although South Africa had committed itself to withdraw its troops from Angola in the Lusaka Accord of February 1984, Pretoria announced in July 1984 that it would halt the operations. One of the pretexts was that SWAPO was continuing to infiltrate fighters through the cease-fire zone.[80] At the same time, South Africa stepped up its support for UNITA which now extended its operations from its traditional stronghold in southeast Angola to the centre, and north of the country.[81]

Continued South African support for UNITA was one of the main factors preventing any substantial diplomatic rapprochement between Luanda and Pretoria. From the Angolan point of view, South African support for Savimbi, in addition to direct attacks from Namibia, prevented the Cubans from leaving the country. The maximum concessions which the Angolan government was prepared to make, was to agree to a partial Cuban withdrawal over three years. In a letter to the UN secretary general in November 1984, known as *Plataforma*, the Angolan president dos Santos suggested that Cuban forces would start to withdraw from the south of Angola once all South African troops – with the exception of 1,500 men as stipulated in Resolution 435 – had left Namibia. However, dos Santos did not propose a complete Cuban withdrawal from Angola. Only 20,000 Cuban troops would leave. The remaining forced would be stationed north of the 13th parallel, which divides the country into half. Their task would be to defend Angola 'against aggression from the north, and northeast, and more especially against Cambinda'.[82]

The *Plataforma* was rejected by South Africa. It nevertheless constituted a shift in Angolan policy. Although Angola continued to reject the idea of linking Namibian independence to a parallel or prior Cuban withdrawal from Angola, it now accepted the principle that the two questions were part of a single negotiation package. From 1984 to 1988, agreement on a *timetable* for Cuban withdrawal – the timetable for South African withdrawal from Namibia had been established in Resolution 435 – became one of the main bones of contention in the negotiations between Angola and South Africa, mediated by Chester Crocker. For the fundamental assumption underlying linkage was that the security concerns of *both* Angola and South Africa had to be satisfied if a settlement of the conflict were to be achieved.[83] Cuban troops helped to protect Angola from South African invasions, and Pretoria was apprehensive of the large number of Cuban troops in Angola. In particular, the South African military were concerned about threats to South Africa's security from a conventional attack on Namibia from Angola. A 1984 South African White Paper on defence, while acknowledging that South Africa's military position towards its neighbouring states was 'reasonably favourable', asserted that the sustained supply of advanced weaponry and of personnel by the Soviet Union to the Frontline states was disturbing the military balance in southern Africa.[84] The then chief of the SADF, General Viljoen warned that the Soviet buildup could easily 'tip the scales' in Angola's favour.[85] And in September 1984, South Africa organized the biggest military exercise since it had entered the Second World War, on the Orange River border between Namibia and South Africa involving 11,000 troops. The fact that the manoeuvres were held on the Namibian-South African border and not in the north of Namibia highlight the debate among South African strategists as to whether the 'total onslaught' on South Africa could be kept at bay at the easily defendable Orange River instead of the more than 1,500 km long border between the mouth of the Cunene river and the Zambezi. The Orange River option was not retained because a South African withdrawal from northern Namibia would expose Botswana and Bophuthatswana to infiltration and attack,[86] one of the main strategic justifications by the South African military to retain control of northern Namibia and the Caprivi strip in particular.[87]

As much as South Africa's security perceptions precluded the military, who dominated the State Security Council, from seriously considering any concessions regarding Namibia, the Angolan government continued to feel threatened by the South African destabilization policy. Under the terms of the Lusaka Accord of February 1984, South Africa withdrew its troops from Angola only in April 1985, with the exception of sixty men who remained at Caluque. But one month later, a South African commando was intercepted by Angolan government troops, when it attempted to blow up oil installations in the Cabinda enclave. In the words of du Toit, the South African officer leading the commando, the attack was designed 'to cause a considerable economic setback to the Angolan government'.[88] And in September, South Africa troops – mainly the 32 Battalion – reentered Southeast Angola in order to save UNITA from defeat while South African aircraft attacked FAPLA forces who had launched an offensive in August 1985.[89] The South African defence minister Magnus Malan admitted for the first time in public that South Africa was assisting UNITA in every way.[90] While the South African intervention ended the FAPLA offensive which was directed by Soviet officers,[91] South African support for UNITA was compounded by a shift in American policy which brought negotiations to a standstill.

American intervention and the Reagan doctrine

Four years after the Reagan administration had introduced linkage, and ten years after the Congress had put an end to American covert aid to Angola by voting the Clark amendment in December 1975, which prohibited American covert aid in support of UNITA, the United States again decided to intervene directly in the Angolan civil war. In July 1985, the American Congress, partly as a result of pressure from the ultraconservative right linked to the Heritage Foundation,[92] repealed the 1975 Clark amendment. In line with an earlier congressional vote for covert military aid of $250 million to the Muyaheddin rebels in Afghanistan, and $27 million 'non-lethal' aid to the Contras in Nicaragua, the repeal of the Clark amendment was a manifestation of the Reagan Doctrine, formulated as the American response to 'Soviet expansionism' in the Third World.

In an address to the UN General Assembly in October 1985, President Reagan strongly denounced Soviet expansionist policy in Afghanistan, Angola, Cambodia, Ethiopia, and Nicaragua. By proposing to discuss these conflicts in a forthcoming meeting with Mikhail Gorbachev in Geneva in November, the American president established a clear link between regional conflicts in Third World countries, and global relations between the United States and the Soviet Union, a link which the Soviet government initially did not accept. For Reagan, 'all of these [regional] conflicts . . . originate in local disputes but they share a common characteristic: they are the consequence of an ideology imposed from without, dividing nations, and creating régimes that are, almost from the day they take power, at war with their own people. And in each case Marxism-Leninism's war with the people becomes war with their neighbours'.[93] While the United States were seeking to resolve these regional conflicts together with the Soviet Union, they were nevertheless prepared to assist 'anti-communist' forces in each of the five countries against Soviet 'domination'. The military doctrine of supporting anti-communist guerrillas in so-called low inten-

164

sity conflicts against an 'expansionist' Soviet Union,[94] and its allies was increasingly supported in Congress. This led to the repeal of the Clark amendment in July 1985, paving the way for direct American intervention in Angola in support of UNITA. President Reagan received Savimbi in January 1986, and the administration announced in March, that UNITA would receive stinger surface-to-air missiles.

Concerning the settlement of the conflicts in Angola and Namibia, the Reagan doctrine highlights a contradiction in American policy. Justified by Freeman, who was the principal deputy assistant secretary of state for African affairs, as a means of leverage to pressurize the Angolan government into negotiations,[95] the State Department recognized that military aid to UNITA could also have the opposite effect, and jeopardize negotiations.[96] American support for UNITA defeated the purpose of linkage which was to obtain the Cuban withdrawal from Angola in exchange for Namibian independence. Cuban troops remained in Angola precisely because of outside support to UNITA. But the Reagan doctrine, which advocated military assistance to anti-communist guerrillas worldwide, prevailed over these objections, even more as secretary of state George Shultz initially defended the doctrine.[97] Not surprisingly, the Angolan government broke off negotiations with the Americans, who had lost their credibility as mediators,[98] and turned to the military option, investing over a billion dollars in weapons and training.[99] At the same time, dos Santos ensured the support of Mikhail Gorbachev during two successive trips to Moscow in February and May 1986, whereby substantial new equipment was delivered under the terms of the friendship treaty of 1976.[100] In addition to new fighter planes, forward military bases were surrounded by surface-to-air missile sites, and equipped with radar systems capable of detecting South African aircraft inside Namibia.[101] And after South African frogmen had sabotaged two Soviet cargo ships in the southern Angolan port of Namibe in June 1986, the Soviet Union warned Pretoria that the South African action 'cannot be left unpunished', and would have far-reaching and dangerous consequences.[102] However, following the advice of Cuban and the Soviet Union, FAPLA did not launch a new offensive against UNITA in southeast Angola.[103] They most probably felt that the Angola forces were not as yet prepared to counter successfully South African air and ground attacks in support of UNITA. But according to Bender, Angola's policy of turning to the military option instead of pursuing negotiations with the United States, was ill-timed. Against the background of falling oil prices, which accounted for 80 per cent of the country's foreign exchange earnings, the government was forced to adopt unpopular economic austerity measures. In addition, there would have to be substantial cuts in military expenditure. One alternative course of action to war would be to resume negotiations, and seek a diplomatic solution to the conflict.[104]

Talks between Angola and the Americans resumed in Brazaville in April 1987. They were followed by the visit of an Angolan government delegation to Washington in June, and a trip by Chester Crocker to Luanda in July. But no progress was made, as the Angolan government simply reiterated its 1984 proposal for a partial withdrawal of Cuban forces. The decisive policy shift in fact came from Cuba. It set the scene for a dynamics of negotiations and war leading to the New York agreements of December 1988 which paved the way for the implementation of Resolution 435.

CHAPTER SEVEN

ANGOLA-NAMIBIA: FROM WAR TO INDEPENDENCE. 1987–90

The devastating effects of the war in Angola which resulted in damages estimated at $12 billion from 1975 to 1987, and had cost over 60,000 lives,[1] as well as economic mismanagement led to a reassessment of Angola's diplomatic and economic options[2]. In April 1987, the Angolan government resumed talks with Chester Crocker in Brazaville. After a delegation of the MPLA government was received in Washington in June, Crocker visited Angola for an inconclusive meeting in July.

But the stalemate reached on the battlefield also provoked a *decisive shift in Cuban policy* as early as July 1987. It was at that time that Cuba approached the United States with a view to joining the talks.[3] On 4 August, President dos Santos met Fidel Castro in Havana. In a joint commuiniqué, the two leaders declared that they were willing to show more flexibility in order to find a 'just and honorable' agreement. And Cuba would like to participate in talks involving Angola, South Africa, SWAPO, and the United States.[4]

Fidel Castro who was personally responsible for the Cuban involvement in Angola, and was involved in directing the operation in Angola,[5] realized that the Angolan war was unwinnable. Furthermore, the cost of the Cuban presence in Angola weighed increasingly on Cuba's economy, the development of which was hampered by a loss of export earnings, an overcentralized bureaucracy, and the end of a five years period of high economic growth as well as growing economic dependency on the Soviet Union.[6] And the increasing cost in lives[7] and health to Cuban soldiers probably made the war unpopular. But Cuba was determined to ensure an honourable exit from Angola for its internationalist troops. South African withdrawal from

Angola and Namibia, and the implementation of Resolution 435 were the conditions.

Following the shift in the Cuban position, Crocker resumed negotiations with the Angolan government in September 1987. Until January 1988, discussions centred on the conditions for Cuban participation in the negotiations.[8] In particular, an important issue was whether a joint Angolan/Cuban delegation would discuss the total withdrawal of Cuban forces from Angola.[9] Luanda's initial position was that the question of Cuban withdrawal north of the 13th parallel was a bilateral issue between Cuba and Angola, and therefore not open to negotiations with other parties. In addition, Luanda refused to talk to Savimbi whom Pretoria and the United States continued to support.[10] And although the Angolan defence minister Pedro Maria Tonha 'Pedale' recognized that there existed no military solution to the war,[11] Luanda's diplomatic initiatives were paralleled by a new military offensive against UNITA, highlighting both Angola's resolve to strengthen its negotiating position, and probably also divisions within the politburo.

According to South African military sources, Luanda had prepared a new offensive against UNITA in southeast Angola in March 1987.[12] The offensive was launched in August, and South African forces, namely the Buffalo Battalion, the 61 Mechanized Battalion, entered Angola in September. 18,000 Angola and Cuban forces, advised by Russian generals and supported by Soviet air craft, and a sophisticated air defence network covering the whole of southern Angola and the northernmost regions of Namibia, were reported to be engaged in battles against South African forces and aircraft along the Lomba river north of the UNITA stronghold of Mavinga.[13] But Angolan troops who incurred the largest military losses of the war, failed to capture Mavinga. The offensive was stopped by South African and UNITA troops who managed to destroy an entire brigade (47 Brigade) in October.[14] As in 1985, South Africa had intervened in order to rescue UNITA from defeat. And Savimbi told the South African field commander that if it had not been for the SADF, Angolan government troops would have taken Mavinga.[15] The South African defence minister Magnus Malan admitted in November 1987 that the SADF had 'saved' UNITA from annihilation.[16] In the logic of the Total National Strategy, Malan justified South African involvement on the grounds that without its intervention, the entire subcontinent could have been 'brought to the brink of the abyss by Communist forces'. According to Malan, South Africa was aware of the risks involved. However, 'the price of peace is high, but cannot be compared with the price of permanent domination of our part of the world by Russian and other alien powers'.[17] And in October 1987, Pretoria decided that Angolan troops should be expelled from the entire territory of southeastern Angola east of the Cuito river,[18] setting the scene for the South African siege of the Cuito Cuanavale region from October 1987 to May 1988.

The battle for Cuito Cuanavale

In November 1987, the South Africans, carried away by their success of preventing Angolan government forces from capturing Mavinga, launched together with Savimbi's troops a counter offensive. Using tanks for the first time since the Second World War,[19] South Africa engaged in what became known as the siege of Cuito Cuanavale, a small but strategic town 300 km north of the Namibian border which served as the staging post for FAPLA's offensive against the UNITA stronghold of Mavinga. The combined South African-UNITA counter offensive signalled Pretoria's resolve not only to prevent UNITA's defeat, but also to affirm South African regional hegemony in the face of a greatly strengthened Angolan army which now enjoyed an air supremacy leaving the aging Mirages of South Africa which could not be replaced because of the 1977 UN arms embargo, at a clear disadvantage. The siege of Cuito Cuanavale, which started in October 1987, took the form of bombing the town, and in particular the bridge over the Cuito river, unsuccessful attempts to destroy the FAPLA brigades which were stationed east of the Cuito river, and to disrupt FAPLA's supply lines from Menongue to Cuito Cuanavale from December 1987 to May 1988. While the shelling of Cuito started on 9 October 1987,[20] the main effort of the SADF was to destroy FAPLA's army east of Cuito Cuanavale from November 1987. However, in spite of incurring heavy losses, the Angolan government forces resisted four South African attempts in November to annihilate them, and managed to regroup east of Cuito Cuanavale, where they established three defence lines.[21]

169

New attempts by the SADF to dislodge two FAPLA brigades in January and February 1988 (Operation 'Hooper') again failed. Moreover, the South Africans did not succeed, either in preventing Angolan government and Cuban troops from crossing the Cuito river at Cuito Cuanavale, or from disrupting the supply line between Menongue and Cuito Cuanavale; attempts which culminated in an unsuccessful attack by the 32 Battalion of the FAPLA air base of Menongue on 14 February 1988 coincided with another attempt to destroy FAPLA forces east of Cuito Cuanavale.[22]

During the second battle of 'Operation Hooper' of 14 February 1988, FAPLA was joined in combat by Cuban troops, who came into direct contact with the South African forces for the first time since 1976.[23] As much as the battle of Mavinga had prompted South Africa to engage in the siege of Cuito Cuanavale, the Angolan-Cuban defeat at Mavinga led to a decisive reorientation of the Cuban military involvement. After a meeting with Angola and the Soviet Union in November 1987, probably held during the celebrations of the October Revolution in Moscow, Fiedel Castro took the crucial decision to send reinforcements to Angola, and to involve Cuban troops directly in the fighting, but this time following Cuban, and not Soviet strategies.[24] Castro blamed misguided Soviet battle strategies for the defeat at Mavinga.[25] And it was this military setback which, according to Fidel Castro, would have required to send reinforcements.[26] Demonstrating a *relative autonomy* in face of Soviet policy, Castro wanted to ensure a major Cuban military victory before withdrawing from Angola. Intended not only to strengthen Cuba's position in the negotiations in which it wanted to participate, this decision no doubt reflected Castro's personal commitment to Cuba's internationalist cause which he had defended for over twenty years, but which his country was not in the position to uphold indefinitely. To illustrate the Cuban resolve, General Arnaldo Ochoa Sanchez, who had commanded the Cuban troops in Angola in 1975 and 1976, left for Angola at the head of Cuban reinforcements in November 1987. In January 1988, Cuban troops had increased to 40,000; and from February, they intervened directly in the fighting, helping FAPLA to resist repeated combined South African/UNITA attacks on, and around Cuito Cuanavale from February to May 1988.

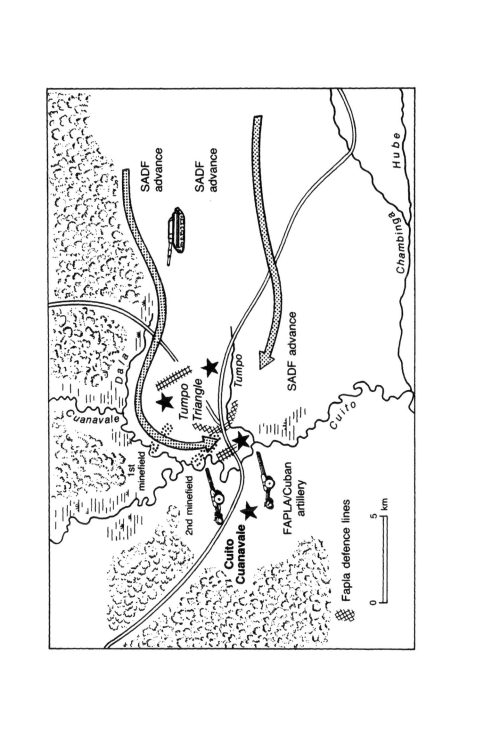

SADF advance

SADF advance

SADF advance

Dala

Cuanavale

Tumpo Triangle

★

★

★

Tumpo

Cuito

1st minefield

2nd minefield

★

FAPLA/Cuban artillery

Cuito Cuanavale

Chambinga

Hube

▨ Fapla defence lines

km

0   5

After the SADF had failed to dislodge FAPLA and Cuban troops from the east of the Cuito river on 14 February 1988, two further tank attacks on a triangle of 30 square km opposite Cuito Cuanavale on the east bank of the Cuito river with an important FAPLA logistics base (Tumpo Triangle) on 25 and 26 February had to be called off after the SADF had been subjected to heavy artillery bombardment from the FAPLA/ Cuban defenses at Cuito Cuanavale.[27] Despite the two failed attacks, caused not only be enemy artillery,but also by failing material, a third attack on FAPLA defence positions east of the Cuito river in the Tumpo Triangle was decided for 23 march. According to Pretoria, continued South African involvement in Angola would be justified on at least five grounds: the importance of supporting UNITA as part of South Africa's attempts to protect her interests in the region; to prevent SWAPO incursions into Okavango, and the Caprivi strip from southeast Angola; to protect these two border regions in Namibia from SWAPO attacks; to oppose the establishment of ANC bases in the south of Angola which would facilitate incursions into South Africa; and to help 'stemming the tide of southward Soviet expansionism from its Angolan stronghold'.[28] Moreover, it was speculated that a South African victory at Cuito Cuanavale would enable UNITA to penetrate deep into Angola with South African air support.[29]

Fresh troops from South Africa crossed into Angola at the beginning of March, and like the previous South African offensive since November 1987, the new attack aimed at driving out all FAPLA forces, and their Cuban advisers from the Tumpo Triangle east of Cuito Cuanavale on the east bank of the Cuito river. Moreover, South African troops would hold the area until dawn of 23 March, while units of UNITA and the 32 Battalion would completely destroy the bridge over the Cuito river, thus preventing new offensive by Angolan government troops on UNITA held Mavinga, and the UNITA headquarters at Jamba in the foreseeable future.

However, the South African/UNITA force was met by units of three FAPLA brigades supported by a Cuban tank battalion, and by artillery positioned near the town of Cuito Cuanavale to the west of the river.[30] At the same time, and more importantly, South African tanks got stuck in a minefield . In the words of the South African officer who commanded the attack

172

on 23 March 1988: 'The enemy had us pinned down in the minefield . . . and they had the chance of shooting out the Olifants [tanks] one by one . . . We were in danger of being well and truly pinned down in a sea of mines'.[31] In the event, the South African lost three tanks which they were unable to recuperate or destroy before they fell into the hands of Fapla/Cuban troops. The South African commander asked for permission 'to break off the attack', a euphemism for acknowledging military defeat.[32]

Faced with the presence of an estimated 800 Cubans around Cuito Cuanavale, and after having repeatedly failed to fulfill the military aim set in October 1987, which was to dislodge Fapla troops from the entire area east of the Cuito river, Pretoria realized that they were unable to achieve this goal, unless they increased substantially the number of South African troops in Angola. However, this was politically not feasible. A confidential report presented to Malan in January pointed out that the only way of taking Cuito Cuanavale speedily was through an infantry attack involving several thousand men. But the drawback to such a plan was that it would lead to the death of up to 300 white soldiers, and several thousand black Namibians from the SWATF.[33] The South Africans continued to bomb positions at Cuito Cuanavale sporadically until May 1988, and according to South African military sources, a force of a thousand men remained in south east Angola until the final withdrawal end of August, in order to prevent a build up of Angolan troops east of the Cuito river.[34] The South African defeat at Cuito Cuanavale was a military, but above all, psychological victory for the Angolan government. Furthermore, South Africa's failure of strengthening UNITA's military position, deprived the South African government of an important leverage in American mediated peace negotiations which had gathered momentum since January 1988.

Towards quadripartite negotiations. January to May 1988

At the end of January 1988, Jorge Risquet, a member of the Cuban politburo who became Cuba's chief negotiator, joined the Angolans for the first time in the talks with Chester Crocker. Most significantly, Angola and Cuba now accepted the principle of a *total* withdrawal of Cuban forces from Angola over four years in exchange for Namibian independence. The Angolan-Cuban policy shift, which was supported by the Frontline states,[35] constituted a breakthrough for Crocker's diplomacy. It meant that linkage as a framework for negotiations had been accepted.

The South Africans, who were fully engaged in their military campaign at Cuito Cuanavale, rejected the Angolan/Cuban proposal. 'Pik' Botha described the Luanda meeting as 'a waste of time',[36] and was irritated that the South African government had not been consulted.[37] But five weeks later, Pretoria accepted the principle of meeting the Cubans and Angolans after discussions between the South African foreign minister and Chester Crocker in Geneva on 14 March 1988. However, the South African government did not readily accept negotiations. The Americans who were eager to ensure a diplomatic success before the end of the Reagan presidency, put pressure on South Africa. Both in Geneva, and at a subsequent meeting in Washington with the South African director of foreign affairs, Neil van Heerden, and the South African ambassador, Crocker 'gave them the bottom line'. By agreeing to the American settlement plan, South Africa had a 'great opportunity' which it should seize. Otherwise there could be consequences which the American government would be unable to prevent. In particular, the Reagan administration could probably not fend off further sanctions which were becoming an issue in the debates leading to the presidential elections.[38]

Contrary to the negotiations between the Contact Group, and South Africa in 1977 and 1978, during which Pretoria knew that the West did not intend to impose sanctions, the spectre of sanctions was this time not an empty threat. Punitive sanctions against South Africa had already been imposed by Congress in October 1986 after it had overruled a veto by the President.[39] The American Congress started considering tougher new sanction bills in March, and the Foreign Affairs Committee of the House of Representatives adopted the so-called Dellums sanctions bill in May. The bill prohibited all imports from South Africa except some strategic minerals, and all exports to South Africa, save humanitarian assistance. Furthermore, it proposed a ban on South African investment in the United States, and an end to all military cooperation between the United States and South Africa.[40] The bill was accepted by the full House of

Representatives in August 1988, and by the Foreign Relations Committee of the Senate in September 1988, although it was not ratified by the full Senate.

The effects of sanctions were felt increasingly inside South Africa despite official denials. According to an estimate by the South African Trust Bank in 1989, sanctions and disinvestment since 1985 had led to a cumulative foreign exchange loss of 40,000 million Rand, or approximately, 15,210 million US dollars. The indirect 'multiplier effects' on production and living standards (for the whole population) were estimated at 80,000 million Rand, and 100,000 million Rand respectively, consumer spending being about 15% lower in 1989 than would have been the case without sanctions.[41] The imposition of sanctions, of financial sanctions in particular, aggravated a severe economic crisis inside South Africa. According to a World Bank expert, output growth which had averaged 5 per cent per annum in the 1960s, fell to 3 per cent in the 1970s, and to 1 per cent in the 1980s. And much of the growth which did take place, was in the government and service sector, while output in agriculture, manufacturing, mining, and construction declined. Likewise personal savings fell from 12 per cent to less than 2 per cent of incomes. As a result of a general fall in incomes, and an increase in the burden of taxation, 'South African whites had to dig deeper into savings in order to maintain their customary life-style'. Corporate savings stagnated, and in 1985–86, the net outflow of capital was estimated at 5 billion US dollars annually, or 6 per cent of the Gross Domestic Product. In addition, apartheid had created structural obstacles to growth, resulting in the low purchasing power of the black population, and as a consequence, in a limited domestic market for South African goods, as well as in acute shortages of skilled labour. Low demand was worsening the problems which resulted from the country's weakening currency, and rising production costs. And declining profitability of mining and manufacturing caused increased financial and balance of payments difficulties.[42] According to the same analyst, the South African government would need to implement a strongly deflationary policy, in which the public sector deficit, running at 8–10 per cent of the Gross Domestic Product in 1987, would be sharply reduced.[43] However, the Total National Strategy with high military expenditure, and the maintenance of the costly apartheid bureaucracy – the cost of financing the homelands amounted to 4.7 billion Rand in 1985/86[44] – precluded the government from pursuing such a policy, a situation which was aggravated by financial sanctions which would make borrowing difficult. To end South African occupation of Namibia, the cost of which was estimated at 1,000 million US dollars in 1987,[45] would thus present substantial savings. According to the director of the South African Institute of Strategic Studies close to the government, 'curtailment of state expenditure in South Africa, and foreign debt repayments[46] may have been one of the single biggest factors putting pressure on South Africa to end its occupation of Namibia.[47] Combined with the failure to drive the FAPLA forces across the Cuito river which, in the eyes of the South Africans, would have prevented them from staging further attacks against UNITA, negotiations for the independence of Namibia now became a serious policy option, rallying both the politicians, and increasingly the military establishment who still feared that, if they abandoned Namibia, and the Caprivi strip in particular, Botswana would be open to 'destabilization' from the north.[48]

But President Botha initially refused to make concessions regarding Namibia in his official statements, and probably also following his personal inclinations. As late as March 1988, he even ruled out South African withdrawal from Angola as long as Cuban troops remained in the country, and he had indicated that South Africa was not prepared to implement Resolution 435 because it would entail an election victory for SWAPO.[49] In 1987, Pretoria had blocked constitutional proposals which had been worked out by the parties of the Transitional Government of National Unity, and which failed to mention 'group rights'. The proposal had been supported by four of the TGNU's six parties who called increasingly for the implementation of Resolution 435. But during a visit to Namibia in April 1988, P. W. Botha tightened South Africa's control over Namibia, notably by increasing the powers of Louis Pienaar, the South African appointed administrator general,[50] who declared at the same time that any political dispensation which was not based on ethnic lies, would be 'totally unacceptable'.[51]

The turning point. Cuban pressures and negotiations. May to June 1988

However, when South Africa, Angola, and Cuba, and the United States met for the first round of quadripartite talks in London from 3 to 5 May 1988, South Africa proposed the implementation of Resolution 435, if agreement could be reached on Cuban withdrawal from Angola.[52] The Angolan-Cuban delegation, for its part, proposed a phased withdrawal of the 20,000 Cuban troops in the south of the country within eighteen months – a shortening of six months compared to the initial timetable offered in January – while the remaining forces would leave Angola over a period of four years.[53] In addition, they signalled to the South Africans that they would be flexible on the timetable.[54] The South Africans rejected the Angolan-Cuban proposal. Nevertheless, in the words of the South African chief negotiator, 'although the London meeting did not provide any concrete results, the delegations had made the first contact, the basic parameters had been demarcated, and all parties appeared to want a solution'.[55]

The fact that Pretoria was now willing to discuss the implementation of Resolution 435, was the reflection of increasing Angolan-Cuban military pressure which was to change the balance of power in southern Angola against South Africa, and in favour of Angola and Cuba, this in addition to the financial burden which continued South African occupation of Namibia presented. In April 1988, combined Cuban-Angolan forces moved southwards to take control of the Cunene, and Namib provinces bordering Namibia,[56] eliminating previous no-go areas as far as FAPLA was concerned. Cuban troops had established a second front against the SADF, and now were close to the Namibian border south of Xangongo in the western Cunene province. They were, however, under strict instructions not to cross the border into Namibia.[57] The South Africans took heavy casualties including the psychologically important number of more than a dozen white South African soldiers who were killed.[58] And as a result of the Cuban-Angolan advance in southwest Angola, the SADF had lost its practically undisputed control over southern Angola since 1980, except for an area between east of Cuito Cuanavale, and the Zambian border to the Caprivi strip.[59] The much feared threat of a conventional war with Cuban forces backed by Soviet material had become a distinct possibility. Together with the defeat suffered at Cuito Cuanavale, the Cuban presence at the Namibian border made the South Africans realize that to continue the war would be very costly.

One week after the London meeting, 'Pik' Botha, alarmed at a Cuban troop buildup in southwest Angola, met with Angolan officials for bilateral talks in Brazzaville, describing the troop deployment as a means of enhancing the Cuban bargaining position before negotiations would start in earnest.[60] To General Malan on the other hand, talks would be meaningless unless the Cuban advance was stopped.[61] Reservists were put on alert. On 23 May, the SADF was reported to have made another attempt at capturing Cuito Cuanavale,[62] and UNITA managed to step up its operations in the north of Angola as Cuban and Angolan government troops were concentrating efforts in the south of the country.

It was against this background of uncertainty that a second round of quadripartite talks was held in Cairo from 24 to 25 June. While the first day of talks was marked by heated, and often rhetorical exchanges between the Angola-Cuban and South African delegations,[63] Angola and Cuba refused to accept new conditions added by the South Africans,[64] such as the completion of Cuban withdrawal from Angola within seven month, and the inclusion of Savimbi in a coalition government within six weeks after the Cairo talks.[65] Nevertheless, the meeting produced what Crocker called 'the parameters of a settlement', or a 'measure of agreement on how to proceed'.[66] Luanda dropped its earlier demand that the end of United States support for UNITA was a precondition for negotiating the withdrawal of Cuban troops,[67] although it continued to call for an end to American support of UNITA. Interviewed on his way back to South Africa, 'Pik' Botha emphasized that his government was ready to grant independence to Namibia. And when asked about his feelings about the Cuban troop concentration along Namibia's border, he hoped that the momentum of the negotiations would be strong enough to prevent a military explosion'.[68]

Botha's remark was a diplomatic euphemism for admitting that South African military activities were under way on the Namibian-Angolan border between Ovamboland and the

Cunene province. While South African commandos of 32 Battalion had started provoking Cuban and FAPLA troops in early June,[69] plans for a conventional attack on the Cuban troops at Techipa, north of the Caluque dam, were finalized on 25 June, the final day of the Cairo meeting. The South African attack, involving tanks and infantry, started in the early morning of 26 June.[70] It is impossible that the South African delegation at Cairo which comprised General Malan, the defence minister as well as General Geldenhuys, the head of the SADF, was not aware of the South African military preparations on the Namibian-Angolan border. This lends credence to the argument of the Angolan government, that the actual decision to attack was taken during the Cairo talks as a means of strengthening Pretoria's bargaining position.[71]

However, South African troops were defeated by Cuban tanks and troops halfway between the Caluque dam and the Cuban stronghold of Techipa in a battle on 27 June, two days after the Cairo talks had ended.[72] Shortly afterwards, Cuban planes bombarded the Caluque dam on the Cunene river just north of the Namibian border inside Angola, killing eleven white South African soldiers, in addition to one white officer killed at the battle south of Techipa.[73] In addition, they destroyed the pipeline from Caluque to Ruacana, cutting the water supply to the north of Namibia.[74] The South African troops inside Angola were ordered to withdraw to Namibia just before midnight of 27 June; and a commander of 32 Battalion declared that he was told 'in no uncertain terms that from that night onward not a toe was to be put across the border into Angola'.[75]

The South African defeat at Techipa, and the Cuban air attack on Caluque were of crucial importance. Coupled with South Africa's setbacks at Cuito Cuanavale, the Cuban action at Techipa, and Caluque for the first time put South Africa in a position of a clear military disadvantage. This threw into question one basic assumption of the Total National Strategy, namely that South Africa could force the governments of neighbouring countries to change their policies towards South Africa.[76] In the absence of economic dependence of Angola on South Africa, economic coercion had never been on the cards, and in the face of an Angolan army which was backed by 50,000 Cuban forces, and protected by a sophisticated air

179

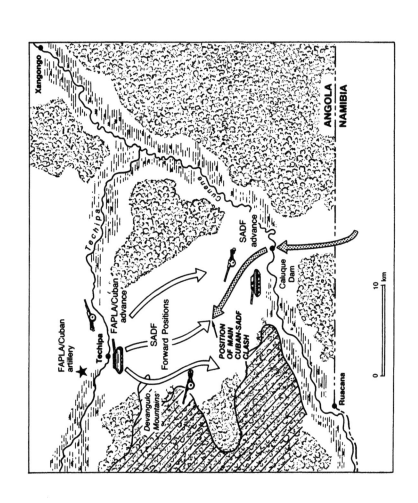

defence system, direct South African intervention had become costly, both in material and human terms. South Africa did not retaliate, and President Botha argued that it would be more prudent to defend the area from the Namibian side of the border.[77] Negotiations for the withdrawal of Cuban troops now were the only real policy option accepted by both the military, and foreign affairs. To give up the financially draining colonial rule over Namibia appeared to be a small price to pay.

The Cuban attack on Caluque which marked a decisive turning point in the negotiations,[78] was a big personal victory for Fidel Castro. The decisive change in the balance of power against South Africa, which made any other course than negotiations unrealistic, was brought about by the Cuban forces thus vindicating Cuban involvement in the Angolan civil war. From now on, it was only a question of time until agreement was reached, paving the way for the implementation of Resolution 435, and the security of Angola from South African attack which had been at the origin of the massive Cuban intervention in Angola in 1975.

From negotiations to settlement. July to December 1988

A breakthrough in the negotiations occurred during the third round of quadripartite talks in New York from 11 to 13 July 1988.[79] In an agreement on 14 'Principles for a peaceful settlement in southwestern Africa', linkage between Namibian independence and Cuban withdrawal from Angola was acknowledged by all parties. While the document also recognized the mediating role of the United States, agreement on a mutually acceptable timetable for South African, and Cuban withdrawal from Angola, and the translation of the 'Principles' into treaty form remained the only important outstanding issue to be resolved.

After secret quadripartite military talks in Cape Verde on 22 and 23 July,[80] South African withdrawal from Angola, and the principle of a cease-fire were agreed on during a fifth round of talks in Geneva from 2 to 5 August.[81] The Geneva meeting produced the first concrete results of the negotiations. Most importantly, the decisions taken in the *Geneva Protocol* concerned both the withdrawal of South African troops from Angola, and efforts by Angola and Cuba to induce SWAPO forces to retreat beyond the 16th parallel,[82] an issue which was to become the centre of controversy between SWAPO and South Africa in April 1989. The Geneva Protocol thus effectively ended the war between South Africa and Angola.[83] On 10 August, South Africa began withdrawing several thousand troops, and the withdrawal was completed on 30 August, when the last 1,000 soldiers crossed into Namibia, after a formal cease-fire agreement had been signed at Ruacana on 22 August.[84]

Agreement on the timetable of Cuban withdrawal from Angola was the object of four inconclusive rounds of talks between August and October. In a separate but indirectly related development, the Secretary-General of the United Nations Javier Pérez de Cuellar visited Pretoria in September. He not only assured the South African government of UN impartiality during the transition phase to Namibian independence, but he also met representatives of some of Namibia's internal parties.[85] Agreement on the timetable for Cuban withdrawal from Angola was reached on 15 November, when Angola, Cuba, and South Africa accepted an American compromise proposal providing for a Cuban withdrawal over 27 months. Finally, they signed a protocol in Brazzaville on 13 December,[86] but only after the South African foreign minister had momentarily walked out of the talks ten days earlier,[87] a move which was criticized by Angola, Cuba, and the United States, and left the outcome of the negotiations in suspense. The Protocol of Brazzaville, as a first step for the formal ratification of the agreement reached on 15 November, fixed 1 April 1989 as the date for the implementation of Resolution 435, and 22 December as the date for the formal signature of a tripartite agreement between Angola, Cuba, and South Africa, and a bilateral agreement between Angola and Cuba concerning the Cuban troop withdrawal. Furthermore, on the insistence of South Africa, who was very much concerned with the verification procedures of any agreement,[88] the Protocol provided for the establishment of a Joint Commission between South Africa, Angola, and Cuba with the United States and the Soviet Union as observers,[89] in order to settle any conflict arising in the implementation of the tripartite agreement. However, the Joint Commission would in no way function as a substitute for the United Nations Transitional Assistance Group (UNTAG).

On 22 December, the tripartite agreement between Angola, Cuba, and South Africa as well as the bilateral agreement between Luanda and Havana were signed in New York. While the implementation of Resolution 435 and the phased withdrawal of Cuban troops until 1 July 1991 were at the centre of the two agreements, the tripartite agreement between Angola, Cuba, and South Africa made no direct reference either to UNITA, or to SWAPO, who had been excluded from the negotiations from the start. The document merely stipulated in its third paragraph that South African and Angolan territories should not be used by 'any state, organization, or person in connection with acts of war, aggression, or violence against the territorial integrity, or inviolability of borders of Namibia, or any other action which could prevent the execution of UNSCR 235/78'.[90] The only mention of South African support to UNITA was that the 'parties shall respect the principle of non-interference in the internal affairs of the states of south-western Africa'.[91] According to Crocker, Pretoria was ready to cease its support for Savimbi in exchange for an undertaking by Luanda that ANC guerillas leave Angola.[92] In January 1989, ANC agreed to the removal of its guerillas from Angola for Tanzania, Uganda, and Ethiopia[93] at the same time as the first 450 Cubans left the country.[94] An agreement had been reached whereby each party could claim with some justification to have emerged victoriously. While Angola and Cuba achieved not only South African withdrawal from Angola but also from Namibia with the implementation of Resolution 435, Pretoria could claim that it had achieved one of the goals of the Total National Strategy, which was to compel Angola to end its material support for ANC. Agreement among the parties that there should be neither looser nor clear winners, coupled as it was with the political will of all parties to come to an agreement, were the main factors accounting for the successful conclusion of the negotiations.[95]

The role of the Soviet Union

Contrary to what is often believed, the Soviet Union did not get actively involved in the peacemaking process before May 1988, in spite of a new Soviet foreign policy orientation which started to emerge at the 27th Congress of the Communist Party in February 1986, and which undoubtedly contributed a lot in weakening the positions of those who argued that the independence of Namibia under a SWAPO led government would inevitably lead to further Soviet expansionism in southern Africa. According to the 'new thinking', international relations are characterized by the *interdependence* of states and peoples based on universal human values. This new approach stressed the global nature of problems of mankind. The common destiny of mankind would replace the conflictual outlook of revolutionary class struggle which had legitimized Soviet support for Third World countries during the Brezhnev era. Support for wars of national liberation was no longer a policy priority. On the contrary, because of the global interdependence, every regional conflict would be a threat to international security, and could degenerate into a conflict between superpowers. Hence the need to defuse existing regional conflicts, and to seek their political solution.[96] In November 1987, Mikhail Gorbachev emphasized that 'we are in favour of stepping up collective searches for ways of defusing conflict situations in the Middle East, in Central America, in Southern Africa, in all the planet's hot spots'.[97] And in his speech before the UN General Assembly in December 1988, Gorbachev reminded the audience that 'the bell of every regional conflict tolls for all of us'.[98]

However, the policy of linking regional conflicts to global concerns, and of supporting a negotiated settlement to the conflicts in Namibia and Angola was slow to materialize. While opposition to the generous but economically often costly support to Third World countries during the Brezhnev era was first articulated at the highest level by his immediate successor Yuri Andropov,[99] a reversal of this policy was not without problems, as it involved a radical revision of the Soviet Union's international strategies.[100] Consequently, the Soviet Union under Gorbachev initially continued to give strong military and economic support to its important allies in the Third World such as Angola.[101] Moreover, the Reagan doctrine, and the related concept of low-intensity conflict was used by those in the Soviet Union, who advocated continuing military assistance to Third World countries, to justify their position. In particular, the United States were accused of double standards. While the Reagan administration stressed the need for global peace, it

184

continued to support 'gangs of bandits operating in Angola, and Afghanistan',[102] and 'it is not the Soviet Union but the United States who ferments regional strife, and it would be very wrong to expect our country to lay the role of a fireman extinguishing the flames of conflicts instigated by Washington'.[103] Furthermore, Soviet Africanists became increasingly aware that southern Africa not only had a low revolutionary potential, but that newly independent Third World countries would increasingly turn to the West, with all ensuing political consequences. 'Experience shows that this trend can be reversed only if the Soviet Union renders large-scale aid tantamount to graciously subsidizing the entire economy of such countries.'[104]

Before 1988, the Soviet Union was accused by the Americans of doing everything to block the negotiations over Angola and Namibia.[105] In June 1987, the deputy-director of the Institute of African Studies of the USSR Academy of Sciences still maintained that linkage was a real stumbling block to a political settlement.[106] The Soviet Union showed an interest in facilitating Crocker's settlement plan for the first time at a meeting between the Soviet deputy minister of foreign affairs, Anatolyi Adamishin, and Chester Crocker in Washington in March 1988.[107] But when Adamishin visited Luanda at the beginning of April, he still supported Angola's position calling for an end to American support to UNITA as a precondition for negotiations. And it was only as late as May 1988 that the Soviet Union actually started cooperating with the United States.[108] After a meeting between Crocker and Adamishin in Lisbon on 18 and 19 May, the Soviet Union declared that it was ready to act as a co-guarantor of any agreement resulting from the quadripartite negotiation. The understanding between the United States and the Soviet Union was underwritten two weeks later at the Moscow summit between Reagan and Gorbachev.[109] From May onwards, the deputy foreign minister Anatoly Adamishin and the head of the southern African section of the foreign ministry Vladillen Vasev now became actively involved behind-the-scenes as mediators in the negotiations.

In addition to the shift in Soviet political thinking, which made cooperation with the United States possible, Soviet experts seemed to doubt MPLA's capability of winning a military victory. Furthermore, the Angolan war put a drain on

Soviet resources, as Luanda stopped paying for the weapons by early 1988 as a result of the fall in oil prices.[110] To support the American mediated negotiations thus presented a means of extricating itself from the Angolan war without having to abandon its allies. From May to the successful conclusion of the negotiations in December 1988, Soviet diplomats played a discreet but active role as observers to the quadripartite negotiations. During the discussions in Cairo of June 1988, they reportedly played a crucial role in preventing the delegations of Angola and Cuba from leaving the negotiation table.[111]

SWAPO

Contrary to other colonial territories where the political parties were directly involved in the agreements leading to independence, neither SWAPO nor any other Namibian political party participated in the quadripartite negotiations. Their exclusion was justified on the grounds that the implementation of Resolution 435, which directly concerned the Namibians, had already been agreed upon in 1978. SWAPO's attitude, however, both towards the war in southern Angola, and the negotiations needs to be further examined.

During the 1987 offensive against UNITA, the Angolan government forces reportedly involved SWAPO in the fighting in central Angola hundreds of kilometres north of the Namibian border.[112] And during the siege of Cuito Cuanavale in 1988, SWAPO as well as ANC fighters worked as scouts for tracking UNITA.[113] In March, PLAN suffered several dozen casualties when it helped Angolan and Cuban troops to recapture the town of Cuemba on the Benguela railway from UNITA.[114] It was also claimed that PLAN fighters assisted the Cubans in their southward offensive from April to June. In particular, the South Africans accused SWAPO of forming three integrated battalions with the Cubans, each consisting of approximately 200 Cubans and 250 PLAN fighters,[115] a claim which was dismissed by western intelligence sources.[116] But South African troops in the Cunene province were surprised by an advance of Angolan and SWAPO forces pushing the SADF back to the Namibian border in May 1988.[117] PLAN fighters were also reported to have assisted the Cuban forces, operating in the south of the country as scouts,[118] and they were involved in the fighting at Caluque after the Cairo conference in June 1988.[119] According to SWAPO's secretary for foreign affairs, Theo-Ben Gurirab, SWAPO was 'ready to give any kind of assistance to the Angolan FAPLA forces whenever necessary'.[120]

On the diplomatic front, SWAPO had affirmed its readiness to hold discussions with South Africa, and after the Cubans had announced that they would now be prepared to negotiate a total withdrawal of Cuban forces from Angola in exchange for Namibian independence, SWAPO was ready to sign a cease-fire.[121] Initially, Angola and Cuba wanted to include SWAPO in the negotiations but dropped their demand, as the South Africans categorically refused to include SWAPO in the discussions.[122] It appears that South Africa made it clear that, if Angola and Cuba insisted on drawing SWAPO into the nego-tiations, Pretoria would request UNITA's participation in the talks.[123] From the outset, SWAPO was excluded from the quadripartite talks which started in London in May 1988. Despite initial protests,[124] SWAPO accepted its position, as the negotiations between Angola, Cuba, and South Africa did not directly concern the implementation of Resolution 435. Nujoma declared that 'SWAPO disagrees with the linkage, but . . . [it] seems to be there'.[125] And after SWAPO had received assur-ances from Angola, Cuba, and the United States that there would be no peace settlement without the independence of Namibia,[126] Nujoma readily conceded, that 'as far as SWAPO is concerned, the only role we are interested in playing is to sign a cease-fire with South Africa, and start the implemen-tation of 435. As far as Namibia is concerned, a formula is already agreed upon. It is up to the other parties to resolve all the other hurdles in order for us to proceed . . . The first phases of the negotiating process have nothing to do with us. We will be around when the time comes for the signing of the cease-fire, and the implementation of 435.'[127] In August, SWAPO – contrary to UNITA – agreed to abide by the cease-fire between Angola, Cuba, and South Africa pending the sign-ing of a formal cease-fire agreement with Pretoria.[128] And after final agreement about the timetable of Cuban withdrawal from Angola had been reached in the quadripartite talks between Angola, Cuba, South Africa, and the United States in Geneva in November 1988, SWAPO reiterated its readiness to sign a formal cease-fire with South Africa to end the war in Namibia.[129] But Pretoria was unwilling to sign a separate agreement with SWAPO, because 'we are not at war with SWAPO. We are dealing here with independent states, and with the United Nations'.[130] The seeds were sown for a series of misunderstandings between SWAPO, South Africa, and the United Nations which nearly prevented the implementation of Resolution 435 from April 1989.

From the 'events' of April 1989 to independence

The implementation of the New York Accords took a promising start. The first 450 Cubans left Luanda on 10 January 1989,[131] followed by the South Africans who started withdrawing their troops from Namibia.[132] On 16 January, the Security Council decided that Resolution 435 of 1978 should start to be implemented on 1 April 1989, and that the UN secretary-general should arrange a cease-fire between South Africa and SWAPO.[133] The first border control post between Namibia and South Africa was established in the town of Ariamsvlei on 16 February. Four days later, the curfew was lifted in Ovamboland, and the cabinet of the Transitional Government of National Unity met for the last time on 28 February when the 'National Assembly' voted to dissolve itself.

However, there were also more ominous developments. Followers of UNITA were reported to have crossed into northern Namibia,[134] and continued UNITA control of southeast Angola north of Okavango, and the Caprivi strip prevented the establishment of all the joint Angolan-South African border monitoring posts provided for in the Geneva Protocol of August 1988.[135] At the same time, the South Africans claimed that 40 per cent of SWAPO forces were still south of the 16th parallel, approximately 150 km north of the Namibian border, in contravention to the same protocol.[136] And the controversial presence of PLAN fighters in northern Namibia and southern Angola threatened to jeopardize the Namibian independence process on the very day Resolution 435 started to be implemented on 1 April 1989.

Only hours after a formal cease-fire had been agreed upon in the form of two separate exchanges of letters with the United Nations secretary-general, serious fighting broke out between SWAPO soldiers, and the South Africans in northern Namibia.

Armed PLAN fighters crossed into Namibia however without any offensive designs before they were attacked by units of the special counterinsurgency police force Koevoet and the SWATF, both backed by regular South African forces. The scene was set for a rapid escalation of the bloodiest battle in the 23 year war. While SWAPO sent reinforcements from southern Angola, the South Africans, with controversial United Nations backing,[137] engaged in a bloody carnage claiming – according to South African sources – more than 300 victims until the beginning of May when SWAPO forces had returned to Angola. Implementation of Resolution 435 resumed after South African troops had regained their bases on 13 May 1989.[138]

The reasons for both the crossing of armed PLAN fighters into Namibia, and the massacres perpetrated by the South Africans have been the object of much legalistic debate as to whether armed SWAPO soldiers were allowed to be in Namibia when Resolution 435 started to be implemented. According to South Africa, whose claim was accepted by most observers, the United Nations as well as Angola, and Cuba, SWAPO acted contrary to article 5 of the Geneva Protocol of 5 August 1988 which stipulated that 'Angola, and Cuba shall use their good offices so that, once the total withdrawal of South African troops from Angola is completed, and within the context also of the cessation of hostilities in Namibia, SWAPO forces will be deployed to the north of the 16th paralle.'[139] As SWAPO had accepted to abide by the Geneva agreement,[140] the presence of PLAN guerrillas north of the Namibian border would have constituted a violation of existing agreements.

SWAPO, on the other hand, argued that the agreements between Angola, Cuba, and South Africa were not binding on SWAPO. They would *not* supersede Security Council Resolution 435, which called for a 'cessation of all hostile acts by all parties, and the restriction of South African, and SWAPO armed forces to base [inside Namibia]',[141] even more as a subsequent resolution of 1989 had called for the implementation of Resolution 435 'in its original, and definitive form'.[142] SWAPO's claim that the PLAN fighters entered Namibia in order to present themselves to United Nations troops after the coming into force of the cease-fire appears more as an ex post justification. The SWAPO leadership must have been well aware that hardly any United Nations troops were present in northern Namibia at that time. SWAPO's decision to have armed PLAN fighters inside Namibia at the beginning of the transitional period leading to independence, gives some credibility to the argument that SWAPO wanted to reestablish its historical role as an active participant in the liberation process from which it had been left out in the final stages. South Africa, on the other hand, was aware of SWAPO's plans to cross the Namibian border just before the coming into force of the ceasefire. South African forces waited to ambush the PLAN fighters in order to be able to discredit SWAPO;[143] and according to a former South African military agent, Nico Basson, South African reports of the massacre of SWAPO guerillas had been prepared *before* the first engagement had taken place.[144]

But irrespective of the reasons underlying SWAPO's action, and South Africa's bloody 'retaliation', and irrespective of the legal merits of the arguments presented by either side, the regional agreements between Angola, Cuba, and South Africa did prevail, highlighting once again both the constraints which SWAPO faced at crucial points in the history of Namibia's decolonization, and the importance of taking the regional dimension into account in any analysis. The work of the Joint Committee established in Brazaville in December 1988, comprising Angola, Cuba, South Africa, the United States, and the Soviet Union, proved to be crucial in resolving the crisis of April 1989. Already at a meeting of the Joint Commission in Havana at the end of March, South Africa had submitted reports of PLAN units moving towards the Namibian border.[145] And when Marrack Goulding, the UN undersecretary-general responsible for peace-keeping operations, visited Luanda two days after the outbreak of the fighting on 3 April, the Angolan government was reported to have agreed that it should persuade SWAPO to withdraw beyond the 16th parallel.[146] The Angolan president Eduardo dos Santos criticized SWAPO for not having fully controlled its forces.[147]

The Joint Commission met again for a crucial meeting inside Namibia from 8 to 9 April, however, *without* SWAPO's participation.[148] Convened at South Africa's request, Cuba, Angola, and South Africa not only reaffirmed their commitment to the New York Agreements of 22 December 1988, but agreed that the Angolan government should ensure that SWAPO forces would be confined beyond the 16th parallel.[149] For in spite of

Angola's basic commitment to the liberation of Namibia, and its support for SWAPO's armed struggle, Luanda was not prepared to see its efforts to reach peace in Angola jeopardized. In a further concession to Pretoria, the Joint Commission, who had met again in Cape Town at the end of April, decided, that the South African security forces would have two weeks after the official deadline set for the return of SWAPO guerillas to Angola had elapsed on 29 April, to locate PLAN fighters still inside Namibia in what was described as 'a process of verification'.[150] And after the Joint Commission, which had met again in Cahama inside Angola on 18/19 May, had agreed that all SWAPO forces – over 5,000[151] – were now confined to base beyond the 16th parallel, the Commission, together with UNTAG,[152] decided to resume the implementation of Resolution 435,[153] thereby underlining its central importance in this final stage of Namibia's decolonization.

The adherence of the Angolan government to the regional agreements with South Africa rather than backing SWAPO, is not surprising. It reflects the Angolan government's difficult position of being torn between its political and ideological support to liberation movements on one hand, and its legitimate need to protect Angola's territorial integrity against South African destabilization on the other. By 1988, South Africa had achieved one aim of the Total Strategy, as reflected in the destabilization of the region. The Angolan government now agreed to end its military support to both SWAPO and ANC. As far as SWAPO was concerned, the MPLA government did not support SWAPO in April 1989. According to the Angolan government, there was no need for PLAN fighters to cross back into Namibia just before the coming into force of the cease-fire between SWAPO and South Africa.[154]

However, Angola's position was *not* shared by all Frontline states. President Mugabe of Zimbabwe might have been personally involved in the unfolding of the 'events' of April. Mugabe would have urged Nujoma to send the PLAN soldiers back into Namibia.[156] Mugabe's traditional attitude of distrust towards the South African government also meant that he probably did not believe that Pretoria would honour its engagement to implement Resolution 435, in which case the return of armed PLAN fighters would have enabled SWAPO to resume the struggle from inside Namibia. After the fighting had erupted in April, Mugabe in his capacity as chairman of the Non-Aligned Movement, accused Martti Attisaari, the secretary-general's special representative, of 'monumental errors of judgement' when he allowed South African forces to oppose the presence of SWAPO guerillas inside Namibia, a decision which 'was welcomed by South Africa as a licence to massacre Namibian people'.[157]

But once the independence process was back on the rails, the 'events' of April became a marginal episode in political terms. If they had any impact on the outcome of the elections for a constituent assembly in November 1989, they probably reinforced the image of SWAPO among the local population in the north of Namibia, to whom SWAPO had been the victim of yet another South African aggression.[158] The first Namibian exiles started to return in May 1989, and nearly 42,000 refugees had been repatriated under the auspices of the United Nations High Commissioner for Refugees (UNHCR) by September.[159] The number of South African forces was reduced to 1,500 by end of June, and the last troops left Namibia in November 1989, at the same time as the last SWAPO military camps were closed down in Angola.[160] Border control posts with Angola and Botswana were officially opened on 1 December 1989.

Most importantly, elections for a Constituent Assembly, which took place over a five day period from 7 to 11 November, were declared free and fair by the UN special representative Athisaari despite sporadic intimidation by Koevoet in the run up to the elections, and the registering of both who were Angolans, accused by SWAPO of being UNITA followers,[161] and 11,000 South Africans who had previously lived in Namibia. Thus, the registration rate of voters compared to the inhabitants was almost 250% in the town of Karasburg near the South African border.[162] However, the presence of 1,700 United Nations electoral supervisors from 27 countries inside every polling station,[163] a figure representing one UN supervisor for every 412 voters, contributed significantly to the smooth running of the elections. With a turnout of 97.04 per cent of the registered voters, the results gave a 57.32 per cent majority to SWAPO with 41 seats in the Constituent Assembly, ensuring a SWAPO controlled government but not the two third majority, which would have enabled SWAPO to adopt its own constitutional proposals without having to secure the agreement of its opponents. The Democratic Turnhalle Alliance (DTA) as major opposition party obtained 28.55 per cent of the votes, and 21 seats in the Assembly.[164] A constitution which reflects a multi-party democracy with entrenched fundamental rights and freedoms as well as an independent judiciary, was adopted on 9 February 1990. One week later, Sam Nujoma was elected as the first president of the country, which became independent as the Republic of Namibia on 21 March 1990.

CONCLUSION:
NAMIBIAN INDEPENDENCE
AND SOUTHERN AFRICA

The analysis of regional dynamics in the decolonization of
Namibia suggests three related questions. Is a focus on southern Africa regional actors, in addition to the South African
colonizer, necessary for the understanding of Namibia's
decolonization from 1945 to 1990? How complete was Namibia's political decolonization, as Pretoria continued to claim
South African sovereignty over the port and surrounding territory of Walvis Bay as well as twelve off-shore islands in the
south of Nambia? How important was Namibia's independence
for further political developments in the region, in Angola and
South Africa in particular?

As the preceding chapters have attempted to show, the role
of regional actors was at times crucial, and complemented significantly the internal dynamics opposing Namibia's nationalist
parties, and SWAPO in particular, to South African control of
the country. While a Botswana chief, Tshekedi Khama, had
been instrumental in making the then South West Africa an
issue of United Nations diplomacy in the wake of the Second
World War, it has been shown that the very formation of
Namibian nationalism had its source in the dynamics of resistance inside South Africa, where opposition parties facilitated
the emergence of SWAPO and SWANU in the late 1950s. Furthermore, SWAPO's politics of exile from the early 1960s cannot
be fully understood without analysing the sometimes complex
relationships with other liberation movements of southern
Africa. More importantly, the study has tried to show that the
analysis of SWAPO's relations with southern African states
supporting its struggle, is essential for the understanding of
the politics of Namibia's decolonization process. In particular,

broad political, and sometimes material support by the Frontline states did not imply that they unconditionally backed
SWAPO. As has been shown in chapter five, SWAPO's policy
options were at times constrained, when SWAPO's strategies
did not correspond to the Frontline states' own policies towards
South Africa. Furthermore, faced with an aggressive South
African regional policy, Frontline states sometimes had to seek
accommodation with Pretoria, often at the expense of the liberation movements which they supported politically.

The regional dimension to Namibia's decolonization became
again apparent and even paramount in the two years preceding
Namibian independence. Contrary to countries such as the
former Portuguese colonies and Zimbabwe, the independence
of Namibia was not the outcome of a settlement between the
South African colonizer and SWAPO as Namibia's strongest
nationalist party. Rather, South African withdrawal from Namibia was dictated by the outcome of a *regional war* between
South Africa, and Angola, compounded as it was by domestic
economic and political constraints on the South African colonizer. This again confirms the crucial importance of the regional
dimension for analysing Namibia's recent history.

But one regional dimension to Namibia's political decolonization, which had been an important point of dispute with
South Africa, continued to influence relations between Namibia
and South Africa beyond Namibia's independence. The long-
standing dispute concerning the sovereignty over Nambia's
only important deep sea harbour of Walvis Bay, and twelve
offshore islands known as the Penguin Islands in the south of
Namibia had not been settled when Namibia attained independence in March 1990. South Africa was not prepared to hand
Walvis Bay over to Namibia, leaving the country's decolonization still unfinished.

However, negotiations between representatives of the Namibian, and South African governments over the Bay's future
status started in Cape Town one year after independence on
14 March 1991. Two months later, the delegations met again
in Windhoek on 17 May 1991, and 'discussed in depth the
possibility of a joint administration as an interim arrangement,
pending an eventual settlement of the . . . question'.[1] Although
the re-incorporation of Walvis Bay into Namibia constituted
a foreign policy priority for the Namibian government,[2] the

Namibian government agreed to establish a joint administration with South Africa in August 1992. Walvis Bay started to be administered jointly by Namibia and South Africa on 1 November 1992, after an agreement had been finalized at the end of October.

It justified its compromise with South Africa on the grounds that it was constitutionally bound to encourage the settlement of international disputes by peaceful means and would favour good relations with South Africa.[3] Namibia thus extended its policy of national reconciliation beyond its borders.[4] In September 1993, the South African government finally announced that it was willing to transfer the sovereignty of Walvis Bay and the offshore islands to Namibia on 1 March 1994.[5]

While the political decolonization of Namibia will be complete in 1994, the country's economic dependence on South Africa is likely to continue even beyond 'majority rule' inside South Africa. At the time of Namibia's independence, ninety per cent of Namibia's trade, imports, and exports, were with South Africa,[6] and Hage Geingob, the prime minister, had pointed out soon after Namibia's independence that his country continued trading with South Africa. 'We do not have any other choice, we are a South African colony'.[7] But in spite of this pattern of dependency with regard to South Africa, the Namibian government believes that the country has an important economic role to play in the region, notably 'by spearheading, and serving as a vehicle for economic development, especially in light of her high quality infrastructure, and favourable geographic location which provides ready access to all regional countries, and the outside world'.[8]

How important then was Namibia's independence for further political developments in the region, in Angola and South Africa in particular? While the New York Accords of December 1988 precipitated the withdrawal of the South African administration from Namibia, the war which opposed the MPLA government and UNITA in Angola continued beyond Namibia's independence in March 1990. Eventually a peace agreement between the government and UNITA was reached in May 1991. But UNITA lost both United Nations monitored presidential and parliamentary elections, which were part of the peace agreement and were held in September 1992. Rather than accepting the outcome of the elections, Savimbi chose to

196

resume war. Subsequent efforts by the United Nations, as well as the United States, Russia and Portugal as guarantors of the 1991 peace agreement, to revive the peace process had failed by May 1993 as a result of UNITA's intransigence.

There are at least two reasons which can explain why the independence of Namibia did not influence the outcome of the civil war in Angola. Linking the decolonization of Namibia to Cuban withdrawal from Angola was an issue of interstate relations between South Africa, Angola and Cuba. Linkage did not address the settlement of the civil war in Angola with UNITA being excluded from the negotiations. Moreover, the conflicts in Namibia and Angola differed qualitatively. The issue in Namibia was decolonization. Pretoria was eventually willing to withdraw from a territory outside South Africa's borders. In Angola, the MPLA government and UNITA are engaged in a post-independence civil war conflict which centers on power. This war is fueled by profound mutual distrust, a culture of political violence, and the intransigence of UNITA's leader Jonas Savimbi. The end of outside governmental support to both UNITA and the government did not seem to affect either their determination or ability to confront each other militarily.

The question then arises whether the independence of Namibia had any direct influence on the dynamics of change inside South Africa? It can be argued that Namibian independence and the country's policy of reconciliation contributed to a psychological break with the past by South Africa's rulers and white minority on one hand, and by a large section of South Africa's black opposition and public opinion in favour of a negotiated transfer of power on the other. In this sense, the independence of Namibia did play a *symbolic role* for the unfolding of a new political dynamics of change inside South Africa. The independence of Namibia, coinciding as it did with the end of the cold war, also brought to an end a balance of forces in southern Africa which had been dominated by Pretoria's economic, military, and political destabilization of neighbouring countries, and the resistance by Frontline states and liberation movements to South African regional expansionism.

NOTES

Introduction

1 On the definition of decolonization, see for example John D. Hargreaves, *Decolonization in Africa*, London/New York, Longman, 1988, p. 1; Prosser Gifford and Wm. Roger Louis, 'Introduction', Prosser Gifford and Wm. Roger Louis (eds), *Decolonization, and African Independence. The Transfer of Power. 1960–1980*, New Haven/London, Yale University Press, 1988, p. x.

2 For the most comprehensive bibliography on Namibia, see Tore Linné Eriksen with Richard Moorsom, *The Political Economy of Namibia. An annotated critical bibliography*, Uppsala, Scandinavian Institute of African Studies, 1989 (second enlarged edition).

3 Hidipo L. Hamutenya and Gottfried H. Geingob, 'African Nationalism in Namibia', in C. Potholm and R. Dale (eds), *Southern Africa in Perspective*, New York, The Free Press, 1972, p. 88.

4 Aquino de Bragança and Jacques Delpechin, 'From the Idealization of Frelimo to the Understanding of the Recent History of Mozambique', *African Journal of Political Economy*, no. 1, 1986, p. 163.

Chapter 1   Incorporation of Namibia into South Africa

1 John S. Galbraith, 'Cecil Rhodes and his Cosmic Dreams: A Reassessment', *Journal of Imperial and Commonwealth History*, vol.1, No.2, January 1973, p. 177–8.

2 Carnarvon to Frere, confidential, 23.1.1878. PRO.CO 879/12/147, No.60.

3 See Ronald Dreyer, *The Mind of Official Imperialism. British and Cape government perceptions of German rule in Namibia from the Heligoland-Zanzibar Treaty to the Kruger Telegram (1890–1896)*. Essen, Reimar Hobbing Verlag, 1987; on British *economic* involvement in Namibia, see Ronald Dreyer, 'Whitehall, Cape Town, Berlin and the Economic Partition of South West Africa: The Establishment of

British Economic Control, 1885–1894', *Journal of Imperial and Commonwealth History*, vol. 15, no.3, May 1987, pp. 264–88.

4 W.K. Hancock, *Smuts*, vol.1: The Sanguine Years, 1870–1919, Cambridge, Cambridge University Press, 1962, p. 380.

5 On the origins of the class C mandate, see for example, Wm. Roger Louis, 'African Origins of the Mandates Idea', *International Organization*, vol.19, no.1, 1965, pp. 20–36.

6 Quoted in *Cape Times*, 18.9.1920.

7 Ronald Hyam, *The Failure of South African Expansion*, New York, Africana Publishing Corporation, 1972, pp. 31–2.

8 Cf. minute Dominions Office, 17.1.1935. PRO.DO 35/160/5(6146)160; *The Times*, 1.4.1937; on Namibia during the inter war period, see Maynard W. Swanson, 'South West Africa in Trust, 1919–1939', in P. Gifford and Wm.R. Louis (eds), *Britain and Germany in Africa: Imperial Rivalry and Colonial Rule*, New Haven, Yale University Press, 1967, chap. 21; for a comparative analysis of South African regional expansionism, see Hyam, *The Failure of South African Expansion*, chapter 2.

9 Quoted in John Dugard, *The South West Africa/Namibia Dispute*. Berkeley/Los Angeles/London, University of California Press, 1972, p. 98.

10 *Ibid.*, p. 101.

11 *The Times*, 23.9.1943.

12 Smuts to Hofmeyr, 6.5.1945, in W.K. Hancock and J. Van de Poel (eds), *Selection of the Smuts Papers*, Cambridge, Cambridge University Press, vol.7, 1973, p. 534.

13 United Nations Charter, art.1.3.

14 Nicholls in Fourth Committee, 23.1.1946. UN.Doc.A/C.4/49.

15 Quoted in Michael Scott, *A Time to Speak*, London, Faber and Faber, 1958, appendix 5.

16 UN.Doc. A/123(1946); Dugard, *South West Africa/Namibia Dispute*, pp. 104–9.

17 The Herero had been forced to leave Namibia at the beginning of the century after the German general von Trotha had issued an extermination order against them in the wake of their rebellion against German colonial rule in 1904; on the Herero uprising, see Horst Drechsler, *Let Us Die Fighting. The Struggle of the Herero and Nama against German Imperialism (1884–1915)*, London, Zed Press, 1980, chapter 3.

18 Hoveka to Moreni, 17.6.1946, encl. in Moreni to Tshekedi, 19.9.1946. PRO.DO 35/1938; see also petitions of the Herero, Nama and Ovambo to the United Nations in 1947. UN.Doc. A/C.4/96, pp. 12–15; only the Rehoboth people, a small mixed blood community living near the capital Windhoek, favoured incorporation (see Mackenzie (district commissioner) to Government Secretary Mafeking, 20.8.1946. Botswana National Archives/(BNA) BT.Adm. 7/7.

19 Katjerengu to Maherero, 20.2.1946, encl. in Tshekedi to Baring, 24.9.1946. BNA/BT.Adm. 7/7.

20 Mackenzie to Government Secretary, 8.8.1946. BNA/BT.Adm. 7/7.
21 Memorandum Herero and Bapandero, n.d., BNA/BT/Adm. 7/7.
22 As regent of his nephew Seretse Khama who was the first president of Botswana from 1966 to 1980.
23 See Michael Crowder, 'Tshekedi Khama, Smuts and the Incorporation of South West Africa', unpublished paper, n.d., in Botswana National Archives, pp. 3–4.
24 In April 1946, the British government decided to back Pretoria's claim for incorporation.
25 Forsyth Thompson, resident commissioner Bechuanaland, to Tshekedi, 20.2.1946. BNA/BT.Adm.7/7.
26 William M. Hailey. *The Republic of South Africa and the High Commission Territories.* London, Oxford University Press, 1963, p. 86.
27 Memorandum from Bechuanaland chiefs to high commissioner, 29.4.1946, in *The Case for Bechuanaland*, encl. in high commissioner to Addison, 27.6.1946. PRO.DO 35/1936.
28 *Ibid.*
29 'Bechuanaland Chief accuses Smuts of aggression', transcript interview with Tshekedi, n.s., 14.7.1946. BNA/BT.Adm.7/10.
30 Tshekedi to Baring, n.d., BNA/BT.Adm.7/11
31 *Ibid.*
32 Notably article 2.2. which stipulated that 'the mandatory shall promote to the utmost the material and moral well-being and the social progress of the inhabitants of the territory subject to the present mandate' (Mandate Agreement for South West Africa, 17.12,1920, reproduced in Dugard. *South West Africa/Namibia Dispute*, pp. 72–3).
33 Memorandum in *The Case for Bechuanaland*; according to British estimates, approximately 8,500 Herero lived in Bechuanaland; see I. Shapera, 'Historical Notes on the Herero of the Bechuanaland Protectorate', in Shapera to Wimbl (Commonwealth Relations Office), 4.9.1951. PRO.DO 35/3826.
34 Memorandum in *The Case for Bechuanaland*.
35 Speech Tshekedi to Bechuanaland chiefs, n.d., BNA/BT.Adm.7/10; see also conclusion in *The Case for Bechuanaland*.
36 Crowder, 'Tshekedi Khama and the Incorporation of South West Africa', p. 10.
37 Xuma to the United Nations, January 1946, in Thomas Karis, Gwendolen M. Carter. *From Protest to Challenge. A Documentary History of African Politics in South Africa, 1884–1964, vol.2*, Stanford, Hoover Institution Press, 1973, pp. 262–3.
38 Xuma to Tshekedi, 23.5.1946. BNA/BT.Adm.7/8; also appendix in *The Case for Bechuanaland*.
39 See Z.K. Matthews. *Freedom for My People. The Autobiography of Z.K. Matthews. South Africa, 1901–1968.* Cape Town, David Philips, 1981, p. 16.
40 Matthews to Tshekedi, n.d., appendix in *The Case for Bechuanaland*.
41 Bokwe to Tshekedi, 20.5.1946, *ibid.*

42 Jabavu to Tshekedi, 23.5.1946, *ibid.*
43 Manifesto ANC Youth League, 1944, in Nelson Mandela, *The Struggle Is My Life*. London, International Defence and Aid Fund for Southern Africa, 1978, p. 16.
44 *Ibid.*, p. 19.
45 H.J. and R.E. Simons, *Class and Colour in South Africa, 1850–1950*, Harmondsworth, 1969, pp. 473–4.
46 *South African Communists Speak. Documents from the History of the South African Communist Party, 1915–1980*, London, Inkululeko Publications, 1981, p. 192.
47 See Tom Lodge, *Black Politics in South Africa since 1945*, London/ New York, Longman, 1983, p. 29.
48 Kotane to Xuma, 30.1.1946, quoted in Karis and Carter. *From Protest to Challenge*, vol.2, p. 263; on the ANC and Communist Party of South Africa before 1950, see for example Lodge, *op. cit.*, chapter 1.
49 CPSA to United Nations, telegram, 23.10.1946, paraphrased in UN.Doc. A/C.4/37/Add.1, p. 5.
50 Greenidge to Tshekedi, 8.3.1946. BNA/BT.Adm.7/7.
51 Cabinet decision, 13.5.1946, quoted in Crowder, 'Tshekedi Khama, Smuts and the Incorporation of South West Africa', pp. 11–12.
52 Tshekedi to Foster (Anti Slavery Society), 14.6.1946. BNA/ BT.Adm.7/9.
53 Baring to Tshekedi, 3.7.1946. BNA/BT.Adm.7/7.
54 Tshekedi to Foster, 14.6.1946. BNA/BT7/9.
55 Tshekedi to Baring, 30.6.1946. BNA/BT.Adm.7/8.
56 Patrick (Indian Office) to Dixon (Dominions Office), secret, 3.7.1946. PRO.DO 35/1935.
57 Krishnamachari, eight meeting Fourth Committee (Trusteeship Council), 29.1.1946. UN.Doc.A/C.4/18.
58 See United Nations, *Yearbook 1946–1947*. New York, United Nations (Department of Public Information), 1947, pp. 144–8.
59 Tshekedi to South African Press Association, 27.7.1946. BNA/ BT.Adm. 7/10.
60 Buchanan to Frew, n.d., BNA/BT.Adm.7/8.
61 See 'Bechuanaland Chief Accuses Smuts of Aggression', transcript interview, n.s., 14.7.1946. BNA/BT.Adm.7/10; interviews given to *Pretoria News*, *The Star* and *Die Vaderland*; cf. Crowder, 'Tshekedi Khama and Incorporation', p. 17.
62 Tshekedi to Archembault, 28.10.1946. BNA/BT.Adm.7/9.
63 Dominions Office to acting high commissioner to South Africa, telegram, 17.12.1946. PRO.DO 35/1938.
64 Smuts in Fourth Committee, 4.11.1946. UN.Doc.A/C.4/41.
65 Smuts to Hofmeyr, 15.10.1946, in *Selection of Smuts Papers*, vol.7, p. 99.
66 Smuts to Gillet, *ibid.*, p. 101.
67 Buchanan to Tshekedi, 24.10.1946. BNA/BT.Adm.7/9.
68 Tshekedi to Buchanan, 12.11.1946, *ibid.*

69 Tshekedi to Buchanan, 10.11.1946. *ibid.*
70 Buchanan to Tshekedi, 17.12.1946, *ibid.*
71 Minute Tait to Machtig, 24.10.1946. PRO/DO 35/1405.
72 See for example 'Rhodesia-Walvis Bay Enquiry Committee (Bulawayo) to Resident Commissioner Bechuanaland, 30.5.1924. BNA/S.5/6/1; Memorandum Rhodesia-Walvis Bay Enquiry Committee,10.12.1924, in PRO/CO 767/4/6198.
73 See Union of South Africa. *Report of the Commission on the Economic and Financial Relations between the Union of South Africa and the Mandated Territory of South West Africa.* Pretoria, Government Printer, 1935, p. 44.
74 Huggins to Cranborne, 9.4.1945. PRO/DO 35/1403; on this point see also debate Legislative Assembly, Salisbury, 23.10.1946, in PRO/DO 35/1406.
75 Tait to Machtig, 24.10.1946. PRO/DO 35/1405; moreover, the establishment of such a corridor would have to be negotiated directly between Pretoria and Salisbury. It would be easier for the South African government to agree to such a deal if Namibia were annexed as this – contrary to the mandate system – would not require any consent by other countries.
76 See Buchanan to Tshekedi, 12.11.1946. BNA/BT.Adm.7/9.
77 See 'Resolutions of the ANC Annual Conference, 14.–17.12.1946', in Karis and Carter, *From Protest to Challenge*, vol.2, pp. 263–4.
78 Xuma to United Nations, 28.11.1946, UN.Doc.A/C.4/37/Add.2; see also Ruth First, *South West Africa*, Harmondsworth, Penguin, 1963, p. 181.
79 Brick and Quarry Workers' Union, Coloured Garment Workers' Union, Chemical and Allied Workers' Union, African Union of Industrial and Commercial Workers, Explosive and Fertilizers Workers' Union.
80 Paraphrased in UN.Doc.A/C.4/37/Add.1 &Add.2.
81 Olisanwuche Esedebe. *Pan-Africanism. The Idea and Movement. 1776–1963*, Washington, Howard University Press, 1982, p. 176.
82 Immanuel Geiss. *The Pan-African Movement. A History of Pan-Africanism in America, Europe and Africa*, London, Methuen, 1974, p. 28.
83 *Ibid.*, p. 408.
84 Esedebe. *Pan-Africanism*, p. 169.
85 Australia, Brazil, France, Greece, New Zealand, Norway, South Africa, Turkey, United Kingdom.
86 Tshekedi to Buchanan, 12.11.1946. BNA/BT.Adm. 7/9.
87 In order to ascertain the exact influence of Tshekedi Khama and South African opposition groups in the Namibian question as far as the Indian delegation at the United Nations was concerned, it will be necessary to consult the Indian archives.
88 Scott. *A Time to Speak*, p. 219–20.
89 See for example, Michael Scott, *Memorandum on South West Africa*, 30.9.1947. UN.Doc. A/C.4/95 Add.1; and background documents compiled by Scott and transmitted by the Fourth Committee to

the International Court of Justice in December 1949, UN.Doc.A/
C.4/L.66.
90 Hidipo Hamutenya and Gottfried H. Geingob, 'African Nationalism in Namibia', in C. Potholm and R. Dale (eds), *Southern Africa
in Perspective*, New York, The Free Press, 1972, p. 88.

Chapter 2   Regional dynamics of Namibian nationalism

1 Ovamboland People's Organization in 1958, and South West
Africa People's Organization from 1960. According to some
authors, OPC was established in 1958 before being transformed
into OPO in 1959 (see Joachim Puetz, Heidi von Egidy, Perri
Caplan, *Namibia Handbook, and Political Who's Who*, 2nd edition,
Windhoek, Magus, 1990, p. 252).
2 Simons, *Class, and Colour in South Africa*, p. 554.
3 Cf. Richard Moorsom, cf. p. 265 868 *Fishing. Exploiting the Sea*,
London, Catholic Institute for International Relations, 1984, chapter 2.
4 Luederitz had already been a centre for trade union organization
in the twenties because of the Industrial and Commercial
Workers' Union (ICU), and Markus Garvey's Universal Nego
Improvement Association (UNIA) which had made of Luederitz
'the centre of the native political movement' (Union of South
Africa), *Report of the Administrator of South West Africa for the Year
1924*, Pretoria, Government Printer, 1925, p. 27); on the influence
of Garveysm in Namibia, see Gregory Pirio, 'The Role of Garveyism in the Making of Namibian Nationalism', in Brian Wood
(ed.), *Namibia. 1884–1984. Readings in Namibia's History, and Society*,
London/Lusaka, Namibia Support Committee, United Nations
Institute for Namibia, 1988, pp. 259–67.
5 Interview with Ray Alexander, Lusaka, 4.8.1987.
6 Alexander quoted in *Clarion*, 17.7.1952.
7 Interview with Alexander, 4.8.1987.
8 Ruth First. *South West Africa*. Harmondsworth, Penguin, 1963,
p. 97.
9 *Report U.N. Committee on South West Africa for 1954*. UN. Doc. A/
2666, pp. 27–8.
10 *Clarion*, 17.7.1952.
11 Interview with Alexander, 4.8.1987.
12 See Gillian and Suzanne Cronje, *The Workers of Namibia*, London,
International Defence and Aid Fund for Southern Africa, 1979,
p. 71; First, *South West Africa*, p. 197.
13 No secondary school for Africans existed in Namibia; cf. *Guardian*
(Cape Town), 27.3.1952; on Bantu Education as applied to Namibia in the fifties and sixties, see for example Justin Ellis, *Education,
Repression, and Liberation: Namibia*, London, World Universities
Service (UK)/Catholic Institute for International Relations, 1984,
pp. 21–6.

14 Other members of the student body's executive were Mburumba Kerina who left Namibia soon after the formation of the body for the United States where he became the first Namibian to testify at the United Nations in 1957, and Zedekia Ngavirue who became an adviser to SWANU's national executive.

15 Hamutenya and Geingob, 'African Nationalism in Namibia', p. 88.

16 First, *South West Africa*, p. 198.

17 *Ibid.*

18 A previous scholarship to the University had been withdrawn by the South West African authorities after Kozonguizi had got involved in the South West African Student Body.

19 David Soggot, *Namibia. The Violent Heritage*, London, Rex Collings, 1980, p. 26; see also interview with Nujoma in *Namibian*, 18.9.1989.

20 Peter H. Katjavivi, *The Rise of Nationalism in Namibia, and its International Dimensions*, Ph.D. dissertation, Oxford, 1987, p. 92; other founding members of OPC were Peter Mueshihange, Solomon Mifima, Andreas Shipanga, Jackson Kshikuka, Jacob Kuhangua, Maxton Joseph Mutongolume.

21 *Ibid.*

22 Hamutenya and Geingob, 'African Nationalism in Namibia', p. 89.

23 See Peter H. Katjavivi, *A History of Resistance in Namibia*, Paris/London, UNESCO/James Currey, 1988, p. 45; First, *South West Africa*, p. 202, in opposition to SWAPO's official birth date, celebrated on 19 April, most probably in commemoration of OPO's launching inside Namibia in April 1959. However, the editors of the *Nambiba Handbook* adhere to 19 April 1960 as the day on which OPO was renamed, and reconstituted as SWAPO (Puetz, Egedy, Caplan, *Namibia Handbook*, p. 253).

24 Interview with Alexander, 4.8.1987.

25 Quoted in J. H. P. Serfontein. *Namibia?*, London, rex Collings, 1976, p. 159.

26 Interview with Randolph Vigne, London, 27.1.1989. Paid-up members of the Liberal Party included Peter Mueshihange, Solomon Mifima, Peter Kaluma, and Andreas Shipanga who also was close to the Non-European Unity Movement.

27 See for example Helao Shityuwete, *Never Follow the Wolf*, London, Cliptown Books, 1990, pp. 41, and 45.

28 C. J. Driver, *Patrick Duncan. South African, and Pan-African*, London, Heinemann, 1980, p. 189.

29 Interview with Neville Rubin, Geneva, 7.3.1989.

30 Interviews with Rubin, and Norah Chase, Geneva, 7.3.1989.

31 Lodge, *Black Politics in South Africa*, p. 86.

32 In response to popular resistance against the authorities' decision to remove the entire black population of the 'Old Location' in Windhoek to a newly built township, Katatura.

33 Tambo in Fourth Committee, 16.11.1960. UN. Doc. A/C.4/SR.

1053; while Kuhangua was deported to Angola, Sam Nujoma, after a week long imprisonment in the wake of the Windhoek shootings, was banned to Ovamboland. Nujoma did not stand trial, but left Namibia for exile on 1st March 1960. With the help of Chief Hosea Kutako of the Herero Chief's Council, and Herero chiefs in Bechuanaland, Nujoma first went to Tanzania where Julius Nyerere, then a member of the legislative Council of Tanganyika, helped him to obtain a passport. In April 1960, Nujoma met Kozunguizi, and Michael Scott in Khartoum, from where he proceeded to Liberia which was preparing the 'Namibia case' it was to submit, together with Ethiopia, to the International Court of Justice (cf. *infra*, chapter 3). With the help of Kwame Nkrumah, Nujoma was able to travel to New York, where he testified before the United Nations from June to November 1960 (Cf. Puetz, von Egidy, Caplan, *Namibia Handbook*, pp. 272–73).

34 *Ibid*.
35 See *Sechaba*, vol. 2, no. 1, 1968; Mary Benson, *South Africa: The Struggle for a Birthright*, Harmondsworth, Penguin, 1966, p. 223.
36 Other Namibian repreentatives were Kuhangua, the Rev. Kooper, Ismael Fortune.
37 See Tambo in Fourth Committee, 16.11.1960. UN. Doc. A/C. 4/ SR. 1053.
38 William Edgett Smith, *Nyerere of Tanzania*, Harare, Zimbabwe Publishing House, 1981, p. 73.
39 *New Age*, 9.3.1961; South Africa decided to declare a Republic on 31 May 1961 after the majority of its white electorate had agreed to such a move in October 1960.
40 *Sechaba*, vol. 1, no. 1, January 1967, p. 9; in March 1961, Julius Nyerere declared that an independent Tanganyika would not join the Commonwealth if South Africa continued to be a member of the organization (David H. Johns, 'The Foreign Policy of Tanzania', in O. Aluko (ed.), *The Foreign Policies of African States*, London/Sydney/Auckland/Toronto, Hodder, and Stoughton, 1977, p. 204).
41 *New Age*, 19.10.1961.
42 Ngakane to Oliver Tambo, telegram, 17.12.1960, in Karis and Carter, *From Protest to Challenge*, vol. 3, p. 628.
43 Cf. *New Age*, 22.3.1962.
44 On this aspect see for example, Lodge, *Black Politics in South Africa*, chapter 9.
45 *New Age*, 22.3.1962.
46 Karis and Carter, *From Protest to Challenge*, vol. 3, p. 351.
47 First, *South West Africa*, p. 200.
48 See Katjavivi, *History of Resistance*, p. 48.
49 *Ibid*., p. 44.
50 Cf. *supra*, chapter 1.
51 Cf. First, *South West Africa* p. 203.
52 Katjavivi, *History of Resistance*, p. 50.

53 Cf. Hamutenya and Geingob, 'African Nationalism in Namibia', p. 90.
54 Cf. *infra*, chapter 3.
55 Katjavivi, *Nationalism in Namibia*, p. 161; Serfontein. *Namibia?*, p. 146.
56 Cherry Gertzel, 'East, and Central Africa', in Michael Crowder (ed.), *The Cambridge History of Africa*, vol. 8, Cambridge, Cambridge University Press, 1984, p. 452.
57 *Ibid.*, p. 453.
58 Richard Cox, *Pan-Africanism in Practice, PAFMECSA, 1958–1964*, London, Oxford University Press, 1964, p. 45.
59 *Ibid.*, p. 54.
60 John Marcum, *The Angolan Revolution. vol. 1. The Anatomy of an Explosion (1950–1962)*, Cambridge, Mass./London, M.I.T. Press, 1969, p. 311.
61 See Joshua Nkomo, 'Southern Rhodesia: Apartheid Country', in James Duffy and Robert Manners (eds), *Africa Speaks*, Princeton, D. van Norstrand Company, Inc., 1961, p. 143.
62 Kenneth W. Grundy, *Confrontation, and Accommodation in Southern Africa. The Limits of Independence*, Berkeley, University of California Press, 1973, p. 194, n. 5; the annual subscription amounted to 50 pounds per organization, and 1,000 pounds per government (Cox, *PAFMECSA*, p. 55).
63 See John A. Marcum, 'The Exile Condition, and Revolutionary Effectiveness: Southern African Liberation Movements', in Potholm and Dale (eds), *Southern Africa in Perspective*, p. 268.
64 Constitution PAFMECSA, in Cox, *PAFMECSA*, appendix C.
65 For the circumstances leading to the launching of the armed struggle in South Africa, see for example, Stephen M. Davis, *Apartheid's Rebels. Inside South Africa's Hidden War*, New Haven/London, Yale University Press, 1987, pp. 14–16; see also Lodge, *Black Politics in South Africa*, chapter 10.
66 *History of Resistance*, p. 46.
67 First, *South West Africa*, pp. 204–5, who argues that the end of 1963 as date for Namibian independence was possibly influenced by PAC's demand for 'independence' of South Africa by this date.
68 Hamutenya and Geingob, 'African Nationalism in Namibia', p. 91; according to SWAPO's official history, this decision had already been taken in 1961 (see SWAPO, *To Be Born a Nation*, London, Zed Press, 1981, p. 176).
69 Hidipo Hamutenya, 'One Century of Imperialist Occupation, and Anti-Colonial Resistance: An Historical Flashback', in Brian Woods (ed.), *Namibia. 1884–1984. Readings in Namibia's History, and Society*, p. 24.
70 Randolph Vigne to the author, 24.2.1989.
71 Interview with Ngarikutuke Tjiriange, Geneva, 21.2.1988.
72 Katjavivi, *Nationalism in Namibia*, p. 265; on this aspect, see for example, Shityuwete, *Never Follow the Wolf*, pp. 95–100.
73 Driver. *Patrick Duncan*, p. 199.

74 Interview with Lev Rytow, researcher at the Africa Institute, Academy of Sciences, USSR, Moscow, 18.7.1988.
75 On the Sino-Soviet rivalry within AAPSO, see *infra*, chapter 3.
76 See Emmanuel M. Dube, 'Relations between Liberation Movements and the OAU', in N. M. Shamuyarira (ed.), *Esays on the Liberation of Southern Africa*, Dar es Salaam, Tanzania Publishing House, p. 39.
77 According to Ruth First, SWAPO members had bursaries from the American Metal Climax Corporation, a subsidiary of Tsumeb Corporation, First, *South West Africa*, pp. 206–7.
78 Maxton Joseph to Africa Bureau, 20.9.1963. RH/AB. MSS. Afr. s. 1681, Box 218/6.
79 Marcum, 'Exile Condition', p. 265.
80 Davis, *Apartheid's Rebels*, p. 16.
81 Nujoma to United Nations, 19.2.1963, UN. Doc. A/AC. 109/PET. 70 (11.3.1963).
82 Kuhangua to United Nations, 12.5.1963. UN. Doc. A/AC. 109/PET 146 (8.8.1963).
83 Nanyemba to United Nations, 4.2.1963. UN. Doc. A/AC. 109/PET 71 (11.3.1963).
84 Hosea Kutako to United Nations, 22.8.1963. UN. Doc. A/AC. 109/ PET 161 (15.10.1963); see also Shityuwete, *Never Follow the Wolf*, p. 86.
85 Nujoma (from Francistown) to United Nations, 19.3.1964. UN. Doc. A/AC. 109/PET 218 (19.4.1964).
86 Shityuwete, *Never Follow the Wolf*, pp. 87, and 89.
87 Marcum, 'Exile Condition', p. 270.
88 Kozonguizi to Africa Bureau, 29.6.1965. RH/AB. MSS Afr. s. 1681. Box 218/6.
89 Statement South African minister of defense in parliament, 22.9.1958, in *Report U.N. Committee on South West Africa for 1959*. UN. Doc. A/4191, p. 12.
90 See *Report U.N. Committee on South West Africa for 1960*. UN. Doc. A/4464, p. 30.
91 On OAU's initial policy towards South Africa, and southern Africa, see Adekunle Ajala, 'The OAU and Southern Africa', in O. Aluko, and T. Shaw (eds), *Southern Africa in the 1980s*, London, George Allen, and Unwin, 1985, chapter 1; Zdenek Cervenka. *The Unfinished Quest for Unity. Africa, and the OAU*, London, Julius Friedman Publishers, 1977, chapter 8; Dube, 'Relations between Liberation Movements and the OAU'.
92 Deon Geldenhuys, *South Africa's Search for Security since the Second World War*, Bramfontein, South African Institute of International Affairs, (Occasional Papr), 1978, p. 6.
93 Abdul Minty, *South Africa's Defence Strategy*, London, Anti-Apartheid Movement, 1969, p. 26.
94 Geldenhuys, *Search for Security*, p. 7.
95 On South African attempts to incorporate the High Commission territories, see for example Jack Spence, 'South Africa, and the

Modern World', in Leonard Thompson and Monica Wilson (eds), *The Oxford History of South Africa*, vol. 2: South Africa. 1870–1966. Oxford, Oxford University Press, 1978., pp. 496–503; Hyam, *The Failure of South African Expansion*, chapter 8.

96 Deon Geldenhuys and Denis Venter. 'Regional Cooperation in Southern Africa: A Constellation of States?', *South African Institute of International Affairs Bulletin*, vol. 3, no. 3, December 1979, p. 45.

97 *Ibid.*, p. 46.

98 Republic of South Africa, *Report of the Commission of Enquiry into South West Africa Affairs. 1962–1963* (Odendaal Report), Pretoria, Government Printer, 1964.

99 Cf. 'Reginald H. Green and Kimmo Kiljunen, 'Unto What End? The Crisis of Colonialism in Namibia', in Reginald Green, Marja-Liias Kiljunen, Kimmo Kiljunen (eds), *Namibia. The Last Colony*, Burnt Mill, Harlow (Essex), Longman, 1981, pp. 6–7.

100 See André du Pisani, *Namibia. From Incorporation to Controlled Change*, paper presented at the Conference 'Namibia. Africa's Last Colony: Prospects for Freedom, and Development', University of Vermont, Burlington (USA), April 1982, p. 5.

101 *Report Committee on South West Africa* (1960), UN. Doc. A/4464, p. 31.

102 Richard Dale, 'Walvis Bay: A Naval Gateway, an Economic Turn-style, or a Diplomatic Bargaining Chip for the Future of Namibia?', *Journal of the Royal United Services Institute for Defence Studies (RUSI)*, vol. 127, no. 1, March 1982, p. 32.

103 International Defence, and Aid Fund (IDAF), *Apartheid's Army in Namibia. South Africa's Illegal Military Occupation*, London, IDAF, 1982, pp. 7–8.

104 *Report Committee on South West Africa* (1960), UN. Doc. A/4464, p. 31.

105 Trade flows between Angola, and South Africa were otherwise insignificant. Angolan imports from South Africa amounted to 0.30% of total imports in 1930, 2.75% in 1944, and 1.87% in 1963; exports to 0.04%, 4.63%, 0.60%; compiled from Instituto Nacional de Estatistica. *Annuario Estatistico, Portugal, Provincia de Angola* (1934–1972).

106 W. G. Clarence-Smith, *Slaves, Peasants, and Capitalists in Southern Angola*, Cambridge, Cambridge University Press, 1979, p. 10; cf. also Shityuwete, *Never Follow the Wolf*, p. 17; for a personal account of recruitment for contract work in Walvis Bay, see *ibid.*, chapter 2.

107 *Report of the South West Africa Native Labourers Commission, 1945–1948*, in UN. Doc. A/C. 4/L. 66 (29.11.1949), p. 44.

108 Cf. Clarence-Smith, *Slaves, Peasants, and Capitalists*, p. 102.

109 John Kane-Berman, *Contract Labour in South West Africa*, Johannesburg, South African Institute of Race Relations, 1972, p. 5.

110 Richard Moorsom, 'Underdevelopment, Contract Labour, and Worker Consciousness in Namibia. 1915–1972', *Journal of Southern African Studies*, vol. 4, no. 1, October 1977, p. 79.

111 Marcum, *Angolan Revolution*, vol. 1, p. 115.
112 *Ibid.*, p. 278, n. 39.
113 On the origins of FNLA, see *ibid.*, chapter 2.
114 Kuhangua in Special Committee on Decolonization, 3.10.1962, UN. Doc. A/AC. 109/SR.103, pp. 4–5.
115 For a detailed account of the rivalry between UPA, and MPLA, see Marcum, *Angolan Revolution, vol. 1*, chapters 7, and 8; on the relationship between SWAPO, and SWANU, see Katjavivi, *Resistance in Namibia*, chapter 8.
116 James Duffy, *Portugal's African Territories: Present Realities*, New York, Carnegie Endowment for International Peace, 1962, p. 37; Marcum, *Angolan Revolution, vol. 1*, pp. 309–10.
117 *Ibid.*, p. 310.
118 *Ibid.*, p. 221.
119 See John Marcum, *The Angolan Revolution, vol. 2: Exile Politics, and Guerilla Warfare (1962–1976)*, Cambridge, Mass./London, M.I.T. Press, 1978, p. 73; on the role played by the Monrovia, and Casablanca groups in the formation of the OAU, see for example Ian Duffield, 'Pan-Africanism since 1940', in *Cambridge History of Africa*, pp. 109–17.
120 Marcum, *Angolan Revolution, vol. 2*, p. 74.
121 David Martin and Phyllis Johnson, *The Struggle for Zimbabwe. The Chimurenga War*, London/Boston, Faber and Faber, 1982, p. 70; see also Anthony R. Wilkinson, *Insurgency in Rhodesia, 1957–1973: An Account and Assessment*, London, The International Institute for Strategic Studies, 1973 (Adelphi Paper 100), p. 6, and p. 31.
122 Marcum, *Angolan Revolution, vol. 2*, p. 75; T. G. Silundika of ZAPU led a short lived Union of Non-independent African States (UNIAS); cf. Marcum, 'Exile Condition', p. 269.
123 Interview with Tjiriange, 21.2.1988.
124 Marcum, *Angolan Revolution, vol. 2*, p. 117; Patrick Duncan who then was a member of PAC, and Mahomo thought that PAC would be able to move from Angola to Namibia, and the borders of Botswana, see Driver, *Duncan*, p. 236; see also Lodge, *Black Politics in South Africa*, pp. 307–8.
125 Marcum, *Angolan Revolution, vol. 2*, p. 118.
126 See for example Duffield, 'Pan-Africanism since 1940', p. 127.
127 Duffy, 'Portugal's African Territories: Present Realities', p. 21.
128 SWAPO. *To Be Born a Nation*. London, Zed Press, 1981, p. 176.
129 Shityuwete, *Never Follow the Wolf*, p. 61.
130 Marcum, *Angolan Revolution, vol. 1*, p. 115, and p. 278, n. 39.
131 See *Report U.N. Committee on South West Africa for 1960*, UN. Doc. A/4464, p. 30.
132 Nujoma in Fourth Committee, 6.11.1962. UN. Doc. A/C. 4/SR. 1374.
133 In early 1961, the Portuguese army in Angola was estimated to comprise approximately eight thousand men, two to three thousand Europeans, and five thousand Africans (Gerald J. Bender, 'The Limits of Counterinsurgency: An African Case', *Comparative*

Politics, vol. 4, no. 3, April 1972, p. 332, n. 6); for a more conservative estimate, see Wilkinson, *Insurgency in Rhodesia*, p. 33.

134 Grundy. *Confrontation and Accommodation*, p. 223; Scott in Fourth Committee, 6.11.1962. UN. Doc. A/C. 4/SR. 1374.

135 Kuhangua in Fourth Committee, 23.10.1963. UN. Doc. A/C. 4/SR. 1456.

136 Interview with Melo Antunes, Paris, 11.5.1989; see also 'Declaration on Overseas Policy', by Antonio Salazar, 12.8.1963, reproduced in Marcum, *Angolan Revolution, vol. 2*, pp. 284–97; on Portugal's Africa policy, see also John Marcum, 'Angola: Perilous Transition to Independence', in Gwendolen M. Carter and Patrick O'Meara (eds), *Southern Africa. The Continuing Crisis*, Bloomington, Indiana University Press, 1982, pp. 187–90.

137 On Pretoria's anti-communism from a South African point of view, see Geldenhuys, *Search for Security*.

138 Quoted in 'International relations of Portugal affecting the territories under its administration', UN. Doc. A/AC. 190/L. 625, 1970, p. 56, para. 189.

139 Basil Davidson, *South Africa and Portugal*, United Nations, Unit on Apartheid (Notes and Documents no. 7/74), 1974, p. 8; see also Wilkinson, *Insurgency in Rhodesia*, p. 39.

140 Vasco Vieira Garin to Special Committee on Decolonization, 31.3.63. UN. Doc. A/AC. 109/36, p. 6.

141 Quoted in Grundy, *Confrontation, and Accommodation*, p. 222.

142 Interview with Antunes, 11.5.1989.

Chapter 3 Cooperation between liberation movements and between colonizers

1 Mainly in response to a decision by the International Court of Justice on the same day to reject an application by Ethiopia, and Liberia in 1960 asking the Court to condemn South African rule in Namibia (for a legal analysis of the Court's judgement, see Dugard; *South West Africa/Namibia Dispute*, pp. 292–375).

2 The first guerrilas of PLAN were reported to have crossed from southern Angola into Namibia in September 1965 where they dispensed basic military training to some Namibians (Willem Steenkamp, *South Africa's Border War, 1966–1989*, Gibralter, Ashanti, 1989, p. 21); and the first skirmish with exchange of fire between SWAPO guerilas and the South African police took place in March 1966 (Shityuwete, *Never Follow the Wolf*, p. 125).

3 Hamutenya and Geingob, 'African Nationalism in Namibia', p. 91.

4 John ya-Otto, *Battlefront Namibia. An Autobiography*, Harare, Zimbabwe Publishing House, 1982, p. 79.

5 Cf. Sogott, *Violent Heritage*, p. 30.

6 SWAPO, *To be Born a Nation*, p. 177.

7 See Katjavivi, *History of Resistance*, p. 61; for a personal account, see ya-Otto, *Battlefront Namibia*, pp. 78–86.

8 On the trial and the conditions of detention in Pretoria, see *ibid.*, chapters 6 to 8.

9 Interview Rytow, 18.7.1988.

10 On the financial constraints on the Liberation Committee, see for example Cervenka, *Unfinished Quest for Unity*, pp. 59–61.

11 See Zaki Laidi, *Les contraintes d'une rivalité. Les superpuissances et l'Afrique*, Paris, La Découverte, 1986, p. 52.

12 Quoted in David Kimche, *The Afro-Asian Movement. Ideology and Foreign Policy of the Third World*, Jerusalem, Israel Universities Press, 1973, p. 165.

13 See Charles Neuhauser, *Third World Politics. China and the Afro-Asian Peoples Solidarity Organization. 1957–1967*, Cambridge, Mass., Harvard University Press, 1968; and 'Open Letter [by the Soviet Union] to Fraternal Communist Parties', 14.7.1963, quoted in *ibid.*, p. 45.

14 In August 1963, the OAU council of foreign ministers proposed to the OAU member states to sign the treaty; see Laidi, *Contraintes d'une rivalité*, p. 55.

15 Kimche, *Afro-Asian Movement*, p. 182.

16 With the exception in Africa notably of Tanzania and Zambia, where China started building the Tan-Zam railroad after an agreement between the three countries had been signed in Peking in September 1967; on Sino-African relations during the Cultural Revolution, see Alaba Ogunsanwo, *China's Foreign Policy in Africa, 1958–1971*, Cambridge, Cambridge University Press, 1974, chapter 5.

17 Article three in *Resolutions on Organizational Questions*, Council Meeting of the Afro-Asian peoples Solidarity Organization, Nicosia, Cyprus, 13 to 17 February 1967; in Deutsches Institut für Zeitgeschichte, *Die afro-asiatische Solidaritätsbewegung*, Berlin (GDR), Staatsverlag der Deutschen Demokratischen Republik, 1968, p. 167.

18 Statement Chinese Afro-Asian Solidarity Committee, 17.3.1967, quoted in Ogunsanwo, *China's Policy in Africa*, p. 231.

19 China did not attempt to set up a rival AAPSO but limited her activities to rival national Afro-Asian solidarity committees.

20 Deutsches Institut für Zeitgeschichte, *Die afro-asiatische Solidaritätsbewegung*, p. 169; the Council also admitted the *Comite de Libertação de São Tome et Principe* (CLSTP).

21 On the controversy over Kozonguizi's Peking speech, see First, *South West Africa*, pp. 206–7, and for a critique of First's assessment, Hamutenya and Geingob, 'African Nationalism in Namibia', pp. 90–1.

22 The conference enlarged the Afro-Asian movement by including Latin America, and establishing a second solidarity movement, the Afro-Asian, and Latin American People's Solidarity Organiz-

ation (OSPAAL) in which Fidel Castro of Cuba played a leading role.

23 Quoted in Richard Gibson, *African Liberation Movements. Contemporary Struggles against White Minority Rule*, London, Oxford University Press, 1972, p. 126.

24 See Kimche, *Afro-Asian Movement*, p. 204.

25 Gibson, *African Liberation Movements*, pp. 128–9; for the resolution on SWANU's expulsion from, and SWAPO's admission to AAPSO, see 'Ratstagung der Organisation für Afro-Asiatische Völkersolidaritäet in Nikosia (Zypern) vom 13. bis 17. Februar 1967: Entschliessungen zu organisatorischen Fragen' (no. 8), in Deutsches Institut für Zeitgeschichte, *Die Afro-asiatische Solidaritätsbewegung* p. 169.

26 See for example joint statement at the fifth OAU summit, Algiers in 1968. Cf. *Sechaba*, vol. 2, no. 12, 1968, pp. 1–3; AAPSO solidarity conference in the German Democratic Republic, May 1968, in *ibid.*, vol. 2, 8, 1968, pp. 12–13.

27 Resolution Khartoum Conference, in *Namibia News*, vol. 2, nos. 4–6, 1969, p. 6.

28 Interview with Brigadier Hashim Mbita, Dar es Salaam, 23.3.1988. However, many nationalist leaders considered aid from the Liberation Committee as being ineffectual (cf. Russell Warren Howe, 'War in Southern Africa', *Foreign Affairs*, vol. 48, no. 1, October 1969, p. 159).

29 Hsinhua News Agency. *Daily Bulletin*, no. 4008, 23.1.1969, quoted in Marcum, 'Exile Condition', p. 383, n. 48; on Chinese assistance to southern African nationalist movements, see also Wilkinson, *Insurgency in Rhodesia*, p. 26.

30 Cf. Marcum, *Angolan Revolution*, vol. 2, pp. 224–5; also Shamuyarira (ZANU) to Roberto, 9.6.1970, in pamphlet GRAE (Dept. of foreign affairs), 1970.

31 Message Oliver Tambo to AAPSO, January 1971, reproduced in Adelaide Tambo (ed.), *Preparing for Power. Oliver Tambo Speaks*, London, Heinemann, 1987, p. 90.

32 Cf. Marcum, *Angolan Revolution*, vol. 1, p. 28; p. 130, n. 200.

33 From January to October 1974, the Soviet Union had again suspended its aid to MPLA because of internal divisions within the movement (see Laidi, *Contraintes d'une rivalité*, pp. 103–4).

34 On the relationship between ANC and the Communist Party of South Africa, see for example, Rob Davies, Dan O'Meara, Sipho Dlamini, *The Struggle for South Africa. A Reference Guide to Movements, Organizations and Institutions*, London, Zed Press, 1984 (vol. 2), pp. 292–4; Lodge, *Black Politics in South Africa, passim.*

35 Davis, *Apartheid's Rebels*, p. 16; on SACP's relationship with the Soviet Union at the end of the 1960's as reflected for example in its approval of the Soviet invasion of Czechoslovakia in 1968, see statements Central Committee SACP, 29.7. and 23.8.1968, in *South African Communists Speak*, pp. 364–6.

36 Marcum, *Angolan Revolution*, vol. 2, p. 74.

37 See Robert Davezies, *Les Angolais*, Paris, Les Editions de Minuit, 1965, p. 258.
38 James Mayall, 'The Soviet Union, Zimbabwe, and South Africa', in Olajide Aluko and Timothy Shaw (eds), *Southern Africa in the 1980s*, London/Boston/Sydney, George Allen & Unwin, 1985, p. 96.
39 See Joint Press release ZAPU-ANC, Lusaka, 19.8.1967; in UN. Doc. A/AC. 109/PET. 904 (27.12.1967); on the ANC-ZAPU alliance in the context of the armed struggle in South Africa, see Joe Slovo, 'The Armed Struggle Spreads', in *Guerilla Warfare*, London, ANC Publicity and Information Bureau, 1970, pp. 33–6; see also Wilkinson, *Insurgency in Rhodesia*, p. 10; Martin and Johnson, *Struggle for Zimbabwe*, p. 10.
40 According to Gibson, an allusion to armed struggle by Kozunguizi in his speech during the AAPSO conference in Havana in 1966 was disapproved by the majority of SWANU's External Council; cf. Gibson, *African Liberation Movements*, p. 127.
41 Katjavivi, *History of Resistance*, pp. 52–3.
42 Puetz, Egedy, Caplan, *Namibia Handbook*, p. 273.
43 Interview with Tjiriange, 21.2.1988.
44 *Ibid.*
45 Personal recollection, Randolph Vigne; Vigne to the author, 24.2.1989.
46 Lodge, *Black Politics in South Africa*, p. 314.
47 Savimbi accused Roberto of being a United States creation, protected by the pro-American Congolese government of Adoula, and accepting American aid; see Basil Davidson, *In the Eye of the Storm. Angola's People*, Harmondsworth, Penguin, 1975, p. 229; on the relationship between Savimbi and Roberto, see also Keith Sommerville, *Angola, Politics, Economics and Society*, London, Frances Pinter, 1986, pp. 35–36; Fred Bridgland, *Jonas Savimbi: A Key to Africa*, London, Hodder & Stoughton, 1988, pp. 73–74; 78–9.
48 Interview with Savimbi by two French journalists: Yves Loiseau and Pierre-Guillaume de Roux, *Portrait d'un révolutionnaire en général. Jonas Savimbi*, Paris, La Table Ronde, 1987, p. 135.
49 Bridgland, *Savimbi*, p. 83.
50 *Ibid.*, pp. 87–8.
51 Discussion with SWAPO activist, Windhoek, 16.2.1991.
52 Dube, 'Relations between Liberation Movements', p. 51.
53 Cf. Katjavivi, *History of Resistance*, p. 86; interview with SWAPO activist, London, 24.1.1989.
54 Bridgland, *Savimbi*, p. 291.
55 Katjavivi, *History of Resistance*, p. 50.
56 Cf. *Africa Confidential*, 23.9.1966; on the recent debate on ethnicity in southern Africa, see for example Leroy Vail (ed.), *The Creation of Tribalism in Africa*, London/Berkeley/Los Angeles, James Currey/ University of California Press, 1989.
57 When in Dar es Salaam, Savimbi used SWAPO's post office box

213

as his mailing address and in 1967 Savimbi managed to re-enter Angola from Zambia from where he had been expelled because UNITA units had derailed trains of the Benguela railway line, with help from SWAPO; cf. Marcum, *Angolan Revolution*, vol. 2, p. 193 and p. 397, n. 88.

58 Katjavivi, *Nationalism in Namibia*, p. 268.

59 Loiseau and de Roux, *Savimbi*, p. 219.

60 Michael Wolfers and Jane Bergerol, *Angola in the Front Line*, London, Zed Books, 1983, p. 11.

61 Interview with SWAPO activist, London, 24.1.1989.

62 Interview with John ya-Otto, Geneva, 21.6.1987.

63 Interview Tjiriange, 21.2.1988.

64 Katjavivi, *Nationalism in Namibia*, p. 269.

65 Interview with Daniel Chipenda by Liberation Support Movement (Canada), 28.8.1969, Richmond (B.C.). LSM Information Centre, 1970, p. 22.

66 On the Tanga Consultative Congress which introduced the first major organizational changes to SWAPO since its formation in 1960, see Katjavivi, *History of Resistance*, p. 104; SWAPO, *To Be Born a Nation*, p. 179.

67 Axel Harneit-Sievers. *SWAPO of Namibia. Entwicklung, Programmatik und Politik seit 1959*. Hamburg, Institut für Afrikakunde, 1985, p. 51.

68 *Financial Times*, 27.5.1975.

69 Interview with Tjiriange, 21.2.1988.

70 'Note to the Zambian Government Regarding the Counterrevolutionary Currents within the Movement', Lusaka, 3.6.1973, reproduced in Marcum, *Angolan Revolution*, vol. 2, p. 203.

71 Cf. response given by Savimbi to a question by the author on the relationship between UNITA amd SWAPO at a public meeting in Geneva on 2.5.1991.

72 See interview Antunes, 11.5.1989; for the correspondence between Savimbi and the Portuguese authorities in 1972, see 'La longue trahison de l'UNITA', *Afrique-Asie*, 8.7.1974; see also William Minter, *Operatin Timber. Pages from the Savimbi Dossier*, Trenton, N.J., Africa World Press, 1988.

73 Marcum, *Angolan Revolution*, vol. 2, p. 271; see *infra*, chapter 4.

74 Interview with Antunes, 11.5.1989.

75 Don Barnett, R. Harvey, *The Revolution in Angola. MPLA Life Stories and Documents*, Indianapolis, New York, Bobbs-Merril Company, 1972, p. 113.

76 *Rhodesia Herald*, 30.9.1966.

77 Deon Geldenhuys. *The Diplomacy of Isolation. South African Foreign Policy Making*. New York, St-Martin's Press, 1984, p. 75.

78 *AfricAsia*, 12–25.4.1971.

79 *Zambia Daily Mail*, 7.8.1971.

80 *Daily News* (Tanz.), 8.6.1972; *Zambia Daily Mail*, 19.5.1972; UN. Doc. A/9023, Rev. 1, p. 202.

81 *25 Setembro* (Information Bulletin, FRELIMO, Political Commissariat), vol. 6, no. 6, 15.7.1971,p. 14.
82 Nujoma in Committee 24, 23.5.1966, UN. Doc. A/AC. 109/SR. 417, p. 5.
83 Press conference Kaunda, 3.6.1965, quoted in Ronald Segall and Ruth First (eds), *South West Africa. Travesty of Trust*, London, André Deutsch, 1967, p. 225.
84 *Zambia Daily Mail*, 13.8.1971.
85 *The Times*, 6./8.10.1971; the South African press qualified the Caprivi strip as South Africa's 'frontline' with black Africa (*Star Weekly*, 19.5.1971).
86 Vorster to Congress Nationalist Party, October 1971, quoted in *Times*, 6.10.1971.
87 Douglas Anglin and Timothy Shaw (eds), *Zambia's Foreign Policy. Studies in Diplomacy and Dependence*, Boulder, Col., Westview Press, 1979, p. 12; on the roots of the secessionist movement in western Zambia, see for example Gerald Caplan 'Barotseland: the secessionist challenge to Zambia', *Journal of Modern African Studies*, vol. 6, no. 3, 1968, pp. 343–60; see also below, chapter 5.
88 In 1961, 1.25% of Angola's total imports were from South Africa, while it sent 0.22% of its total exports to South Africa, (percentage of total value); see *Annuario estatistico*, Portugal, Provincia de Angola, 1962.
89 See Basil Davidson, 'Portuguese Speaking Africa', in *Cambridge History of Africa*, p. 774; Jane Cotter, 'West European Economic Interests in Angola', World Council of Churches, *Program to Combat Racism: Cunene Dam Symposium*, Arnoldshain, 29.–3.3.1972, pp. 14–15.
90 Mario de Andrade and Marc Ollivier, *The War in Angola. A Socio-Economic Study*, Dar es Salaam, Tanzania Publishing House, 1975, p. 73; on western interests in Angola, see for example, Cotter, 'European Economic Interests', pp. 29–32.
91 *Financial Times*, 8.8.1972; *Jeune Afrique* (Tunisia), 16.9.1972; South African capital notably participated in a cardboard packing plant and in the acquisition of Angola's largest coffee export firm. And a consortium of South African companies participated with the Angolan petroleum company ANGOL and TEXACO in operating a concession; cf. Report London Support Committee, *International Conference in Support of the Peoples of Portuguese Colonies*, Rome, 27.–29.6.1970, p. 18.
92 *Star*, 27.5.1972.
93 *Financial Times*, 8.8.1972.
94 In 1964, 2.13%/0.60% of Angola's total imports/exports as compared to 4.58%/1.10% in 1972. The corresponding figures were 36.9%/35.2% for metropolitan Portugal, 10.4%/11.2% for West Germany and 10.5%/10.9% for the United States; see Banco de Angola, *Economic and Financial Survey*, Luanda, 1970, p. 108.
95 Marcum, *Angolan Revolution*, vol. 1, p. 278.
96 De Andrade and Ollivier, *War in Angola*, p. 85; other joint infra-

structure projects were a Cape to Lisbon telephone cable inaugurated in 1969, and regular flights from Luanda to Windhoek.

97 Associacão das Empresas do Ultramar, *The Cunene Development Plan*, Lisbon, Overseas Companies of Portugal, 1973 (?), p. 1.

98 *Odendaal Report*, paras 1466 and 1473.

99 On the history of the Cunene dam project, see World Council of Churches (WCC), *The Cunene Dam scheme and the Struggle for the Liberation of Southern Africa*, Geneva, World Council of Churches, 1971, pp. 3–5; Eduardo de Sousa Ferreira, *Portuguese Colonialism from South Africa to Europe*, Freiburg i.B., Aktion Dritte Welt, 1972, pp. 106–10.

100 Twice the cost of the Cabora Bassa scheme in Mozambique for one tenth of its output (see World Council of Churches, *Cunene Dam scheme*, p. 28 and *African Development*, 19.7.1972).

101 World Coucil of Churches, *Cunene Dam Scheme*, p. 30.

102 On white settlement in Angola, see Gerald Bender, *Angola under the Portuguese: The Myth and the Reality*, London, Heinemann, 1978, chapters 3 and 4.

103 De Andrade and Ollivier, *War in Angola*, p. 81.

104 On the economic implications of the Cunene and Cabora Bassa schemes for Portugal, see Eduardo de Sousa Ferreira, 'Cunene and Carbora Bassa – Signs of the New Portugese Land Settlement Policy', World Council of Churches, Unit 2, *Program to Combat Racism: Cunene Dam Symposium*. Arnoldshain, 29.2.–3.3.1972, doc. no. 2, p. 5.

105 'Angola: un barrage contre les hommes', *Afrique-Asie*, 1.11.1971.

106 On the resettlement programme, and its impact on southern Angola, see Bender, *Angola under the Portuguese*, chapter 6; and Bender, 'Limits of Counterinsurgency', pp. 350–2; see also Wilkinson, *Insurgency in Rhodesia*, p. 37.

107 Statement UNITA in World Council of Churches, *Cunene Dam Scheme*, appendix 3, pp. 44–5.

108 Statement SWAPO, 29.1.1971, *ibid.*, appendix 1.

109 Nujoma in UN Fourth Committee, 26.10.1970, UN. Doc. A/C. 4/SR. 1987.

110 Interview with Paulo Jorge by Don Barnett, December 1972, in Liberation Support Movement (Canada), *Interviews in Depth: MPLA/Angola*, no. 4. Paulo Jorge, Richmond, B.C., LSM Information Centre, 1973, p. 28; see also statement MPLA in World Council of Churches, *Cunene Dam Scheme*, appendix 2; interview Agostinho Neto by FRELIMO, in *Mozambique Revolution*, no. 49, Oct.-Dec. 1971, p. 8.

111 On the origins of the strike, see for example Moorsom, 'Underdevelopment, Contract Labour and Worker Consciousness', pp. 81–83; Rauha Voipio, 'Contract Work through Ovambo Eyes', in *Namibia. The Last Colony*, chapter 6.

112 Contract workers were distributed as follows: 14,000 in government, commerce, and industry; 12,800 in mining; 10,900 in farm-

ing; 3,000 in fishing; 2,700 in domestic service: cf. Kane-Berman, *Contract Labour*, p. 5.

113 Moorsom, 'Underdevelopment, Contract Labour and Worker Consciousness', p. 85.

114 Ya-Otto, *Battlefront Namibia*, p. 143; also interview with ya-Otto, 21.6.1987.

115 Cf. SWAPO, *To Be Born a Nation*, pp. 199 and 202.

116 Liberation Support Movement, *Interviews in Depth: Paulo Jorge*, p. 10; see also MPLA, 'War Communiqué', 17.2.1972, in *Angola in Arms* (information organ MPLA), Jan./Feb./March 1972, p. 9; *Angola in Arms*, June/July 1972, pp. 13–14.

117 See Clarence-Smith, *Slaves, Peasants and Capitalists*, pp. 77–81; W. G. Clarence-Smith and R. Moorsom, 'Underdevelopment and Class Formation in Ovamboland, 1845–1915', *Journal of African History*, vol. 16, no. 3, 1975, p. 380; Moorsom, 'Underdevelopment, Contract Labour and Worker Consciousness', p. 85.

118 *Ibid.*, p. 85, n. 21.

119 On the revised contract system, see Kane-Berman, *Contract Labour*, pp. 5–11.

120 International Defence and Aid Fund, *Apartheid's Army in Namibia*, p. 9; officially, the SADF assumed responsibility for counter-insurgency operations in northern Namibia in April 1974 (Steenkamp, *Border War*, p. 26).

121 Kane-Berman, *Contract Labour*, p. 33.

122 *Guardian*, 24.1.1972.

123 *Times of Zambia*, 2.3.1972.

124 See *Jeune Afrique* (Tunisia), 15.4.1972.

125 *Financial Times*, 8.2.1972.

126 Liberation Support Movement, *Interviews in Depth: Paulo Jorge*, p. 10.

127 Cf. 'War Communique MPLA', 17.2.1972, p. 9; *Jeune Afrique*, (Tunisia), 15.4.1972.

128 Moorsom, 'Underdevelopment, Contract Labour and Worker Consciousness', p. 85.

129 Ya-Otto, *Battlefront Namibia*, p. 144.

130 Hamutenya and Geingob, 'Nationalism in Namibia', p. 89.

131 Kimmo Kiljunen, 'The Ideology of National Liberation', in Green and Kiljunen, *Namibia. The Last Colony*, p. 190.

132 Katjavivi, *History of Resistance*, p. 70.

133 Moorsom, 'Underdevelopment, Contract Labour and Worker Consciousness', pp. 81–2.

134 Statement Daniel Chipenda, 16.2.1972, quoted in *Standard* (Tanzania), 17.2.1972.

135 MPLA, 'War Communiqué' p. 9.

136 Liberation Support Movement, *Interviews in Depth: Paulo Jorge*, p. 10. According to Bender, MPLA had been active in the region since 1968; see Bender, 'Limits of Counterinsurgency', p. 352; in 1975, military activities of MPLA in southern Angola were still very limited and of mainly symbolic nature (Franz-Wilhelm

Heimer. *Der Entkolonisierungskonflikt in Angola.* Munich/London, Weltforum Verlag, 1979, p. 186).
137 Wolfers and Bergerol, *Angola in the Front Line*, p. 11; see *infra*, chapter 4.

Chapter 4 Namibia – Angola, shifting alliances

1 Cf. Kenneth Maxwell, 'Portugal and Africa: The Last Empire', in Prosser Gifford and Wm. Roger Louis (eds), *The Transfer of Power in Africa*, New Haven/London, Yale University Press, 1982, pp. 337–85; Maxwell, 'The Thorns of the Portuguese Revolution', *Foreign Affairs*, vol. 54, no. 2, 1976, pp. 250–70.
2 See for example Patrick O'Meara, 'Zimbabwe: The Politics of Independence', in Gwendolen M. Carter and Patrick O'Meara (eds), *Southern Africa. The Continuing Crisis*, Bloomington, Indiana University Press, 1982, pp. 32–3.
3 Robert Davies and Dan O'Meara, 'The Total Strategy in Southern Africa. An Analysis of South African Regional Policy since 1978', *Journal of Southern African Studies*, vol. 11, no. 2, 1985, p. 187; see also UN Special Committee Against Apartheid, 'Recent Developments in the Build-Up of South African Military Forces', *Notes and Documents* (Unit on Apartheid), no. 31/75, September 1975.
4 See Geldenhuys and Venter, 'Constellation of States', p. 49.
5 Quoted in Colin Legum, *Southern Africa. The Secret Diplomacy of Détente – South Africa at the Cross Roads*, London, Rex Collings, 1975, p. 8.
6 Robert Jaster, *South Africa in Namibia. The Botha Strategy*, Lanham/New York/London, University Press for America, 1985, p. 7.
7 On the origins of Zambia's attempts of rapprochement with South Africa, see Anglin and Shaw, *Zambia's Foreign Policy*, chapter 7.
8 Martin and Johnson, *Struggle for Zimbabwe*, pp. 127–8; de Villiers, a South African living in London who had been contacted by Rowland, informed Vorster about the contacts between Kaunda and Portuguese officers who were negotiating a hand-over of power.
9 *Ibid.*, p. 140.
10 For the following, see Martin and Johnson, *Struggle for Zimbabwe*, pp. 141–2, who are in the possession of the document.
11 *Ibid.*, p. 144.
12 Carol B. Thompson *Challenge to Imperialism. The Frontline States in the Liberation of Zimbabwe.* Harare, Zimbabwe Publishing House, 1985, p. 14.
13 Elizabeth Landis and Michael I. Davis, 'Namibia: Impending Independence?', in Carter and O'Meara (eds), *Southern Africa, Continuing Crisis*, p. 118.
14 SC Resolution 366 (17.12.1974).
15 Geldenhuys, 'Search for Security', p. 9.
16 Quoted by Katjavivi, *Resistance*, p. 95.

17 SWAPO, *Born A Nation*, p. 218.
18 Katjavivi, *Resistance*, p. 82.
19 The relative high turnout of 70% of voters for the elections of the Ovamboland assembly in January 1975 has been ascribed to large-scale intimidation by SADF (*ibid*. p. 76).
20 International Defence and Aid Fund, *Apartheid's Army in Namibia*, p. 11 and note 23.
21 Within five months, 2,500 Namibians left for Angola and Zambia from June 1974 (see Katjavivi, *Resistance*, pp. 82–3; *The Rise of Nationalism in Namibia*, p. 231; for a personal account of the exodus, see Ya-Otto, *Battlefront Namibia*, chapter 9).
22 International Defence and Aid Fund, *Apartheid's Army in Namibia*, p. 30.
23 Regional ethnic administrations had been established in Ovamboland in 1968, in Okavango in 1970 and in Eastern Caprivi in 1973.
24 Statement de Wet, despatch *Agence France Press*, 28.1.1975.
25 *Africa Confidential*, 5.3.1976; see also Robin Hallett, 'The South African Intervention in Angola. 1975–6', *African Affairs*, vol. 77, no. 308, 1978, p. 359.
26 *Ibid.*, p. 351.
27 *Observer*, 8.2.1976.
28 Quoted in *Star Weekly* (S.A.), 19.7.1975.
29 As a result of the Alvor Agreement between Portugal, MPLA, FLNA, and UNITA.
30 *Star Weekly*, 19.4.1975.
31 Interview with John Ya-Otto, 21.6.1987.
32 The idea lingered and still seemed to be alive among Pretoria's strategists in the early 1980s (*Economist*, 16.7.1983, p. 17). In 1982, there was talk of creating a state of Ovimbundu called after the ethnic group to which Savimbi belonged and which would also comprise northern Namibia (Colin Legum, 'The Southern African Crisis. The Making of a Second Middle East', *Africa Contemporary Record (1982–1983)*, New York/London, Africana Publishers, A.12).
33 Geldenhuys, *Isolation*, p. 78.
34 Hallett, 'Intervention', p. 352.
35 Steenkamp, *Border War*, p. 44.
36 Geldenhuys, *Isolation*, p. 78.
37 Marcum, *Angolan Revolution*, vol. 2, p. 248.
38 *Times of Zambia*, 5.2.1975.
39 Hallett, 'Intervention', p. 358.
40 Marcum, *Angolan Revolution*, vol. 2, p. 440, n. 220.
41 *Star Weekly*, 3.5.1975.
42 Hallett, 'Intervention', pp. 354–5; Marcum, *Angolan Revolution*, vol. 2, p. 268.
43 *Ibid.*, p. 441, n. 225.
44 Legum, Colin, 'Foreign Intervention in Angola', *Africa Contemporary Record*, vol. 8, 1975–6, London, Rex Collings, 1976, A 8; see also *Star Weekly*, 13.12.1975.
45 Marcum, *Angolan Revolution*, vol. 2, p. 441, n. 225.

46 Cf. Steenkamp, *Border War*, p. 43.
47 Heimer, *Entkolonisierungskonflikt*, p. 188; on the escalation of the conflict between MPLA and FLNA in 1975, see also Franz-Wilhelm Heimer, *The Decolonization Conflict in Angola. 1974–76. An Essay in Political Sociology*. Geneva, Graduate Institute of International Studies, 1979, pp. 65–71.
48 *Ibid.*, p. 69.
49 Hallett, 'Intervention', p. 357.
50 Heimer, *Decolonization*, p. 74.
51 Loiseau, and de Roux, *Savimbi*, p. 218; he did of course not anticipate the dramatic increase in Cuban and Soviet assistance to MPLA from November 1975.
52 Maxwell, 'Portugal and Africa', p. 374.
53 *Ibid.*, pp. 374–5.
54 John A. Marcum, 'Lessons of Angola', *Foreign Affairs*, vol. 54, no. 3, 1976, p. 416.
55 Maxwell, 'Portugal and Africa', pp. 374, and 375.
56 Marcum, 'Lessons of Angola', p. 414; in January 1975, the Committee did not extend its help to UNITA.
57 See for example Laidi, *Contraintes d'une rivalité*, pp. 112–13.
58 Minter, *Operation Timber*, p. 24.
59 Cf. Nathaniel Davis, 'The Angola Decision of 1975: A Personal Memoir', *Foreign Affairs*, vol. 57, no. 1, 1978, pp. 109–24.
60 Marcum, 'Lessons of Angola', p. 416.
61 On the CIA involvement, see John Stockwell, *In Search of Enemies: A CIA Story*. New York, André Deutsch, 1978, p. 187; for an assessment of American policy in Angola in 1975, see for example Marcum, 'Lessons of Angola', pp. 407–25.
62 The House of Representatives followed the Senate in refusing further covert aid to Angola by 323 to 99 votes (Tunney Amendment) in January 1976 (see Marcum, 'Lessons of Angola', p. 419).
63 Heimer, *Decolonization*, p. 74.
64 Marcum, *Angolan Revolution*, vol. 2, p. 269.
65 Wolfers and Bergerol, *Angola*, p. 15.
66 Steenkamp, *Border War*, p. 44.
67 Marcum, *Angolan Revolution*, vol. 2, p. 271; *Washington Post*, 26.11.1976.
68 Heimer, *Entkolonisierungskonflikt*, p. 200.
69 Geldenhuys, *Isolation*, p. 79.
70 Holden Roberto was a relative of the Zairean president Mobutu who had committed a substantial number of Zairean troops to assist FNLA in their offensive against MPLA in the north of Angola. President Kaunda's policy was ambivalent. On one hand, he supposedly opposed foreign interference in Angola (see 'Zambia's Basic Principles in Angola', in Legum, 'Foreign Intervention', A27–28). On the other hand, he was keen to prevent MPLA from coming to power (cf. Hallett, 'Intervention', p. 355). Furthermore, UNITA controlled large parts of the Benguela railway which was vital for the export of Zambian, and Zairean copper to the sea.

71 Geldenhuys, *Isolation*, p. 79.
72 Cf. Steenkamp, *Border War*, p. 43.
73 Wolfers, and Bergerol, *Angola*, p. 12; Robert Scott Jaster, *The Defence of White Power. South African Foreign Policy under Pressure*, Basingstoke, Macmillan (with International Institute for Strategic Studies), 1988, p. 70.
74 *Financial Times*, 23.8.1975; Steenkamp, *Border War*, p. 39; while the official figure given was 30 men, some argue that the force consisted of 'over 1,000 regular soldiers, armoured cars, and helicopters (Wolfers, and Bergerol, *Angola*, p. 12).
75 For a detailed account of the South African attack, see *ibid.*, pp. 13–14.
76 Geldenhuys, *Isolation*, p. 79.
77 *Ibid.*, p. 80.
78 Hallett, 'Intervention', p. 369; Steenkamp, *Border War*, p. 41.
79 Stockwell, *In Search of Enemies*, p. 187.
80 Steenkamp, *Border War*, p. 47.
81 Geldenhuys, *Isolation*, p. 78.
82 Heimer, *Decolonization*, p. 78; MPLA estimates at the time put the figure at between 1,000 and 6,500 troops.
83 Steenkamp, *Border War*, p. 49.
84 Loiseau and de Roux, *Savimbi*, pp. 217–18.
85 Steenkamp, *Border War*, pp. 48–49; see also Hallett, 'Intervention', pp. 375–76.
86 For accounts of the FNLA attack on Luanda, see Wolfers, and Bergerol, *Angola*, pp. 17–20; from the South African perspective on the SADF involvement in the attack, see Steenkamp, *Border War*, p. 50.
87 Hallett, 'Intervention', p. 371.
88 Marcum, 'Lessons of Angola', p. 417.
89 On this aspect, see for example Daniel R., Kempton, *Soviet Strategy toward Southern Africa. The National Liberation Movement Connection*, New York/Westport/London, Prager, 1989, pp. 5, and 8; Maxwell, 'Thorns of the Portuguese Revolution', pp. 258–65.
90 David E. Albright, 'The USSR and the Third World in the 1980s', *Problems of Communism*, vol. 38, nos. 2–3, March-June 1989, pp. 55–6; S. Neil MacFarlane, 'The Soviet Union and Southern African Security', *Problems of Communism*, vol. 38, nos. 2–3, March-June 1989, p. 74; from a Soviet point of view, see Y. Tarabrin, 'The National Liberation Movement: Problems and Prospects', *International Affairs* (Moscow), February 1978, pp. 59–68; G. Kim, 'The Successes of the National Liberation Movement and World Politics', *International Affairs* (Moscow), February 1979, p. 86.
91 Cf. speech by Leonid Brezhnev, 25.10.1976, reprinted in 'Discours à la session plénière du Comité central du parti communiste de l'Union soviétique' (25 October 1976), Moscow, Novosti Press Agency, 1976, p. 37.
92 Anatoli Gromyko, 'La révolution d'octobre et les destinées de l'Afrique', in *L'U.R.S.S. et l'Afrique*, Moscow, Academy of Sciences

USSR, 1982, p. 15; see also V. Sofinsky, and A. Khazanov, 'Angola's Chronicle of the Peking Betrayal', *International Affairs* (Moscow), July 1978, pp. 61–9; K. Uralov, 'Angola: The Triumph of the Right Cause', *International Affairs* (Moscow), May 1976, pp. 54–5.

93 Laidi, *Contraintes d'une rivalité*, p. 104; on Chinese involvement, see also Legum, 'Foreign Intervention', A15–16; Charles Ebinger, 'External Intervention in Internal War: the Politics and Diplomacy of the Angolan Civil War', *Orbis*, vol. 20, no. 3, 1976, pp. 681–82.

94 MacFarlane, 'The Soviet Union, and Southern African Security', pp. 73, and 76.

95 See *supra*, chapter 3.

96 Jorge I. Dominguez, *To Make a World Safe for Revolution. Cuban Foreign Policy*. Cambridge (Mass.)/London, Harvard University Press, 1989, p. 131.

97 Maxwell, 'Last Empire', p. 379; Neto also requested Cuban help during a visit of a Cuban government delegation to Luanda in the same month (Wolfers, and Bergerol, *Angola*, p. 29).

98 Cf. Marcum, *Angolan Revolution*, vol. 2, p. 443, n. 257.

99 *Ibid.*, p. 273.

100 Jorge I. Dominguez, 'Cuban Foreign Policy', *Foreign Affairs*, vol. 57, no. 1, 1978, p. 96.

101 Cf. Wolfers, and Bergerol, *Angola*, p. 31; Steenkamp, *Border War*, p. 50.

102 Dominguez, *Cuban Foreign Policy*, pp. 152, and 321, n. 13.

103 Excerpts reproduced in Zdenek Cervenka, 'Cuba and Africa', *Africa Contemporary Record* (1976–7) London, Rex Collings, 1977, A87.

104 Fidel Castro, *Nothing Can Stop the Course of History. Interview by Jeffrey M. Elliot, and Mervin M. Dymally*, New York/London/Sydney, Pathfinder Press, 1986, p. 172, n. 566; Wolfers, and Bergerol refer to a group of Namibians recruited by UNITA (Wolfers and Bergerol, *Angola*, p. 14).

105 See for example Laidi, *Contraintes d'une rivalité*, p. 114; who argues that the decision to increase assistance to MPLA was taken in response to Portugal's refusal to commit new troops to Angola in the transitional period before independence.

106 Arkady N. Shevchenko, *Breaking with Moscow*, New York, Alfred Knopf, 1985, p. 136.

107 Interview Antunes, 11.5.1989; see also Dominguez, *Cuban Foreign Policy*, pp. 144–5.

108 *Ibid.*, pp. 114–15.

109 Private discussion with Cuban diplomat, Maputo, 22.8.1987.

110 Tony Hodges, 'How the MPLA Won in Angola', in Colin Legum Tony Hodges (eds), *After Angola: The War over Southern Africa*, London, Rex Collings, 1976, p. 58.

111 Steenkamp, *Border War*, p. 54.

112 Geldenhuys, *Isolation*, p. 81.

113 *Guardian*, 16.2.1976; Marcum, *Angolan Revolution*, vol. 2, p. 277.

114 Hodges, 'How the MPLA Won in Angola', p. 58.
115 Alex Callinicos and John Roger, *Southern Africa after Soweto*, London, Pluto Press, 1978, p. 156; Ebinger, 'External Intervention in Internal War', p. 696; according to Steenkamp, the working of the Cunene dam was also discussed at a meeting between South African, and Angolan officials at Caluque on 5 April 1976 (Steenkamp, *Border War*, p. 60).
116 Estimation by the author who at that time was Delegate of the International Committee of the Red Cross (ICRC) in Rundu, and southern Angola, and involved in the administration of refugee camps in the Angolan towns of Calai and Cuangar on the Namibian border. Both localities were then occupied by the South African Defence Force.
117 Quoted in Jaster, *White Power*, p. 74.
118 Brigadier Roos to the author in Rundu, February 1976.
119 Quoted in Geldenhuys, *Search for Security*, p. 10; he was echoed by P.W. Botha who argued that South Africa wanted to stem the imperialist expansion of the Soviet Union whose goal would be the control of Angola's natural resources, and the sea route around the Cape (see Legum, 'Foreign Intervention', p. 37).
120 See for example *Star Weekly*, 6.12.1975; J.H.P. Serfontein, *Namibia?*, London, Rex Collings, 1976, p. 335; the military notably thought that they were in a position to eliminate SWAPO militarily. This in turn would enable the South African government to put into practice its strategy of setting up an anti-SWAPO, and pro-South African government structure in Namibia. This would have been an expression of a South African controlled transition to the eventual independence of the territory. In the words of Constand Viljoen who commanded the South African troops in Namibia, and Angola in 1976, 'we had in mind the short-term aim of giving SWAPO a coup de grace so that the SWA strategy could unfold' (quoted in Steenkamp, *Border War*, p. 43).
121 John Barratt, *The Angolan Conflict. Internal and International Aspects*. Bramfontein, South African Institute of International Affairs, 1976, pp. 19–20.
122 Geldenhuys, *Isolation*, p. 80.
123 *Ibid.*, p. 79; see also James Barber, and John Barratt, *South Africa's Foreign Policy. The Search for Status and Security. 1945–1988*, Cambridge/New York/Port Chester/Melbourne/Sydney, Cambridge University Press, 1990, p. 192.
124 Geldenhuys, *Search for Security*, p. 10.
125 Geldenhuys, *Isolation*, p. 81.
126 See *infra*, chapters 5, 6 and 7.
127 José Eduardo dos Santos to *Le Monde*, 14.12.1976.
128 Harneit-Sievers, *SWAPO of Namibia*, p. 53.
129 Hallett, 'Intervention', p. 352.
130 *Financial Times*, 27.9.1975; Heimer, *Entkolonisierungskonflikt*, p. 200, n. 564.
131 'Mystère sur la frontière', *Afrique-Asie*, 20.10.1975.

132 Heimer, *Entkolonisierungskonflikt*, p. 200, n. 566; Wolfers and Bergerol refer to a group of Namibians recruited by UNITA (Wolfers
and Bergerol, *Angola*, p. 14).

133 Loiseau, and de Roux, *Savimbi*, p. 219.

134 Hallett, 'Intervention', p. 377.

135 Statement Jorge Sangumba (UNITA secretary for foreign affairs),
Zambia Daily Mail, 5.2.1976.

136 *Africa Confidential*, 4.11.1977.

137 Andreas Shipanga, *In Search of Freedom. The Andreas Shipanga Story
as Told to Sue Armstrong*. Gibraltar, Ashanti Publishing, 1989,
pp. 101–2.

138 *Africa Confidential*, 4.11.1977.

139 *Rhodesia Herald*, 2.6.1976; for accounts of the SWAPO crisis, see
Harneit-Sievers, *SWAPO*, pp. 56–75; Katjavivi, *History of Resistance*, pp. 105–8; on Zambia's involvement in the crisis, see *infra*,
chapter 5.

140 Radio Lusaka, 13.12.1975.

141 *Observer*, 8.2.1976.

142 Interview Nujoma, in *Granma* (Cuba), 14.3.1976.

143 *Daily Telegraph*, 30.4.1976.

144 Wolfers and Bergerol, *Angola*, p. 224.

145 *Africa Development* (Britain), June 1976.

146 Cf. Heimer, *Entkolonisierungskonflikt*, p. 200, n. 64.

147 Bridgland, *Savimbi*, p. 292.

148 'Namibia guerillas deny joint action with Angola forces', *The
Times*, 5.10.1976.

149 See *Jornal de Angola*, 12.6.1976.

150 *Financial Times*, 12.6.1976.

151 For the location of ANC camps, see Davis, *Apartheid's Rebels*,
p. 48.

152 Quoted in Katjavivi, *Resistance*, pp. 108–9; for a discussion of the
development of SWAPO's ideological perspective, see Kimmo Kiljunen, 'The Ideology of National Liberation', in Green, and Kiljunen (eds), *Namibia. The Last Colony*, pp. 183–95.

153 Cf. interviews with Mtshana Ncube, and Billy Modise, Lusaka
(United Nations Institute for Namibia), 3 and 4 August 1987.

Chapter 5   Regional dynamics of negotiations

1 A 420 km long border security fence from Ruacana to the Kavango
river was erected in 1977 (Cf. Jaster, *Botha Strategy*, p. 20).

2 *Financial Times*, 30.6.1976.

3 Green, and Kiljunen, *Last Colony*, p. 158; see also Steenkamp,
Border War, p. 70.

4 International Defence and Aid Fund for Southern Africa, *Namibia.
The Facts*, London, International Defence and Aid Fund,1980,
p. 53.

5 Cf. International Defence and Aid Fund, *Apartheid's Army in Namibia*, pp. 31–2.

6 See below, chapter 6.

7 SWAPO, *Political Programme of The South West Africa People's Organisation*, Lusaka, SWAPO Department of Publicity, and Information, 1976, p. 10.

8 Internal SWAPO document, quoted in Katjavivi, *History of Resistance*, p. 95.

9 The proposed representation was: 12 Ovambos, 6 Whites, 5 Damaras, 5 Hereros, 5 Kavangos, 5 Coloureds, 5 Nama, 5 Caprivians, 4 Bushmen, 4 Rehobothers, 4 Tswanas.

10 The second-tier 'representative authorities' would be responsible regionally for primary, and secondary education, traditional administration of justice, social welfare, housing, etc. The third tier was to be the equivalent of local, and municipal authorities.

11 Cf. Landis, and Davis, 'Namibia', p. 167.

12 SWAPO, *Political Programme*, p. 8.

13 The great-grandson of Chief Hendrick Witbooi who had led the Nama resistance to German colonial rule from 1904 to 1907.

14 Statement Witbooi, October 1976, quoted in *Namibia News*, vol. 9, no. 12, December 1976, p. 3; in 1977, SWAPO was also joined by a section of the Herero community, the Association for the Preservation of the Royal House of Tjamuaha/Maherero (see Puetz, Egidy, Caplan, *Namibia Handbook*, p. 207; Katjavivi, *History of Resistance*, p. 100.

15 It also included the Damara Council, the Mbanderu group of the Hereros, the Coloured National Independence Party, and the liberal white Federal Party.

16 On Mudge's political career, see Puetz, Egidy, Caplan, *Namibia Handbook*, p. 225.

17 Besides the Republican Party of Mudge which had split from the National Party in 1977, the DTA comprised 14 parties in 1981 (see André du Pisani, 'SWA/Namibia: 1980 Review', *Bulletin Africa Institute of South Africa*, vol. 21, no. 4, 1981, p. 32.

18 The U.N. General Assembly recognized SWAPO as the sole, and authentic representative of the Namibian people in December 1976.

19 As related by Kissinger to the then Portuguese foreign minister Melo Antunes (interview with Antunes, 11.5.1989).

20 *Le Monde*, 5.2.1976.

21 According to Option 2 of the National Security Council Study Memorandum no. 39 (1969) which had been updated in January 1970 (cf. Thomas Karis, 'United States Policy towards South Africa', in Carter, and O'Meara, *Continuing Crisis*, p. 334; see also M.M. Ncube, 'The United States, South Africa, and Destabilization in Southern Africa', in Michael Sefali, and John Bardill (eds), *Development, and Destabilization in Southern Africa*, Roma (Lesotho), Institute of Southern African Studies, 1985, p. 44.

22 MacFarlane, 'The Soviet Union, and Southern African Security', p. 74.
23 'Cuba pledges support to Namibians in fight against South Africa', *The Times*, 24.2.1976.
24 Cf. Colin Legum, 'International Rivalries', in Carter, and O'Meara (eds), *Continuing Crisis*, p. 11.
25 Security Council Resolution 385 (30.1.1976).
26 Statement Kissinger, Lusaka, 27.4.1976, in *Africa Contemporary Record (1976–1977)*, London, Rex Collings, 1977, C 159–163. But the American secretray of state made no reference to majority rule in South Africa.
27 Geldenhuys, *Diplomacy of Isolation*, p. 212.
28 Statement Kissinger Lusaka, 27.4.1976, *Africa Contemporary Record (1976–77)*, C 161.
29 Interview with Bernard Muganda, Dar es Salaam, 19.2.1987; on the origins of the Frontline states, see Carol B. Thompson, *Challenge to Imperialism. The Frontline States in the Liberation of Zimbabwe*, Harare, Zimbabwe Publishing House, 1985, chapter 2; Bernhard Weimer, *Die Allianz der Frontlinien-Staaten im südlichen Afrika: Vom 'Mulungusi- Club' (1974) zum 'Nkomati-Akkord'. Bedingungen und Dynamik von Befreiung, Dialog und Integration in einer Krisenregion*, Ebenhausen, Stiftung Wissenschaft und Politik, 1985, pp. 23–31.
30 Samora Machel was accorded the status of head of 'state before the formal independence of Mozambique in 1975.
31 See appendix 1.
32 Interview Muganda, 19.2.1987.
33 Malawi was the only state who had established diplomatic relations with South Africa in 1967.
34 Cf. Adekune Ajala, 'The OAU, and Southern Africa', in Aluko, and Shaw (eds), *Southern Africa in the 1980s*, pp. 10–11.
35 Cf. appendix 1, point 12.
36 Botswana's only direct contact with majority ruled African countries was through a ferry over the Zambezi where the borders of Namibia, Zambia, Zimbabwe, and Botswana met in the middle of the river. While the 'freedom ferry' enabled South African and Namibian refugees in Botswana to reach Zambia, and the rest of Africa, it also became a major trade route between Zambia, and South Africa with the repeated closures of the border between Zambia, and Rhodesia from 1973.
37 International Defence and Aid Fund, *Namibia. The Facts*, p. 58.
38 Christian M. Rogerson, 'A Future University of Namibia? The Role of the United Nations Institute for Namibia', *Journal of Modern African Studies*, vol. 18, no. 4, 1980, p. 675.
39 General Assembly Resolution 3296 (29), 13.12.1974.
40 United Nations Institute for Namibia, *A Decade of Progress, 1976–1986*, Lusaka, United Nations Institute for Namibia, 1986, p. 4.
41 Cf. *ibid.*, p. 29; on UNIN, see also Hage Geingob, 'The role of

research in the Namibian struggle against colonialism', in Brian Wood (ed.), *Namibia. 1884–1984*, pp. 27–31.

42 Katjavivi, *History of Resistance*, p. 106.

43 Quoted in *ibid.*

44 Martin and Johnson, *Struggle for Zimbabwe*, p. 142.

45 Andreas Shipanga, *In Search of Freedom. The Andreas Shipanga Story as Told to Sue Armstrong*, Gibraltar, Ashanti Publishing, 1989, p. 117.

46 Harneit-Sievers, *SWAPO of Namibia*, p. 60.

47 *Ibid.*, pp. 60–1.

48 *Africa Confidential*, 26.9.1975.

49 Harneit-Sievers, *SWAPO*, p. 61.

50 Katjavivi, *History of Resistance*, p. 106.

51 *Africa Confidential*, 4.11.1977.

52 Katjavivi, *History of Resistance*, pp. 106–7.

53 Cf. Harneit-Sievers, *SWAPO*, p. 67.

54 For a personal account of the arrest, and subsequent detention, see Shipanga, *In Search of Freedom*, chapters 29, 31, and 32.

55 *Africa Confidential*, 22.10.1976.

56 Harneit-Sievers, *SWAPO*, p. 73.

57 Press Conference Nyerere, Washington, 5.8.1977, in Julius Nyerere. *Crusade for Liberation*. Dar es Salaam/ Nairobi/Oxford/New York, Oxford University Press, 1978, p. 17.

58 Quoted in C. Munhamu Botsio Utete, 'Zimbabwe, and Southern African 'Détente', in Seiler (ed.), *Southern Africa Since the Portuguese Coup*, pp. 67–8; see also 'Sesay, 'The Roles of the Front Line States in Southern Africa', in Aluko, and Shaw (eds), *Southern Africa in the 1980s*, 1985, p. 27.

59 Regulations which restricted operations of liberation movements had been issued as early as 1965 (see Marcum, *Angolan Revolution*, vol. 2, p. 303, 307–8).

60 On the ZANU rebellion, see Martin, and Johnson, *The Struggle for Zimbabwe*, chapter 9; by the same authors, *The Chitepo Assassination*, Harare, Zimbabwe Publishing House, 1985.

61 Britain, France, and the United States had vetoed a Security Council resolution calling for an arms embargo against South Africa because of its continued occupation of Namibia.

62 Margaret P. Karns, 'Ad hoc multilateral diplomacy: the United States, the Contact Group, and Namibia', *International Organization*, vol. 41, no. 1, 1987, pp. 99–100.

63 Legum, 'International Rivalries', p. 10.

64 Cyrus Vance, *Hard Choices. Critical Years in America's Foreign Policy*, New York, Simon & Schuster, 1983, p. 283.

65 André Du Pisani and Klaus von der Ropp, 'The Western/Namibian Initiatives: Past, Present-and Future?', *International Affairs Bulletin* (South Africa), vol. 12, no. 2, 1988, p. 7; on the interests of Britain, Canada, France, and the Federal Republic of Germany in Namibia, see I. William Zartman, *Ripe for Resolution. Conflict, and*

Intervention in Africa, New York/Oxford, Oxford University Press, 1985, p. 164.

66 Vance, *Hard Choices*, p. 276.

67 Quoted in Gerald Bender, 'Angola, the Cubans, and American Anxieties', *Foreign Policy*, no. 31, Summer 1978, p. 6.

68 Vance, *Hard Choices*, p. 274. But the view that Namibian independence should precede Cuban withdrawal from Angola was never accepted by Carter.

69 *Ibid.*, p. 257.

70 *Ibid.*, p. 274.

71 *Ibid.*, p. 275.

72 Karns, 'Contact Group', p. 104.

73 Thompson, *Challenge to Imperialism*, p. 16.

74 Robert Jaster, *A Regional Security Role for Africa's Front-Line States: Experience, and Prospects* (Adelphi paper no. 180). London, International Institute for Strategic Studies, 1983, p. 6.

75 Vance, *Hard Choices*, p. 278.

76 Interview Muganda, 19.2.1987; cf. also Julius K. Nyerere, 'America, and Southern Africa', *Foreign Affairs*, vol. 55, no. 4, 1977, p. 673.

77 Vance, *Hard Choices*, p. 277; although Pretoria realized that the western countries were reluctant to impose sanctions, the South African government took the threat seriously (Geldenhuys, *Isolation*, p. 223). In June 1977, Pretoria appointed an administrator general for the territory during the transition period to independence.

78 Interview with Mark Bomani, Lusaka, 4.8.1987.

79 Thompson, *Challenge to Imperialism*, p. 65.

80 Interview Bomani, 4.8.1987.

81 Vance, *Hard Choices*, p. 275.

82 Address to the UN General Assembly, September 1969, paras. 13–16, Institute of Commonwealth Studies (London), JX 1584. B2 BOT.

83 Seretse Khama *From the Frontline (Speeches)*, edited by Gwendolen M. Carter and E.Philip Morgan, London, Rex Collings, 1980, p. 171.

84 Address to the 14th Annual Conference of the Botswana Democratic Party, Mahalapye, 28.3.1975, in *ibid.*, p. 195.

85 *Ibid.*,pp.142–3.

86 Interview with A.M. Mogwe, Gaborone, 1.12.1987.

87 Address at the opening of the Fifteenth Annual Conference of the Botswana Democratic Party, 16.4.1976, in Khama, *From the Frontline*, p. 226.

88 Interview Mogwe, 1.12.1987.

89 Interview with José Maria Lopes, Maputo, 20.8.1987.

90 Allen and Barbara Isacman, *Mozambique. From Colonialism to Revolution. 1900–1982*, Harare, Zimbabwe Publishing House, 1985, p. 175.

91 On Tanzanian foreign policy, see S.S. Mushi and K. Mathews

(eds), *Foreign Policy of Tanzania, 1961–1981: A Reader*, Dar es Salaam, Tanzania Publishing House, 1981; David H. Johns, 'The Foreign Policy of Tanzania', in Aluko (ed.), *Foreign Policies of African States*, pp. 196–219.

92 Vance, *Hard Choices*, p. 280.

93 Interview Muganda, 19.2.1987.

94 Interview with Musinga Bandora, Dar es Salaam, 21.2.1987.

95 Nyerere, *Crusade for Liberation*, p. 34.

96 Interview Bandora, 21.2.1987.

97 See for example Nathan Shamuraya 'The Dangers of the Lusaka Manifesto', *Africa Review* (Dar es Salaam), vol. 1, no. 1, March 1971, in Acquino de Bragança and Immanuel Wallerstein (eds), *The African Liberation Reader*, vol. 3: 'The Strategy of Liberation', London, Zed Press, 1982, pp. 88–90.

98 Kurt M. Campbell, *Southern Africa in Soviet Foreign Policy* (Adelphi Paper no. 227), London, International Institute for Strategic Studies, 1987/88, p. 23.

99 James Mayall, 'The Soviet Union, Zimbabwe, and Southern Africa', in O. Aluko and T. Shaw (eds), *Southern Africa in the 1980s*, London, George Allen & Unwin, 1985, p. 102.

100 Interview Bomani, 4.8.1987.

101 Statement Nujoma, World Conference for Action against Apartheid, Lagos, 22–26.8.1977, UN. Doc. UN Centre against Apartheid, Conf. 2, Oct.1977, p. 21.

102 Press statement SWAPO in *Daily News*, 30.11.1977.

103 *Daily News*, 8.2.1977.

104 Interview Tjiriange, Geneva, 21.2.1988.

105 For a comprehensive discussion of the dispute over Walvis Bay, see Lynn Berat, *Walvis Bay. The Last Frontier*, Wynberg/New Haven, Radix/Yale University Press, 1990. See also Richard Moorsom, *Walvis Bay. Namibia's Port*. London, International Defence and Aid Fund for Southern Africa/United Nations Council for Namibia, 1984; Ronald Dreyer, 'Dispute over Walvis Bay. Origins, and Implications for Namibian Independence', *African Affairs*, vol. 83, no. 333, October 1984, pp. 497–510.

106 Vance, *Hard Choices*, p. 279.

107 *Ibid.*, p. 280.

108 *Ibid.*.

109 *Ibid.*, p. 281.

110 Statement Nujoma to World Conference for Action against Apartheid, Lagos, 22.–26.8.1977, pp. 25–6.

111 Vance, *Hard Choices*, p. 282.

112 *Ibid.*, p. 283.

113 See I. William Zartman, *Ripe for Resolution. Conflict, and Intervention in Africa*, New York/Oxford, Oxford University Press, 1985.

114 Vance, *Hard Choices*, p. 303.

115 Jaster, *Botha Strategy*, p. 12.

116 André du Pisani, 'Namibia: On Brinkmanship, Conflict, and Self-

interest. The Collapse of the UN Plan', *Politikon*, vol. 8, no. 1, June 1981, p. 7.

117 The South Africans blamed SWAPO for the assassination. But SWAPO leaders denied any responsibility, and hinted at a South African inspired ploy (Landis 'Namibia', p. 171).

118 Vance, *Hard Choices*, p. 303.

119 'Proposal for a settlement of the Namibian situation', encl. in Letter dated 10 April 1978 from the representatives of Canada, France, Federal Republic of Germany, the United Kingdom of Great Britain and Northern Ireland, and United States of America addressed to the president of the Security Council, UN. Doc. S/12636, 10.4.1978; see appendix 2.

120 Vance, *Hard Choices*, pp. 303–4.

121 Du Pisani, 'Namibia: Brinkmanship', p. 8; Jaster, *Botha Strategy*, p. 12.

122 Vance, *Hard Choices*, p. 302.

123 Geldenhuys, *Isolation*, p. 226; the author discusses in detail the South African negotiating strategy over Namibia.

124 On the role of Nigeria, see Olajide Aluko, 'Nigeria, Namibia, and Southern Africa', in Aluko, and Shaw (eds), *Southern Africa in the 1980s*, pp. 41–60.

125 Vance, *Hard Choices*, p. 304.

126 Cf. International Defence and Aid Fund, *Namibia: the Facts*, p. 56; for an account of the attack from a South African point of view, see Steenkamp, *Border War*, pp. 74–80.

127 Vance, *Hard Choices*, p. 305.

128 See Geldenhuys, *Isolation*, p. 83.

129 Interview Muganda, 19.2.1987; see also *Africa Confidential*, 23.6.1978, p. 1.

130 Vance, *Hard Choices*, p. 305.

131 Interview with M. Ribeiro, New York, 30.3.1982; Vance, *Hard Choices*, p. 305.

132 Statement Peter Mueshihange to OAU Standing Committee on Defence, General Policy, Information, and Finance, 29.5.–2.6.1978, Archives Daily News, Dar es Salaam.

133 Interview Tjiriange, 21.2.1988.

134 Pretoria had previously warned the Contact Group that the negotiations would be terminated if the Group changed its position on Walvis Bay.

135 Vance, *Hard Choices*, p. 306; it was reported at that time that the American state department was planning to formally recognize the MPLA government (*Africa Confidential*, 7.7.1978).

136 Muganda to the author, 26.7.1988; interview Muganda, 23.8.1989.

137 Interview Bomani, 4.8.1987.

138 *Ibid*.

139 SWAPO, *Born a Nation*, p. 242.

140 Security Council Resolution 432 (27.7.1978); see appendix 3.

141 Explanation of vote on Resolution 432 by Cyrus Vance, 27.7.1978, in Foreign and Commonwealth Office, 'Memorandum on Walvis

Bay', reprinted in the *Minutes of Evidence taken before the Foreign Affairs Committee of the House of Commons*, 13.5.1981. London, HMSO, 1981, pp. 97–8.

142 Interview with N. Tjiriange, New York, 9.4.1982.

143 Interview Bomani, 4.8.1987.

144 See *Africa Confidential*, 23.6.1978; 4.11.1979.

145 Interview Tjiriange, 21.2.1988.

146 Interview Ya-Otto, 21.6.1987.

147 Interview Bandora, 21.2.1987.

148 Cf. *The Times*, 7.4.1978.

149 Security Council Resolution 431 (27.7.1978).

150 B.J. Vorster, 'Statement on South West Africa', 20.9.1978, London, Director of Information, South Africa House, 1978, p. 2.

151 Zartman, *Ripe for Resolution*, p. 178; du Pisani, 'Brinkmanship', p. 12.

152 *Times*, 16.9.1978; PLAN guerillas had successfully attacked a South African base at Katima Mulilo in August in response to which South Africa attacked Zambian territory killing twelve civilians.

153 Zartman, *Ripe for Resolution*, p. 178.

154 With a turnout of over 80%, DTA won 82% of the votes. SWAPO's internal wing, SWAPO-D led by Andreas Shipanga who had been released from jail in Tanzania in May 1978, and the Namibian National Front boycotted the elections.

155 Vance, *Hard Choices*, p. 311.

156 Brian Urquhart, *A Life in Peace, and War*, New York, Harper & Row Publishers, 1987, p. 309.

157 UN. Doc. S/12636, 10.4.1978, p. 3.

158 Vance, *Hard Choices*, p. 311.

159 Karns, 'Contact Group', p. 110.

160 Vance, *Hard Choices*, p. 312.

161 *Africa Contemporary Record* (1978–79), A7.

162 *Guardian*, 14.8.1979.

163 Vance, *Hard Choices*, p. 312.

164 *Guardian*, 14.8.1979; statement Van Dunem (M'Binda), Unesco, International Conference of Solidarity with the People of Namibia, Paris,11.–13.5.1980, United Nations Institute for Namibia, archives.

165 Jaster, *Frontline States*, p. 25.

166 André du Pisani, *SWA/Namibia: The Politics of Continuity, and Change*, Johannesburg, Jonathan Ball, 1986, p. 438.

167 Urquhart, *Peace, and War*, p. 310.

168 Interview Muganda, 23.8.1989.

169 Urquhart, *Peace, and War*, p. 310.

170 On the South African position, see Mike Hough, 'DMZ Proposals for SWA/Namibia', *Africa Insight*, vol. 10, no. 2, 1980, pp. 91–4.

171 Urquhart, *Peace, and War*, p. 311.

172 *Ibid.*, p. 312.

173 Cf. MPLA Special Congress, *Report of the Central Committee of the MPLA-Workers' Party*, Luanda, 1980, p. 57.

174 Urquhart, *Peace, and War*, pp. 312–13.
175 Cf. Vance, *Hard Choices*, p. 283.
176 *Africa Confidential*, 23.5.1979, and 1.8.1979; work on the Ruacana hydroelectric complex on the Angolan side of the border had been briefly interrupted after the South African troop withdrawal from Angola in March 1976 in the wake of the South African invasion of 1975. Work on the Caluque dam started again in April 1976 after secret talks between South African, and Angolan officials (*Guardian*, 7.4.1976). The dam was not completed, and the sluices which were kept open prevented a regular water supply to the electric generator at Ruacana on the Namibian side of the border outside the rainy season. The hydroelectric complex only worked at a fourth of its capacity in 1980. In addition, PLAN frequently sabotaged the power line which led from the border south into Namibia.
177 Zartman, *Ripe for Resolution*, p. 185.
178 See Jaster, *Botha Strategy*, p. 70.
179 Geldenhuys, *Isolation*, p. 140.
180 White Paper of Defence, 1973, quoted in Geldenhuys, *Search for Security*, p. 11.
181 The concept of a total counterinsurgency strategy mobilizing the totality of the state structures, and not only the military element, for defeating a guerilla movement, had been put forward by the French general André Beaufre (see Philip H. Frankel, *Pretoria's Praetorians. Civil-Military Relations in South Africa*, Cambridge, Cambridge University Press, 1984, p. 46).
182 Davies, and O'Meara, 'Total Strategy', p. 194.
183 Geldenhuys, *Isolation*, p. 141.
184 Botha to party congress, National Party, 15.8.1979, quoted in *ibid.*
185 Davies and O'Meara, 'Total Strategy', p. 191.
186 On CONSAS, see Deon Geldenhuys and Denis Venter, 'Constellation of States'.
187 'Southern Africa: Towards Economic Liberation' (Lusaka Declaration of April 1980), reproduced in Iddi Simba, and Francis Wells, *Development Co-operation in Southern Africa. Structures, and Procedures*. Paris, OECD, 1984, p. 41.
188 Davies and O'Meara, 'Total Strategy', p. 198.
189 This was to be the case in January 1986 when Chief Jonathan of Lesotho was overthrown in a coup; for a detailed account of South Africa's destabilization policies, see Joseph Hanlon, *Beggar Your Neighbours. Apartheid Power in Southern Africa*, London, Catholic Institute for International Relations/James Currey, 1986.
190 Geldenhuys, *Isolation*, p. 145; see also Deon Geldenhuys, 'The Destabilisation Controversy: An Analysis of a High Risk Foreign Policy Option for South Africa', in D. Geldenhuys, and W. Gutteridge (eds), *Instability, and Conflict in Southern Africa*, London, Institute for the Study of Conflict, 1983, pp. 11–26.
191 'De Klerk moves to dismantle security management system', *Southscan*, 8.12.1989.

192 See above, chapter 3.
193 Hanlon, *Beggar Your Neighbours*, p. 244.
194 Wolfers and Bergerol, *Angola*, p. 223; see also International Defence, and Aid Fund, *Apartheid's Army in Namibia*, p. 56.
195 The attack took place during Kissinger's shuttle diplomacy over southern Africa, and the Zambian government took South Africa to the Security Council over the issue (Serfontein, *Namibia?*, p. 358).
196 In the context of SWAPO's internal crisis of 1976, the SWAPO leadership claimed that dissident PLAN fighters had given the information to the SADF (Katjavivi, *History of Resistance*, p. 107).
197 Anglin, and Shaw, *Zambia's Foreign Policy*, p. 12.
198 Hanlon, *Beggar Your Neighbours*, p. 244.
199 *Daily News*, 26.8.1976.
200 *Daily News*, 27.5.1977; according to Steenkamp, South African forces had responded to a mortar attack by the Zambian army (Steenkamp, *Border War*, p. 71).
201 *Ibid.*, p. 83.
202 *Times*, 24.8.1978, *Guardian*, 26.8.1978; see also International Aid, and Defence Fund, *Apartheid's Army in Namibia*, p. 57.
203 *Rhodesia Herald*, 26.8.1978.
204 'Frontline States: developments', week of 17.9.1979, Library Ministry of Information (Zimbabwe), file 6.3.'Pan African Organizations, PAFMECA, vol. 5.
205 Steenkamp, *Border War*, p. 86.
206 International Defence and Aid Fund, *Apartheid's Army in Namibia*, p. 57.
207 Hanlon, *Beggar Your Neighbours*, p. 244.
208 William Minter, 'Account from Angola. UNITA as described by ex-participants and foreign visitors' (Minter Report on UNITA, in *Facts, and Reports*, vol. 20, no. L, 15.6.1990, p. 8).
209 International Defence and Aid Fund, *Apartheid's Army*, p. 43; *Sunday Times*, 29.5.1977; Marcum, *Angolan Revolution*, vol. 2, p. 277.
210 Steenkamp, *Border War*, p. 63.
211 Minter, 'Account from Angola', p. 8.
212 Hanlon, *Beggar Your Neighbours*, p. 158.
213 People's Republic of Angola, *White Paper on Acts of Aggression by the Racist South African Regime Against the People's Republic of Angola (1975–1982)*, Luanda, Ministry of External Relations, 1982, pp. 79–83.
214 See 'South Africa backs secret plan to invade Angola', *Sunday Times*, 29.5.1977 which revealed details of the plan.
215 Wolfers and Bergerol, *Angola*, p. 218.
216 *Sunday Times*, 29.5.1977.
217 Steenkamp, *Border War*, p. 71, who provides a detailed account of 'Operation Reindeer', *ibid.*, pp. 74–80.
218 Geldenhuys, *Isolation*, p. 83.
219 *To the Point International* (South Africa), 9.3.1979.

220 On the South African perception of the sanctions issue, see Geld-enhuys, *Isolation*, p. 223.
221 Jaster, *Botha Strategy*, p. 44.
222 On the 'Muldergate' affair, see Geldenhuys, *Isolation*, pp. 84–9.
223 Wolfers and Bergerol, *Angola*, p. 233.
224 *Guardian*, 14.6.1980.
225 International Aid and Defence Fund, *Namibia. The Facts*, p. 57.
226 Hanlon, *Beggar Your Neighbours*, p. 162.

Chapter 6   Namibia-Angola, 'Linkage' and war

1 'U.S. Seeks Angola Compromise as Price for Accord on Namibia', *New York Times*, 1.6.1981.
2 Chester Crocker, 'South Africa: A Strategy for Change', *Foreign Affairs*, vol. 59, no. 2, 1980, p. 345.
3 Chester A. Crocker. *A U.S. Policy for the 80s* (Occasional Paper), Braamfontein, South African Institute of International Affairs, May 1981, p. 10.
4 In 1978, he sharply attacked the American Angola specialist Gerald Bender for condoning Cuban and Soviet intervention. Chester A. Crocker, 'Comment: Making Africa Safe for the Cubans' (reply to Bender, 'Angola, the Cubans, and American Anxieties'), *Foreign Policy*, no. 31, 1978, pp. 31–33.
5 Interview with Chester Crocker, Geneva, 31.5.1990.
6 Colin Legum, 'The Southern African Crisis', *Africa Contemporary Record (1981–82)*, New York/London, Africana Publishing Company, 1982, A18.
7 United Nations Council for Namibia, *Report Conference Paris*, UN. Doc. A/AC.131/94, 31.3.1983, p. 17, para. 82.
8 *Ibid.*, p. 19, para. 88.
9 Cf. Julio Faundez, 'Namibia: the relevance of international law', *Third World Quarterly*, vol. 8, no. 2, April 1986, p. 555; see also 'SWAPO's response to the proposal of the 'Contact Group' on a one vote-two count system presented to SWAPO on 1 April 1982', appendix 2 in *Africa Contemporary Record* (1981–82), A 58.
10 UN. Doc. S/15287, 12.7.1982.
11 'Principles concerning the Constituent Assembly, and the Constitution for an independent Namibia', annex, in 'Letter Dated 12 July 1982 from the Representatives of Canada, France, the Federal Republic of Germany, the United Kingdom of Great Britain and Northern Ireland, and the United States of America Addressed to the Secretary-General', UN. Doc. S/15287, 12.7.1982.
12 Interview Crocker, 31.5.1990.
13 See Colin Legum, *The Battlefronts of Southern Africa*, New York/London, Africana Publishing Company, 1988, pp. 224–25.
14 *Ibid.*, p. 262.
15 Cf. *Africa Contemporary Record (1982–3)*, vol. 15, New York/London, Africana Publishing Company, 1984, A 30.

16 Cf. Legum, *Battlefronts*, p. 339.
17 *Africa Contemporary Record (1981–2)*, vol. 14, New York/London, Africana Publishing Company, 1981, A19.
18 Legum, *Battlefronts*, p. 368.
19 *Ibid.*, p. 385.
20 Geldenhuys, *Isolation*, p. 226; for a detailed account of the meeting, see 'America and South Africa. Anti-apartheid without tears', *Economist*, 30.3.1985, p. 19.
21 Interview Crocker, 31.5.1990.
22 Hanlon, *Beggar Your Neighbours*, p. 159; see also Steenkamp, *Border War*, pp. 98–9.
23 South Africa also attempted to mobilize a few ex-ZIPRA fighters known as 'Super-ZAPU' against the Zimbabwean government (cf. Hanlon, *Beggar Your Neighbours*, pp. 181–2).
24 International Defence and Aid Fund, *Apartheid's Army in Namibia*, p. 43; *Sunday Times*, 29.5.1977; Marcum, *Angolan Revolution, vol. 2*, p. 277.
25 William Minter, 'Account from Angola. UNITA as described by ex-participants and foreign vistors' (Minter Report on UNITA), *Facts and Reports*, vol. 20, no. L, 15.6.1990, p. 8; according to a pro-South African account, this help was already forthcoming in 1977 (see Steenkamp, *Border War*, p. 68).
26 International Defence and Aid Fund, *Apartheid's Army in Namibia*, p. 56.
27 *Ibid.*
28 Cf. William Minter (ed.), *Operation Timber. Pages from the Savimbi Dossier*, Trenton, New Jersey, Africa World Press, 1988, p. 108.
29 Steenkamp, *Border War*, p. 87.
30 *Guardian*, 19.5.1979.
31 Jaster, *Botha Strategy*, p. 48.
32 Kimmo Kiljunen, 'National Resistance and the Liberation Struggle', in Green and Kiljunen (eds), *Namibia. The Last Colony*, p. 159.
33 Jaster, *Botha Strategy*, p. 105.
34 Verbatim record of the meeting, 15–16.4.1981, reproduced in Karis, 'United States Policy towards South Africa', in Carter and O'Meara, *Continuing Crisis*, p. 359.
35 International Defence and Aid Fund, *Apartheid's Army*, p. 50.
36 Cf. John Seiler, 'South Africa in Namibia: Persistence, Misperception, and Ultimate Failure', in T. Callaghy (ed.), *South Africa in Southern Africa. The Intensifying Vortex of Violence*. New York, Praeger Publishers, 1984, pp. 178–9.
37 Statement Jan Klopper, Acting Commander SWATF, March 1982, in 'Namibia. Shifting sands: Desertification of an economy', *Africa Contemporary Record (1982–3)*, vol. 15, B 683.
38 *Ibid.*; following the SWAPO offensive of April 1982, South Africa escalated the raids into Angola.
39 Steenkamp, *Border War*, p. 101.
40 On this aspect, see A.K. Mhina, *Liberation Struggles in Southern*

Africa after Zimbabwe, paper submitted to International Conference on Peace, and Security in Southern Africa, Arusha (Tanzania), 24–31.5.1985.

41 Statement Ahmed Salim in *Daily News*, 17.9.1983.

42 See Report of the United Nations Council for Namibia, *International Conference in Support of the Struggle of the Namibian People for Independence*, Paris, 25–29.4.1983, in UN. Doc. A/AC. 131/94, 31.3.1983, p. 20, para 96.

43 Legum, *Battlefronts*, p. 266.

44 Interview Crocker, 31.5.1990.

45 Gilbert M. Khadiagala, 'The Front Line States, Regional Interstate Relations, and Institution Building in Southern Africa', in Harvey Glickman (ed.), *Toward Peace and Security in Southern Africa*, New York, Gordon, and Breach Science Publishers, 1990, p. 147; see also Jaster, *Regional Security Role*, p. 24; Michael Evans, 'The Frontline States, South Africa, and Southern African Security. Military Prospects, and Perspectives', Offprint from *Zambezia*, vol. 12, no. 5, 1984, p. 5

46 Legum, *Battlefronts*, p. 266.

47 *Ibid.*, p. 339.

48 *Ibid.*, p. 310.

49 See Marga Holness, 'Angola: The Struggle Continues', in Phillis Johnson and David Martin (eds), *Destructive Engagement. Southern Africa at War*, Harare, Zimbabwe Publishing House, 1986, p. 100.

50 Jaster, *Botha Strategy*, p. 57.

51 Cf. Geldenhuys, *Isolation*, p. 145.

52 Davies and O'Meara, 'Total Strategy in Southern Africa', p. 201.

53 For an account of South African military operations in Angola from 1981 to 1983, see for example Steenkamp, *Border War*, pp. 99–113.

54 'America, and South Africa. Anti-apartheid Without Tears', *Economist*, 30.3.1985, p. 21.

55 'Angola. The MPLA at the Nadir of its Fortunes', *Africa Contemporary Record (1982–83)*, B 602.

56 'Destabilisation in Southern Africa', *The Economist*, 16.7.1983, p. 17.

57 Cf. *Africa Confidential*, 4.7.1984.

58 Hanlon, *Beggar Your Neighbours*, p. 161.

59 See statements José Eduardo dos Santos, 8.3.1984, and 6.4.1984, Statement of the Central Committee of the MPLA-Workers' Party, 18.4.1984;in *Angola Information* (Bulletin), no. 66, 12.3.1984, pp. 1–3; 6.6.1984, p. 1; 2.5.1984, p. 14; see also Holness, 'Angola', pp. 102–3.

60 *Economist*, 30.3.1985, p. 21.

61 Statement Paulo Jorge, Angolan Press Agency (ANGOP), 7.3.1984, in *Angola Information*, no. 66, 12.3.1984, p. 4.

62 Jaster, *Botha Strategy*, p. 22.

63 Weimer, *Frontlinienstaaten*, p. 61.

64 Steenkamp, *Border War*, p. 194.

NOTES

65 On Nkomati, see Hanlon, *Beggar Your Neighbours*, pp. 142–44;
David Martin and Phyllis Johnson, 'Mozambique: To Nkomati an
Beyond', in Johnson and Martin (eds), *Destructive Engagement*,
pp. 1–41; for the text of the Accord, see Ibrahim Msabaha, and
Timothy M. Shaw (eds), *Confrontation and Liberation in Southern
Africa*. Boulder(Col.)/ London/Westview Press/Gower, 1987,
appendix 1.
66 Davies and O'Meara, 'Total Strategy', pp. 204–5.
67 Geldenhuys, 'Destabilization Controversy', p. 25.
68 The South African government also released Andimba Toivo ya
Toivo, one of the founders of SWAPO, from prison on Robben
Island in South Africa.
69 Summit meeting Frontline states, Maputo, 29.11.1984, final communiqué, in Daily News archives, Dar es Salaam.
70 *Daily News*, 4.3.1984.
71 Embassy Tanzania, Stockholm, to Tanzanian delegation, confidential memorandum 'Talking points in relation to the meeting
of the foreign minister of the Nordic countries, and the Frontline
states (20.–21.6.1984)', 15.6.1984, in *Daily News* archives.
72 Cf. interview Crocker, 31.5.1990.
73 On the Lusaka talks on Namibia, see Legum, *Battlefronts*,
pp. 284–8; Brian Hackland, Anne Murray-Hudson, Brian Wood,
'Behind the Diplomacy: Namibia, 1983–5', *Third World Quarterly*,
vol. 8 no. 1, 1986, p. 69; see also interview Nujoma, in *Daily
News*, 29.7.1984.
74 Legum, *Battlefronts*, p. 312.
75 SWAPO-D of Andreas Shipanga, National Party [of South West
Africa], SWANU-Katjiuongua, the Labour Party, and the Rehoboth Liberation Front.
76 See for example special report on Namibia, *International Herald
Tribune*, 1.11.1984.
77 Hackland, Murray-Hudson, Wood, 'Behind the Diplomacy', p. 70;
on the TGNU, see André du Pisani, 'Namibia: A New Transitional
Government', *South Africa International*, vol. 16, no. 2, 1985,
pp. 66–73.
78 Deon Geldenhuys, *What Do we Think? A Survey of White Opinion
on Foreign Policy Issues. (Number 2)*, Braamfontein, South African
Institute of International Affairs (Occasional Paper), 1984,
pp. 14–15.
79 Cf. United Nations Council for Namibia (Standing Committee II),
The Military Situation in, and relating to Namibia. New York, United
Nations, 1985, p. 6.
80 Jaster, *White Power*, p. 97.
81 See Hanlon, *Beggar Your Neighbours*, p. 163.
82 'Message from the Angolan Head of State to the United Nations
Secretary-General on the Problems of Southern Africa', reproduced in *Destructive Engagement*, appendix 2, p. 329.
83 Cf. Gerald J. Bender, 'Peacemaking in Southern Africa: the

237

Luanda Pretoria Tug-of-War', *Third Word Quarterly*, vol. 11, no. 2, April 1989, p. 19.

84 Robert. S. Jaster, *South Africa, and its Neighbours: the Dynamics of a Regional Conflict* (Adelphi Paper 209), London, International Institute for Strategic Studies, 1986, p. 19.

85 Christopher Cocker, *South Africa's Security Dilemma* (The Washington Papers), New York, Prager, 1987, p. 36.

86 Jaster, *South Africa, and its Neighbours*, p. 19.

87 Mike Hough (Director South African Institute for Strategic Studies), to conference 'Namibia: zwischen Entwicklungsnotwendigkeit und Unabhängigkeit', Wildbad Kreuth (Germany), 28.11.1988.

88 Quoted in Steenkamp, *Border War*, p. 131.

89 *Ibid.*, pp. 135–7; Jaster, *White Power*, p. 99.

90 *Neue Zürcher Zeitung*, 26/27.10.1985; the South African air force had intervened to rescue UNITA for the first time in August 1983, when UNITA attempted to take the town of Cangamba in the Moxico province in eastern Angola (Holness, 'The Struggle Continues', p. 101.).

91 Olga Nazario, 'Cuba's Angolan Operation', in Sergio Diaz-Briquets (ed.), *Cuban Internationalism in Sub-Saharan Africa*. Pittsburgh (Penns.), Duquesne University Press, 1989, p. 109.

92 Pierre Abramovici, 'L'engagement des groupes privés derrière M. Reagan. Des millions de dollars pour 'les combattants de la liberté', *Le Monde diplomatique*, April 1985, pp. 3–5.

93 Ronald Reagan to United Nations General Assembly, 24.10.1985, UN. Doc. A/40/PV. 48, 24.10.1985, p. 9; on the Reagan doctrine, see also Ibbo Mandaza, 'Southern Africa: US Policy, and the Struggle for National Independence', *African Journal of Political Economy*, no. 1, 1986, pp. 120–41.

94 On this aspect, see Michael T. Klare, 'Les conflits de faible intensité: la nouvelle doctrine d'intervention américaine', *Le Monde diplomatique*, March 1986, pp. 1/3.

95 Chas. W., Freeman, Jr., 'The Angola/Namibia Accords', *Foreign Affairs*, vol. 68, no. 3, 1989, p. 132.

96 Bender, 'Peacemaking in Southern Africa', p. 21.

97 *Ibid.*, n. 9; Klare, 'Les conflits de faible intensité', p. 3.

98 Interview Venacia de Moura, in *AfricAsia*, no. 38, February 1987, p. 29.

99 Bender, 'Peacemaking in Southern Africa', p. 21.

100 Kurt M. Campbell, *Southern Africa in Soviet Foreign Policy* (Adelphi Paper no. 227), London, International Institute for Strategic Studies, 1987/88, p. 14; see also *Guardian*, 7.5.1986.

101 Jaster, *White Power*, p. 100.

102 Campbell, *Southern Africa in Soviet Policy*, pp. 13–14; see also *Namibian*, 13.6.1986.

103 *Guardian*, 2.9.1986.

104 Bender, 'Peacemaking in Southern Africa', pp. 21–2.

Chapter 7 Angola-Namibia: from war to independence

1 Bender, 'Peacemaking in Southern Africa', p. 24.
2 The government also adopted a new economic course, notably by announcing the reduction of state involvement in the country's economy, and its intention to join the International Monetary Fund.
3 Interview Crocker, 31.5.1990.
4 See Alain Gresh, 'Afrique australe: une priorité pour les Etats-Unis: la capitulation du régime angolais', Le Monde diplomatique, February 1988, p. 11; 'Glasnost à l'angolaise', Le Monde, 22.9.1987.
5 Olga Nazario, 'Cuba's Angolan Operation', in Sergio Diaz-Briquets (ed.), Cuban Internationalism in Sub-Sahran Africa. Pittsburgh (Penns.), Duquesne University Press, 1989, p. 110.
6 A 7 per cent annual economic growth between 1980, and 1985 fell by 4 per cent in 1987; ('Cuba: Financial Times Survey', Financial Times, 17.2.1989) on Cuban-Soviet economic relations in the 1980s, see Jorge I. Dominguez, To Make a World Safe for Revolution. Cuban Foreign Policy, Cambridge (Mass.)/London, Harvard University Press, 1989, pp. 87–92.
7 10,000 according to the the Cuban general Rafale del Pino who defected from Cuba in 1987, but only 1,000 according to Cuban Politburo member Jorge Risquet.
8 Interview Crocker, 31.5.1990.
9 Freeman, 'Angola/Namibia Accords', p. 134.
10 The South African resolve to intervene in Angola was underligned by a personal visit of President Botha to South African troops inside Angola in November 1987.
11 Le Monde, 22.9.1987.
12 Mike Hough, Military Reasons for Recent Developments in the Angolan Namibian Question, paper presented to conference 'Namibia: zwischen Entwicklungsnotwendigkeit und Unabhängigkeit', Wildbad Kreuth (Germany), 28.11.1988, p. 1.
13 Africa Confidential, 7.10.1987; Guardian Weekly, 11.10.1987.
14 Hough, Military Reasons, p. 2.; for a detailled decription of the South African operations inside Angola from September to October 1987, see Fred Bridgland, The War for Africa. Twelve Months that Transformed a Continent, Gibraltar, Ashanti, 1990, pp. 48–164.
15 Ibid., p. 81.
16 Ibid., p. 254.
17 Quoted in Guardian, 13.11.1987.
18 See Steenkamp, Border War, p. 151; Bridgland, War for Africa, p. 172.
19 Hough, Military Reasons, p. 2; 13 tanks entered Angola from Namibia on 30 October 1987 (Bridgland, War for Africa, p. 182).
20 Steenkamp, Border War, p. 151.
21 For a detailed description of the South African-UNITA operations in November, and December 1987, see Bridgland, War for Africa, pp. 191–252.

22 On the South African attacks in January, and February 1988 ('Operation Hooper'), see *ibid.*, pp. 254–83; on the South African-UNITA operations near Menongue, see *ibid.*, pp. 244–52; on the unsuccessful attack on Menongue, see *ibid.*, pp. 286–92.
23 *Ibid.*, p. 279.
24 Cf. interview Crocker, 31.5.1990; Bridgland, *War for Africa*, p. 341.
25 Cf. Bender, 'Peacemaking in Southern Africa', p. 26; see also Freeman, 'Angola/Namibia Accords', p. 136.
26 *Economist*, 17.12.1988, p. 53.
27 For an account of the two South African attacks, see Bridgland, *War for Africa*, pp. 293–314.
28 Hough, *Military Reasons*, pp. 5–6.
29 *Guardian*, 15.3.1988; UNITA, which also received American aid through neigbouring Zaire, had already managed to occupy several towns on the Benguela railway line including Savimbi's birthplace Munhango.
30 Cf. Bridgland, *War for Africa*, p. 327.
31 Quoted in *ibid.*, p. 328.
32 Bridgland, in his South Africa biased account, qualifies the battle of 23 March as 'the only clear defeat the SADF suffered in the War for Africa [from August 1987 to May 1988]' (*Ibid.*, p. 330).
33 *Africa Confidential*, 1.4.1988; see also Bender, 'Peacemaking', p. 27; according to Bridgland, South African field commanders had wanted to launch an attack on Cuito Cunanavale from the west since November 1987 (Bridgland, *War for Africa*, p. 292).
34 *Ibid.*, pp. 332–3.
35 *Daily News*, 25.3.1988.
36 *Africa Confidential*, 5.2.1988.
37 *Financial Times*, 3.2.1988.
38 Interview Crocker, 31.5.1990; on the Reagan administration's perception of American relations with the Botha government in the 1980s, see Chester A. Crocker, 'Southern Africa: Eight Years Later', *Foreign Affairs*, vol. 68, no. 4, 1988, pp. 158–61.
39 For a detailed account of the sanction campaign, see Ben L. Martin, 'Attacking Reagan by Way of Pretoria', *Orbis*, vol. 31, no. 3, 1987, pp. 293–311; Gerald Braun and Heribert Weiland, 'Sanctions against South Africa: Punitive Action or Placebo Politics?', in John D. Brewer (ed.), *Can South Africa Survive. Five Minutes to Midnight*, London, Macmillan, 1989, pp. 44–5.
40 *International Herald Tribune*, 7/8.5.1988.
41 *S.A. Report (SA)*, 10.11.1989; for a detailed analysis regarding the effects of sanctions, see *Independent Expert Study on the Evaluation of the Application, and Impact of Sanctions. Final Report to the Commonwealth Committee of Foreign Ministers on Southern Africa*, London, Commonwealth Secretariat, confidential, April 1989.
42 Chandra Hardy, 'The Prospects for Growth, and Structural Change in Southern Africa', *Development Dialogue* (Uppsala), 1987, no. 2, p. 35.
43 *Ibid.*, p. 37.

44 Axel J. Halbach, 'Folgen der südafrikanischen Homeland-Politik: Durch getrennte Entwicklung gemeinsam in die Krise'. *IFO Schnelldienst*, Munich, no. 37, 1987, p. 27.
45 Reginald H. Green, *Namibia: the state of the struggle*, paper presented at conference, International Institute of Strategic Studies (London)/University of Zimbabwe, Harare, June 1987, p. 7; the daily cost of military operations inside Namibia alone was estimated by South African sources at $500,000 per day (Hough, *Military Reasons*, p. 10).
46 The South African foreign debt amounted to $24,000 million in 1988 (*Independent*, 12.10.1988), out of which $12 billion were due to be repaid in 1990–91 (John A. Marcum, 'A Continent Adrift', *Foreign Affairs*, vol. 68, no. 1, 1989, p. 173).
47 Hough, *Military Reasons*, pp. 10–11.
48 Hough at Conference, 'Namibia zwischen Entwicklungsnotwendigkeit und Unabhängikeit', 28.11.1988.
49 *Weekly Mail*, 18.3.1988.
50 The Administrator-general was empowered to call for ethnically based elections which had previously been the 'prerogative' of the 'Transitional Government of National Unity' formed in 1985, and to repress the local media (*Financial Times*, 9.4.1988).
51 *Windhoek Advertiser*, 6.4.1988.
52 Interview Crocker, 31.5.1990.
53 *Times*, 2.5.1988; Pretoria initially wanted the timetable of Cuban withdrawal to coincide with South African withdrawal from Namibia over twelve months.
54 *Financial Times*, 12.5.1988.
55 Neil P. van Heerden, *Negotiating the 1988 New York Accord: Motives, Rationale, Experiences*, paper presented to 'Workshop on Cooperation, and Security in Post-Apartheid Southern Africa', Maputo, 3–6 September 1991, p.9.
56 *Guardian*, 6.5.1988; *International Herald Tribune*, 17.5.1988; according to Jaster, Castro had ordered the move of 15,000 troops to the border on 10 March 1988 (Robert Jaster, *The 1988 Peace Accords, and the Future of South-western Africa* (Adelphi paper no. 253), London, International Institute for Strategic Studies, 1990, p. 21).
57 *Independent*, 10.6.1988.
58 *Guardian Weekly*, 22.5.1988.
59 Cf. *Africa Confidential*, 27.5.1988.
60 Interview 'Pik' Botha with Reuter, 19.5.1988 in *Southern Africa Record*, no. 50, 1988, pp. 55–60; see also *The Times*, 16.5.1988.
61 *Independent*, 24.5.1988.
62 *Africa Confidential*, 15.7.1988.
63 *Financial Times*, 27.6.1988.
64 Cf. Interview with Antonio Pitra Neto, Maputo, 5.9.1991; van Heerden, *Negotiating the 1988 New York Accord*, p. 10.
65 See Bridgland, *War for Africa*, p. 340.
66 Quoted in *Financial Times*, 27.6.1988.
67 *Financial Times*, 24.6.1988.

68 Interview with 'Pik' Botha in *BBC World Service*, 26.6.1988.
69 Bridgland, *War for Africa*, pp. 349–350, 363.
70 *Ibid.*, p. 358.
71 Interview Pitra Neto, 5.9.1991.
72 See Bridgland, *War for Africa*, p. 360.
73 Twenty-six according to the Angolan government; for a detailed decription of the attack on Caluque, see *ibid.*, pp. 361–2.
74 *Independent*, 30.6.1988; *Namibian*, 1.7.1988.
75 Quoted in Bridgland, *War for Africa*, p. 364.
76 Cf. Geldenhuys, *Isolation*, p. 145.
77 Cf. Bender, 'Peacemaking in Southern Africa', p. 29; see also *Citizen*, 2.2.1989.
78 Bender, 'Peacemaking in Southern Africa', p. 30.
79 Interview Crocker, 31.5.1990, van Heerden, *Negotiating the 1988 New York Accord*, pp. 10–11.
80 See *Financial Times*, 25.7.1988.
81 See *Independent*, 6.8.1988, and 9.8.1988.
82 See appendix 5: Protocol of Geneva, 5.8.1988. The Geneva protocol also established a Joint Military Monitoring Committee with eleven Joint Monitoring Border Posts (Cf. *Southern Africa Record* (South African Institute for International Affairs), no. 51, 1988, pp. 5–7).
83 Interview Crocker, 31.5.1990.
84 Steenkamp, *Border War*, p. 176,; Jaster, *Peace Accords*, p. 26.
85 Cf. *International Herald Tribune*, 23.9.1988; see also 'Further Report of the Secretary-General Concerning the Implementation of Security Council Resolution 435 (1978) Concerning the Question of Namibia', UN. Doc. S/20412, 23.1.1989, paras. 17–27.
86 See appendix 6.
87 Unhappy over the issue of the verification of the Cuban withdrawal, Botha returned to Pretoria for consultations on 2 December.
88 Cf. *Financial Times*, 23.11.1988.
89 Namibia would be invited to join the commission after independence.
90 Tripartite Agreement of 22 December, para. 3 (appendix 7).
91 *Ibid.*, para. 6. The agreement also stipulated that the territories of Angola, and South Africa should not be used by any organization for acts which would violate the territorial integrity of any state of southwestern Africa, an implicit reference to ANC bases in Angola (*Ibid.* para. 5).
92 Interview with Crocker in *Schweizerische Handels-Zeitung*, 2.11.1989.
93 *Southscan*, 11.1.1989, Jaster, *Peace Accords*, p. 65.
94 *International Herald Tribune*, 11.1.1989.
95 Van Heerden, *Negotiating the 1988 New York Accord*, p. 14; Pitra Neto to 'Workshop on Cooperation, and Security in Post-Apartheid Southern Africa', Maputo, 6.9.1991.
96 Interview Rytow, 18.7.1988; see also Igor Belikov, 'Perestroika,

the Soviet Union, and the Third World', *Review of African Political Economy*, no. 50, 1991, p. 33.
97 Speech Gorbachev, 70th anniversary October revolution, Moscow, 2.11.1987, in *Southern Africa Record* , no. 49, 1987, pp. 15–6.
98 Quoted in Robert Legvold, 'The Revolution in Soviet Foreign Policy', *Foreign Affairs*, vol. 68, no. 1, 1989, p. 86; on the Soviet doctrine, see Mikhail Gorbachev, *Perestroika: New Thinking for Our Country and the World*, New York, Harper & Row, 1987; with particular reference to southern Africa, see Vladimir Sokolov, 'Soviet Foreign Policy: A reply to Nabudere', *Southern Africa Political and Economic Monthly*, no. 11, August 1988, pp. 7–9; Alexei Vassiliev, 'A la recherche d'alternatives régionales', *Les Nouvelles de Moscou*, 7.8.1988; interview Youri Youkalov (head of Africa section Soviet ministry of foreign affairs), 'Moscou-Pretoria: vers les relations diplomatiques', *Les Nouvelles de Moscou*, 16.4.1989.
99 Francis Fukuyama, 'Gorbachev, and the Third World', *Foreign Affairs*, vol. 64, no. 4, 1986, p. 718.
100 Alexei Izyumov, and Andrei Kortunov, 'The Soviet Union in the Changing World', *International Affairs* (Moscow), August 1988, p. 52.
101 See Fukuyama, 'Gorbachev, and the Third World', pp. 716, 724, 725, 727; when Gorbachev met the Angolan president dos Santos in May 1986, he made it clear that the Soviet Union would honour its commitments to Angola.
102 Anatoli Gromyko, and Vladimir Lomeiko, 'New Way of Thinking, and "New Globalism", *International Affairs* (Moscow), May 1986, p. 19.
103 Nikolai Kapchenko, 'The CPSU Foreign Policy, and Today's World', *International Affairs*, October 1987, p. 73.
104 Izyumov and Kortunov, 'The Soviet Union in a Changed World', p. 52.
105 Freeman, 'Angola/Namibia Accords', p. 137.
106 Cf. *Southern Africa Record*, nos. 47, and 48, 1987, p. 82; Adamishin was apparently disavowed for earlier disagreement with Crocker (interview Rytow, 18.7.1988).
107 Cf. Freeman, 'Angola/Namibia Accords', p. 134.
108 Interview Crocker, 31.5.1988.
109 Cf. Winrich Kühne, 'Frieden im südwestlichen Afrika? Der Durchbruch bei den Verhandlungen um die Unabhaengigkeit Namibias', *Europa Archiv*, vol. 44, no. 4, 25.2.1989, p. 109; Pisani and von der Ropp, 'Western/Namibian Initiatives', p. 14.
110 Cf. Bender, 'Peacemaking in Southern Africa', p. 27; in early 1988, Angola's debt to the Soviet Union stood at 2.5 to 3 billion dollars out of a total foreign debt of 4 billion.
111 S. Neil MacFarlane, 'The Soviet Union, and Southern African Security', *Problems of Communism*, vol. 38, no. 2–3, March-June 1989, p. 71, n. 2.
112 *Africa Confidential*, 27.5.1987. According to South African sources,

an estimated 8,000 SWAPO guerillas were operating from Angola (*Namibian*, 6.11.1987).

113 *Africa Confidential*, 5.2.1988.
114 *Africa Confidential*, 1.4.1988.
115 Hough 'Military Reasons', p. 7; one battalion code named 'Tiger' would have been based at Xangongo in the Cunene province, the other battalions, 'Zebra', and 'Lion' at Mupa, and Cahama to the northeast, and northwest of Xangongo (*Namibian*, 27.5.1988).
116 *Independent*, 10.6.1988.
117 *Guardian Weekly*, 22.5.1988; at the same time ANC guerillas were reported to have assisted FAPLA in fighting UNITA in the north (*Africa Confidential*, 27.5.1988).
118 *Africa Confidential*, 15.7.1988.
119 *Namibian*, 1.7.1988.
120 'SWAPO cannot confirm or deny presence at Caluque', *Namibian*, 1.7.1988.
121 *Daily News*, 22.3.1988.
122 Interview Crocker, 31.5.1990.
123 Franz Ansprenger, 'Die SWAPO als Regierungspartei', *Das Parlament*, 16.2.1990, p. 15.
124 *Times*, 2.5.1988.
125 Quoted in *Windhoek Advertiser*, 6.5.1988.
126 See *Namibian*, 20.5.1988.
127 Interview Nujoma in *Namibian*, 3.6.1988.
128 *Times*, 10.8.1988; see also letter Sam Nujoma to U.N. Secretary-General, 17.8.1988, UN. Doc. S/20129.
129 *Financial Times*, 18.11.1988.
130 Press Conference R.F. Botha, 22.11.1988 in *Backgrounder*, no. 43/1988, South African Embassy, London, 24.11.1988.
131 *Independent*, 11.1.1989.
132 According to Resolution 435, only 1,500 troops would remain in the country at independence day.
133 Resolution 629 (16.1.1989).
134 *Namibian*, 3.2.1989; *Southscan*, 1.3.1989.
135 *International Herald Tribune*, 14/15.1.1989.
136 *Namibian*, 17.2.1989.
137 Faced with the threat by Pretoria that it would abort the independence process, the United Nations agreed to the redeployment of South African forces in northern Namibia (see *Guardian*, 2.4.1989; *Independent*, 4.4.1989; *Namibian*, 7.4.1989).
138 Cf. Report of the Secretary-General on the Implementation of Security Council Resolution 640 (1989) Concerning the Question of Namibia, 6.10.1989, UN. Doc. S/20883, para. 6, p. 3.
139 Protocol of Geneva, 5.8.1988, see appendix 5.
140 See letter Nujoma to UN secretary-general, 17.8.1988, UN. Doc. S/20129.
141 'Proposal for a settlement of the Namibian situation', in Letter from the representatives of Canada, France, FRG, United States,

and United Kingdom to president Security Council, 10.4.1978, UN. Doc. S/12636, p. 4 (see appendix 2).

142 Security Council Resolution 632 (16.2.1989); cf. letter Helmut Angula (SWAPO Observer Mission at the United Nations, New York) to *Namibian*, 28.4.1989); on SWAPO's view of the events, see also interview with Nujoma in *Southern Africa Political, and Economic Monthly*, November 1989.

143 Cf. David Simon, *Independent Namibia One Year On* (Conflict Studies no. 239), London, Research Institute for the Study of Conflict, and Terrorism, 1991, p. 4.

144 *Southscan*, 12.4.1991, p. 127.

145 *Financial Times*, 4.4.1989.

146 *Independent*, 4.4.1989.

147 *Neue Zürcher Zeitung*, 8/9.4.1989.

148 SWAPO, and the South Africans met as late as 18 April 1989 at Ruacana on the Namibian-Angolan border (*Southscan*, 26.4.1989, p. 121).

149 Mount Etjo Declaration, Annexure, 9.4.1989, see appendix 8.

150 *Guardian*, 29.4.1989. 151 *Southscan*, 17.5.1989.

152 United Nations officials participated at the Cahama meeting.

153 Cf. *International Herald Tribune*, 20.5.1989.

154 Interview Pitra Neto, 5.9.1991.

155 *Foreign Report Confidential* (Economist, London), 17.5.1990.

156 Interview with Frontline state diplomat, Geneva, 19.7.1990.

157 Cf.*Herald* (Zimbabwe), 6.4.1989.

158 Cf. Jaster, *Peace Accords*, p. 39; the fact that SWAPO had detained several hundred of its members in Angola probaly cost the movement votes, especially in the south of the country (cf. Heribert Weiland. *Namibia – wohin?*. Bonn, Deutsche Kommission Justitia et Pax, 1990, p. 10).

159 See UN. Doc. S/20883, 6.10.1989, p. 48.

160 *Windhoek Advertiser*, 28.11.1989.

161 *Southscan*, 19.7.1989; on the election campaign, see Jaster, *Peace Accords*, pp. 40–45; Ansprenger, 'SWAPO als Regierungspartei', pp. 19–20.

162 *Namibia Today*, 23.9.1989; an estimated 100,000 South African citizens who had lived for four consecutive years in Namibia, were eligible for voting. However, only 11,000 persons registerted out of whom only 6,000 voted in the elections of November 1989 (Jaster, *Peace Accords*, p. 43).

163 Cf. UN. Doc. S/20967, 14.11.1989, p. 1.

164 Other minority parties in the Assembly were the Action Christian National (ACN) (three seats), Federal Convention of Namibia (FCN) (one seat), National Patriotic Front (NPF) (one seat), and United Democratic Front (UDF) (fours seats). The Christian Democratic Action for Social Justice (CDA), the Namibia National Democratic Party (NNDP), and SWAPO-D(emocrats) led by Andreas Shipanga did not obtain sufficient votes to have any deputy; for the detailed election results, see UN. Doc. S/20967, 14.11.1989,

pp. 2, and 10; for an analysis of the elections, see Weiland. *Namibia – wohin?*, pp. 6–11.

Conclusion: Namibian independence ans Southern Africa

1 Ministry of Foreign Affairs (Namibia), *Joint Statement*, Windhoek, 17th May 1991; the two governments agreed at the meeting that the the middle of the Orange River should be the boundary between the two countries, instead of the north bank as decided by Germany when it had declared its protectorate over south west Africa in 1884.
2 See 'Foreign Policy Perspectives of the Republic of Namibia: An Overview', *Southern African Political, and Economic Monthly*, vol.4, no.6, March 1991, p.13; the issue of *sovereignty* over Walvis Bay, and the offshore islands, however, is not negotiable as it is enshrined in the constitution (art.1.4.) (cf. interview with Andreas Guibeb, Permanent Secretary Foreign Affairs, Windhoek, 14 February 1991).
3 Citizen, 4.4.1992.
4 On national reconciliation, see for example Ronald Dreyer, 'La Namibie indépendante: la réconciliation nationale l'épreuve', in Dominique Darbon (ed.), *Année africaine 1990–1991*, Bordeaux, Institut d'études politiques (Centre d'étude d'Afrique noire, and Centre de recherche et d'étude sur les pays d'Afrique orientale), 1992, pp. 261–83; Kenneth W. Grundy, 'Namibia's First Year of Independence', *Current History*, vol. 90, no. 556, May 1991, pp. 213–16, and 226–7; Simon, *Independent Namibia*.
5 *Southscan*, 10.9.1993.
6 S.K.B. Asante, and W.W. Asombang, 'An Independent Namibia? The Future Facing SWAPO', *Third World Quarterly*, vol. 11, no. 3, 1989, p. 12.
7 Quoted in *Windhoek Advertiser*, 24.4.1990.
8 Statement Ben Amathila at *Meeting on Southern Africa*, World Economic Forum, Geneva, 27–28.10.1991.

BIBLIOGRAPHY

Archives

Arquivo Histrico Ultramarino, Lisbon
Instituto Nacional de Estatistica. *Annuario Estatistico, Portugal, Provincia de Angola* (1934–72).
Botswana National Archives (BNA), Gaberone
BTA. 7/7–11:   Bamangwato Tribal Administration, 1946

S. 5/6:   Railways, 1924.

Daily News archives, Dar es Salaam
Box: Namibia (1978): Frontline States (1984)

Institute of Commonwealth Studies (ICS), London
JX 1584. B2 BOT: Botswana, 1969.

Ministry of Information of Zimbabwe, Harare
File 6.3.:   'Pan African Organizations, PAFMECA', vol. 5.

Public Record Office (PRO), London
CO 879/12: Colonial Office, Africa, confidential print, 1878.
DO 35: Dominions Office, original correspondence, 1935, 1945, 1946, 1951.
Rhodes House, Oxford
MSS Afr.S.1681, Box 218/6 Africa Bureau, 1963, 1965.
United Nations Institute for Namibia, Lusaka
Unesco, International Conference of Solidarity with the People of Namibia, Paris, 11.–13.5.1980.

Interviews

With Ray Alexander, Lusaka, 4 August 1987.
With Melo Antunes, Paris, 11 May 1989.
With Musinga Bandora, Dar es Salaam, 21 February 1987.

247

With Mark Bomani, Lusaka, 4 August 1987.
With Norah Chase, Geneva, 7 March 1989.
With Chester Crocker, Geneva, 31 May 1990.
With Andreas Guibeb, Windhoek, 14 February 1991.
With José Maria Lopes, Maputo, 20 August 1987.
With Brigadier Hashim Mbita, Dar es Salaam, 23 March 1988.
With Billy Modise, Lusaka, 4 August 1987.
With A. M. Mogwe, Gaberone, 1 December 1987.
With Bernard Muganda, Dar es Salaam, 19 February 1987 and 23 August 1989.
With Mtshana Ncube, Lusaka, 3 August 1987.
With Antonio Pitra Neto, Maputo, 5 September 1991.
With M. Ribeiro, New York, 30 March 1982.
With Neville Rubin, Geneva, 7 March 1989.
With Lev Rytow, Moscow, 18 July 1988.
With Ngarikutuke Tjiriange, New York, 9 April 1982; Geneva, 21 February 1988.
With Randolph Vigne, London, 27 January 1989.
With John Ya-Otto, Geneva, 21 June 1987.

Published Interviews

With 'Pik' Botha by Reuter, 19.5.1988 in *Southern Africa Record*, no. 50, 1988, pp. 55–60.
With 'Pik' Botha by *BBC World Service*, 26.6.1988.
With Fidel Castro by Jeffrey M. Elliot and Mervyn M. Dymally, in *Fidel Castro. Nothing Can Stop the Course of History*. New York/London/Sydney, Pathfinder Press, 1986.
With Daniel Chipenda by Don Barnett, Liberation Support Movement (Canada), 28.8.1969, Richmond (B.C.). LSM Information Centre, 1970.
With Chester Crocker in *Schweizerische Handelszeitung*, 2.11.1989.
With Paulo Jorge by Don Barnett, December 1972, in Liberation Support Movement (Canada). *Interviews in Depth: MPLA/Angola, no. 4. Paulo Jorge*, Richmond, B.C., LSM Information Centre, 1973.
With Venancia de Moura, in *AfricAsia*, no. 38, February 1987, p.29.
With Sam Nujoma, in *Daily News*, 29.7.1984.
With Sam Nujoma, in *Granma* (Cuba), 14.3.1976.
With Sam Nujoma, in *Namibian*, 3.6.1988.
With Sam Nujoma in *Namibian*, 18.9.1989.
With Sam Nujoma in *Southern Africa Political and Economic Monthly*, November 1989.
With Jonas Savimbi by Yves Loiseau and Pierre-Guillaume de Roux, in *Portrait d'un rvolutionnaire en général. Jonas Savimbi*. Paris, La Table Ronde, 1987.
With Youri Youkalov, in 'Moscou-Pretoria: vers les relations diplomatiques', *Les Nouvelles de Moscou*, 16.4.1989.

United Nations documents

General assembly

Resolutions: 65(1), 14.12.1946; 2145 (21), 27.10.1966; 2375 (22), 12.6.1968, 3111 (28), 12.12.1973; 3296 (29), 13.12.1974; 31/146 (31), 20.12.1976.
A/ General Assembly, working documents, 1946.
A/2666 Report of the Committee on South West Africa for 1954.
A/4191 Report of the Committee on South West Africa for 1959.
A/4464 Report of the Committee on South West Africa for 1960.
A/A/40/PV.48 Speach Ronald Regan to General Assembly, 24.10.1985.

Committees of the General Assembly

Fourth Committee:
A/C.4: working documents, 1946, 1947; hearing of petitioners, 1960, 1962, 1963, 1970.
A/C.4/L: draft reports and resolutions, 1949, 1970.
Special Committee on the Situation with regard to the Implementation of the Declaration of the Granting of Independence to Colonial Countries and Peoples:
A/AC. 109: working documents, 1966, 1970.
A/AC. 109/PET: petitions, 1962, 1963, 1964, 1967.
A/AC. 109/L: draft reports and resolutions, 1970.
United Nations Council for Namibia: A/AC.131: 1983.
Special Committee Against Apartheid:
Notes and Documents (Unit on Apartheid), no. 7/74 (1974); no. 31/75 (1975); Centre against Apartheid: Conf.2 (1977).

Security council

Resolutions:
366 (17.12.1974); 385 (30.1.1976); 431 (27.7.1978); 432 (27.7.1978); 435 (29.9.1978); 626 (20.12.1988); 629 (16.1.1989). 632 (16.2.1989).
Letters to Council, reports and notes by the secretary-general (S/):
12636 (10.4.1978); 12827 (29.8.1978); 15287 (12.7.1982); 17658 (29.11.1985); 20109 (8.8.1988); 20129 (17.8.1989); 20345 (22.12.1988); 20346 (22.12.1988); 20412 (23.1.1989); 20566 (4.4.1989); 20579 (17.4.1989); 20883 (6.10.1989); 20967 (14.11.1989).

Official Publications

Annuario estatistico, Portugal, Provincia de Angola, 1962.
Banco de Angola. *Economic and Financial Survey*, Luanda, 1970.
Brezhnev, Leonid I., *Discours à la session plénière du Comité central du*

Parti Communiste de l'Union soviétique (25 octobre 1976), Moscow, Novosti Press Agency, 1976.

Foreign and Commonwealth Office (U.K.), 'Memorandum on Walvis Bay', reprinted in the *Minutes of Evidence taken before the Foreign Affairs Committee of the House of Commons* London, HMSO, 13.5.1981.

MPLA Special Congress, *Report of the Central Committee of the MPLA-Workers' Party*, Luanda, 1980.

Ministry of Foreign Affairs (Namibia), *Joint Statement* (governments of the Republic of Namibia, and the Republic of South Africa), Windhoek, 17.5.1991.

People's Republic of Angola. *White Paper on Acts of Aggression by the Racist South African Regime Against the People's Republic of Angola. 1975–1982.* Luanda, Ministry of External Relations, 1982.

Republic of South Africa, *Backgrounder*, no. 43/1988, South African Embassy, London, 24.11.1988.

Republic of South Africa. *Report of the Commission of Enquiry into South West Africa Affairs. 1962–1963* (Odendaal Report). Pretoria, Government Printer, 1964.

United Nations, *Yearbook 1946–1947*. New York, United Nations (Department of Public Information), 1947.

United Nations Institute for Namibia, *A Decade of Progress, 1976–1986*, Lusaka, United Nations Institute for Namibia, 1986.

Union of South Africa, *Report of the Administrator of South West Africa for the Year 1924*. Pretoria, Government Printer, 1925.

Union of South Africa, *Report of the Commission on the Economic and Financial Relations between the Union of South Africa and the Mandated Territory of South West Africa*, Pretoria, Government Printer, 1935.

United States Department of State, Bureau of Public Affairs, *Agreements for Peace in Southwestern Africa*, Washington, December, 1988.

Vorster, B.J., 'Statement on South West Africa', 20.9.1978, London, Director of Information, South Africa House, 1978.

Published documents

Hancock, W.K., *Smuts, vol. 1: The Sanguine Years, 1870–1919*, Cambridge, Cambridge University Press, 1962.

Hancock W.K. and Van de Poel, J. (eds), *Selection of the Smuts Papers*, Cambridge, Cambridge University Press, vol. 7, 1973.

Karis, Thomas and Carter, Gwendolen M., *From Protest to Challenge. A Documentary History of African Politics in South Africa, 1884–1964*, vol. 2, Stanford, Hoover Institution Press, 1973.

Mandela, Nelson, *The Struggle Is My Life*. London, International Defence and Aid Fund for Southern Africa, 1978.

Minogue, Martin and Molloy, Judith (eds), *African Aims and Attitudes. Selected Documents*. Cambridge, Cambridge University Press, 1974.

Minter, William, *Operation Timber. Pages from the Savimbi Dossier*. Trenton, N.J., Africa World Press, 1988.

South African Communists Speak. Documents from the History of the South

African Communist Party, 1915–1980, London, Inkululeko Publications, 1981.

Newspapers, periodicals

Africa Confidential, 1966, 1975, 1976, 1977, 1978, 1979, 1984, 1987, 1988.
Africa Development (Britain), 1972, 1976.
AfricAsia, 1971, 1987.
Afrique-Asie, 1971, 1974, 1975.
Agence France Press, 1975.
Angola Information, 1984.
Cape Times, 1920.
Citizen, 1989, 1990.
Clarion, 1952.
Daily News (Tanz.), 1972, 1976, 1977, 1983, 1984, 1988.
Daily Telegraph, 1976.
Economist, 1983, 1985, 1988.
Financial Times, 1972, 1975, 1976, 1988, 1989.
Foreign Report Confidential (Economist), 1990.
Granma (Cuba), 1976.
Guardian (Cape Town), 1952.
Guardian (London), 1972, 1976, 1978, 1979, 1986, 1987, 1988, 1989, 1990.
Guardian Weekly, 1987, 1988.
Herald (Zimbabwe), 1989.
Independent, 1987, 1988, 1989.
International Herald Tribune, 1984, 1986, 1988, 1989.
Jane's Defence Weekly, 1989.
Jeune Afrique, 1972.
Jornal de Angola, 1976.
Le Monde, 1976, 1987.
Le Monde diplomatique, 1985, 1986, 1988, 1991.
Namibian, 1986, 1987, 1988, 1989, 1990.
Namibia Today, 1989.
Neue Zürcher Zeitung, 1985, 1988, 1989.
New Age, 1962.
New York Times, 1981.
Novosti Press Agency, 1976.
Nouvelles de Moscou, 1988, 1989.
Observer, 1976.
Rhodesia Herald, 1966, 1976, 1978.
SA Report (South Africa), 1988, 1989.
Schweizerische Handelszeitung, 1989.
Southern Africa Political and Economic Monthly, 1989, 1990, 1991.
Southern Africa Record (S.A.), 1987, 1988, 1993.
Southscan, 1988, 1989, 1990, 1991.
Standard (Tanz.), 1972.
Star, 1972.

Star Weekly, 1971, 1975.
Sunday Times, 1977.
The Times (London), 1937, 1943, 1971, 1976, 1978, 1988.
Times of Zambia, 1972, 1975.
To the Point International (South Africa), 1979.
Washington Post, 1976.
Weekly Mail, 1988.
West Africa (U.K.), 1988.
Windhoek Advertiser, 1988, 1989, 1990.
Zambia Daily Mail, 1971, 1972, 1976.

Books

Aluko, Olajide and Shaw, Timothy M. (eds), Southern Africa in the 1980s, London, George Allen & Unwin, 1985.
Aluko, Olajide (ed.), The Foreign Policies of African States, London/ Sydney/Auckland/Toronto, Hodder & Stoughton, 1977.
Anglin, Douglas and Shaw, Timothy (eds), Zambia's Foreign Policy. Studies in Diplomacy and Dependence. Boulder, Col., Westview Press, 1979.
Ansprenger, Franz, Die SWAPO. Profil einer afrikanischen Befeiungsbew- egung. Munich/Mainz, Kaiser/Grünewald, 1984.
Azicri, Max, Cuba. Politics, Economics and Society. London/New York, Pinter Publishers, 1988.
Barber, James, Barratt, John, South Africa's Foreign Policy. The Search for Status and Security. 1945–1988, Cambridge/New York/Port Chester/ Melbourne/Sydney, Cambridge University Press, 1990.
Barnett, Don and Harvey, R., The Revolution in Angola. MPLA Life Stories and Documents, Indianapolis, New York, Bobbs-Merril Com- pany, 1972.
Bender, Gerald, Angola under the Portuguese: The Myth and the Reality, London, Heinemann, 1978.
Benson, Mary, South Africa: The Struggle for a Birthright, Harmond- sworth, Penguin, 1966.
Berat, Lynn, Walvis Bay. The Last Frontier, Wynberg/New Haven, Radix/Yale University Press, 1990.
Bragança, Acquino de and Wallerstein, Immanuel (eds), The African Liberation Reader, vol. 3: 'The Strategy of Liberation', London, Zed Press, 1982.
Brewer, John D. (ed.), Can South Africa Survive. Five Minutes to Mid- night, London, Macmillan, 1989.
Bridgland, Fred, Jonas Savimbi: A Key to Africa, London, Hodder & Stoughton, 1988.
Bridgland, Fred, The War for Africa. Twelve Months that Transformed a Continent, Gibraltar, Ashanti, 1990.
Callaghy, T. (ed.), South Africa in Southern Africa. The Intensifying Vortex of Violence, New York, Praeger Publishers, 1984.

Callinicos, Alex and Roger, John, *Southern Africa after Soweto*. London, Pluto Press, 1978.

Carter, Gwendolen M. and O'Meara, Patrick (eds), *Southern Africa. The Continuing Crisis*, Bloomington, Indiana University Press, 1982.

Cervenka, Zdenek, *The Unfinished Quest for Unity. Africa and the OAU*, London, Julius Friedman Publishers, 1977.

Clarence-Smith, W.G., *Slaves, Peasants and Capitalists in Southern Angola. 1840–1926*, Cambridge, Cambridge University Press, 1979.

Cox, Richard, *Pan-Africanism in Practice, PAFMECSA, 1958–1964*, London, Oxford University Press, 1964.

Crowder, Michael (ed.), *The Cambridge History of Africa, vol. 8: ca.1940 to ca.1975*, Cambridge, Cambridge University Press, 1984.

Davezies, Robert, *Les Angolais*. Paris, Les Editions de Minuit, 1965.

Davidson, Basil, *In the Eye of the Storm. Angola's People*. Harmondsworth, Penguin, 1975.

Davies, Rob, O'Meara, Dan and Dlamini, Sipho *The Struggle for South Africa. A Reference Guide to Movements, Organizations and Institutions*, London, Zed Press, 1984 (vol.II).

Davis, Stephen M., *Apartheid's Rebels. Inside South Africa's Hidden War*, New Haven/London, Yale University Press, 1987.

De Andrade Mario and Ollivier, Marc, *The War in Angola. A Socio-Economic Study*, Dar es Salaam, Tanzania Publishing House, 1975.

De Sousa Ferreira, Eduardo, *Portuguese Colonialism from South Africa to Europe*, Freiburg i.B., Aktion Dritte Welt, 1972.

Diaz-Briquets, Sergio (ed.), *Cuban Internationalism in Sub-Sahran Africa*. Pittsburgh (Penns.), Duquesne University Press, 1989.

Dominguez, Jorge I., *To Make a World Safe for Revolution. Cuban Foreign Policy*. Cambridge (Mass.)/London, Harvard University Press, 1989.

Drechsler, Horst, *Let Us Die Fighting. The Struggle of the Herero and Nama against German Imperialism (1884–1915)*, London, Zed Press, 1980.

Dreyer, Ronald, *The Mind of Official Imperialism. British and Cape Government Perceptions of German Rule in Namibia from the Heligoland- Zanzibar Treaty to the Kruger Telegram (1890–1896)*, Essen, Reimar Hobbing Verlag, 1987.

Driver, C.J., *Patrick Duncan. South African and Pan-African*. London, Heinemann, 1980.

Deutsches Institut für Zeitgeschichte. *Die Afro-asiatische Soldaritätsbewegung*. Berlin (GDR), Staatsverlag der Deutschen Demokratischen Republik, 1968.

Duffy, James and Manners, Robert (eds), *Africa Speaks*. Princeton, D. van Nostrand Company, Inc., 1961.

Dugard, John, *The South West Africa/Namibia Dispute. Documents and Scholarly Writings on the Controversy Between South Africa and the United Nations*. Berkeley/Los Angeles/London, University of California Press, 1972.

Du Pisani, André, *SWA/Namibia: The Politics of Continuity and Change*. Johannesburg, Jonathan Ball, 1986.

Elliot, Jeffrey M. and Dymally, Mervyn M., *Fidel Castro. Nothing Can*

Stop the Course of History. New York/London/Sydney, Pathfinder Press, 1986.

Eriksen, Tore Linné with Moorsom, Richard, *The Political Economy of Namibia. An annotated critical bibliography.* Uppsala, Scandinavian Institute of African Studies, 1989 (second enlarged edition).

Esedebe, Olisanwuche, *Pan-Africanism. The Idea and Movement. 1776–1963*, Washington, Howard University Press, 1982.

First, Ruth, *South West Africa*, Harmondsworth, Penguin, 1963.

Frankel, Philip H., *Pretoria's Praetorians. Civil-Military Relations in South Africa*, Cambridge, Cambridge University Press, 1984.

Geiss, Immanuel, *The Pan-African Movement. A History of Pan-Africanism in America, Europe and Africa.* London, Methuen, 1974.

Geldenhuys, Deon, *The Diplomacy of Isolation. South African Foreign Policy Making*, New York, St-Martin's Press, 1984.

Geldenhuys, Deon and Gutteridge William (eds), *Instability and Conflict in Southern Africa*, London, Institute for the Study of Conflict, 1983.

Gibson, Richard, *African Liberation Movements. Contemporary Struggles against White Minority Rule.* London, Oxford University Press, 1972.

Gifford, Prosser and Louis, Wm. Roger (eds), *Britain and Germany in Africa: Imperial Rivalry and Colonial Rule*, New Haven, Yale University Press, 1967.

Gifford, Prosser and Louis, Wm. Roger (eds), *The Transfer of Power in Africa*, New Haven/London, Yale University Press, 1982.

Gifford, Prosser and Louis, Wm. Roger (eds), *Decolonization and African Independence. The Transfer of Power. 1960–1980*, New Haven/London, Yale University Press, 1988.

Glickman, Harvey (ed.), *Toward Peace and Security in Southern Africa*, New York, Gordon & Breach Science Publishers, 1990.

Gorbachev, Mikhail, *Perestroika: New Thinking for Our Country and the World.* New York, Harper & Row, 1987.

Green, Reginald, Kiljunen, Marja-Liisa, Kiljunen, Kimmo (eds), *Namibia. The Last Colony*, Burnt Mill, Harlow (Essex), Longman, 1981.

Grundy, Kenneth W., *Confrontation and Accomodation in Southern Africa. The Limits of Independence*, Berkeley, University of California Press, 1973.

Grundy, Kenneth W., *The Militarization of South African Politics*, Oxford, Oxford University Press, 1988.

Hailey, William M., *The Republic of South Africa and the High Commission Territories*, London, Oxford University Press, 1963.

Hanlon, Joseph, *Beggar Your Neighbours. Apartheid Power in Southern Africa*, London, Catholic Institute for International Relations/James Currey, 1986.

Hargreaves, John D., *Decolonization in Africa.* London/New York, Longman, 1988.

Harneit-Sievers, Axel, *SWAPO of Namibia. Entwicklung, Programmatik und Politik seit 1959*, Hamburg, Institut für Afrikakunde, 1985.

Heimer, Franz-Wilhelm, *Der Entkolonisierungskonflikt in Angola.* Munich/London, Weltforum Verlag, 1979.

BIBLIOGRAPHY

Hyam, Ronald, *The Failure of South African Expansion*, New York, Africana Publishing Corporation, 1972.

Isaacman, Allen and Barbara, *Mozambique. From Colonialism to Revolution. 1900–1982*. Harare, Zimbabwe Publishing House, 1985.

Jaster, Robert, *South Africa in Namibia. The Botha Strategy*. Lanham/New York/London, University Press for America, 1985.

Jaster, Robert Scott, *The Defence of White Power. South African Foreign Policy under Pressure*. Basingstoke, Macmillan (with International Institute for Strategic Studies), 1988.

Johnson, Phyllis and Martin, David (eds), *Destructive Engagement. Southern Africa at War*, Harare, Zimbabwe Publishing House, 1986.

Katjavivi, Peter H., *A History of Resistance in Namibia*. Paris/London, UNESCO/James Currey, 1988.

Kempton, Daniel R., *Soviet Strategy toward Southern Africa. The National Liberation Movement Connection*, New York/Westport/London, Prager, 1989.

Khama, Seretse, *From the Frontline (Speeches)*, edited by Gwendolen M. Carter and E.Philip Morgan, London, Rex Collings, 1980.

Kimche, David, *The Afro-Asian Movement. Ideology and Foreign Policy of the Third World*. Jerusalem, Israel Universities Press, 1973.

Laidi, Zaki, *Les contraintes d'une rivalité. Les superpuissances et l'Afrique*. Paris, La Découverte, 1986.

Legum, Colin (ed.), *Africa Contemporary Record (1981–2)*, vol. 24, New York/London, Africana Publishing Company, 1982.

Legum, Colin (ed.), *Africa Contemporary Record (1982–3)*, vol. 25, New York/London, Africana Publishing Company, 1984.

Legum, Colin, *The Battlefronts of Southern Africa*, New York/London, Africana Publishing Company, 1988.

Legum, Colin, Hodges, Tony (eds), *After Angola: The War over Southern Africa*, London, Rex Collings, 1976.

Lodge, Tom, *Black Politics in South Africa since 1945*. London/New York, Longman, 1983.

Loiseau, Yves and de Roux, Pierre-Guillaume, *Portrait d'un révolutionnaire en général. Jonas Savimbi*, Paris, La Table Ronde, 1987.

Marcum, John, *The Angolan Revolution. vol. 1. The Anatomy of an Explosion (1950–1962)*, Cambridge, Mass./London, M.I.T. Press, 1969.

Marcum, John, *The Angolan Revolution. vol. 2: Exile Politics and Guerilla Warfare (1962–1976)*, Cambridge, Mass./London, M.I.T. Press, 1978.

Martin, David and Johnson, Phyllis, *The Chitepo Assassination*, Harare, Zimbabwe Publishing House, 1985.

Martin, David and Johnson, Phyllis, *The Struggle for Zimbabwe. The Chimurenga War*, London/Boston, Faber and Faber, 1982.

Matthews, Z.K., *Freedom for My People. The Autobiography of Z.K. Matthews. South Africa, 1901–1968*. Cape Town, David Philips, 1981.

Minter, William (ed.), *Operation Timber. Pages from the Savimbi Dossier*. Trenton, New Jersey, Africa World Press, 1988.

Msabaha, Ibrahim and Shaw, Timothy M. (eds). *Confrontation and*

Liberation in Southern Africa. Boulder(Col.)/ London/Westview Press/ Gower, 1987.

Mushi, S.S. and Mathews, K. (eds), *Foreign Policy of Tanzania, 1961–1981: A Reader*, Dar es Salaam, Tanzania Publishing House, 1981.

Neuhauser, Charles, *Third World Politics. China and the Afro-Asian Peoples Solidarity Organization. 1957–1967*. Cambridge, Mass., Harvard University Press, 1968.

Nyerere, Julius, *Crusade for Liberation*. Dar es Salaam/ Nairobi/Oxford/ New York, Oxford University Press, 1978.

Potholm, Christian P. and Dale, Richard (eds) *Southern Africa in Perspective*, New York, The Free Press, 1972.

Ogunsanwo, Alaba, *China's Foreign Policy in Africa. 1958–1971*, Cambridge, Cambridge University Press, 1974.

Puetz, Joachim, Von Egidy, Heidi, Caplan, Perri, *Namibia Handbook and Political Who's Who*, 2nd edition, Windhoek, Magus, 1990.

Scott, Michael, *A Time to Speak*, London, Faber and Faber, 1958.

Sefali, Michael and Bardill, John (eds), *Development and Destabilization in Southern Africa*, Roma (Lesotho), Institute of Southern African Studies, 1985.

Segall, Ronald and First, Ruth (eds), *South West Africa, Travesty of Trust*, London André Deutsch, 1967.

Seiler, John (ed.), *Southern Africa Since the Portuguese Coup*, Boulder, Col., Westview Press, 1980.

Serfontein, J.H.P., *Namibia?*. London, Rex Collings, 1976.

Shamuyarira N.M. (ed.), *Essays on the Liberation of Southern Africa*, Dar es Salaam, Tanzania Publishing House, 1972.

Shevchenko, Arkady N., *Breaking with Moscow*, New York, Alfred Knopf, 1985.

Shipanga, Andreas, *In Search of Freedom. The Andreas Shipanga Story as Told to Sue Armstrong*. Gibraltar, Ashanti Publishing, 1989.

Shityuwete, Helao, *Never Follow the Wolf*, London, Cliptown Books, 1990.

Simba, Iddi and Wells, Francis, *Development Co-operation in Southern Africa. Structures and Procedures*. Paris, OECD, 1984.

Simons, H.J. and R.E., *Class and Colour in South Africa, 1850–1950*, Harmondsworth, Penguin, 1969.

Smith, William Edgett, *Nyerere of Tanzania*, Harare, Zimbabwe Publishing House, 1981.

Soggot, David, *Namibia. The Violent Heritage*, London, Rex Collings, 1980.

Sommerville, Keith, *Angola, Politics, Economics and Society*, London, Frances Pinter, 1986.

Steenkamp, Willem, *South Africa's Border War, 1966–1989*, Gibraltar, Ashanti, 1989.

Stockwell, John, *In Search of Enemies: A CIA Story*. New York, Andr Deutsch, 1978.

SWAPO, *To Be Born a Nation*, London, Zed Press, 1981.

Tambo, Adelaide (ed.), *Preparing for Power. Oliver Tambo Speaks*. London, Heinemann, 1987.

Thompson, Carol B., *Challenge to Imperialism. The Frontline States in the Liberation of Zimbabwe*, Harare, Zimbabwe Publishing House, 1985.

Thompson, Leonard and Wilson, Monica (eds), *The Oxford History of South Africa*, vol. 2: South Africa. 1870–1966, Oxford, Oxford University Press, 1978.

United Nations Institute for Namibia, *A Decade of Progress, 1976–1986*, Lusaka, United Nations Institute for Namibia, 1986.

Urquhart, Brian, *A Life in Peace and War*. New York, Harper & Row Publishers, 1987.

Vail, Leroy (ed.), *The Creation of Tribalism in Africa*, London/ Berkeley/ Los Angeles, James Currey/University of California Press, 1989.

Vance, Cyrus, *Hard Choices. Critical Years in America's Foreign Policy*. New York, Simon & Schuster, 1983.

Wolfers, Michael and Bergerol, Jane, *Angola in the Front Line*. London, Zed Books, 1983.

Wood, Brian (ed.), *Namibia. 1884–1984. Readings in Namibia's History and Society*, London/Lusaka, Namibia Support Committee, United Nations Institute for Namibia, 1988.

Ya-Otto, John *Battlefront Namibia. An Autobiography*, Harare, Zimbabwe Publishing House, 1982.

Zartman, I. William, *Ripe for Resolution. Conflict and Intervention in Africa*. New York/Oxford, Oxford University Press, 1985.

Articles and chapters in books

Ajala, Adekunle, 'The OAU and Southern Africa', in O. Aluko and T. Shaw (eds), *Southern Africa in the 1980s*, London, George Allen & Unwin, 1985, pp. 3–17.

Albright, David E., 'The USSR and the Third World in the 1980s', *Problems of Communism*, vol. 38, nos 2–3, March–June 1989, pp. 50–70.

Aluko, Olajide, 'Nigeria, Namibia and Southern Africa', in O. Aluko and T. Shaw (eds), *Southern Africa in the 1980s*, London, George Allen & Unwin, pp. 41–60.

Ansprenger, Franz, 'Die SWAPO als Regierungspartei', *Das Parlament*, 16.2.1990, pp. 14–23.

Asante, S.K.B. and Asombang, W.W., 'An Independent Namibia? The Future Facing SWAPO', *Third World Quarterly*, vol. 11, no. 3, 1989, pp. 1–19.

Belikov, Igor, 'Perestroika, the Soviet Union and the Third World', *Review of African Political Economy*, no. 50, 1991, pp. 33–7.

Bender, Gerald, 'Angola, the Cubans and American Anxieties', *Foreign Policy*, no. 31, Summer 1978, pp. 3–33.

Bender, Gerald J., 'Peacemaking in Southern Africa: the Luanda Pretoria Tug-of-War', *Third World Quarterly*, vol. 11, no. 2, April 1989, pp. 15–30.

Bender, Gerald J., 'The Limits of Counterinsurgency: An African Case', *Comparative Politics*, vol. 4, no. 3, April 1972, pp. 331–60.

Bragança, Aquino de and Delpechin, Jacques, 'From the Idealization of Frelimo to the Understanding of the Recent History of Mozambique', *African Journal of Political Economy*, no. 1, 1986, pp. 162–80.

Braun, Gerald and Weiland, Heribert, 'Sanctions against South Africa: Punitive Action or Placebo Politics?', in John D. Brewer (ed.), *Can South Africa Survive. Five Minutes to Midnight*, London, Macmillan, 1989, pp. 35–56.

Caplan, Gerald, 'Barotseland: the secessionist challenge to Zambia', *Journal of Modern African Studies*, vol. 6, no. 3, 1968, pp. 343–60.

Cervenka, Zdenek, 'Cuba and Africa', *Africa Contemporary Record (1976–7)*, London, Rex Collings, 1977, A84–A90.

Clarence-Smith, W.G. and Moorsom, R., 'Underdevelopment and Class Formation in Ovamboland, 1845–1915', *Journal of African History*, vol. 16, no. 3, 1975, pp. 365–81.

Crocker, Chester A., 'Comment: Making Africa Safe for the Cubans' (reply to Bender, 'Angola, the Cubans and American Anxieties'), *Foreign Policy*, no. 31, 1978, pp. 31–3.

Crocker, Chester A., 'South Africa: A Strategy for Change', *Foreign Affairs*, vol. 59, no. 2, 1980, pp. 323–51.

Crocker, Chester A., 'Southern Africa: Eight Years Later', *Foreign Affairs*, vol. 68, no. 4, 1989, pp. 144–64.

Crocker, Chester A., 'Southern African Peace-Making', *Survival*, vol. 32, no. 3, 1990, pp. 221–32.

Crowder, Michael, 'Tshekedi Khama, Smuts, and South West Africa', *Journal of Modern African Studies*, vol. 25, no. 1, 1987, pp. 25–42.

Dale, Richard, 'Walvis Bay: A Naval Gateway, an Economic Turnstyle, or a Diplomatic Bargaining Chip for the Future of Namibia?', *Journal of the Royal United Services Institute for Defence Studies (RUSI)*, vol. 127, no. 1, March 1982, pp. 31–6.

Davidson, Basil, 'Portuguese Speaking Africa', in Michael Crowder (ed.), *The Cambridge History of Africa*, Cambridge, Cambridge University Press, 1984, pp. 753–810.

Davies, Robert and O'Meara, Dan, 'The Total Strategy in Southern Africa. An Analysis of South African Regional Policy since 1978', *Journal of Southern African Studies*, vol. 11, no. 2, 1985, pp. 183–211.

Davis, Nathaniel, 'The Angola Decision of 1975: A Personal Memoir', *Foreign Affairs*, vol. 57, no. 1, 1978, pp. 109–24.

Diaz-Briquets, Sergio and Pérez-Lopez, Jorge, 'Internationalist Civilian Assistance: The Cuban Presence in Sub-Saharan Africa', in Sergio Diaz-Briquets (ed.), *Cuban Internationalism in Sub-Sahran Africa*. Pittsburgh (Penns.), Duquesne University Press, 1989, pp. 48–77.

Diedrichsen, Telse, 'Wettlauf der Elefanten. In Angola kämpfen die ehemaligen Bürgerkriegsgegner nun um Wählerstimmen', *Überblick*, no. 1, 1992, pp. 49–53.

Dominguez, Jorge I., 'Cuba in the 1980s', *Foreign Affairs*, vol. 65, no. 1, 1986, pp. 118–35.

Dominguez, Jorge I., 'Cuban Foreign Policy', *Foreign Affairs*, vol. 57, no. 1, 1978, pp. 83–108.

Dreyer, Ronald, 'Dispute over Walvis Bay. Origins and Implications for Namibian Independence', *African Affairs*, vol. 83, no. 333, October 1984, pp. 497–510.

Dreyer, Ronald, 'La Namibie indépendante: la réconciliation nationale à l'épreuve', in Dominique Darbon (ed.), *Anné africaine 1990–1991*, Bordeaux, Institut d'tudes politiques (Centre d'étude d'Afrique noire, and Centre de recherche et d'étude sur les pays d'Afrique orientale), 1992, pp. 261–83.

Dreyer, Ronald, 'Whitehall, Cape Town, Berlin and the Economic Partition of South West Africa: The Establishment of British Economic Control, 1885–1894', *The Journal of Imperial and Commonwealth History*, vol. 15, no. 3, May 1987, pp. 264–88.

Dube, Emmanuel M., 'Relations between Liberation Movements and the OAU', in N.M. Shamuyarira (ed.), *Essays on the Liberation of Southern Africa*, Dar es Salaam, Tanzania Publishing House, 1972, pp. 25–68.

Duffield, Ian, 'Pan-Africanism since 1940', in Michael Crowder (ed.), *The Cambridge History of Africa*, vol. 8: from c.1940 to c.1975, Cambridge, Cambridge University Press, 1984, pp. 95–141.

Du Pisani, André, 'Namibia: A New Transitional Government', *South Africa International*, vol. 16, no.2, 1985, pp. 66–73.

Du Pisani, André, 'Namibia: On Brinkmanship, Conflict and Self-interest. The Collapse of the UN Plan', *Politikon*, vol. 8, no. 1, June 1981, pp. 1–16.

Du Pisani, André 'SWA/Namibia: 1980 Review', *Bulletin Africa Institute of South Africa*, vol. 21, no. 4, 1981, pp. 25–32.

Du Pisani, André, and von der Ropp, Klaus, 'The Western/Namibian Initiatives: Past, Present and Future?', *International Affairs Bulletin* (South Africa), vol.12, no. 2, 1988, pp. 4–22.

Ebinger, Charles, 'External Intervention in Internal War: the Politics and Diplomacy of the Angolan Civil War', *Orbis*, vol. 20, no. 3, 1976, pp. 669–99.

Evans, Michael, 'The Frontline States, South Africa, and Southern African Security. Military Prospects and Perspectives', *Zambezia*, vol. 12, no. 5, 1984, pp. 1–19.

Faundez, Julio, 'Namibia: The Relevance of International Law', *Third World Quarterly*, vol. 8, no. 2, April 1986, pp. 540–58.

Freeman, Jr., Chas. W., 'The Angola/Namibia Accords', *Foreign Affairs*, vol. 68, no. 3, 1989, pp. 126–41.

Fukuyama, Francis, 'Gorbachev and the Third World', *Foreign Affairs*, vol. 64, no. 4, 1986, pp. 715–31.

Galbraith, John S., 'Cecil Rhodes and his Cosmic Dreams: A Reassessment', *Journal of Imperial and Commonwealth History*, vol. 1, no. 2, January 1973, pp. 173–89.

Geingob, Hage, 'The Role of Research in the Namibian Struggle against Colonialism', in Brian Wood (ed.), *Namibia. 1884–1984. Readings in Namibia's History and Society*, London/Lusaka, Namibia Support Committee, United Nations Institute for Namibia, 1988, pp. 27–31.

Geldenhuys, Deon, 'The Destabilisation Controversy: An Analysis of a High Risk Foreign Policy Option for South Africa', in D. Geldenhuys and W. Gutteridge (eds), *Instability and Conflict in Southern Africa*, London, Institute for the Study of Conflict, 1983, pp. 11–26.

Geldenhuys, Deon and Venter, Denis, 'Regional Cooperation in Southern Africa: A Constellation of States?', *South African Institute of International Affairs Bulletin*, vol. 3, no. 3, December 1979, pp. 36–72.

Gertzel, Cherry, 'East and Central Africa', in Michael Crowder (ed.), *The Cambridge History of Africa*, vol. 8, Cambridge, Cambridge University Press, 1984, pp. 383–457.

Green, Reginald H. and Kiljunen, Kimmo, 'Unto What End? The Crisis of Colonialism in Namibia', in Reginald Green, Marja-Liisa Kiljunen, Kimmo Kiljunen (eds), *Namibia. The Last Colony*, Burnt Mill, Harlow (Essex), Longman, 1981, pp. 1–23.

Gromyko, Anatoli, 'La révolution d'octobre et les destinées de l'Afrique', in *L'U.R.S.S. et l'Afrique*, Moscow, Academy of Sciences USSR, 1982, pp. 8–23.

Gromyko, Anatoli and Lomeiko, Vladimir, 'New Way of Thinking and "New Globalism" ', *International Affairs* (Moscow), May 1986, pp. 17–27.

Grundy, Kenneth W., 'Namibia's First Year of Independence', *Current History*, vol. 90, no. 556, May 1991, pp. 213–16, and 226–7.

Hackland, Brian, Murray-Hudson, Anne, Wood, Brian, 'Behind the Diplomacy: Namibia, 1983–5, *Third World Quarterly*, vol. 8. no. 1, 1986, pp. 51–77.

Halbach, Axel J., 'Folgen der südafrikanischen Homeland-Politik: Durch getrennte Entwicklung gemeinsam in die Krise', *IFO Schnelldienst*, Munich, no. 37, 1987, pp. 17–29.

Hallett, Robin, 'The South African Intervention in Angola. 1975–6', *African Affairs*, vol. 77, no. 308, 1978, pp. 347–86.

Hamutenya, Hidipo, 'One Century of Imperialist Occupation and Anti-Colonial Resistance: An Historical Flashback', in Brian Wood (ed.), *Namibia. 1884–1984. Readings in Namibia's History and Society*, London/Lusaka, Namibia Support Committee, United Nations Institute for Namibia, 1988, pp. 14–26.

Hamutenya, Hidipo L. and Geingob, Gottfried H., 'African Nationalism in Namibia', in C.Potholm and R.Dale (eds) *Southern Africa in Perspective*, New York, The Free Press, 1972, pp. 85–94.

Hardy, Chandra, 'The Prospects for Growth and Structural Change in Southern Africa', *Development Dialogue* (Uppsala), 1987, no. 2, pp. 33–58.

Herbst, Jeffrey, 'The Angola-Namibia Accords: An Early Assessment', in Sergio Diaz-Briquets (ed.), *Cuban Internationalism in Sub-Sahran Africa*, Pittsburgh (Penns.), Duquesne University Press, 1989, pp. 144–53.

Hodges, Tony, 'How the MPLA Won in Angola', in Colin Legum,

Tony Hodges (eds), *After Angola: The War over Southern Africa*, London, Rex Collings, 1976, pp. 47–64.

Holness, Marga, 'Angola: The Struggle Continues', in Phillis Johnson and David Martin (eds), *Destructive Engagement. Southern Africa at War*, Harare, Zimbabwe Publishing House, 1986, pp. 73–109.

Hough, Mike, 'DMZ Proposals for SWA/Namibia', *Africa Insight*, vol. 10, no. 2, 1980, pp. 91–4.

Howe, Russell Warren, 'War in Southern Africa', *Foreign Affairs*, vol. 48, no. 1, October 1969.

Izyumov, Alexei and Kortunov, Andrei, 'The Soviet Union in the Changing World', *International Affairs* (Moscow), August 1988, pp. 46–56.

Johns, David H., 'The Foreign Policy of Tanzania', in O. Aluko (ed), *The Foreign Policies of African States*, London/Sydney/Auckland/Toronto, Hodder & Stoughton, 1977, pp. 196–219.

Kapchenko, Nikolai, 'The CPSU Foreign Policy and Today's World', *International Affairs* (Moscow), October 1987, pp. 65–74.

Karis, Thomas, 'United States Policy towards South Africa', in Gwendolen M. Carter and Patrick O'Meara (eds), *Southern Africa. The Continuing Crisis*, Bloomington, Indiana University Press, 1982, pp. 213–63.

Karns, Margaret P., 'Ad hoc multilateral diplomacy: the United States, the Contact Group, and Namibia', *International Organization*, vol. 41, no. 1, 1987, pp. 93–123.

Khadiagala, Gilbert M., 'The Front Line States, Regional Interstate Relations, and Institution Building in Southern Africa', in Harvey Glickman (ed.), *Toward Peace and Security in Southern Africa*, New York, Gordon and Breach Science Publishers, 1990, pp. 131–61.

Kiljunen, Kimmo, 'National Resistance and the Liberation Struggle', in Reginald Green, Marja-Liisa Kiljunen, Kimmo Kiljunen (eds), *Namibia. The Last Colony*, Burnt Mill, Harlow (Essex), Longman, 1981, pp. 145–71.

Kiljunen, Kimmo, 'The Ideology of National Liberation', in Reginald Green, Marja-Liisa Kiljunen, Kimmo Kiljunen (eds), *Namibia. The Last Colony*, Burnt Mill, Harlow (Essex), Longman, 1981, pp. 183–95.

Kim, G., 'The Successes of the National Liberation Movement and World Politics', *International Affairs* (Moscow), February 1979, pp. 84–89.

Kühne, Winrich, 'Frieden im südwestlichen Afrika? Der Durchbruch bei den Verhandlungen um die Unabhängigkeit Namibias', *Europa Archiv*, vol. 44, no. 4, 25.2.1989, pp. 105–14.

Landis, Elizabeth and Davis, Michael I., 'Namibia: Impending Independence?', in Gwendolen M. Carter and and Patrick O'Meara (eds), *Southern Africa. The Continuing Crisis*, Bloomington, Indiana University Press, 1982, pp. 141–74.

Legum, Colin, 'Foreign Intervention in Angola', *Africa Contemporary Record*, vol. 8, 1975–76, London, Rex Collings, 1976, A 3–38.

Legum, Colin, 'International Rivalries', in Gwendolen M. Carter and

261

Patrick O'Meara (eds), *Southern Africa: the Continuing Crisis*, Bloomington, Indiana University Press, 1982, pp. 3–17.

Legum, Colin 'The Southern African Crisis', *Africa Contemporary Record (1981–82)*, New York/London, Africana Publishing Company, 1982, A3–62.

Legum, Colin, 'The Southern African Crisis. The Making of a Second Middle East', *Africa Contemporary Record (1982–1983)*, New York/ London, Africana Publishers, A 3–41.

Legvold, Robert, 'The Revolution in Soviet Foreign Policy', *Foreign Affairs*, vol. 68, no. 1, 1989, pp. 82–98.

Louis, Wm. Roger, 'African Origins of the Mandates Idea', *International Organization*, vol. 19, no. 1, 1965, pp. 20–36.

MacFarlane, S. Neil, 'The Soviet Union and Southern African Security', *Problems of Communism*, vol. 38, nos. 2–3, March-June 1989, pp. 71–89.

Mandaza, Ibbo, 'Southern Africa: US Policy and the Struggle for National Independence', *African Journal of Political Economy*, no. 1, 1986, pp. 120–41.

Marcum, John A., 'A Continent Adrift', *Foreign Affairs*, vol. 68, no. 1, 1989, pp. 159–79.

Marcum, John A., 'Angola: Perilous Transition to Independence', in Gwendolen M. Carter and Patrick O'Meara (eds), *Southern Africa. The Continuing Crisis*, Bloomington, Indiana University Press, 1982, pp. 175–98.

Marcum, John A. 'Lessons of Angola', *Foreign Affairs*, vol. 54, no. 3, 1976, pp. 407–25.

Marcum, John A., 'The Exile Condition and Revolutionary Effectiveness: Southern African Liberation Movements', in C.Potholm and R.Dale (eds), *Southern Africa in Perspective*, New York, The Free Press, 1972, pp. 262–75.

Martin, Ben L., 'Attacking Reagan by Way of Pretoria', *Orbis*, vol. 31, no. 3, 1987, pp. 293–311.

Martin, David and Johnson, Phyllis, 'Mozambique: To Nkomati and Beyond', in Phyllis Johnson and David Martin (eds), *Destructive Engagement*, Harare, Zimbabwe Publishing House, 1986, pp. 1–41.

Maxwell, Kenneth, 'Portugal and Africa: The Last Empire', in Prosser Gifford and Wm. Roger Louis (eds), *The Transfer of Power in Africa*, New Haven/London, Yale University Press, 1982, pp. 337–85.

Maxwell, Kenneth, 'The Thorns of the Portuguese Revolution', *Foreign Affairs*, vol. 54, no. 2, 1976, pp. 250–270.

Mayall, James, 'The Soviet Union, Zimbabwe and Southern Africa', in O. Aluko and T. Shaw (eds), *Southern Africa in the 1980s*, London, George Allen & Unwin, 1985, pp. 89–119.

Moorsom, Richard, 'Underdevelopment, Contract Labour and Worker Consciousness in Namibia. 1915–1972', *Journal of Southern African Studies*, vol. 4, no. 1, October 1977, pp. 52–87.

Nazario, Olga, 'Cuba's Angolan Operation', in Sergio Diaz-Briquets (ed.), *Cuban Internationalism in Sub-Sahran Africa*. Pittsburgh (Penns.), Duquesne University Press, 1989, pp. 102–23.

Nazario, Olga, Benemelis, Juan, 'Cuba's Relations with Africa: An Overview', in Sergio Diaz-Briquets (ed.), *Cuban Internationalism in Sub-Sahran Africa*, Pittsburgh (Penns.), Duquesne University Press, 1989, pp. 11–26.

Ncube, M.M., 'The United States, South Africa and Destabilization in Southern Africa', in Michael Sefali and John Bardill (eds), *Development and Destabilization in Southern Africa*, Roma (Lesotho), Institute of Southern African Studies, 1985, pp. 39–58.

Nkomo, Joshua, 'Southern Rhodesia: Apartheid Country', in James Duffy and Robert Manners (eds), *Africa Speaks*. Princeton, D. van Norstrand Company, Inc., 1961, pp. 130–43.

Nyerere, Julius K., 'America and Southern Africa', *Foreign Affairs*, vol. 55, no. 4, 1977, pp. 671–84.

O'Meara, Patrick, 'Zimbabwe: The Politics of Independence', in Gwendolen M. Carter and Patrick O'Meara (eds), *Southern Africa. The Continuing Crisis*, Bloomington, Indiana University Press, 1982, pp. 18–56.

Pirio, Gregory, 'The Role of Garveyism in the Making of Namibian Nationalism', in Brian Wood (ed.), *Namibia. 1884–1984. Readings in Namibia's History and Society*, London/Lusaka, Namibia Support Committee, United Nations Institute for Namibia, 1988, pp. 259–67.

Ribeiro-Kabulu, A. Bento, 'Demokratie – die Basis für Versöhnung. Angola auf dem Weg zum Frieden', *Der Überblick*, no. 1, 1992, pp. 46–9.

Rogerson, Christian M., 'A Future University of Namibia? The Role of the United Nations Institute for Namibia', *Journal of Modern African Studies*, vol. 8, no. 4, 1980, p. 675.

Seiler, John, 'South Africa in Namibia: Persistence, Misperception and Ultimate Failure', in T. Callaghy (ed.), *South Africa in Southern Africa. The Intensifying Vortex of Violence*. New York, Praeger Publishers, 1984, pp. 165–89.

Sesay, Amadu, 'The Roles of the Front Line States in Southern Africa', in Olajide Aluko, and Timothy M. Shaw (eds), *Southern Africa in the 1980s*, London, George Allen & Unwin, 1985, pp. 19–40.

Shamuraya Nathan, 'The Dangers of the Lusaka Manifesto', *Africa Review* (Dar es Salaam), vol. 1, no. 1, March 1971, in Acquino de Braganç and Immanuel Wallerstein (eds), *The African Liberation Reader*, vol. 3: 'The Strategy of Liberation', London, Zed Press, 1982, pp. 88–90.

Slovo, Joe, 'The Armed Struggle Spreads', in *Guerilla Warfare*, London, ANC Publicity and Information Bureau, 1970, pp. 32–44.

Sofinsky, V., Khazanov, A., 'Angola's Chronicle of the Peking Betrayal', *International Affairs* (Moscow), July 1978, pp. 61–9.

Sokolov, Vladimir, 'Soviet Foreign Policy: A reply to Nabudere', *Southern Africa Political and Economic Monthly*, no. 11, August 1988, pp. 7–9.

Spence, Jack, 'South Africa and the Modern World', in Leonard Thompson and Monica Wilson (eds), *The Oxford History of South*

263

Africa, vol. 2: South Africa. 1870–1966, Oxford, Oxford University Press, 1978, pp. 477–527.

Stevens, Christopher, 'The Soviet Role in Southern Africa', in John Seiler (ed.), *Southern Africa since the Portuguese Coup*, Boulder, Col., Westview Press, 1980, pp. 45–60.

Swanson, Maynard W., 'South West Africa in Trust, 1919–1939', in Prosser Gifford and Wm. Roger Louis (eds), *Britain and Germany in Africa: Imperial Rivalry and Colonial Rule*, New Haven, Yale University Press, 1967, pp. 631–65.

Tarabrin, Y., 'The National Liberation Movement: Problems and Prospects', *International Affairs* (Moscow), February 1978, pp. 59–68.

Uralov, K., 'Angola: The Triumph of the Right Cause', *International Affairs* (Moscow), May 1976, pp. 51–56.

Utete, C. Munhamu Botsio, 'Zimbabwe and Southern African "Détente" ', in John Seiler (ed.), *Southern Africa Since the Portuguese Coup*, Boulder, Col., Westview Press, 1980, pp. 61–77.

Vigne, Randolph, 'SWAPO of Namibia: A Movement in Exile', *Third World Quarterly*, vol. 9, no. 1, 1987, pp. 85–107.

Voipio, Rauha, 'Contract Work through Ovambo Eyes', in Reginald Green, Marja-Liisa Kiljunen, Kimmo Kiljunen (eds), *Namibia. The Last Colony*, Burnt Mill, Harlow (Essex), Longman, 1981, chapter 6.

Von der Ropp, Klaus Frhr., 'Friedensinitiativen im Südwesten Afrikas', *Aussenpolitik*, vol. 40, no. 2, 1989, pp. 193–205.

Weimer, Bernhard, 'South Africa and the Frontline States: From Confrontation to Confidence Building', *Southern Africa Political and Economic Monthly*, vol. 3, no. 10, 1990, pp. 22–8.

Monographs and reports

Barratt, John, *The Angolan Conflict. Internal and International Aspects*. Bramfontein, South African Institute of International Affairs, 1976.

Campbell, Kurt M,. *Southern Africa in Soviet Foreign Policy* (Adelphi Paper no. 227), London, International Institute for Strategic Studies, 1987/88.

Cocker, Christopher, *South Africa's Security Dilemmas* (The Washington Papers), New York, Praeger, 1987.

Commonwealth Secretariat, *Independent Expert Study on the Evaluation of the Application, and Impact of Sanctions. Final Report to the Commonwealth Committee of Foreign Ministers on Southern Africa*, London Commonwealth Secretariat, confidential, April 1989.

Crocker, Chester A., *A U.S. Policy for the 80s* (Occasional Paper), Braamfontein, South African Institute of International Affairs, May 1981.

Cronje, Gillian and Suzanne, *The Workers of Namibia*, London, International Defence and Aid Fund for Southern Africa, 1979.

Davidson, Basil, *South Africa and Portugal*. United Nations, Unit on Apartheid (Notes and Documents no. 7/74), 1974.

Dreyer, Ronald, *Namibia and Angola. The Search for Independence and*

BIBLIOGRAPHY

Regional Secuity (1966–1988). Geneva, Graduate Institute of International Studies, 1988.

Duffy, James, *Portugal's African Territories: Present Realities*. New York, Carnegie Endowment for International Peace, 1962.

Ellis, Justin, *Education, Repression and Liberation: Namibia*. London, World University Service (UK)/Catholic Institute for International Relations, 1984.

Geldenhuys, Deon, *South Africa's Search for Security since the Second World War*, Bramfontein, South African Institute of International Affairs (Occasional Paper), 1978.

Geldenhuys, Deon, *What Do we Think? A Survey of White Opinion on Foreign Policy Issues*. *(Number 2)*, Braamfontein, South African Institute of International Affairs (Occasional Paper), 1984.

Heimer, Franz-Wilhelm, *The Decoloniziation Conflict in Angola. 1974–76. An Essay in Political Sociology*. Geneva, Graduate Institute of International Studies, 1979.

International Defence and Aid Fund, *Apartheid's Army in Namibia. South Africa's Illegal Military Occupation*. London, IDAF, 1982.

International Defence and Aid Fund for Southern Africa. *Namibia. The Facts*, London, International Defence and Aid Fund, 1980.

Jaster, Robert, *A Regional Security Role for Africa's Front-Line States: Experience and Prospects*. (Adelphi paper no. 180), London, The International Institute for Strategic Studies, 1983.

Jaster, Robert. S., *South Africa and its Neighbours: the Dynamics of a Regional Conflict* (Adelphi Paper 209), London, International Institute for Strategic Studies, 1986.

Jaster, Robert. S., *The 1988 Peace Accords and the Future of South-western Africa* (Adelphi Paper 253), London, International Institute for Strategic Studies, 1990.

Kane-Berman, John, *Contract Labour in South West Africa*, Johannesburg, South African Institute of Race Relations, 1972.

Legum, Colin, *Southern Africa. The Secret Diplomacy of Détente – South Africa at the Cross Roads*, London, Rex Collings, 1975.

Minter, William, 'Account from Angola. UNITA as described by ex-participants and foreign visitors' (Minter Report on UNITA), in *Facts and Reports*, vol. 20, no. L, 15.6.1990.

Minty, Abdul, *South Africa's Defence Strategy*. London, Anti-Apartheid Movement, 1969.

Moorsom, Richard, *A Future for Namibia 5: Fishing. Exploiting the Sea*, London, Catholic Institute for International Relations, 1984.

Moorsom, Richard, *Walvis Bay. Namibia's Port*. London, International Defence and Aid Fund for Southern Africa/United Nations Council for Namibia, 1984.

Overseas Development Institute (ODI), *Economic Prospects for Namibia* (Briefing Paper), Overseas Development Institute, London, August 1989.

Simon, David, *Independent Namibia One Year On* (Conflict Studies 239), London, Research Institute for the Study of Conflict and Terrorism, 1991.

265

United Nations Council for Namibia (Standing Committee II), *The Military Situation in and relating to Namibia*, New York, United Nations, 1985.

Weiland, Heribert, *Namibia – wohin?* Bonn, Deutsche Kommission Justitia et Pax, 1990.

Weimer, Bernhard, *Die Allianz der Frontlinien-Staaten im südlichen Afrika: Vom 'Mulungusi-Club' (1974) zum 'Nkomati-Akkord'. Bedingungen und Dynamik von Befreiung, Dialog und Integration in einer Krisenregion,* Ebenhausen, Stiftung Wissenschaft und Politik, 1985.

Wilkinson, Anthony R., *Insurgency in Rhodesia, 1957–1973: An Account and Assessment* (Adelphi Paper no. 100), London, The International Institute for Strategic Studies, 1973.

World Council of Churches (WCC), *The Cunene Dam scheme and the Struggle for the Liberation of Southern Africa*, Geneva, World Council of Churches, 1971.

Conference papers, theses, unpublished manuscripts

Amathila, Ben, Statement at *Meeting on Southern Africa*, World Economic Forum, Geneva, 27–28.10.1991.

Cotter, Jane, 'West European Economic Interests in Angola', World Council of Churches, *Program to Combat Racism: Cunene Dam Symposium*, Arnoldshain, 29.2–3.3.1972.

Crowder, Michael, 'Tshekedi Khama, Smuts and the Incorporation of South West Africa', unpublished m., n.d., in Botswana National Archives.

De Sousa Fereira, Eduardo, 'Cunene and Cabora Bassa – Signs of the New Portuguese Land Settlement Policy', World Council of Churches, Unit II, *Program to Combat Racism: Cunene Dam Symposium*, Arnoldshain, 29.2–3.3.1972, doc. no. 2.

Du Pisani, André, *Namibia. From Incorporation to Controlled Change*, paper presented at the Conference 'Namibia. Africa's Last Colony: Prospects for Freedom and Development', University of Vermont, Burlington (USA), April 1982.

Green, Reginald H., *Namibia: the state of the struggle*, paper presented at conference, International Institute of Strategic Studies (London)/ University of Zimbabwe, Harare, June 1987.

Hough, Mike, *Military Reasons for Recent Developments in the Angolan Namibian Question*, paper presented to conference 'Namibia: zwischen Entwicklungsnotwendigkeit und Unabhängigkeit', Wildbad Kreuth (Germany), 28.11.1988.

Katjavivi, Peter H., *The Rise of Nationalism in Namibia and its International Dimensions*, Ph.D. dissertation, Oxford, 1987.

London Support Committee, Report to the *International Conference in Support of the Peoples of Portuguese Colonies*, Rome, 27.–29.6.1970.

Mhina, A.K., *Liberation Struggles in Southern Africa after Zimbabwe*, paper submitted to International Conference on Peace and Security in Southern Africa, Arusha (Tanzania), 24–31.5.1985.

Van Heerden, Neil P., *Negotiating the 1988 New York Accord: Motives, Rationale, Experiences*, paper presented to Conference 'Cooperation and Security in Post-Apartheid Southern Africa', Maputo, 3–6 September 1991.

Pamphlets

Angola in Arms, 1972.
Associção das Empresas do Ultramar. *The Cunene Development Plan.* Lisbon, Overseas Companies of Portugal, 1973(?).
Mozambique Revolution, 1971.
Namibia News, 1969, 1976.
Sechaba, 1967, 1968.
SWAPO. *Political Programme of The South West Africa People's Organisation.* Lusaka, SWAPO Department of Publicity and Information, 1976.
25 Setembro (Moz.), 1971.

APPENDIX ONE

MANIFESTO ON SOUTHERN AFRICA, LUSAKA, 16 APRIL 1969 (EXTRACTS)

Reproduced in: Martin Minogue and Judith Molloy (eds), *African Aims and Attitudes. Selected Documents*, Cambridge, Cambridge University Press, 1974.

[. . .]17 Just as a settlement of the Rhodesian problem with a minimum of violence is a British responsibility, so a settlement in *South-West Africa* with a minimum of violence is a United Nation's responsibility. By every canon of international law, and by every precedent, South-West Africa should by now have been a sovereign, independent State with a Government based on majority rule. South-West Africa was a German colony until 1919, just as Tanganyika, Rwanda and Burundi, Togoland, and Cameroon were German colonies. It was a matter of European politics that when the Mandatory System was established after Germany had been defeated, the administration of South-West Africa was given to the white minority Government of South Africa, while the other ex-German colonies in Africa were put into the hands of the British, Belgian, or French Governments. After the Second World War every mandated territory except South-West Africa was converted into a Trusteeship Territory and has subsequently gained independence. South Africa, on the other hand, has persistently refused to honour even the international obligation it accepted in 1919, and has increasingly applied to South-West Africa the inhuman doctrines and organisation of apartheid.

18 The United Nations General Assembly has ruled against this action and in 1966 terminated the Mandate under which South Africa had a legal basis for its occupation and domination of South-West Africa. The General Assembly declared that the territory is now the direct responsibility of the United Nations and set up an *ad hoc* Committee to recommend practical means by which South-West Africa would be administered, and the people enabled to exercise self-determination and to achieve independence.

19 Nothing could be clearer than this decision – which no permanent member of the Security Council voted against. Yet, since that time no effective measures have been taken to enforce it. South-

West Africa remains in the clutches of the most ruthless minority government in Africa. Its people continue to be oppressed and those who advocate even peaceful progress to independence continue to be persecuted. The world has an obligation to use its strength to enforce the decision which all the countries co-operated in making. If they do this there is hope that the change can be effected without great violence. If they fail, then sooner or later the people of South-West Africa will take the law into their own hands. The people have been patient beyond belief, but one day their patience will be exhausted. Africa, at least, will then be unable to deny their call for help. [. . .]

APPENDIX TWO

PROPOSAL FOR A SETTLEMENT OF THE NAMIBIAN SITUATION UN. DOC. S/12636, 10 APRIL 1978

I Introduction

1 Bearing in mind their responsibilities as members of the Security Council of the United Nations, the Governments of Canada, France, the Federal Republic of Germany, the United Kingdom and the United States have consulted with the various parties involved with the Namibian situation with a view to encouraging agreement on the transfer of authority in Namibia to an independent government in accordance with resolution 385 (1976), adopted unanimously by the Security Council on 30 January 1976.

2 To this end, our Governments have drawn up a proposal for the settlement of the Namibian question designed to bring about a transition to independence during 1978 within a framework acceptable to the people of Namibia and thus to the international community. While the proposal addresses itself to all elements of resolution 385 (1976), the key to an internationally acceptable transition to independence is free elections for the whole of Namibia as one political entity with an appropriate United Nations role in accordance with resolution 385 (1976). A resolution will be required in the Security Council requesting the Secretary-General to appoint a United Nations Special Representative whose central task will be to make sure that conditions are established which will allow free and fair elections and an impartial electoral process. The Special Representative will be assisted by a United Nations Transition Assistance Group.

3 The purpose of the electoral process is to elect representatives to a Namibian Constituent Assembly which will draw up and adopt the Constitution for an independent and sovereign Namibia. Authority would then be assumed during 1978 by the Government of Namibia.

4 A more detailed description of the proposal is contained below. Our Governments believe that this proposal provides an effective basis for implementing resolution 385 (1976) while taking adequate account

of the interests of all parties involved. In carrying out his responsibilities the Special Representative will work together with the official appointed by South Africa (the Administrator-General) to ensure the orderly transition to independence. This working arrangement shall in no way constitute recognition of the legality of the South African presence in and administration of Namibia.

II The electoral process

5 In accordance with Security Council resolution 385 (1976), free elections will be held, for the whole of Namibia as one political entity, to enable the people of Namibia to freely and fairly determine their own future. The elections will be under the supervision and control of the United Nations in that, as a condition to the conduct of the electoral process, the elections themselves, and the certification of their results, the United Nations Special Representative will have to satisfy himself at each stage as to the fairness and appropriateness of all measures affecting the political process at all levels of administration before such measures take effect. Moreover the Special Representative may himself make proposals in regard to any aspect of the political process. He will make at his disposal a substantial civilian section of the United Nations Transition Assistance Group, sufficient to carry out his duties satisfactorily. He will report to the Secretary-General of the United Nations, keeping him informed and making such recommendations as he considers necessary with respect to the discharge of his responsibilities. The Secretary-General, in accordance with the mandate entrusted to him by the Security Council, will keep the Council informed.

6 Elections will be held to select a Constituent Assembly which will adopt a Constitution for an independent Namibia. The Constitution will determine the organization and powers of all levels of government. Every adult Namibian will be eligible, without discrimination or fear of intimidation from any source, to vote, campaign and stand for election to the Constituent Assembly. Voting will be by secret ballot, with provisions made for those who cannot read or write. The date for the beginning of the electoral campaign, the date of elections, the electoral system, the preparation of voters rolls, and other aspects of electoral procedures will be promptly decided upon so as to give all political parties and interested persons, without regard to their political views, a full and fair opportunity to organize and participate in the electoral process. Full freedom of speech, assembly, movement and press shall be guaranteed. The official electoral campaign shall commence only after the United Nations Special Representative has satisfied himself as to the fairness and appropriateness of the electoral procedures. The implementation of the electoral process, including the proper registration of voters and the proper and timely tabulation and publication of voting results will also have to be conducted to the satisfaction of the Special Representative.

271

7 The following requirements will be fulfilled to the satisfaction of the United Nations Special Representative in order to meet the objective of free and fair elections:

A Prior to the beginning of the electoral campaign, the Administrator General will repeal all remaining discriminatory or restrictive laws, regulations, or administrative measures which might abridge or inhibit that objective.

B The Administrator General shall make arrangements for the release, prior to the beginning of the electoral campaign, of all Namibian political prisoners or political detainees held by the South African authorities so that they can participate fully and freely in that process, without risk of arrest, detention, intimidation or imprisonment. Any disputes concerning the release of political prisoners or political detainees shall be resolved to the satisfaction of the Special Representative acting on the independent advice of a jurist of international standing who shall be designated by the Secretary-General to be legal adviser to the Special Representative.

C All Namibian refugees or Namibians detailed or otherwise outside the territory of Namibia will be permitted to return peacefully and participate fully and freely in the electoral process without risk of arrest, detention, intimidation or imprisonment. Suitable entry points will be designated for these purposes.

D The Special Representative with the assistance of the United Nations High Commissioner for Refugees and other appropriate international bodies will ensure that Namibians remaining outside of Namibia are given a free and voluntary choice whether to return. Provision will be made to attest to the voluntary nature of decisions made by Namibians who elect not to return to Namibia.

8 A comprehensive cesssation of all hostile acts shall be observed by all parties in order to ensure that the electoral process will be free from interference and intimidation. The annex describes provisions for the implementation of the cessation of all hostile acts, military arrangements concerning the United Nations Transition Assistance Group, the withdrawal of South African forces, and arrangements with respect to other organized forces in Namibia, and with respect to the forces of SWAPO. These provisions call for:

A A cessation of all hostile acts by all parties and the restrictions of South African and SWAPO armed forces to base.

B Thereafter a phased withdrawal from Namibia of all but 1500 South African troops within 12 weeks and prior to the official start of the political campaign. The remaining South African force would be restricted to Grootfontein or Oshivello or both and would be withdrawn after the certification of the election.

C The demobilization of the citizen forces, commandos, and ethnic forces, and the dismantling of their command structures.

D   Provision will be made for SWAPO personnel outside of the territory to return peacefully to Namibia through designated entry points to participate freely in the political process.

E   A military section of the United Nations Transition Assistance Group to make sure that the provisions of the agreed solution will be observed by all parties. In establishing the military section of UNTAG, the Secretary-General will keep in mind functional and logistical requirements. The Five Governments, as members of the Security Council, will support the Secretary-General's judgement in his discharge of this responsibility. The Secretary-General, will, in the normal manner, include in his consultations all those concerned with the implementation of the agreement. The Special Representative will be required to satisfy himself as to the implementation of all these arrangements and will keep the Secretary-General informed of developments in this regard.

9   Primary responsibility for maintaining law and order in Namibia during the transition period shall rest with the existing police forces. The Administrator General to the satisfaction of the United Nations Special Representative shall ensure the good conduct of the police forces and shall take the necessary action to ensure their suitability for continued employment during the transition period. The Special Representative shall make arrangements when appropriate for United Nations personnel to accompany the police forces in the discharge of their duties. The police forces would be limited to the carrying of small arms in the normal performance of their duties.

10   The United Nations Special Representative will take steps to guarantee against the possibility of intimidation or interference with the electoral process from whatever quarter.

11   Immediately after the certification of election results, the Constituent Assembly will meet to draw up and adopt a Constitution for an independent Namibia. It will conclude its works as soon as possible so as to permit whatever additional steps my be necessary prior to the installation of an independent Government of Namibia during 1978.

12   Neighbouring countries shall be requested to ensure to the best of their abilities that the provisions of the transitional arrangements, and the outcome of the election, are respected. They shall also be requested to afford the necessary facilities to the United Nations Special Representative and all United Nations personnel to carry out their assigned functions and to facilitate such measures as may be desirable for ensuring tranquility in the border areas.

APPENDIX THREE

SECURITY COUNCIL RESOLUTION 432 (1978) 27 JULY 1978

The Security Council,

Recalling its resolutions 385 (1976) of 30 January 1976 and 431 (1978) of 27 July 1978,

Reaffirming in particular the provisions of resolution 385 (1976) relating to the territorial integrity and unity of Namibia.

Taking note of paragraph 7 of General Assembly resolution 32/9 D of 4 November 1977, in which the Assembly declares that Walvis Bay is an integral part of Namibia.

1 *Declares* that the territorial integrity and unity of Namibia must be assured through the reintegration of Walvis Bay within its territory:

2 *Decides* to lend its full support to the initiation of steps necessary to ensure early reintegration of Walvis Bay into Namibia;

3 *Declares* that, pending the attainment of this objective, South Africa must not use Walvis Bay in any manner prejudicial to the independence of Namibia or the viability of its economy;

4 *Decides* to remain seized of the matter until Walvis Bay is fully reintegrated into Namibia.

Adopted unanimously at the 2082nd meeting.

APPENDIX FOUR

SECURITY COUNCIL RESOLUTION 435, 29 SEPTEMBER 1978

The Security Council,

Recalling its resolutions 385 (1976) and 431 (1978), and 432 (1978),

Having considered the report submitted by the Secretary-General pursuant to paragraph 2 of resolution 431 (1978) (S/12827) and his explanatory statement made in the Security Council on 29 September 1978 (S/12869),

Taking note of the relevant communications from the Government of South Africa addressed to the Secretary-General,

Taking note also of the letter dated 8 September 1978 from the President of the South West Africa People's Organization (SWAPO) addressed to the Secretary-General (S/12841),

Reaffirming the legal responsibility of the United Nations over Namibia,

1 *Approves* the report of the Secretary-General (S/12827) for the implementation of the proposal for a settlement of the Namibian situation (S/12636) and his explanatory statement (S/12869);

2 *Reiterates* that its objective is the withdrawal of South Africa's illegal administration of Namibia and the transfer of power to the people of Namibia with the assistance of the United Nations in accordance with resolution 385 (1976);

3 *Decides* to establish under its authority a United Nations Transition Assistance Group (UNTAG) in accordance with the above-mentioned report of the Secretary-General for a period of up to 12 months in order to assist his Special Representative to carry out the mandate conferred upon him by paragraph 1 of Security Council resolution 431 (1978), namely, to ensure the early independence of Namibia through free and fair elections under the supervision and control of the United Nations;

4 *Welcomes* SWAPO's preparedness to co-operate in the implementation of the Secretary-General's report, including its expressed readiness to sign and observe the cease-fire provisions as manifested in the letter from the President of SWAPO dated 8 September 1978 (S/12841);

5 *Calls on* South Africa forthwith to co-operate with the Secretary-General in the implementation of this resolution;

6 *Declares* that all unilateral measures taken by the illegal administration in Namibia in relation to the electoral process, including unilateral registration of voters, or transfer of power, in contravention of Security Council resolutions 385 (1976), 431 (1978) and this resolution are null and void;

7 *Requests* the Secretary-General to report to the Security Council no later than 23 October 1978 on the implementation of this resolution.

APPENDIX FIVE

PROTOCOL OF GENEVA, 5 AUGUST 1988

Reproduced in UN. Doc. S/20566, 4 April 1989

Delegations representing the Governments of the People's Republic of Angola/Republic of Cuba, and the Republic of South Africa, meeting in Geneva, Switzerland, 2–5 August 1988, with the mediation of Dr. Chester A. Crocker, Assistant Secretary of State for African Affairs, United States of America, have agreed as follows:

1   Each side agrees to recommend to the Secretary-General of the United Nations that 1 November 1988 be established as the date for implementation of UNSCR 435/78.

2   Each side agrees to the establishment of a target date for signature of the tripartite agreement among Angola, South Africa, and Cuba not later than 10 September 1988.

3   Each side agrees that a schedule acceptable to all parties for the redeployment toward the North and the stages and total withdrawal of Cuban troops from Angola must be established by Angola and Cuba, who will request on-site verification by the Security Council of the United Nations. The parties accept 1 September 1988 as the target date for reaching agreement on that schedule and all related matters.

4   The complete withdrawal of South African forces from Angola shall begin not later than 10 August 1988 and be completed not later than 1 September 1988.

5   The parties undertake to adopt the necessary measures of restraint in order to maintain the existing de facto cessation of hostilities. South Africa stated its willingness to convey this commitment in writing to the Secretary-General of the United Nations. Angola and Cuba shall urge SWAPO to proceed likewise as a step prior to the ceasefire contemplated in resolution 435/78 which will be established prior to 1 November 1988. Angola and Cuba shall use their good offices so that, once the total withdrawal of South African troops from Angola is completed, and within the context also of the cessation of hostilities in Namibia, SWAPO's forces will be deployed to the north of the 16th parallel. The parties deemed it appropriate that, during the period before 1 November 1988, a representative of the United

Nations Secretary-General be present in Luanda to take cognizance of any disputes relative to the cessation of hostilities and agreed that the combined military committee contemplated in paragraph 9 can be an appropriate venue for reviewing complaints of this nature that may arise.

6   As of 10 August 1988, no Cuban troops will deploy or be south of the line Chitado-Ruacana-Calueque-Naulila-Cuamato-N'Giva. Cuba furthermore stated that upon completion of the withdrawal of the South African troops from Angola not later than 1 September 1988 and the restoration by the People's Republic of Angola of its sovereignty over its international boundaries, the Cuban troops will not take part in offensive operations in the territory that lies east of meridian 17 and south of parallel 15 degrees, 30 minutes, provided that they are not subject to harassment.

7   Following the complete withdrawal of South African forces from Angola, the Government of Angola shall guarantee measures for the provision of water and power supply to Namibia.

8   With a view toward minimizing the risk of battlefield incidents and facilitating exchange of technical information related to implementations of the agreements reached, direct communications shall be established not later than 20 August 1988 between the respective military commanders at appropriate headquarters along the Angola/Namibia border.

9   Each side recognizes that the period from 1 September 1988, by which time South African forces will have completed their withdrawal from Angola, and the date established for implementation of UNSCR 435, is a period of particular sensitivity, for which specific guidelines for military activities are presently lacking. In the interest of maintaining the ceasefire and maximizing the conditions for the orderly introduction of UNTAG, the sides agree to establish a combined military committee to develop additional practical measures to build confidence and reduce the risk of unintended incidents. They invite United States membership on the committee.

10   Each side will act in accordance with the Governors Island principles, including paragraph E (non-interference in the internal affairs of states not to allow their territory to be used for acts of war, aggression, or violence against other states).

FOR THE GOVERNMENT
OF THE PEOPLE'S
REPUBLIC OF ANGOLA:

FOR THE GOVERNMENT
OF THE REPUBLIC OF
CUBA:

FOR THE GOVERNMENT
OF THE REPUBLIC OF
SOUTH AFRICA:

APPENDIX SIX

PROTOCOL OF BRAZZAVILLE, 13 DECEMBER 1988

Reproduced in United States Department of State, Bureau of Public Affairs, *Agreements for Peace in Southwestern Africa*, Washington, December 1988.

Delegations representing the Governments of the People's Republic of Angola, the Republic of Cuba, and the Republic of South Africa.

Meeting in Brazzaville with the mediation of the Government of the United States of America.

Expressing their deep appreciation to the President of the People's Republic of the Congo, Colonel Denis Sassou-Nguesso, for his indispensable contribution to the cause of peace in Southwestern Africa and for the hospitality extended to the delegations by the Government of the People's Republic of the Congo.

Confirming their commitment to act in accordance with the Principles for a Peaceful Settlement in South-western Africa, initialled at New York on 13 July 1988 and approved by their respective Governments on 20 July 1988, each of which is indispensable to a comprehensive settlement: with the understandings reached at Geneva on 5 August 1988 that are not superseded by this document; and with the agreement reached at Geneva on 15 November 1988 for the redeployment to the North and the staged and total withdrawal of Cuban troops from Angola.

Urging the international community to provide economic and financial support for the implementation of all aspects of this settlement.

Agree as follows:

1 The parties agree to recommend to the Secretary General of the United Nations that 1 April 1989 be established as the date for implementation of UNSCR 435 78.

2 The parties agree to meet on 22 December 1988 in New York for signature of the tripartite agreement and for signature by Angola and Cuba for their bilateral agreement. By the date of signature, Angola and Cuba shall have reached agreement with the Secretary General

of the United Nations on verification arrangements to be approved by the Security Council.

3 The parties agree to exchange the prisoners of war upon signature of the tripartite agreement.

4 The parties agree to establish a Joint Commission in accordance with the annex attached to this protocol.

Annex on the Joint Commission

1 With the objective of facilitating the resolution of any dispute regarding the interpretation or implementation of the tripartite agreement the parties hereby establish a Joint Commission. Which shall begin its work upon signature of the tripartite agreement.

2 The Joint Commission shall serve as a forum for discussion and resolution of issues regarding the interpretation and implementation of the tripartite agreement, and for such other purposes as the parties in the future may mutually agree.

3 The parties invite the United States of America and the Union of Soviet Socialist Republics to participate as observers in the work of the Commission. Furthermore, the parties agree that, upon the independence of Namibia, the Namibian Government should be included as a full member of the Joint Commission. To that end, the parties will extend a formal invitation to the Namibian Government to join the the Joint Commission on the date of Namibian independence.

4 The Joint Commission shall be constituted within thirty days of the signing of the tripartite agreement. The Joint Commission shall establish its own regulations and rules of procedure for regular meetings and for special meetings which may be requested by any party.

5 The decision by a party to discuss or seek the resolution of an issue in the Joint Commission shall not prejudice the right of that party to raise the issue, as it deems appropriate, before the Security Council of the United Nations or to pursue such other means of dispute resolution as are available under international law.

6 The Joint Commission shall in no way function as a substitute for UNTAG (including the monitoring of UNTAG outside Namibia) or for the UN entity performing verification in Angola.

APPENDIX SEVEN

AGREEMENT BETWEEN ANGOLA, CUBA AND SOUTH AFRICA (NEW YORK ACCORDS), 22 DECEMBER 1988

Reproduced in UN.Doc.S/20346, 22 December 1988.

The Governments of the People's Republic of Angola, the Republic of Cuba, and the Republic of South Africa, hereinafter designated as 'the Parties'.

Taking into account the 'Principles for a Peaceful Settlement in Southwestern Africa', approved by the Parties on 20 July 1988, and the subsequent negotiations with respect to the implementation of these Principles, each of which is indispensable to a comprehensive settlement.

Considering the acceptance by the Parties of the implementation of United Nations Security Council resolution 435 (1978), adopted on 29 September 1978, hereinafter designated as 'UNSCR 435/78'.

Considering the conclusion of the bilateral agreement between the People's Republic of Angola and the Republic of Cuba provided for the redeployment toward the North and the staged and total withdrawal of Cuban troops from the territory of the People's Republic of Angola.

Recognizing the role of the United Nations Security Council in implementing UNSCR 435/78 and in supporting the implementation of the present agreement.

Affirming the sovereignty, sovereign equality, and independence of all States of southwestern Africa.

Affirming the principle of non-interference in the internal affairs of States.

Affirming the principle of abstention from the threat or use of force against the territorial integrity or political independence of States.

Reaffirming the right of the peoples of the southwestern region of Africa to self-determination, independence, and equality of rights, and of the States of southwestern Africa to peace, development, and social progress.

Urging African and international co-operation for the settlement of the problems of the development of the southwestern region of Africa.

Expressing their appreciation for the mediating role of the Government of the United States of America.

Desiring to contribute to the establishment of peace and security in southwestern Africa.

Agree to the provisions set forth below.

1 The Parties shall immediately request the Secretary-General of the United Nations to seek authority from the Security Council to commence implementation of UNSCR 435/78 on 1 April 1989.

2 All military forces of the Republic of South Africa shall depart Namibia in accordance with UNSCR 435/78.

3 Consistent with the provisions of UNSCR 435/78, the Republic of South Africa and the People's Republic of Angola shall co-operate with the Secretary-General to ensure the independence of Namibia through free and fair elections and shall abstain from any action that could prevent the execution of UNSCR 435/78. The Parties shall respect the territorial integrity and inviolability of borders of Namibia and shall ensure that their territories are not used by any State, organization, or person in connection with acts of war, aggression, or violence against the territorial integrity or inviolability of borders of Namibia or any other action which could prevent the execution of UNSCR 435/78.

4 The People's Republic of Angola and the Republic of Cuba shall implement the bilateral agreement, signed on the date of signature of this agreement, providing for the redeployment toward the North and the staged and total withdrawal of Cuban troops from the territory of the People's Republic of Angola, and the arrangements made with the Security Council of the United Nations for the on-site verification of that withdrawal.

5 Consistent with their obligations under the Charter of the United Nations, the Parties shall refrain from the threat or use of force, and shall ensure that their respective territories are not used by any State, organization, or person in connection with any acts of war, aggression, or violence, against the territorial integrity, inviolability of borders or independence of any State of southwestern Africa.

6 The Parties shall respect the principle of non-interference in the internal affairs of the States of southwestern Africa.

7 The Parties shall comply in good faith with all obligations undertaken in this agreement and shall resolve through negotiation and in a spirit of co-operation any disputes with respect to the interpretation or implementation thereof.

8 This agreement shall enter into force upon signature.

Signed at New York in triplicate in the Portuguese, Spanish and English languages, each language being equally authentic, this 22nd day of December 1988.

282

FOR THE PEOPLE'S
REPUBLIC OF ANGOLA:
(Signed)
Afonso VAN DUNEM
M'BINDA

FOR THE REPUBLIC OF
CUBA:

(Signed)
Isidoro MALMIERCA
PEOLI

FOR THE REPUBLIC OF
SOUTH AFRICA:

(Signed)
Roelof F. BOTHA

APPENDIX EIGHT

MOUNT ETJO DECLARATION, 9 APRIL 1989

Reproduced in UN. Doc.S/20579, 17 April 1989.

The Joint Commission created by the Protocol of Brazzaville of 13 December 1988 met at Mount Etjo, Namibia, on 8 and 9 April 1989 in an extraordinary session.

Delegations of the People's Republic of Angola, the Republic of Cuba and the Republic of South Africa, parties to the New York Accord of 22 December 1988, attended this meeting.

Delegations from the United States of America and the Union of Soviet Socialist Republics participated in their capacity as observers.

(a) The parties reaffirm their commitment to fulfil the obligations undertaken in the Accord of 22 December 1988 for the peaceful resolution of the conflict in the south-western region of Africa and in conformity with United Nations Security Council resolution 632 (1989) of 16 February 1989;

(b) In order to facilitate the restoration of peace and to promote the full application of resolution 435 (1978) of the Security Council of the United Nations and the subsequent agreements subscribed to by the parties, as well as the restoration of the situation in existence on 31 March 1989, and taking into account in this regard the declaration by the leadership of SWAPO on 8 April 1989, the parties agree to a package of recommendations which are reflected in the attached annexure;

(c) The parties urge the Secretary-General of the United Nations urgently to adopt all the necessary measures for the most rapid and complete deployment of UNTAG so that it can fully and effectively carry out it mandate. They likewise urge all Member States of the United Nations, particularly those who are members of the Security Council, to extend to the Secretary-General their full co-operation with the carrying out of UNTAG's tasks.

Enclosure 1
Annexure to the Mount Etjo declaration

Principles

1. The withdrawal procedure has as its purpose the restoration of the situation in existence on 31 March 1989.
2. The Administrator-General and UNTAG shall verify the departure of SWAPO troops from Namibia.
3. The security and protection of the SWAPO elements and of the security forces in Namibia-enjoy the highest level of importance.
4. A period will be established during which SWAPO forces will be granted free passage to the border assembly points and those assembly points south of the border which are contained in the annexure to this document.
5. As of the signing of this document it will be considered that the SWAPO forces will be able to deploy with full safety to the established assembly points.
6. The procedure will be simple and practical to allow its implementation in the shortest time possible.
7. This procedure will be executed under UNTAG supervision.

Sequence

1. The People's Republic of Angola commits itself to receive on its territory the forces of SWAPO which leave Namibia and to ensure that these forces and others on its territory are confined north of latitude 16°S under UNTAG supervision.
2. As of 9 April 1989 SWAPO troops who are still in the territory of Namibia should present themselves to the border assembly points or to the assembly points south of the border herein established, enjoying the right of freedom of passage
3. All assembly points shall be under UNTAG supervision and shall contain personnel drawn from UNTAG and personnel authorized by the Administrator-General. SWAPO shall utilize the normal chain of command for the communications as well as the broadcast on commercial networks to notify its members of said arrangements.
4. The Joint Military Monitoring Commission shall be temporarily reactivated without Cuban representation, unless requested by both parties, until the situation existing on 31 March 1989 has been re-established.
At the border assembly points which appear in the annexure to this document, joint border control posts manned by forces of the People's Republic of Angola and the Republic of South Africa will be established with the presence of UNTAG to guarantee the control of the crossing of SWAPO forces.
5. The terms of this agreement, the assembly points on the border

as well as the assembly points south of the border herein established shall be communicated to SWAPO forces by all means possible.

6. SWAPO forces which turn themselves over to the custody of UNTAG shall lay down their weapons with UNTAG.

7. SWAPO members who present themselves to the assembly points south of the border shall be transferred by air to north of latitude 16°S by UNTAG or by Angola under the supervision of UNTAG.

8. SWAPO members who present themselves to assembly points on the border will be transferred to bases north of latitude 16°S by Angola under the supervision of UNTAG.

9. The Administrator-General and the Special Representative shall be notified as to the number of SWAPO forces which return to the bases north of latitude 16°S from the territory of Namibia.

10. By 15 April 1989, the Special Representative will be informed by SWAPO about the conclusion of the removal of its forces from the territory of Namibia.

11. The end of this process will be based on two essential points:

– Information provided by SWAPO to the Special Representative upon the conclusion of the removal of its forces from Namibian territory;

– Joint verification by the Administrator-General and the Special Representative of the exit of all SWAPO forces from Namibian territory.

Once these two conditions are met, the situation existing on 31 March 1989 will be considered to have been restored.

12. Having agreed to the foregoing principles and procedure the three Governments take note of a press release by the SWAPO leadership announcing the withdrawal of SWAPO forces from the northern part of Namibia to Angola. The three Governments recommend that the Administrator-General and the Special Representative give immediate attention as to how SWAPO's decision can be put into effect within the framework of the agreed withdrawal procedure with a view to ensuring that lives are spared.

MOUNT ETJO
NAMIBIA
9 April 1989

INDEX

References to Namibia and South Africa will not be found in this index as they occur on practically every page. References to Angola have been restricted to main headings only, for the same reason. Organizations appear alphabetically in their abbreviated form, e.g. ANC, OAU, SWAPO.